Background to Crisis

Other Titles in This Series

Agricultural Policies in the USSR and Eastern Europe, edited by Ronald A. Francisco, Betty A. Laird, and Roy D. Laird

The Social Context of Soviet Science, edited by Linda L. Lubrano and Susan Gross Solomon

The Future of the Soviet Economy: 1978-1985, edited by Holland Hunter

The Future of Agriculture in the Soviet Union and Eastern Europe: The 1976-1980 Five-Year Plans, edited by Roy D. Laird, Joseph Hajda, and Betty A. Laird

The Soviet Agrarian Debate: A Controversy in Social Science, 1923-1929, Susan Gross Solomon

The Jewish Minority in the Soviet Union, Thomas E. Sawyer

Soviet Involvement in the Middle East: Policy Formulation, 1966-1973, Ilana Kass

Civil-Military Relations in Communist Systems, edited by Dale R. Herspring and Ivan Volgyes

Perspectives for Change in Communist Societies, edited by Teresa Rakowska-Harmstone

Innovation in Communist Systems, edited by Andrew Gyorgy and James A. Kuhlman

A Case Study of a Soviet Republic: The Estonian SSR, edited by Tönu Parming and Elmar Järvesoo

A Short History of the Hungarian Communist Party, Miklós Molnár

Yugoslavia After Tito: Scenarios and Implications, Gavriel D. Ra'anan

Hungary: An Economic Geography, György Enyedi

The Liberated Female: Life, Work, and Sex in Socialist Hungary, Ivan Volgyes and Nancy Volgyes

Westview Special Studies on the Soviet Union and Eastern Europe

Background to Crisis: Policy and Politics in Gierek's Poland

edited by
Maurice D. Simon and Roger E. Kanet

The 1970s in Poland were marked by rapid social, economic, and political change that included the phenomenal expansion of Polish industry, the growth of economic ties with the West, food shortages, and substantial domestic unrest. The Polish government was faced with a large number of problems--foreign as well as domestic--that to date have not been amenable to lasting solutions. Efforts to solve one problem often have merely exacerbated difficulties in other areas.

The authors of this volume examine many of the policy-related developments in Poland during Gierek's regime, from his accession to power in late 1970 to his dismissal in 1980. The book begins with an overview of Poland's recent political evolution and concludes with an analysis of the nation's status at the end of the 1970s. The chapters describe political participation and integration, the role of various groups in the Polish political process, and major policy issues facing the Polish government.

Maurice D. Simon is an assistant professor of political science at the University of North Carolina at Greensboro. He has been conducting research on the attitudes of Polish youth and political change in Poland. Roger E. Kanet is a professor of political science and a member of the Russian and East European Center at the University of Illinois at Urbana/Champaign. He is author or editor of numerous publications on the foreign policies of the Soviet Union and East European countries. All of the contributors to this volume lived in or visited Poland during the 1970s.

Background to Crisis: Policy and Politics in Gierek's Poland

edited by
Maurice D. Simon and Roger E. Kanet

Routledge
Taylor & Francis Group
LONDON AND NEW YORK

First published 1981 by Westview Press, Inc.

Published 2018 by Routledge
52 Vanderbilt Avenue, New York, NY 10017
2 Park Square, Milton Park, Abingdon, Oxon OX14 4RN

Routledge is an imprint of the Taylor & Francis Group, an informa business

Library of Congress Cataloging in Publication Data
Main entry under title:

Background to Crisis: Policy and politics in Gierek's Poland.
(Westview special studies on the Soviet Union and Eastern Europe)
1. Poland--Politics and government--1945- 2. Poland--Foreign relations--1945- I. Simon, Maurice David. II. Kanet, Roger E., 1936-
DK4440.P63 320.9438 80-24078
ISBN 13: 978-0-367-02078-1 (hbk)

Contents

PART 3
GROUP ACTIVITY AND ATTITUDES:
THEIR IMPACT ON POLICY

PART 4
ISSUES IN ECONOMIC AND FOREIGN POLICY

PART 5
CONCLUSION

Tables and Figures

Tables

Figures

Preface

The 1970s have witnessed a degree of social, economic, and political change in Poland that was unprecedented in the first two decades of communist rule--i.e., after the consolidation of power by the Polish United Workers' Party in the late 1940s. The riots of December 1970, which resulted in the political overthrow of Wladislaw Gomulka, also ushered in a period of substantial policy change under the leadership of new party chief Edward Gierek. The decade of the 1970s was marked by the almost phenomenal expansion of Polish industrial development; by the closely related growth of Polish economic ties with the West and the resulting balance of payments problems; by substantial domestic unrest--a consequence, in part, of increased shortages in foodstuffs and consumer goods on the domestic market; by the development of open opposition groups, such as the Workers' Defense Committee (KOR); and by the continued integration of the Polish economy with those of the Soviet Union and the other members of the Council for Mutual Economic Assistance. The Polish government has been faced with a large number of problems--in domestic and foreign relations, in the economic, political, and social realms--that have to date not proven to be amenable to lasting solutions. Often, efforts to solve one problem have merely exacerbated difficulties in other areas.

The essays included in the present volume examine a substantial portion of the policy-relevant developments in Poland since the accession to power by Gierek in late 1970. The volume begins with an introductory overview of Poland's recent political evolution and concludes with a summary of the nation's status at the end of the 1970s. It includes sections dealing with political participation and integration, the role of various "groups" in the Polish political process, and a number of major policy issues presently facing the Polish government.

The present volume was conceived in the coffee shop of Warsaw's Hotel Europejski in the fall of 1976 when the coeditors, both residing and conducting research in Poland, met for the first time. Among other topics, they discussed the glaring need for a current study of Polish politics and noted the positive fact that there was then a substantial number of North American scholars in Poland carrying out research on a variety of topics. Out of this original discussion evolved the idea of a co-authored book on recent Polish politics and public policy. Fortunately, the coeditors were able to interest a substantial number of those American and Canadian scholars in participating in the project.

The coeditors wish to express their appreciation to a number of individuals for their role in the preparation and completion of the present volume. First, they wish to thank the authors of the individual chapters for their submission of interesting manuscripts and for their willingness to accept suggestions for revisions and condensation. In addition, they wish to express their appreciation for financial assistance from the Department of Political Science of the University of North Carolina at Greensboro and the Russian and East European Center of the University of Illinois at Urbana-Champaign that covered the costs of typing and retyping the manuscript. Maurice Simon wishes to express his deep gratitude to his wife,Judy, his son,Jason, and his parents for their support and patience throughout this project. Finally, the editors extend sincere thanks to Ms. Maggie Davis, who worked so relentlessly typing the final version of the manuscript and to Ms. Lynn Clawson who assisted in its preparation.

Maurice D. Simon
Greensboro, North Carolina

Roger E. Kanet
Champaign, Illinois

Addendum to the Preface

The research and writing of the articles that constitute this book were completed prior to the political upheavals that have resulted in the apparent restructuring of the relationship between the Polish United Workers Party and society in Poland and in the wholesale replacement of top political officials, including First Secretary Edward Gierek and Prime Minister Edward Babiuch. However, these developments have served to support the validity of the analyses presented here, for they confirm the existence of the fundamental problems that beset the Polish Political and economic system. The decision announced on 2 July 1980 concerning an increase in the basic price of meat led to a series of uncoordinated strikes throughout the country during the next month. Although this first wave of worker unrest was resolved through negotiations resulting in increased wages in specific enterprises, by mid-August the government and Party were faced with a well-organized strike by workers in the major industrial centers of the Baltic Coast region. The result of these strikes was the removal of a number of high-ranking officials and the eventual capitulation of the regime to the basic demands of the workers--increased wages and, most important, the right to labor unions independent of direct Party control. On 1 September, after a seventeen-day strike that threatened to bring about the collapse of the entire economy and the intervention of the Soviet Union, workers in Gdansk and other northern cities returned to work.

Yet the agreement in Gdansk did not end the unrest. During the past week, miners in Silesia have struck briefly in order to obtain new benefits, and at 1:30 A.M. (Warsaw time) on 6 September 1980 the official Polish news agency reported that First Secretary Gierek had been replaced by Stanislaw Kania, whose recent career has included overseeing the activities of the police and security forces. For the second time in less than a decade, labor unrest had brought down the highest ranking political official in Poland. As these lines are being written, news reports indicate that new strikes have occurred and that the new political leadership is threatening to cancel the agreements reached in Gdansk and elsewhere unless all workers return to their jobs.

It is much too soon to assess the long-term implications of recent events in Poland. However, the existence of truly independent unions could mean that the Party will be forced to share power in the making of decisions concerning the allocation of resources. Such a development--assuming that the agreements are, in fact, implemented--will result in a major shift in the communist system in Poland.

M.D.S. and R.E.K.
8 September 1980

The Contributors

JACK BIELASIAK is Assistant Professor of Political Science and Associate of the Russian-East European Institute at Indiana University, Bloomington. A native of Lodz, he was educated in Poland, France, and the United States and holds a Ph.D. from Cornell University. His publications include articles on modernization and political elites in Eastern Europe that have been published in Studies in Comparative Communism (1979) and East European Quarterly (forthcoming). He is currently completing a book-length study of Soviet and East European political elites in the post-Stalin period.

ADAM BROMKE is Professor of Political Science and Chairman of the Department at McMaster University in Hamilton, Ontario. He has also been President of the International Committee for Soviet and East European Studies since its creation in 1974. His numerous publications include Poland's Politics: Idealism vs. Realism (Harvard, 1967); Gierek's Poland (Praeger, 1973, coedited with John W. Strong); a number of edited volumes on East European foreign and domestic politics; and various articles on Polish politics that have appeared in such journals as Foreign Affairs (1971), Problems of Communism (1972, 1976, 1978), The World Today (1969, 1978), and International Journal (1978).

VINCENT CHRYPINSKI is Professor Emeritus of Political Science at the University of Windsor. He has written widely on Polish politics, in particular on the relationship of the Roman Catholic Church to the Polish political system. Among his publications are "Recent Polish Nationalism: A Commentary," in George W. Simmonds, ed., Nationalism in the USSR and Eastern Europe in the Era of Brezhnev and Kosygin (1977); "Polish Catholicism and Social Change," in B. Bociurkiw and J.W. Strong, eds., Religion and Atheism in the U.S.S.R. and Eastern Europe (1975); and "Political Changes Under Gierek," Canadian Slavonic Papers (1973).

JANE LEFTWICH CURRY, of the Research Institute of East-Central Europe of Columbia University, is currently a recipient of a grant from the Rockefeller Foundation and is engaged in research on human rights in Poland. She was recently awarded a Ph.D. at Columbia University where her dissertation dealt with the role of journalists in Polish society.

ZBIGNIEW M. FALLENBUCHL is Professor of Economics and Head of the Department of Economics at the University of Windsor. He has edited Economic Development in the Soviet Union and Eastern Europe (Praeger, 1975, 1976, two volumes). His recent publications include "Internal Migration and Economic Development Under Socialism: The Case of Poland," in A. Brown and E. Neuberger, eds., Internal Migration: A Comparative Perspective (Academic Press, forthcoming); "The Polish Economy in the 1970s," in J.P. Hardt, ed., East European Economies Post-Helsinki (Joint Economic Committee, U.S. Congress, 1977); "The Commodity Composition of Intra-COMECON Trade and the Industrial Structure of the Member Countries," In COMECON: Progress and Prospects (NATO Directorate of Economic Affairs, 1977); and "Integration économique en Europe de l'Est," Revue d'Études Comparatives Est-Ouest (1977).

JOHN P. FARRELL is Associate Professor of Economics at Oregon State University. His publications include articles on banking and the monetary system in Poland that have appeared in Soviet Studies (1975), Economics of Planning (1973), and Yearbook of East European Economics (1975, 1977).

DALE R. HERSPRING is a Foreign Service Officer with the Department of State. He is the author of East German Civil-Military Relations: The Impact of Technology, 1949-1972 (Praeger, 1973), and senior editor of Civil-Military Relations in Communist Systems (Westview, 1978). He has also published numerous articles and essays in journals such as

Problems of Communism, Studies in Comparative Communism, Armed Forces and Society, the Journal of Political & Military Sociology, as well as chapters in books on the GDR published in this country and the FRG.

ROGER E. KANET is Professor of Political Science and a member of the Russian and East European Center of the University of Illinois at Urbana-Champaign. He is the editor of and contributor to several books on Soviet foreign policy and the author of numerous articles on Soviet and East European politics, including articles on Polish foreign trade in Revue d'Études Comparatives Est-Ouest (forthcoming), continuity and change in Soviet-East European relations in Alexander Rabinowitch, Robert Sharlet and Stephen Cohen, eds., Continuity and Change Since Stalin (Indiana, forthcoming), and East-West trade in Charles Gati, ed., The International Politics of Eastern Europe (Praeger, 1976).

ANDRZEJ KORBONSKI is Professor of Political Science and Chairman of the Department of Political Science at the University of California, Los Angeles. He holds a B.S. in economics from the University of London and an M.A. and Ph.D. in public law and government from Columbia University. He is the author of Politics of Agriculture in Poland, 1945-1960 and has published numerous articles on various aspects of East European politics and economics that have appeared in scholarly journals and books.

DANIEL N. NELSON is Assistant Professor of Political Science at the University of Kentucky. His publications include articles on local government in Poland and Romania, as well as related topics, that have appeared in World Politics, Polity, and Journal of Politics. He has edited a volume on Local Politics in Communist Countries (University of Kentucky Press, 1979).

CHRISTINE M. SADOWSKI is Assistant Professor of Sociology at Trinity College, Hartford, Connecticut. In 1970-1971 she was a Kosciuszko Foundation exchange student at the Sociology Institute of the Jagiellonian University of Cracow. Her doctoral dissertation from the University of Michigan is on the function of voluntary associations in contemporary Poland--the result of research that she conducted through the Sociology Institute of Warsaw

University while on a Fulbright Fellowship in 1976-1977.

MAURICE D. SIMON is Assistant Professor of Political Science at the University of North Carolina at Greensboro. He has spent considerable time conducting research in Poland, having received research grants in the academic years 1966-1967, 1972-1973, 1976-1977. His research has been concerned with youth, higher educational policy, and political change in socialist societies. He has contributed articles recently to *Legislative Studies Quarterly*, *Problems of Communism*, and to Donald E. Schulz and Jan S. Adams, *Political Participation in Communist Systems* (Pergamon Press, Inc., forthcoming). He is currently working on a study of the concept of developed socialism, as it has emerged in post-1970 Poland.

SARAH MEIKLEJOHN TERRY is Assistant Professor of Political Science and an Associate Dean at Tufts University. She has taught at Harvard University where she remains an Associate of the Russian Research Center. Recent publications include "External Influences on Political Change in Eastern Europe: A Framework for Analysis," in Jan F. Triska and Paul M. Cocks, eds., *Political Development in Eastern Europe* (Praeger, 1977) and a monograph for the Department of State on "The Implications of Interdependence for Soviet-East European Relations: A Preliminary Analysis of the Polish Case," (1977). She is currently completing a study of the wartime origins of the Oder-Neisse boundary.

Part 1

Introduction

1 Policy and Politics in Gierek's Poland

Adam Bromke

The Polish People's Republic is in the throes of the most serious crisis in its entire existence. The present difficulties do not just reflect erroneous policies, but strike at the roots of the system itself. The ruling Polish United Workers' Party (PUWP) seems uncertain as to how to cope with the situation, and Gierek is fighting for his political life. The opposition, in contrast, displays a mood of self-assurance, perhaps over-confidence. For the first time since the 1940s, demands for a change of the system itself are openly and boldly articulated.

The workers' riots in Ursus and Radom in June 1976, in protest against drastic food price increases, left the Gierek regime badly shaken.[1] For several months afterward the government conveyed the impression of being totally disoriented--moving in different, and often contradictory, directions at once. The objectionable price increases were hastily revoked, but the authorities insisted that they were still necessary and would have to be reintroduced at a later date. The need for closer consultations with the workers was acknowledged, but severe repressions were nevertheless applied against the participants in the June demonstrations. Amid widespread rumors of police brutality, several

---

This chapter is largely based on two articles: "Poland at the Crossroads," The World Today, Vol. 34, No. 4 (April 1978); and "Opposition in Poland," Problems of Communism, Vol. XXVII, No. 5 (September/ October 1978). The author is grateful to the Royal Institute of International Affairs and the U.S. International Communication Agency for their permission to use these materials.

groups of workers from Ursus and Radom were tried and sentenced to lengthy terms of imprisonment. At mass rallies staged to demonstrate support for the communist authorities, Gierek emphasized the need for national unity, while at the same time the press mounted a campaign against "hooligans and firebrands." Despite the admission of a major error of judgment on its part, no changes in the government were forthcoming.

ECONOMIC RETRENCHMENT

It was only late in the year that the Gierek regime regained its composure and tried to come to grips with the problems. A meeting of the Central Committee held on December 1-2, 1976, addressed itself to the task of bolstering the sagging economy. In his speech on that occasion, Gierek defended the economic policies of the first part of the 1970s as "fruitful and creative", but he admitted that tensions had developed in the Polish economy.[2] These he blamed on adverse climatic conditions, which had resulted in poor grain harvests and a decline in livestock, and difficulties in foreign trade because of the recession in the West. There were also other shortcomings, such as an obsolete price structure, a tendency towards overinvestment, a lack of coordination among various branches of industry, and inefficiencies which often resulted in a poor quality of goods. To cope with the deteriorating situation a "New Economic Maneuver" was adopted. In the next few months several further meetings of the Central Committee were devoted to elaborating and expanding on this economic adjustment.

The New Economic Maneuver was directed as much toward the preservation of calm in the country as to economic recovery. The price increases of basic foodstuffs were shelved and top priority for 1977 was given to improving the supply of the home market. To that end a drastic reduction in the overall level of investments was announced, but a greater proportion of investment was allocated to consumer industries. Substantial additional funds were also allocated to housing construction. Imports of industrial equipment, but significantly not of meats and grain, were reduced. More authority over distribution of profits was delegated to industrial units. At the same time, encouragement was given to private farming. Prices of agricultural produce were increased. Individual farmers were offered pension plans, and their prospects of acquiring more land were re-emphasized. The small private enterprises that provide many crucial consumer goods and services were also promised more support.

All of these measures were in the right direction, but they failed to bring about the desired results. If anything, in 1977 the situation at the market deteriorated even further. Another bad harvest, due to heavy rainfalls, necessitated increased grain imports from the West. In addition to the chronic shortages of meat, many other foodstuffs such as coffee or citrus fruits fell into short supply. Although Poland is the world's largest _per capita_ producer of coal, there was even a shortage of this commodity. For the first time since the war, sugar was rationed and the queues became a familiar sight all over the country. Dissatisfaction and grumbling were evident. There were reports of scattered strikes in the coal mines, steel works, and other factories.

Obviously, the government had overestimated the speed with which it could accomplish economic recovery. When in October 1977 the Central Committee met to review the results of the New Economic Maneuver, its mood was somber. There were still complaints about poor coordination of various industrial activities and gross waste due to inefficiency. On November 5, an influential Warsaw weekly, _Polityka_ (Politics), proposed as a remedy a greater decentralization of economic decision making. In an article written by Editor-in-Chief Mieczyslaw Rakowski, this was stated very clearly: "Excessive centralization may result in harmful curtailing of individual initiative...Overcoming the existing difficulties ought to be linked as much as possible to decentralization."

There is no evidence, however, that _Polityka's_ advice was heeded. At the Party Conference held on January 9-10, 1978, Gierek once again criticized the economy for inefficiency and insufficient coordination among its various branches, but he proposed no new measures to cope with those problems. No reforms of the price-wage structure nor of the methods of planning and management were undertaken. Consequently, throughout 1978 economic conditions continued to worsen. Price increases of basic foodstuffs were officially postponed once more but, nevertheless, they were carried out in practice. Prices of various commodities were increased under the guise of improving their quality, and special "commercial shops" with a quality assortment of goods at steeply higher costs were introduced all over the country. Thus, many essential commodities still remained beyond the reach of the ordinary public. At the same time, Poland's heavy debts to various western countries--estimated at the end of 1978 at $14.8 billion in long-term and about $2 billion in short-term credits--not only drastically reduced the country's imports, but also compelled it to export many goods badly needed at home.[3]

Despite the signs that the roots of the crisis reach beyond specific policies into the heart of the economic system, the Gierek regime has stubbornly resisted introducing into it any basic changes. What the government hopes for is that the results of the New Economic Maneuver, combined with the coming to fruition of the substantial investments in industry made in the past, will eventually ease the situation. But this is not going to take place soon. If, under the staggering foreign debts, the country's economy is not going to collapse altogether, several lean years are clearly ahead for Poland.

THE RISE OF OPPOSITION

After coming into power in 1970, Gierek adopted a new political style which emphasized greater respect on the part of the communist authorities for the citizens' rights and a readiness to enter into dialogue with the Polish people.[4] This, coupled with improvements in the standard of living, won the Gierek regime a measure of genuine popular sympathy. In the mid-1970s, however, with the return to more orthodox communist policies, the goodwill among various segments of the society was largely squandered. There was a tightening of religious freedom, and church-state relations deteriorated visibly. Cultural freedom was also curbed, and when, early in 1976, amendments to the Polish Constitution were introduced, bringing it closer to the Soviet document, there were massive protests by the intellectuals.

The persecutions of the Ursus and Radom workers, after the government had withdrawn the controversial food price increases, were the last straw. At that stage, various discontented groups coalesced into a united opposition. In July 1976 a prominent writer, Jerzy Andrzejewski, praised the persecuted workers as "fighters for the true socialist democracy", and pledged to persevere in the efforts on their behalf.[5] On September 27, a "Committee for the Defense of the Workers' (KOR) was established.

The composition of KOR reflected the various layers of opposition in Poland. Among its members (fourteen originally and thirty-one at present), there are several prominent prewar social democrats such as Professor Edward Lipinski, a respected economist, and Antoni Pajdak, one of the defendants in the trial of the Polish leaders in Moscow in 1945. They are all now in their seventies or even eighties. Another group is composed of well-known leaders of the wartime resistance movement. The youngest of these is a literary historian, Jan Jozef Lipski, who is now in his early fifties.

The largest, and also the most active, group in KOR consists of leaders of the 1968 students' rebellion.[6] Except for a former teacher, Jacek Kuron, who is in his forties, these people are all in their early thirties or even their late twenties. The most widely known among them is a talented historian, Adam Michnik, who spent several months in Western Europe in 1976 and 1977. Beyond KOR itself, among its supporters are many other student activists of 1968. Hardened by the years of imprisonment, more mature and experienced, they are determined to carry on their struggle for freedom.

KOR has developed rather ingenious methods for its activities. It has declared itself to be merely a social, not political, body; and it has refrained, in order to avoid submitting itself to public control by the communist authorities, from adopting a formal organizational structure. It has been operating simply as a group of citizens who spontaneously cooperate in promoting common goals. The Committee's main activity has consisted of assisting the people exposed to persecutions by the Communist authorities. They have been offered moral encouragement, legal advice, and financial aid. To that end, money has been collected all over the country. The major vehicles of KOR's influence have been the communiques, declarations, and appeals circulated throughout the country in samizdat form. In the same way, it has regularly published its own paper, the Biuletyn informacyjny (the Information Bulletin) named, significantly, after an influential organ of the Polish wartime resistance.

KOR's initial aims were modest. Its first communiques reported on the persecutions of the imprisoned workers--with detailed accounts of police brutality--and announced public campaigns to raise funds for medical and legal aid. Gradually, however, the Committee's goals became more ambitious. They came to include amnesty for all the imprisoned workers, their reinstatement in the same positions they had held before June 1976, and punishment of those police officers guilty of abusing their powers. On January 16, 1977, KOR appealed to the Polish parliament to appoint a special committee to investigate charges of beatings and torturing of prisoners.

The Committee has gained widespread sympathy in the country. Its demand for the establishment of a parliamentary committee to investigate police abuses was supported by close to two thousand people, among them many distinguished intellectuals. Cardinal Wyszynski also threw his enormous authority behind the Committee's objectives. Although stressing the need to preserve calm in the country, he strongly denounced the workers' persecutions. "It is painful", he declared in one of his sermons, "when workers must struggle for their rights from a workers' government."[7]

The government responded to the new challenge by zigzagging between concessions and repressions. Special efforts were made to appease the Catholic church. On August 3, 1976, Premier Jaroszewicz ostentatiously sent Cardinal Wyszynski a bouquet of white and red flowers for his seventy-fifth birthday. In a speech in Mielec on September 3, Gierek declared that there was no conflict between the state and the church and that all the outstanding problems could be easily resolved. The church reacted coolly to the communist overtures. Late in November the Episcopate issued a letter complaining about "a secret conspiracy against God" and presented a veritable litany of grievances. In exchange for its cooperation, the Episcopate demanded the removal of obstacles against building new churches, the unimpeded right to hold catechism classes for the children, the termination of atheistic propaganda in the schools and universities, access to public media, and an end to discrimination against Catholics holding public office.

Conciliatory gestures were also made toward the intellectuals. Late in January 1977, Gierek received the Chairman of the Writers' Union, and a few weeks later he held "frank and open" discussions with a group of representatives of artistic circles. Early in March a film by Andrzej Wajda, "The Marble Man"--highly critical of the Stalinist era and not without some contemporary political overtones--was shown in all the major cities in Poland. Some overtures were made toward the workers too. On February 3, Gierek visited Ursus and promised clemency for the imprisoned workers. Indeed, most of them were soon released. On March 26, Polityka, in an article entitled "The Roots of Democracy", emphasized the need for more effective consultations with the workers. Meanwhile, however, five workers still stayed in prison. A campaign against the Committee for the Defense of the Workers was mounted in the press, and the younger members of KOR were systematically submitted to police harassment and intimidation.

On May 7, Stanislaw Pyjas, a Cracow student and an active supporter of KOR, was found dead. The circumstances strongly suggested political assassination (although it is doubtful that it was in fact a premeditated murder). Students all over the country rose in protest. Requiem masses were celebrated in all the university cities and some 2,000 Cracow students staged a candlelight procession. Tension was high--it was feared that clashes between students and police might spark an open revolt. The government responded by promptly arresting ten persons: six younger members of KOR and four of its active supporters. This led to new protests from the intellectuals and the church hierarchy. In the face of the mounting wave of popular indignation, the government relented. On June 30, in a speech to the Polish parliament, Gierek pledged to respect the citizens' dignity and to uphold the rule of law. On July 23, the KOR people, as well as the remaining five workers, were all released from imprisonment.[8]

The opposition activities, however, did not stop there. If anything, they were even further intensified. On September 29, 1977, the Committee for the Defense of Workers announced its transformation into a permanent body called the "Committee for Social Self-Defense--KOR" (KSS-KOR). The composition and the structure of the new Committee remained basically unchanged. The goals of KSS-KOR were defined as combating violations of the law, fighting for institutional guarantees of civil rights, and assisting in all similar social initiatives. Around these activities the Committee has built an impressive popular following. There are now official KSS-KOR representatives in nine cities and active supporters in many other centers. It is estimated that about a thousand people, a good many of them students, are involved in its work in one way or another.

OPPOSITION CONSOLIDATED

The achievements of KOR went beyond rallying a great number of people in defense of the persecuted workers and, through popular pressure, compelling the communist government to abandon its reprisals. Perhaps even more important were the psychological consequences of this achievement. The Committee demonstrated that there is room in contemporary Poland for successful political action. By standing up to the communist authorities, KOR overcame the political inertia among various segments of Polish society, and its example led to a proliferation of similar activities in many other spheres of life.

On March 25, 1977, the founding of a new group, called the Movement for the Defense of Human and Civil Rights (ROPCiO) was announced. Its eighteen founding members were predominantly from Warsaw and Lodz. The most visible among them was Leszek Moczulski, a former journalist and historian of World War II, who is now in his mid-forties. For the most part, however, ROPCiO, like KOR, is composed of distinctly separate prewar and postwar generations. Among its older members are a prewar general, Mieczyslaw Boruta-Spiechowicz, and a leader of the former Christian Democratic party, Stefan Kaczorowski. The younger members are mostly former participants in the clandestine group Ruch, who were discovered and tried in 1971 but were subsequently released. The best known of the latter is Andrzej Czuma, who in the spring of 1978 pushed Moczulski aside and emerged as the leading personality in ROPCiO.

In contrast to KSS-KOR, the Movement has no Marxist leanings; if anything, it has reverted to the political traditions of interwar Poland. It is more critical of the communist system and is more far reaching in its proposals for political change. The objectives of ROPCiO are to fight for respect for human and civil rights, to assist persons whose rights have been infringed upon, to publicize violations of the laws, and to strive for institutional safeguards of basic freedoms.

To promote these ends, the Movement has established offices in eleven Polish cities, where free advice is offered to citizens aggrieved by the communist authorities. By the fall of 1977, they had a current docket of forty-three such complaints. ROPCiO's organ is a _samizdat_ monthly, _Opinia_ (Opinion). In addition to publicizing the Movement's program and activities, the paper covers current domestic and international events quite extensively. On June 5, 1977, ROPCiO sponsored the first reunion of former political prisoners, and, on August 6, it organized a patriotic demonstration by the grave of prewar Polish Marshall Edward Rydz-Smigly. On December 30, an _Opinia_ correspondent tried unsuccessfully to attend the Warsaw press conference of US President Jimmy Carter.

In addition to KSS-KOR and ROPCiO, various other groups and _samizdat_ publications representing a wide diversity of opinion have appeared in Poland in the last year. About the same time that ROPCiO was set up, a Polish chapter of Amnesty International was founded, with some overlapping of key personalities. In the fall of 1977, the Polish Committee for the Defense of Life and Family was formed. It soon collected over 6,000 signatures on an appeal to parliament to abolish the existing, extremely liberal abortion laws. In the spring of 1978, it came out with its own publication, _Samoobrona Polska_ (The Polish Self-Defense), in which, in addition to continuing its anti-abortion campaign, it openly reverted to the political tradition of prewar National Democracy. In the summer of 1978, Moczulski and some of his followers, after leaving ROPCiO, established a new organization called the Initiative Groups of the Citizens' Defense Movement (ZiNO) and started publishing their own monthly, _Droga_ (The Road).

At the time of the demonstrations in Krakow in May 1977, the Students' Solidarity Committee (SKS) spontaneously came into existence. Its declared objective is to replace the Communist-dominated student organization with a body that truly represents the Polish students. SKS now has branches at virtually every university in the country and publishes two papers, _Bratniak_ (Fraternity) and _Indeks_ (Index). In the autumn of 1977, an independent journal of young Catholics, _Spotkania_ (Encounters), covering religious as well as social and political topics, was founded. At about the same time, the first issue of _Robotnik_ (The Worker), a publication whose name was borrowed from the respected organ of the old Polish Peasant Party (PPS), appeared. It pledged to strive for replacement of the official trade unions with genuine workers' representation. This journal was soon followed by _Gospodarz_ (The Farmer), addressed to the peasants and urging them to continue their opposition to collectivization of agriculture. Meanwhile, two literary samizdat periodicals, Zapis (The Record) and Puls (Pulse), entered into circulation. Zapis was issued by NOWA (Independent Publishing House), which at the same time announced that it intended to undertake publication of books banned by censorship. By the spring of 1978, thirteen such volumes, six in belles-lettres and seven in the social sciences, had come out.

Side by side with the emergence of open opposition groups, the clandestine Polish Coalition for Independence (PPN), which made its first appearance by issuing a programmatic declaration in the spring of 1976, has continued its work. It has published critical analyses against the Catholic Church, the lack of respect for the law, the widespread corruption among the ruling elite, and the apathy among the people. To oppose these negative phenomena, the PPN has prepared several practical guides to action that outline, for example, how to cope with the security police and how to collect true information about the situation in the country. In the fall of 1977, another clandestine group gave evidence of its existence with the first issue of a bimonthly, Polska Walczaca (Fighting Poland), whose name, significantly, was a cryptonym used for the Polish wartime underground.

On October 20, 1977, a Declaration of the Domestic Movement, signed by 110 people, was published in still another samizdat paper, Glos (The Voice). The declaration observed with satisfaction that, in the preceding two years, communist attempts to break the Movement had not only failed but had, in fact, made it even more popular, to the point that it now had "thousands" of adherents. The time had come, the declaration stated, for the Democratic Movement to undertake the the struggle for Poland's democracy and sovereignty.[9]

POPULAR FERMENT SPREADS

Along with the flourishing of samizdat publications came a proliferation of discussion groups of all sorts, especially among the young people. Some of them have been sponsored by SKK-KOR, ROPCiO, or the SKS, while others have sprung up quite spontaneously. They have met in private homes and also occasionally on local church premises. In Warsaw and in some other major cities, veritable intellectual salons have emerged, where prominent writers read their works and well known scholars give lectures.

In November 1977, at the initiative of the students' committees, an effort was made to transform some of these occasional lectures into systematic courses. The aim was to supplement the education offered at regular universities, especially in those fields where communist ideology had placed political limitations on objective scholarship--i.e., in modern history, literature, philosophy, and the social sciences. This new venture has been designated the "Flying University" (UL), after a similar institution in Warsaw at the turn of the century that played an important role in rekindling national consciousness among Polish students attending Russianized schools by giving secret training in native history and literature. Unlike its distinguished predecessor, the present Flying University is an open institution. It is sponsored by the Society for Educational Courses (TKN), which was founded on January 22, 1978, and is composed of sixty-one persons, including many prominent writers and scholars. To supervise the quality of courses offered at the UL, the Society has established an Education Council from among its members.

In the first "trimester", the Flying University offered five courses on an experimental basis, but by the third "trimester", that number had risen to thirteen. These lectures took place in Warsaw as well as in other major university cities. Although the UL offers no diplomas, its courses have proved to be quite popular. Attendance has averaged thirty to forty students but has run as high as one hundred for lectures on subjects such as Polish postwar history. As an aid to students, "flying libraries" of books banned from the regular university collections have been established. To cap things off, a Free Association of Research and Studies was founded in the spring of 1978. Composed of scholars who have been prevented from working at official institutions, it seeks to foster research free of political influence and to disseminate the results in the form of samizdat publications.

The communist authorities have charged that the objectives of the Flying University are not educational but political, that its main aim is to spread opposition ideas among the young people. Consequently, the authorities have tried hard to restrict the scope of UL activities. Students participating in the courses have been warned by regular university officials about possible adverse consequences for them, and some SKS activists have been interrogated by the police. Several lectures, especially outside of Warsaw, have actually been broken up. Moreover, a few younger lecturers have been arrested and detained long enough to prevent them from meeting their classes. Owners of apartments where lectures have been taking place have been fined for holding "illegal gatherings", and some have even been threatened with eviction from their dwellings.

Despite all the persecutions, the activities of UL continued. In the fall of 1978, its second "academic year" was solemnly inaugurated by a lecture given at St. Martin's Church in Warsaw. At the same time, the official pressure relented, and for the rest of the year the Flying University was largely left alone. In addition a curious official initiative was also launched. An attempt was made to organize an ongoing colloquium sponsored by the Polish Academy of Sciences, on the current social problems. Among some one hundred individuals invited to participate were many well known Catholic and liberal intellectuals (some of whom had been prominently linked with UL). Evidently, however, this was too much for some party leaders for the project was abruptly shelved.

So far the opposition activities have basically remained confined to the intellectuals and the student youth. Two attempts to organize a free trade union movement--the first in Katowice in February 1978 and the second in Gdansk the following April--were both met with immediate and severe reprisals. Yet, in December, workers' demonstrations commemorating the eighth anniversary of their rebellion against the Gomulka regime were staged in Gdansk. Also, there was evidence of swelling unrest among the peasants. In protest against what they consider an unsatisfactory pension scheme, the farmers in some scattered parts of the country organized Peasants' Self-Defense Committees and threatened to stop deliveries of their produce.[10]

The new, more openly nationalistic and assertive atmosphere in the country was underlined by the demonstrations in Warsaw on the occasion of the sixtieth annivarsary of Poland's independence. On November 11, 1978, after a solemn mass at St. John's Cathedral, a crowd of some three thousand people marched to the Tomb of the Unknown Soldier to place several wreaths there. Patriotic and religious hymns were sung and spontaneous speeches, praising independence and democracy, were given.[11] On January 2, 1979, another high mass was consecrated at the Warsaw Cathedral, this time to commemorate the fortieth anniversary of the death of the leader of the National Democratic party, Roman Dmowski. While singing the ancient Polish national anthem, the crowd, composed of some five hundred people. spontaneously reverted to the words which had been used in the century when Poland had been enslaved by its neighbors: "God return us our freedom." On both occasions the communist authorities carefully refrained from any interference whatsoever with the participants.

DISARRAY IN THE PARTY

In the face of the mounting economic and political difficulties, the leadership of the Polish United Workers' Party has maintained an outward facade of unity. To some extent, unity has, in fact, been there. After his coming to power, Gierek skillfully disposed of all his potential rivals in the party, and at the Seventh Congress in December 1975, he filled the key positions with his own men. Since that time there have been surprisingly few personnel changes. The only event of any consequence was the shifting in December 1976 of a young and able Politburo member, Stefan Olszowski, from the post of Minister of Foreign Affairs to the Party Secretariat, where he was entrusted with the task of overseeing the New Economic Maneuver. Premier Piotr Jaroszewicz, despite the fact that since the fiasco of the price increases his popularity in the country plummeted, has managed to retain his post. Gierek evidently has been reluctant to oust the Prime Minister, perhaps fearing that the changes at the top might not stop there.

It has been a <u>secret de polichinelle</u> in Warsaw, however, that beneath the surface serious differences exist among the PUWP leaders. There has been no revival of clearly identifiable factions such as existed in the 1960s, but there have been increasingly sharp divisions in the Politburo and the Secretariat over some specific issues. The most significant among them, of course, have been the methods of dealing with the economic crisis and of coping with political opposition. The moderate wing has favored economic decentralization, expansion of cultural and religious freedoms, and expanded consultations with the workers. In contrast, the hardline wing has advocated centralized economic planning and management and tougher measures towards the opposition. The split has often, although not uniformly, reflected the professional preoccupations of various individuals. Persons responsible for culture, science, agriculture, and foreign affairs have leaned towards a moderate course, while those concerned with ideology, party affairs, and internal security have favored the hard line. Gierek and his closest supporters have oscillated between the two groups, although, since the spring of 1977, they have moved closer to the moderate wing.

The tug of war between the opposing party wings has from time to time surfaced in the press. The showing of "The Marble Man" resulted in a controversy over permissible limits of cultural expression. On April 4, 1977, the paper identified closely with the hardliners, Zycie Warszawy (the Warsaw Daily) denounced the film as a one-sided and distorted presentation of the Stalinist era. It was also revealed in the press, no doubt intentionally, that the attack continued at the meeting of the Central Committee on April 14. On that occasion the Secretary of the party organization in Lodz, where the main center of the Polish film industry is located, criticized "The Marble Man" for serious ideological errors.

Even more heated polemics ensued over Rakowski's article in Polityka, in which he advocated decentralization of the economic system. On November 8, 1977, Zycie Warszawy published an article in which Dr. Wladyslaw Ratynski, an obscure social scientist but one who was evidently well-connected among the party hardliners, viciously attacked Rakowski. He even accused the Editor-in-Chief of Polityka of an ideological deviation. In a pointed allusion to the economic reforms in Czechoslovakia during the Dubcek era, Ratynski equated "decentralized socialism" with a "market economy socialism" which, he concluded, inevitably leads to "revisionism". In the November 19 issue of Polityka, Rakowski, clearly stung by the gravity of the charges, hit back hard at Ratynski. He categorically repudiated the accusation that he wanted to go beyond the limits of the socialist system. If all proposals to improve the existing situation were branded as political deviations, he argued, harmful stagnation would result. Indeed, Rakowski turned the tables on Ratynski and charged him with an attempt, by reviving the atmosphere of mutual recriminations, to undermine the unity of the party. Such practices, Rakowski concluded, had been compromised and repudiated a long time ago, while for the past several years the PUWP unity had been fully restored.

Rakowski's assurances about the unity of the party may have been tactically sound, but obviously do not truly reflect the situation there. On the contrary, a widespread expectation exists in Poland that a struggle between the moderate and the hardline wings in the party may erupt at any time, resulting in sweeping personnel changes. Indeed, during Gierek's conspicuous absence from public performances for a good part of the autumn of 1978, apparently due to ill health, rumors about his impending resignation were flying in Warsaw.[12] With the return of the First Secretary to public life at the end of November these were put to rest, but the scathing attack against the party policies delivered at the meeting of the Central Committee on December 13 by the Konin District Secretary, Tadeusz Grabski, reopened speculations about the widening split at the top.

There are good reasons to anticipate a forthcoming revival of the intra-party struggle. In the PUWP leadership, for the time being, the moderates and the hardliners are stalemated. The zigzagging in government policies has largely been a reflection of this situation. As economic conditions in the country deteriorate and popular pressures for changes mount, however, sooner or later the hard choices will have to be made. At this point the rivalry in the PUWP is likely to be intensified with, ultimately, either one wing or the other gaining the upper hand.

The tug of war in the PUWP is delicately interlinked with the activities of the opposition. Popular pressure, as long as it remains confined to proposals for reform within the existing system, is useful to the moderates. Too much pressure, however, could be counterproductive. The demands for a change of the communist system itself play into the hands of hardliners. In an article in Polityka on September 10, 1977, Rakowski subtly warned the opposition against this danger. He noted that there are people in Poland who, by presenting an excessively pessimistic picture of the situation, create a climate of nervousness and tensions. Such activities, in Rakowski's opinion, are not in the interests of the country.

PROSPECTS AND PORTENTS

Both the communist government and the democratic opposition are well aware that the outcome of their confrontation may be determined not only by internal, but also by external, forces. The opposition is confident that, if the danger of Soviet intervention in Poland were removed, they would prevail over the government.[13] The opposition leaders also believe that, if pressed to the wall, Gierek would not invite Soviet troops, but that he would offer substantial concessions to the Polish people. This is because he understands that he could not survive such a major crisis. Soviet intervention would be a tragedy for the Polish nation, but it would be a catastrophy for the Gierek regime. In this respect the interests of the government and the opposition run parallel.

Furthermore, the opposition is convinced that even if the Polish Communists did turn to Moscow for help, in the present international climate the Soviet leaders would be extremely reluctant to oblige. If Moscow refrained from intervening in Poland with force in 1956 and again in 1970 (when, reportedly, Gomulka pleaded with Brezhnev for assistance), it is even less likely to take such a step today. The Poles would resist the invasion with arms and this would lead to a small-scale Soviet-Polish war. Poland, of course, would lose the conflict, but it would have grave consequences for the progress of East-West detente. Indeed, at least so far, Moscow's response to the new crisis in Poland has been remarkably circumspect. The Soviet leaders have continued to voice their full confidence in Gierek, and have abstained from any public references to the activities of the Polish opposition. In November 1976 Moscow even offered substantial economic aid to Warsaw. In addition to granting a one billion ruble low-interest loan, Soviet deliveries of grain and of some raw materials and consumer goods were considerably increased.

Nevertheless, there are limits beyond which Soviet patience had best not be tried by the Poles. Moscow probably would tolerate substantial changes in the existing system in Poland, as long as they were carried out in an orderly fashion and under the aegis of the PUWP. Yet, the Soviet Union is unlikely to accept, as some of the Polish opposition groups have demanded, Poland's assertion of sovereignty and adoption of democracy. The Russians, who are at present flexing their muscles in such faraway places as Ethiopia and Angola, would not easily suffer, regardless of the consequences to East-West detente, a major setback in their own backyard. Should the need arise, as Ratynski's article clearly illustrated, they would also have little difficulty in finding in Warsaw the Polish Husaks.[14]

It is not only the opposition, but also the communist government, which has been using East-West detente to its advantage. Gierek is well aware of the fact that rubbing shoulders with the western leaders enhances his prestige in the eyes of the Poles, and this he has been exploiting to the full. Since mid-1976 he has exchanged visits with President Giscard d'Estaing and has received at home Chancellor Schmidt and President Carter. During his visit to Italy on December 1, 1977, Gierek had an audience, especially widely publicized by the Polish media, with Pope Paul VI.

Gierek's visit to the Vatican marked a new relaxation in state-church relations in Poland. Even earlier, on October 29, Gierek held talks with Cardinal Wyszynski. This was their first meeting, and it was conducted in a style as if negotiations between two sovereigns were taking place. The official communique issued on this occasion emphasized that the Polish Communist leader and the Primate of Poland exchanged views on "the most important problems of the nation". The formal aspect of the meeting accurately reflected political reality. Cardinal Wyszynski today is undoubtedly the most respected man in the country. His courageous defense of religious freedom and human rights has won him enormous prestige among the Polish people. At the same time, he has consistently followed a thoroughly realistic course, and whenever the danger of Soviet intervention has arisen, as in 1956 and 1970, he has appealed to the Poles for calm and restraint.[15] Cardinal Wyszynzki is probably the only person in the country who could effectively check excessive demands on the part of the opposition.[16] Yet he would be unlikely to do so unless, in return, Gierek would curb the hardliners in the party and introduce popular reforms into the country.

The elevation on October 16, 1978, of the Archbishop of Cracow, Karol Cardinal Wojtyla, to the papacy has introduced momentous new elements into state-church relations in Poland. The communist government reacted to this historic event with considerable grace by declaring itself, at least ostensibly, to be delighted to see that a Pole has ascended to the Throne of St. Peter. The Chairman of the State Council, Henryk Jablonski, led the Polish delegation to Rome and the entire inauguration ceremony was shown live on Polish television. Yet there is no question that the election of John Paul II has complicated the situation of the Gierek regime even further. It has given a tremendous moral boost to the Polish Catholics and it has encouraged them in their demands for greater religious and civic freedoms. It has also diminished the credibility of the Soviet threat; knowing that such an action would turn against them the Catholics all over the world, the Russians would be doubly careful to avoid intervening in Poland with force. At the same time, the enhanced prestige of the Catholic Church need not necessarily have only adverse effects for the communist government; for if the state-church *modus vivendi* were to be preserved, and possibly even expanded, it would contribute to the strengthening of the forces of moderation in the country.

As one of the writers for the *samizdat* paper, *Opinia,* Andrzej Woznicki, observed early in 1978, Poland stands at the crossroads. There is no return to the situation which existed prior to June 1976. The communist regime has little choice but to offer meaningful concessions to the Polish people. Nothing short of this will defuse the present crisis. This reality was underlined by a group of veteran communists, headed by a former PUWP First Secretary, Edward Ochab. In a letter issued in October 1977, they urged the present Party leaders to adopt a broad program of democratization.

Should the Gierek regime fail to carry out popular reforms, pressure from the opposition will probably increase. In such a situation, political forces in the country would become sharply polarized, with the danger that political events might overtake them all and necessitate Soviet intervention. Yet this would not solve anything. Moscow's direct involvement in Poland would only defer, but not eliminate, the existing problems. Indeed, by intensifying the Poles' resentment against the Russians, it would precipitate another, even more bitter, political confrontation at some future date.

By 1979, the turning point in Poland still had not been reached, but the tensions continued to buildup. On several occasions in the past, Gierek has proved to be a cleaver politician with a good sense of timing. There is still an odd chance that he may do it once again, and by getting rid of some of his particularly unpopular collaborators, he would restore the prestige of the government, as well as his own. There is a strong possibility, however, that Gierek eventually will be deposed by a palace revolution in the upper echelons of the party or by popular explosion, or both. As the decade of the seventies drew to its conclusion, the inefficaciousness of the Polish political system remained and tempers among the people were short.

NOTES

1. For an account of the events leading to the June 1976 workers' outbreak and the Communist government's initial reaction to it, see Adam Bromke, "A New Juncture in Poland," Problems of Communism (September/October 1976).

2. An excellent analysis of economic developments in Poland in the 1970s is presented by Zbigniew M. Fallenbuchl, "The Polish Economy in the 1970s," in East European Economics Post-Helsinki, Joint Economic Committee, Congress of the United States.

3. Ann Crittendon, "Poland in Bid for Loan, Will Let West's Banks Monitor Economy," The New York Times, January 26, 1978. For a penetrating analysis of Poland's indebtedness to the West see: Richard Portes, "East Europe's Debt to the West: Interdependence is a Two-Way Street," Foreign Affairs (July 1977), pp. 757-780.

4. The early policies of the Gierek regime are discussed in Adam Bromke and John W. Strong (eds.), Gierek's Poland. New York: Praeger, 1973; and also in Adam Bromke, "Poland Under Gierek, A New Political Style," Problems of Communism (September/October 1972).

5. Aneks (London), (December 1976), pp. 43-44.

6. Political developments in Poland in the late 1960s are discussed in Adam Bromke, "Poland's Political Crisis," The World Today (March 1969),

and "Beyond the Gomulka Era," Foreign Affairs (April 1971).

7. Dissent in Poland, Reports and Documents in Translation, December 1975-July 1977 (London, 1977), p. 157.

8. For an interesting, although perhaps over-optimistic account of the developments in Poland in 1977, see Peter Osnos, "The Polish Road to Communism," Foreign Affairs (October 1977).

9. Reprinted in Kultura (December 1977), pp. 138-141.

10. Sue Masterman, "Tide of protest by Polish farmers," The Times (October 6, 1978).

11. For an account of the demonstration see: Bernard Margueritte, "Pologne: manifestation spontanee pour le 60e anniversaire de l'independence," Le Figaro (November 13, 1978).

12. Paul Hoffman, "Polish Rumors About Gierek Fly," The New York Times (November 26, 1978).

13. A concise exposition of the opposition strategy was presented by Adam Michnik on December 16, 1976 in Le Monde. For some other programmatic statements by leading members of the opposition see Ruch Oporu (Paris, 1977) and Aneks (London), No. 13-14, 1977.

14. For more detailed analysis of Soviet attitude toward the changes in Poland see Adam Bromke, "Czechoslovakia 1968-Poland 1978: a dilemma for Moscow," International Journal, Vol. XXXIII, No. 4 (Autumn 1978).

15. For a penetrating analysis of state-church relations in Poland see Thomas E. Heneghan, "The Loyal Opposition: Party Programs and Church," RFE Research, February 28, 1978 (mimeographed).

16. Unfortunately, Cardinal Wyszynski's health is not good; in 1977 he twice underwent serious surgery. The communist government seems to be as much concerned about it as is the entire Polish society. When the Cardinal was hospitalized, official bulletins about his medical progress were issued regularly.

Part 2

The Party, Institutions, Participation, and the Policy Process

2
The Sejm as Symbol: Recent Polish Attitudes Toward Political Participation

Sarah Meiklejohn Terry

"It is already a truism that the activity of the Sejm . . . is a kind of barometer of the general climate and pulse of political life (in Poland). Just as an intensification of its activity and an expansion of its role in the system is an expression of accelerated social change and democratic development, so too a waning of the Sejm's activity and a diminution of its authority is a sympton of stagnation and set backs in the development of social and political relations."[1]

"You see, our representative institutions really <u>are</u> democratic--even the deputies to the Sejm didn't know what was going on until the last moment! (Comment of a nonparty deputy to the Sejm on the secrecy surrounding the June 1976 decision to raise food prices.")[2]

The purpose of this essay is twofold: to provide an overview of current Polish thinking on questions of participation and representation, most recently in the context of "developed socialism"; and to examine the extent to which the rhetoric of socialist democracy has been reflected in the performance of the single most important representative institution in Poland, the Sejm. I

The author wishes to express her appreciation to the International Research and Exchanges Board for its support of part of the research on which this chapter is based. She is also grateful for the research assistance of Beth Holmgren, of the Slavic Department and Russian Research Center, Harvard University.

have chosen the Sejm in part because it is designated in the Constitution as "the highest organ of state power." The more important reason however, is that, as the first quotation above indicates, the vicissitudes in the Sejm's fortunes over the past few decades have been an accurate barometer of the seriousness with which Poland's communist leadership at any point in time has regarded the need for meaningful participation in the decision-making process, and thus provide an important aspect of the political context in which the more general question of popular participation is being discussed today.

THE SEJM 1956-1970

Indeed, so striking are some of the parallels in the Sejm's fortunes between the periods following Gomulka's return in 1956 and his fall in 1970 that the salient features of the earlier era bear a brief review here. Already a forum for open criticism by the spring of 1956, the Sejm's revitalization received official sanction at the October Plenum of the PUWP's Central Committee. "The Party," stated the resolution of the plenum, "will strive to create both the political and legal conditions to enable the Sejm, the leading organ of state authority in a people's democracy, to execute its fundamental constitutional task"--i.e., to create conditions in which "parliament will become an effective instrument of society's control over the actions of the government and state administration."[3] In January of the following year, the official slate sponsored by the Front of National Unity for election to the new Sejm included for the first time an element of choice; that is, the number of candidates exceeded the number of seats to be filled by approximately percent and included a larger number of fifty noncommunist representatives.[4] In addition, a new set of rules designed to raise the Sejm's effectiveness as a legislative and oversight body introduced the concept of two readings, strengthened the provisions for deputy interpellations, and increased the number of standing committees from eleven to nineteen. The new rules also introduced so-called "desiderata," a mechanism giving committees the right to request information from the government or an individual agency--a right which the committees invoked more than 2,500 times over the next four years.[5]

Overall, during the next several years the activity of the Sejm was, by most indicators, four to five times greater than it had been at the height of Stalinism. During the 1956-1958 period, for instance, the Sejm sat in plenary session for an average of twenty days per year, compared with a mere four days per year from 1952-1955; during the same period it enacted an average of forty laws per year, compared with a total of eleven for the previous four years. Conversely, the number of decrees issued by the Council of State during periods when the Sejm was not in session dropped from a high of fifty-two in 1953 to twelve in 1957, and then to zero in 1958. Moreover, the Sejm no longer served as an automatic and unanimous rubber stamp for government bills. Committee meetings for the entire second term (1957-1961) totalled 1,203, compared with 247 for the 1952-1956 term; and nearly half of the 160 laws enacted during the second Sejm were substantively amended in committee, while four were rejected altogether. In addition, more than two-thirds of the bills remained under consideration for a month or more (55 percent for one to three months, another 13 percent for more than three months), compared with a mere 15 percent in the first term; and ten of the laws enacted originated within the Sejm rather than in the government.[6]

Beyond these improvements in legislative practice, reformers pressed for more far-reaching changes of a structural nature. Legal scholars began calling for a clarification of constitutional provisions pertaining to the Sejm; the existing wording of its relationship to other organs of state was, they argued, characterized by excessive "brevity," "imprecision," and "flabbiness," which had effectively undermined its theoretical supremacy. Of particular concern were the decree power, indiscriminate use of which had virtually stripped the Sejm of its legislative functions, and the elimination of its investigative arm, the Supreme Control Chamber (Najwyzsza Izba Kontroli), which had been dissolved in 1952 because there was "no longer any place for an organ of state control independent of the Government."[7]

Politically more explosive, however, were the views of Julian Hochfeld, professor of philosophy and a former socialist, as well as deputy to the Sejm. Writing in the April 1957 issue of the Central Committee's theoretical journal, Nowe Drogi, Hochfeld launched a stinging attack on the "monistic" character of the socialist state.[8] While the principles of democratic centralism as "traditionally conceived" might suit the needs of a communist party in opposition or in the process of consolidating its revolution, he argued that historical experience no longer "permits blind faith in the revolutionary honesty and wisdom of the party leadership as the sole defense against the bureaucratization of socialist governments"--that unfettered power in the hands of a single party will lead to an "anti-democratic degeneration" of the state, which can be averted or overcome only through the introduction of institutionalized "checks and balances" on the arbitrary power of the apparat. Though rejecting the idea of an opposition party as opening the door for a reversal of socialist achievements, he nonetheless favored a genuine restoration of parliament's authority and independence within the political system:

> Elections and control over their regularity, the organs of the Sejm and deputy caucuses, the normalization of Sejm procedure and deputy privileges, the openness of debate and interpellations--all this has meaning from the point of view of the popular masses only insofar as it is not pure fiction, a facade, behind which is hidden the mechanism of an institutionally uncontrolled government.[9]

As one means of ensuring that the restoration of parliamentary norms would be more than a fiction, Hochfeld proposed that the communist delegation within the Sejm be granted limited autonomy from the central party leadership. The party's caucus would continue to exercise discipline over its members and would continue to be guided in its actions by the decisions of the Central Committee and party congress; however, "within certain limits--namely, in the course of debates (not votes!), in committees of the Sejm, and in written interpellations--freedom could remain with the party deputies." "The guiding idea of this conception," he continued:

> is the thought that <u>the caucus should be the body entrusted with the collective realization of the leading role of the party in the Sejm,</u> and not merely an executive arm of such classical central party authorities as the Politburo and CC Secretariat. By this means it would undoubtedly be possible to build a system

which--without jeopardizing the state leadership of our party, but likewise without equating that leadership with the undivided control of the central organs of the party--would begin to function as a system of "checks and balances."[10]

While under no illusions that implementation of his proposals would bring about "government by the people," Hochfeld did believe that they would make it impossible for the state to govern in total disregard of the diverse interests within society, and that they would guarantee a basic minimum of democratic rights and freedoms. Moreover, although his primary concern in this article was with the role the Sejm could play in curbing the arbitrary power of the state, he also recognized that other forms of institutionalized interest articulation and participation were an integral part of this process:

> Today as in the past the struggle for democratic rights and freedoms is accompanied by, and culminates in, the emergence of various types of voluntary associations and organizations, thanks to which society ceases to be "atomized" in the face of the power of the state and becomes "articulated." Particular classes, strata and social groups impart a distinctive character to these associations and organizations and leave their imprint on the rights and freedoms won as a result of their struggle. If one speaks of an institutional guarantee of civil rights and freedoms, then the emergence and functioning of such institutions as local self-government, trade unions, economic associations, scientific organizations, etc., play an extraordinarily important role. . . . (On the other hand), it is a characteristic phenomenon that the liquidation or absorption by the state of all public associations--of all the traditional forms through which particular classes, strata and social groups are "articulated"--as a rule accompanies every policy of eliminating democratic rights and freedoms, (every) dictatorial, totalistic policy.[11]

Despite the undeniable gains made in the post-October period (and with the exception of the Supreme Control Chamber which was reestablished in December 1957), none of these proposals--neither those for a clarification of the Sejm's constitutional position nor Hochfeld's appeal for a system of checks and balances--made any headway. On the contrary, instead of a loosening of centralized control over the party's delegation in the Sejm, the Third Congress of the PUWP in 1959 mandated a tightening of discipline.[12] Moreover, even the modest improvements in the Sejm's performance fell far short of the initial pledge of transforming it into "an effective instrument of society's control over the actions of the government and state administration"--thus confirming Hochfeld's fears of another "anti-democratic degeneration" in the absence of institutionalized controls. The element of electoral choice has turned out to be little more than an elaborate facade; for, with the exception of a single instance in the 1957 election in which a seat temporarily went unfilled because no candidate received the required 50 percent of the votes,[13] in no election since then has a favored candidate to the Sejm failed to be elected, and by an overwhelming majority. In fact, in the last three elections (1969, 1972, and 1976), only a handful of candidates below the line--i.e., those in excess of the number of seats to be filled in each district--have received as much as 5 percent of the votes.[14] In addition, as the 1960s progressed, the various indicators of Sejm activity--whether numbers of days in plenary session, bills passed, committee meetings held, bills initiated within the Sejm, interpellations or formal requests (desiderata) presented to the government--all showed a persistent decline; what little leverage had been gained over such crucial policy areas as the annual economic plan and budget was lost.[15] Gradually the most outspoken deputies found themselves stricken from the list for the next election--or in a few cases removed themselves, not wishing to take part any longer in what they viewed as a charade.[16]

To be sure, not all of the post-October gains were lost: use of the decree power was not revived; though their total number was constantly declining, a large percentage of the bills reaching the Sejm were still being considered for one to three months or longer; and more than half were still undergoing substantive revision in committee. Yet, by the end of the Gomulka era, the mood and performance of the Sejm were clearly symptomatic of the stagnation and alienation that had overtaken the political life in Poland in general.

THE SEJM 1971-1976

At least in the area of parliamentary activity, the advent of the Gierek regime witnessed a replay of the scenario of fifteen years earlier. First at the Eighth Central Committee Plenum in February of 1971, and later at the Sixth Party Congress in December of that year, the new First Secretary stressed the urgency of "raising the role and authority of the Sejm and . . . (its) committees" and--in a comment that reveals as much about the lethargy and neglect into which that body had fallen as it does about Gierek's intention to revive it--of "establishing the principle that the government should present to the Sejm the general directions of (its) work and that these matters should be discussed in plenary sessions of the Sejm."[17]

Not surprising in the wake of such pronouncements, the Sejm's vital signs again surged upward to their highest levels since the immediate post-1956 period (see Table 2.1). Once again, formal parliamentary procedures were revived or strengthened--e.g., the use of interpellations and the practice of two readings, both of which had fallen into disuse. And once again, the Sejm's rules were revised--this time permitting committees to initiate legislation, increasing the effectiveness of "desiderata" by setting a thirty day limit for the government's response, introducing "deputy questions" (a streamlined form of interpellation for "less complicated matters"), and even empowering deputies to intervene on behalf of aggrieved constituents with administrative agencies.[18] In addition, new departures of an organizational nature seemed to attest to Gierek's sincerity in wanting to improve the quality of legislation, as well as the degree of legislative-administrative coordination. The newly created Legislative Committee of the Sejm (Komisja Prac Ustawodawczych), on the one hand, and Legislative Council (Rada Legislacyjna) attached to the Council of Ministers, on the other, were to coordinate the legislative activities of their respective branches, provide technical legal assistance to other committees or agencies of government, ensure the relevancy and consistency of legislative proposals with existing law, and draw up long-range plans for updating and recodfying the law. The number of Sejm committees was again expanded, from nineteen to twenty-two, and their jurisdictions redrawn to better correspond to ministerial divisions. For their part, the min-

TABLE 2.1
Basic Data on the Sejm's Activity, 1952-1976, By Term[a]

	I[b] 1952-56 (1956 only)	II[b] 1957-61	III[b] 1961-65	IV[b] 1965-69	V[b] 1969-72 (1971 only)	VI[d] 1972-76 (1972 only)[b]
No. of Deputies to Sejm	425	459	460	460	460	460
From PUWP (% of total)	273 (64.2)	239 (52.0)	256 (55.7)	255 (55.4)	255 (55.4)	255 (55.4)[e]
No. Plenary Sittings	39 (22)	59	32	23	18 (8)	32 (8)
Days Plenary Debate	39 (22)	71	44	40	22 (11)	38 (12)
Laws Passed	42 (31)	174	93	60	36 (21)	103 (46)
Decrees Issued	161 (46)	13	1	1	0	11
Bills Rejected by Sejm	0	4	5	2	2 (na)	0
Deputy Interpellations	69 (69)	139	13	15	37 (36)	na (7)
No. Committee Meetings	247 (na)	1203	887	801	538 (213)	1060
Subcommittee Meetings	na	na	na	835	na (194)[c]	847
Field Trips by Committees	na	na	na	336	248 (na)	523

Desiderata Addressed to Government	--	2539	1842	1298	611(288)[c]	442
No. Bills Substantively Amended in Committee	23(na)	75	59	32	20(na)	na(12)
Bills Remaining in Sejm:						
Less Than 1 Week	16(na)	9	1	2	2(na)	na(17)
More Than 1 Month	6(na)	109	68	44	26(na)	na(18)

a Elections to the Sejm held: November 1952, January 1957, April 1961, May 1965, June 1969, March 1972 and March 1976.

b Data for the I through V terms, plus the first year of the VI term, compiled from <u>Sejm PRL</u>, pp. 344-45, 445, 452, 457, and 504-23.

c Data for 1971 only from Sokolewicz, "Changes in the Structure and Functions of the Polish Sejm," <u>East Central Europe</u>, II, No. 1 (1975), pp. 86-89.

d Data for VI term from Jarosz, "Niektore nowe elementy" and "Dzialalnosc ustawodawcza Sejmu."

e Communist representation rose slightly in the VII Sejm, elected in March 1976, to 261 of 460, or 56.7%.

istries were instructed to consult with the appropriate Sejm committees in drafting their legislative proposals; likewise, the committees were urged to cooperate more among themselves and to open their deliberations both to outside experts as well as to local authorities and relevant public opinion groups.[19]

Not surprising also, legal scholars were quick to take advantage of the more receptive political climate to renew their demands for constitutional reform. Although by no means unanimous in their views, and generally more circumspect in their criticisms than Hochfeld had been a decade and a half earlier--one finds no repetition of such phrases as "anti-democratic degeneration," no direct criticism of democratic centralism, no references to a "system of checks and balances" or to the necessary "articulation" of society--nonetheless they based their proposals on essentially the same premise: to wit, the need for institutionalized restraints on the arbitrary power of the state, including an enlarged and more autonomous role for representative organs. As one proponent of reform wrote, "the real role of representative organs in our constitutional system is dependent upon the extent to which the leading role of the Party is implemented through the representative system, and the extent to which it is implemented outside it."[20] Another analyzed the failure of the system to develop institutionalized guarantees of legality, noting that the disdain for such guarantees shown by "the ideology of the 'personality cult'" was rooted in the "mistaken assumption" that:

> in a socialist society an atmosphere of complete trust is automatically created between the working masses and the state leadership. . . . Rejected out of hand was the simple notion that, in every social system in which relations of authority exist among people, tests of the mutual trust between rulers and ruled are essential. Thus also in a socialist state it is not possible to speak of some kind of unlimited trust, for no system is able to mould the perfect human type free of weakness and susceptibility to error. . . . The superiority of state organs over society can in no case become a political axiom, for all people are fallible and frequently commit errors in the performance of their functions. . . . Therefore the homogeneity of

> society and state apparatus, with respect to social class, is an insufficient guarantee of the correct expression of the will of the proclaimed master of the state by those exercising power.[21]

Among the more frequent targets of criticism were the long-familiar ones of the unlimited decree power and the inadequacy of the provisions securing the Sejm's theoretical supremacy over other organs of state.[22] But to these were added new concerns and suggestions, based in part on the example of recent constitutional changes in other East European states.[23] First (and the apparent contradiction notwithstanding), there was a growing realization that the most serious challenge to the Sejm's legislative prerogatives came, not from the decree power in the hands of the State Council, but from the unchecked growth of administrative law. In part because the decree power was only rarely invoked during the 1960s, in part because it was deemed to have a residual utility for emergency measures or supplementary legislation--but mostly because the decline in the number of decrees had not been matched by a comparable increase in the legislative authority of the Sejm--the focus of attention shifted to the question of controlling the myriad orders and regulations issuing from the ministries and administrative agencies. There were suggestions, for instance, that laws passed by the Sejm in the future be more comprehensive and detailed, thereby effectively increasing the body's control over the interpretation and implementation of policy and reducing the latitude left to the government; also that the supremacy of both constitutional and parliamentary law over administrative law be clearly spelled out, as well as those matters to be regulated solely by legislative act.[24] Closely related to the problem of administrative law was that of ensuring the conformity of all forms of law with the constitution. Citing a 1968 addition to the Czechoslovak constitution which specified that "the interpretation and application of all legal rules must be in agreement with the constitution and constitutional acts of the federation, one writer commented that, while such a principle could be deduced from earlier constitutions and legal doctrine, the fact that it had not been explicitly incorporated in the fundamental law "could not remain without influence on practice." The obvious implication of this passage was that Poland's constitution was similarly deficient and should be amended to provide for a review of the constitutionality of all normative acts, whether through the courts, a special committee of parliament or some alternative mechanism.[25]

Despite scant progress toward resolving these fundamental structural issues (a subject to which I shall return below), some of the early results of the procedural and organizational innovations in the Sejm's activities were modestly encouraging. Apart from the purely statistical indicators of increased legislative activity--e.g., 103 laws enacted during the sixth term (1972-1976) compared with 36 in the fifth (of which 21 were passed in 1971 after the advent of the Gierek regime)--there is other evidence to suggest that the deputies were eager to take advantage of their increased latitude. Out of the total of 103 bills enacted, the newly formed Legislative Committee participated in an advisory capacity in the deliberations on all 87 referred to committee, reportedly contributing to their internal clarity and consistency with existing law.[26] Although the vast majority of legislative proposals continued to emanate from the government, informal consultations between the initiating ministries or agencies and the corresponding committees of the Sejm not only offered deputies the possibility of influencing bills in the drafting stage, as well as sufficient lead time to produce a comprehensive and considered piece of legislation,[27] but (according to one unofficial source) occasionally served as a channel for quashing particularly offensive proposals at an early stage and without incurring the risks of an open confrontation.[28] In addition, while the plenary sessions remained, in the words of one close observer, "the most painful problem in the whole mechanism of the Sejm's functioning," even here there was some improvement, particularly in the frequency of participation by the Premier and other government ministers.[29]

Perhaps the most intriguing departure from past practice was the initiation by the leadership of the Sejm itself of a series of wide-ranging policy reviews. Beginning in early 1974, and continuing through the end of 1975, groups of committees (numbering in each case from seven to fifteen) investigated seven different policy areas for periods ranging from five months to two years. The topics studied spanned the gamut of socio-economic problems from investment policy and raw material supply to environmental protection and consumer services; the most extensive undertaking of this sort was the two-year review of Poland's family code, involving all thirteen Sejm committees as well as consultations at the provincial level and with outside experts, and leading eventually to substantial revisions of the code.[30]

To be sure, all of these developments together comprised, at best, a first hesitant step on the road to a working parliamentary system. Nonetheless, it was enough to evoke the following bit of self-congratulatory rhetoric at the Party's Seventh Congress in December of 1975:

> In the system of institutions of socialist democracy, the Sejm occupies a special place as the highest organ of state authority, which through the making of laws and the exercise of control functions creates the basis for the operational legal activity of the state apparatus. The Sejm has become an important forum for the practical realization of the principle of cooperation of our party with the allied parties and nonparty representatives in implementing the program of socialist construction. . . . The fundamental functions of the Sejm were invested with content and actions, which contributed to raising its status and authority. Likewise, the function of the Sejm as an organ integrating socialist authority with society has been developed. . . .[31]

Yet, within the next six months the Gierek regime was confronted with two crises, both of which served to spotlight the essential impotence of the Sejm as well as the marginal and superficial nature of all forms of officially sanctioned participation. The first of these was the row in the winter of 1975-1976 over the regime's proposed constitutional amendments, in which none of the provisions so long sought to strengthen the Sejm's position were included. Indeed, the manner in which the amendments were introduced--as a *fait accompli* requiring only pro forma public "discussion" and ratification by the Sejm--provided a classic example of precisely those procedures the constitutional reformers had hoped to eliminate. In the end, it was not the provisions (or more accurately the paucity of provisions) pertaining to the Sejm which aroused opposition, nor was it the Sejm which demanded and obtained concessions in the pending amendments;

rather, it was the combined and unofficial forces of the Church and dissident intellectuals.[32]

The second crisis came, of course, in June 1976 when the Gierek regime, despite all of its pious protestations about participation and consultations, made virtually the same mistake Gomulka has made six and a half years earlier, by imposing unexpectedly high increases in food prices on an unprepared population. Once again, it was not the Sejm which forced the government to first revise and then withdraw its proposals but, for the third time in twenty years, widespread protests and rioting among the workers. In fact, so little advance notice of the increases were the deputies given that one member was prompted to make the facetious remark quoted at the beginning of this chapter, implying that the people's representatives were as powerless and uninformed as the people themselves.

EVALUATION OF THE SEJM'S PERFORMANCE SINCE 1970

What had gone wrong? Why was it that, despite assurances to the contrary, proposals of such major import were presented to the Sejm--and to the public at large--with a minimum of preparation and consultation, and in a form and context which implied that they would be accepted without alteration or delay? And how was it that Gierek could so badly misjudge the mood of the nation on precisely the issue that had destroyed his predecessor and brought him to power? The answer to these questions would seem to be twofold, relating first to persistent deficiencies in the structure and functioning of the Sejm and, second, to a shift away from the Sejm (and representative institutions in general) as the mode of "participation" preferred by the regime as it moves toward the stage of "developed socialism."

Looking first at what I have just called "persistent deficiencies" in the Sejm's operations, it is not my intention to belittle the very real gains made by that institution in the early 1970s and which I have briefly outlined above. Yet, on closer examination, it becomes clear that the benefits of these gains have been concentrated overwhelmingly in areas peripheral to the central policy concerns of the regime, and that parliamentary influence over the latter has remained negligible. For example, although more than half of the Sejm's legislative activity during its sixth term involved "socio-economic questions" (56 of the

103 laws passed), according to one authoritative review, "'economic' laws for the most part concerned the private economy (e.g., the performance and organization of the crafts, management of nonstate-owned forests, retail trade by the nonsocialized sector, etc.) and only to a small degree the main branches of the socialized economy." To illustrate his point, the author noted that, during the entire four years of the sixth term, none of the three committees responsible for virtually all industrial production in the socialized sector (i.e., those for Mining, Energy and Chemicals, for Heavy and Machine Industry, and for Light Industry) was once designated as the committee with primary jurisdiction over a bill--because, as one of their final reports stated, "the need did not arise." Of course, he continued:

> one should keep in mind the special role of acts of socio-economic planning, as the main form in which the Sejm influences the direction of development of the basic branches of the economy. The fact remains, however, that the fundamental elements of the structure as well as of the methods and forms of the planning and functioning of the economic system have not to this day undergone comprehensive legislative regulation.[33]

Moreover, even for those measures that were brought before the Sejm, the tendency to push the more important bills through with only the most perfunctory consideration persisted. Indeed, on a single day, March 29, 1972 (less than two weeks after the election of the sixth Sejm and the same day on which its rules were amended to ensure more thorough scrutiny of legislative proposals), no fewer than sixteen bills were rushed through plenary session without amendment or even token referral to committee. Of these, seven dealt with the establishment of new top-level administrative agencies and, in a blanket grant of authority, delegated to the Council of Ministers the power to define their jurisdictions.[34] Overall only 11 of the 103 bills received the mandated two readings; and when it did occur, the first reading was more often than not a mere formality. Although the majority of bills were referred to committee, deputies frequently complained of being "taken by surprise" and of having too little time for careful consideration. The adverse consequences of this excessive haste and poor coordination were several: on only one occasion did the committees exercise their newly acquired right to initiate legislation (the revisions of the family code); out of a total of 1,060 committee meetings during the sixth term, only 52 involved the use of outside expertise; rather than attempt to assert their authority through more comprehensive lawmaking, committees tended to settle for pledges on the part of the ministries to keep them better informed of executive rulings; and, finally, the sixth term saw a partial revival of the decree power (eleven decrees issued compared with none in the fifth term).[35] Again, these negative phenomena should not be allowed to obscure the positive achievements of the Sejm in this period; but they can hardly be said to constitute best evidence of the regime's promises of better legislative planning or of "establishing the principle that the government should present to the Sejm the general directions of (its) work and that these matters should be discussed in plenary session."

One obvious reason for the haste and superficiality which continue to mar the Sejm's performance is the fact that, with few exceptions, deputies hold full-time jobs elsewhere in the economy or political structure (and for the most part elsewhere in the country). This may well, as is claimed, give them a closer sense of identification with their constituents; however, it also means that they have neither the time nor, in many cases, the expertise, to deal effectively with the complexities of a modern industrial state.[36] Equally problematic are the real or potential conflicts of interest arising from the Sejm's composition and organization. To take just one example: according to one highly authoritative study, while nearly 95 percent of Sejm deputies serve on at least one committee, members of the Presidium of the Sejm (consisting of four members and not to be confused with the State Council) and "certain other deputies who hold the highest party and state positions" are presumably excluded.[37] Full committee rosters are not available; yet a review of data for the current (i.e., seventh) term reveals the following high officials, who serve not merely as ordinary committee members but as chairmen: three Secretaries of the Central Committee of the PUWP (Zdzislaw Zandarowski, CC Secretary for party organization, as chairman of Mandate and Rules; Jozef Pinkowski, a former first deputy chairman of the Planning Commission and a CC Secretary since February 1974, of Economic Plan,

Budget and Finance; and Ryszard Frelek, of Foreign Affairs); two directors of departments in the CC Secretariat (Zbigniew Zielinski, director of the Economic department, as chairman of the Committee on Foreign Trade; and Jarema Maciszewski, director of the Department of Science and Education, of the Education Committee); and Zdzislaw Grudzien, a full member of the Politburo and long-time associate of 1st Secretary Gierek in Silesia, as chairman of the Committee on National Defense. (Gierek himself chaired this committee from 1957 to 1971). In addition, a seventh committee (Labor and Social Affairs) is chaired by a top official in the Central Council of Trade Unions, in effect an arm of the government; while two others (Heavy and Machine Industry and Administration, Local Economy and Environmental Protection) are chaired by deputies who are also members of the State Council, and who therefore could be called upon to review in their capacity as chairmen decree actions in which they participated as members of the State Council. The number of such conflicts (especially of chairmen who are simultaneously full CC Secretaries) is somewhat higher in the seventh than in the sixth Sejm; but the problem has existed in all previous terms and has involved more or less the same committees, while others of a less sensitive nature are sometimes entrusted to noncommunist deputies and/or professionals (e.g., a physician as chairman of Health and Physical Culture, or the rector of a polytechnical institute for the Committee on Science and Technical Progress, etc.)[38]

Behind these deficiencies of an operational and structural nature, the more basic reason for the Sejm's continuing lackluster performance, as well as for Gierek's disastrous misjudgement of the popular mood, lies in his regime's approach to the whole question of participation--and more specifically in a distinct, if subtle, retreat from its early emphasis on the Sejm as the primary institutional forum for popular participation in policy discussions. In retrospect, Gierek, on coming to power, behaved much as Gomulka had in the 1950s, boosting the Sejm's visibility and nominal authority as a symbolic gesture in a time of political unrest only to balk at implementing genuine reform once the situation has stabilized. Nor should this be surprising. After all, a properly functioning parliament implies, as Hochfeld so clearly stated in 1957, the introduction of a "system of checks and balances" that is fundamentally at odds with the existing power structure.

In somewhat oversimplified terms--but without, I think, doing too much violence to reality--one can describe recent Polish thinking on participation as a partially obscured tug of war between those, on the one hand, who stress "consultations" with the working masses and other forms of "direct" participation as the highest form of socialist democracy and, on the other hand, those who place greater weight on "indirect democracy" and who advocate structural reforms for the purpose of improving the effectiveness and influence of representative organs, in both their policy-making and oversight functions. This is not meant to suggest that Poles of either persuasion view direct and indirect forms of participation as mutually exclusive (indeed they are often mentioned in the same breath), any more than either side openly challenges the "need to improve socialist democracy." Rather, it is a battle of nuances--of emphasis and priorities--in which the key phrases have become code words for radically differing approaches to all forms of participation.

For example, it is clear (to me at least) that those who come down on the side of direct "consultations"--and especially those who stress the superiority of "consultative democracy" over "bourgeois (i.e., parliamentary) democracy"--tend to be the conservatives, who are resisting meaningful changes in the status quo. I say this because the consultation process leaves both the initiative and control in the hands of the leadership. It is they who decide: on which issues to seek consultations; with whom to consult (which too often means only with local party functionaries or carefully selected groups); how much information to divulge; and finally, how to interpret the results of the consultation (presumably representing the "will of the people"). It is, in short, a process that provides neither established institutionalized channels through which the populace can articulate views and demands on its own initiative, nor alternative centers of authority which could serve as effective restraints on the concentrated power of the state. On the other hand, those reformers who stress the need to strengthen the system of indirect representation do so not because they reject the utility and desirability of many forms of direct participation,[39] but because of the implied limitations on social initiative and control.

Recognizing that the average citizen has neither the expertise nor the clout to influence policy through an informal consultative process, they see precisely the kinds of institutionalized mechanisms not provided for by that process as essential both to a more responsive political system as well as to a more responsible citizenry.

The issue is further complicated by the fact that this debate is frequently couched in the ideological rhetoric of "developed socialism," a term which itself has become something of a bone in the dog-fight and which, to the extent that it has any specific meaning, implies a need to adapt the present system to meet the demands of post-industrial society and the attendant scientific-technological revolution.[40] As elsewhere in the international communist movement, the differences are reflected on the domestic Polish scene in a polarization of views between those who perceive the future as a streamlined, more efficient extension of the present and, on the other hand, those who see the emergence of a "developed socialist society" as opening the way for, and indeed necessitating, substantive changes in the political structure and political processes. For those of the more conservative outlook, such a society requires not a restructuring of political relationships, but an enhanced role for the professional bureaucracy (the "experts") at the center, accompanied by greater discipline and guided activism in what is depicted as an increasingly homogeneous society; while the opposing view holds that modern technological society is becoming ever more dependent on "human initiative, resourcefulness, and responsibility," which can only be elicited "in a system in which employees feel themselves (to be) truly comanagers" and, therefore, that the political structure must be reformed to reflect the growing complexity and diversity of society.[41]

Although the distinctions between these two approaches are rarely, if ever, as baldly stated in Polish writings as they have been here,[42] there can be little doubt that, until the June 1976 disturbances, it was the first view which predominated. For example, despite gestures in the direction of the Sejm, it was the notion of "consultations"--ironically including promises of consultations on the food price question--that ran through the deliberations of the seventh Party Congress.[43] Again, it was the principle of "consultations" that was incorporated into the revised constitution a few months later,[44] while none of the several proposals to operationalize the Sejm's theoretical primacy was adopted. (Indeed, one could argue that the principle of parliamentary supremacy actually lost ground as a result of two amendments, the first of which placed the Sejm's investigative arm, the Supreme Control Chamber, under the joint supervision of the Sejm and the Council of Ministers; the second not only did not define or limit the decree power of the State Council, but entrusted to that body the power to determine the constitutionality of laws).[45]

Just how little genuine participation and influence over policy "consultations" might afford in practice was rudely demonstrated by the prelude to the June riots. According to the accounts of both Polish and Western observers on the scene,[46] such consultations as took place were confined to local officials and party committees in the factories. In addition, the magnitude of the increases revealed apparently ranged from 25 to 30 percent (scarcely more than had been rumored among the general population for more than a year), rather than the average 70 percent on meat and 100 percent on sugar that were finally announced.[47] A good indication of the restrictions imposed on public discussion of food price policy was the cancellation, about two weeks before the announcement of the increases, of an article scheduled to appear in the leading political weekly, <u>Polityka</u>, advocating a gradual elimination of state food subsidies. Even within the Sejm, the true magnitude of the proposed increases began to reach the deputies only hours before the official pronouncement; the fact that the new prices were to go into effect a mere four days later (from Thursday to the following Monday) hardly left time for judicious parliamentary consideration.

REPRESENTATION AND PARTICIPATION

The shock effect of June 1976 was caused, not so much by the realization that the process of consultations had failed to inform the public and give them a say in the price increase decision, as that it had failed utterly to forewarn the leaders of the likely consequences of their high-handedness.[48] Thus it is not surprising that, as in the wake of previous crises, the 1976 riots have precipitated yet another swing of the pendulum in the direction of renewed tolerance for reformist ideas. While it is not possible in the space available to do more than scratch the surface of recent literature, the three articles reviewed below are representative of the outer limits of official or quasi-official thinking on questions of participation.[49]

The first of these articles, appearing in the September 1976 issue of Nowe Drogi under the deceptively uninspired title "From the Problems of Socialist Democracy," was written by Professor Sylwester Zawadzki, editor-in-chief of Poland's leading legal journal Panstwo i Prawo, a member of the Sejm, and a long-time advocate of the revitalization of representative organs as instruments of control over the professional state bureaucracy.[50] Zawadzki begins by evaluating Poland's political system at her present stage of socialist development and as she prepares for the transition to "developed socialism." Rather like the early proponents of political reform in Czechoslovakia,[51] he defines this new stage as one in which outright class struggle is being replaced by "nonantagonistic contradictions." In other words, there now exists in Poland a broad consensus as to the overall goals of society; yet divergent interests and opinions remain as to the proper means toward those ends, and these divergent views have a legitimate place in the political process. Zawadzki stops short of stating that Poland is faced with a Marxian dilemma: to wit, that of having an obsolete political superstructure which has been outstripped by the development of the socio-economic base. But he does warn that:

> the development of the political and legal superstructure should not lag behind socio-economic development. Together with the potential possibilities and favorable conditions, objective needs for a further development of socialist democracy arise. These are, first requirements of an economic nature, connected with the dominance of socialist ownership as the basis of the socio-economic and political structure. . . . with the scale of the tasks of the socio-economic development program, and with the program for joint management and joint responsibility which is unrealizable without an improvement in the conditions for social initiative.[52]

In essence, what is involved here is a recognition

of the fact that the social structure (and therefore the structure of social interests) does not, as Marx predicted, become increasingly simplified with the development of socialism and, therefore, that "politics" (as the process by which diverse interests are reconciled) cannot give way to Marx's notion of the "mere administration of things."

Zawadzki's special interest is the system of representation, and it is here that he makes his most important and specific contribution. Attacking head-on the notion that the crucial issues of social and economic policy in modern technological society can be resolved only by experts and, therefore, that a rise in the role of specialists "must inevitably mean a curtailment of the influence of the masses and the degradation of democratic institutions," he argues skillfully that the newly adopted constitutional principle of consultations cannot be "based on obtaining directly the opinions of the whole of society"--which in any event is "a practical impossibility short of a nationwide referendum"--"but on seeking the opinion of the widest possible representation of society or the constituencies concerned." Thus "it can be assumed that, likewise in a developed socialist society, indirect forms of democracy will predominate; hence, the special significance of actions aimed at raising the standing and improving the model for all forms of socialist representation." It becomes then, he concludes:

> a question of representation being truly representative, and having the possibility of expressing the broad gamut of views, of submitting the whole range of considerations and proposals to thorough examination and consideration. . . . In conditions of the formation of a developed socialist society, the representative system is confronted by new tasks. For, the period in which contradictions of an antagonistic variety dominated in society is gradually passing into history. Together with the strengthening of the moral and political unity of the nation, social contradictions will take on a predominantly nonantagonistic character. This essential difference cannot not find reflection in the functions of the representative system and its procedures, in the climate for discussing problems and expressing opinions. . . .[53]

At this point, Zawadzski cautiously asks whether "the evolution of criteria for the selection of representatives as well as the further development of electoral system (shouldn't) be considered," and specifically:

> whether in conditions of a developed socialist society--and without resigning one iota from the fundamental principle of ensuring the socialist direction of development--it is not necessary to seek solutions which will enrich the existing electoral system through broader possibilities for expressing preferences with respect to candidates. . . Recognizing elections as an expression of attitude toward the the electoral program, we should strive toward (a situation in which) they are also an expression of attitude toward different candidates who represent that program. . . .[54]

While far less explicit and forceful than Hochfeld had been twenty years earlier in proposing limited autonomy for Sejm deputies from central party direction,[55] Zawadzki's proposal nonetheless carries the same implication. And, indeed, he goes on to remind his readers that democratic centralism is comprised of two elements--democracy as well as centralism--and that any deviation from the proper balance between them will have negative social and political consequences.[56]

A second article, appearing in mid-1977, on the "socio-economic foundations of the socialist political system" is more explicit in its endorsement of the kinds of institutionalized "checks and balances" Hochfeld had advocated. In it author Jerzy Kowalski, another of Poland's leading legal scholars, suggests that, especially in a socialist system, direct forms of participation may be inadequate to offset the concentrated power of the state. "In striving to develop the socialist system," he states:

> we must keep in mind the distinctness of its socio-economic foundations (from those of the capitalist system), and thus the distinctness of the principles of social action. National ownership of the means of production, as the main factor unifying the social structure in the socialist state, imposes specific requirements for institutional solutions. . . .

> The socialist political structure and its operational principles are closely tied to the requirements of economic organization. This is manifested in a high degree of concentration of economic and political power in a single center. Such a situation demands institutional safeguards against the possibility of the abuse of such great power, abuse not necessarily caused by ill will. Some look to self-management as the solution to the problem of institutional safeguards against the negative consequences of an excessive concentration of power. . . . (However) it cannot play the role with which we are concerned here (i.e., a mechanism ensuring the proper functioning of authority), although in other questions its significance is of first-rank importance. In my opinion, protection against the abuse of power must be sought in more contemporary solutions. Among them are: a strictly observed division of tasks, corresponding more or less to the idea of a "separation of powers"; the institution of rotation (in office); prohibition against the joining of certain functions; a proper role for expertise in the process of decision making; and, finally, the functioning of public opinion (the technical, organizational, legal possibility for its expression) through the channel of representative organs as well as other known forms; meetings, consultations, and the mass media.[57]

Moreover, while sharing Zawadzki's tolerance for the continuing diversity of views within socialist society, Kowalski goes even further to imply that, through its attempts to ignore or stifle conflicting interests in society, the leadership has failed to build a sense of common social purpose and should, therefore, revise the way it interprets the "leading" or "guiding" role of the party:

> It is essential to master the art of using egotistical motives and the play of group interests (not necessarily based on politically conflicting classes) for broader social purposes. Rather than using the play of these interests as a tool, we frequently resort to administrative methods and various appeals which when too often applied, are of limited efficacy.

Suggesting that "the method of nondisclosure and administrative stifling" of conflicting interests--rather than their open confrontation and resolution--"not only does not eliminate social tensions but causes them to accumulate, provoking their spontaneous, uncoordinated and anarchical manifestation," he concludes:

> The party can and should to a greater degree step forward publicly in the role of the coordinator (or) mediator of conflicting interests, and not exclusively as the spokesman of an abstract general interest. The burden of power would through the use of this method be lighter, although the difficulties of leadership would be greater.[58]

The third and in some respects most interesting, of the three articles examined here is by a young sociologist, Krzysztof Jasiewicz, and is entitled: "Interest Articulation in the Polish Political System: A Tentative Model." It was first presented in draft form to a meeting of the Polish Political Science Association, in November 1976 and was the subject of discussion the following month at a small conference sponsored by the Political Sociology Section of the Academy of Sciences.[59] In a sense, Jasiewicz picks up where Zawadzki and Kowalski leave off; that is, he implicitly accepts their premises concerning the existence of a broad consensus in society and, within that framework, the legitimacy of diverse interests in a socialist society as well as the negative consequences of repressing such interests in the name of some abstract general good. The most striking point of the article itself is the author's explicit use of Western interest group theory as an objective, or neutral, tool for describing the Polish political system. His approach to the whole notion of "groups" is remarkably free of the traditional Marxist preoccupation with class analysis. In fact, he describes the range of potential groups in Polish society very much as an American might for his own; that is, group identity might indeed be based on class, but might just as easily be based on other criteria: e.g., more narrowly defined professional ties, territorial or regional identities; institutional or organizational associations; demographic criteria (youth, the elderly, women); or "according to the most diverse characteristics, such as automobile owners, dog owners, parents of small children, etc."

More interesting than the article itself, however, was the discussion it provoked. The treatment of the Polish political system in the article is largely descriptive, and does not include a critique of how existing institutions actually perform as channels for participation and interest articulation. By contrast, the discussion was entirely taken up with the question of performance. Here the consensus of the group was clearly that political and social institutions have failed to function as channels for effective participation, have failed to represent their constituencies--and that (as Kowalski also suggests) it is this failure that is responsible for the emergence of such extra-legal forms of interest articulation as strikes, riots and protest groups. The only feasible remedy, in the opinion of the discussants, is not the suppression of such extra-legal forms, but the development of more adequate channels within the legal institutional structure, thereby rendering these disruptive extra-legal forms unnecessary. It was apparent also that they view the process of group formation as a dynamic one--that the structure of groups and interests in society will constantly change, and therefore that the political system must also be sufficiently flexible and responsive to reflect these changes. One discussant even suggested the legalization of ad hoc organizations to represent emerging interests, a proposal that would seem to be one step short of legal opposition groups. (It is worth noting that Zawadzki, too, emphasized the dynamic nature of socialist development and wrote that "socialist democracy must be viewed not as a congealed state but as a constantly ascending process"--although he in no way associated himself with notions of autonomous interest groups).[60]

TOWARD SOCIALIST DEMOCRACY

Whether this latest round of reformist thinking will produce more lasting results than preceding ones is problematical to say the least. As of this writing (mid-1978), the picture is mixed and not especially promising. On the positive side, publication of articles such as those just reviewed is apparently being encouraged by some officials at a very high level in the Gierek regime, for whom the disruptive effects of unorganized "participation" outside the existing institutional structure have demonstrated the wisdom of finding more orderly and systematic channels for interest articulation.[61] Once again the leadership claims to have rediscovered the virtues of genuine socialist democracy, has promised more extensive and open consultations as well as a more central role for the Sejm in policy formulation, and has boosted the visibility of the two subsidiary parties.[62] In addition, a rather novel development is the quasi-parliamentary role assumed by the Warsaw branch of the Polish Sociological Association whose meetings, frequently attended by state officials as well as association members, serve as an unofficial forum for open discussions on current policy issues.[63]

In a gloomier vein, the recent flap over peasant pensions suggests that, promises notwithstanding, the regime has learned little in the past two years about the process of "consultations"--in this case, failing to inform the peasants of the basis on which their payments into the plan would be based.[64] In the Sejm also, legislative activity in the current seventh term has slowed to less than half the pace of the previous term (twenty-nine bills passed during the first thirty months of this term compared with sixty-nine during the same period in the sixth)--a fact which, in the words of one official, reflects " a progressive shift in the center of gravity (of the Sejm's activities) away from strictly legislative work toward control functions, toward more influence over day-to-day administration."[65] Although in principle a positive trend in that it implies greater emphasis on the important and hitherto neglected area of legislative oversight, in practice such a shift will inevitably distract the limited energies of part-time deputies from the unfinished task of improving basic legislative procedures. Moreover, it is apparent that the Sejm is not being given sufficient latitude to enable it to begin to serve as the kind of "institutional safeguard against the negative consequences of an excessive concentration of power" suggested by Professor Kowalski.[66] On the contrary, when asked whether their expanded oversight role might bring Sejm committees into conflict with administrative agencies, this same official dissented vehemently, stating that "there is no tendency toward an adversarial stance; among the deputies a sense of participation predominates."[67]

Certainly it would be shortsighted to deny that the Sejm has undergone internal structural improvements and a regularization of its operations in the interim. (And it is well to remember that

Parliament, too, evolved slowly from the dependent status of an advisory body to the Court). Yet the fact that these improvements have not measurably increased its influence over the crucial matters of state has sapped the credibility of the institution, and, by extension, of all officially sponsored forms of participation, in the eyes of an increasingly apathetic and alienated population.[68] That many within the party are seriously concerned about the level of popular alienation is evident from the letter sent to Gierek in October 1977 by fourteen more or less formerly prominent politicians and intellectuals, and occasioned by the approach of the National Party Conference in January 1978. Calling the relative political stability since June 1976 "superficial and shallow," the signers described the regime's "vaunted policy of consultation" as a "sham" and appealed to the First Secretary to implement a policy of genuine democratic reform "that would make it possible for the nation to take part in the decision-making processes affecting the country's life."[69]

While it may still be too soon to conclude that the present leadership's promises of good faith have faded with the sense of immediate crisis, the fact that Poland is now in its third cycle of crisis, reform, and retrenchment is scant cause for optimism. Indeed, one of the most striking (and depressing) aspects of the views being expressed by moderate reformers today on questions of participation and parliamentary reform is how little their criticisms and proposals differ from those of Julian Hochfeld twenty-odd years ago, and how meager the progress since 1957 has been. The danger now confronting the regime is that the sands of moderation are again running low in the hourglass--and that, the longer concrete action is put off, the more likely it becomes that whatever concessions Gierek (or his successor) might reasonably be expected to offer will be perceived as "too little, too late."

NOTES

1. Zdzislaw Jarosz, "Niektore nowe elementy w organizacji o formach dzialania Sejmu VI kadencji," *Panstwo i Prawo*, XXXI, No. 8-9 (August-September 1976), p. 4.

2. Personal interview, Warsaw, November 1976.

3. Quoted in Julian Hochfeld, "Z zagadnien parlamentaryzmu w warunkach demokracji ludowej, *Nowe Drogi*, XI, No. 4 (April 1957), p. 71.

4. See, e.g., H. Gordon Skilling, *The Governments of Communist East Europe*. New York: Crowell, 1966, p. 132.

5. For the Sejm rules adopted in 1952, 1957, and amended in 1972, see Andrzej Burda, et. al., *Sejm Polskiej Rzeczypospolitej Ludowej* (hereafter *Sejm PRL*). Wroclaw: Ossolineum, 1975, pp. 473-501; also Andrzej Burda, "Niektore zagadnienia regulaminu sejmowego w Polsce Ludowej," *Panstwo i Prawo*, XII, No. 6 (June 1957).

6. *Sejm PRL*, pp. 445-57 and 511-12.

7. See, e.g., Witold Zakrzewski, "Zagadnienie rewizji Konstytucji," *Panstwo i Prawo*, XII, No. 4-5 (April-May 1957); and Jerzy Stembrowicz, "Konstytucja a ustroj panstwowy i spoleczny," *Panstwo i Prawo*, XXVI, No. 8-9 (August-September 1971), especially p. 235.

8. Hochfeld, "Z zagadnien parlamentaryzmu," pp. 69-80.

9. *Ibid*., p. 76.

10. *Ibid*., pp. 79-80 (emphasis added).

11. *Ibid*., p. 71.

12. Adam Bromke, *Poland's Politics: Idealism vs. Realism*. Cambridge, Massachusetts: Harvard University Press, 1967, p. 168.

13. Stefan Rozmaryn, *The Seym and People's Councils in Poland*. Warsaw: Polonia, 1958, p. 135.

14. For lists of candidates and election results, see the following issues of *Trybuna Ludu*: April 27, May 1-12, and June 3, 1969; February 20 and March 21, 1972; and February 28/29 and March 23, 1976. See also Jerzy Ptakowski, "Parliamentary Elections in Poland," *East Europe*, XIV, No. 8 (August 1965), pp. 15-19.

15. For a detailed treatment of the Sejm's role (or lack of a role) in shaping the national economic plan and budget, see *Sejm PRL*, pp. 418-39, especially 434-35.

16. For instance, the well-known Catholic writer and critic Stefan Kisielewski removed himself from the running in the 1965 elections; personal interview, Warsaw, November 1976.

17. Jarosz, "Niektore nowe elementy," pp. 4-5.

18. Andrzej Gwizdz, "O zmianach w regulaminie Sejmu," *Panstwo i Prawo*, XXVII, No. 10 (October 1972), pp. 4-18; and Wojciech Sokolewicz, "Changes in the Structure and Functions of the Polish Sejm," *East Central Europe*, II. No. 1 (1975), pp. 78-91.

19. Gwizdz, "O zmianach w regulaminie," pp. 13-16; Wlodzimierz Berutowicz, "Doskonalenie prawa--obiektywna koniecznosc rozwoju socjalistycznego," *Nowe Drogi*, No. 10 (October 1973), pp. 86-95; Jerzy Bafia, "Dorobek i doswiadczenia Komisji Prac Ustawodawczych Sejmu PRL," *Panstwo i Prawo*, XXXI, No. 7 (July 1976), pp. 14-16; also Jarosz, "Niektore nowe elementy," and Sokolewicz, "Changes in the Structure," especially pp. 82-84.

20. Witold Zakrzewski, "System przedstawicielski w praktyce," Miesiecznik Literacki, No. 6 (1972), p. 93; quoted in Sokolewicz, "Changes in the Structure," p. 79.

21. Andrzej Burda, "Instytucjonalne gwarancje praworzadnosci i ich rola w panstwie socjalistycznym," Panstwo i Prawo, XXVI, No. 8/9 (August-September 1971), pp. 223-24.

22. See, e.g., ibid., especially pp. 227-30; Stembrowicz, "Konstytucji a ustroj," pp. 231-42; and Kazimierz Dzialocha, "System zrodel prawa w Konstytucji PRL po 20 latach jej obowiazywania," Panstwo i Prawo, XXVII, No. 12 (December 1972), pp. 19-32. See also Sejm PRL, pp. 119ff.

23. Andrzej Gwizdz, "Glowne kierunki rozwoju wspolczesnego konstytucjonalizmu socjalistycznego," Panstwo i Prawo, XXVI, No. 8-9 (August-September 1971), pp. 244-55; Jerzy Stembrowicz, "Zmiany konstytucji w europejskich panstwach socjalistycznych," Panstwo i Prawo, XXVII, No. 5 (May 1972), p. 3-22; Kazimierz Dzialocha, "Zmiany w systemie zrodel prawa w nowych konstytucji socjalistycznych," Panstwo i Prawo, XXVIII, No. 8-9 (August-September 1973), pp. 101-112.

24. Berutowicz, "Doskonalenie prawa"; Andrzej Gwizdz, "Z zagadnien organizacji procesu legislacyjnego," Panstwo i Prawo, XXX, No. 12 (December 1975), pp. 72-82; Jerzy Bafia, "Podstawowe zalozenie tworzenia prawa," Panstwo i Prawo, XXX, No. 7 (July 1975), pp. 3-15; also Sejm PRL, pp. 119-20.

25. Dzialocha, "Zmiany w systemie," pp. 103-106.

26. Concerning the work of this committee, see: Bafia, "Dorobek i doswiadczenia," pp. 17-18; and Zdzislaw Jarosz, "Dzialalnosc ustawodawcza Sejmu PRL VI kadencji," Panstwo i Prawo, XXXII, No. 3 (March 1977), pp. 27-29. In part as a result of its activity, some 1900 amendments, mostly of a technical and editorial nature, were incorporated into the bills considered.

27. E.g., early in the 6th term, several committees elicited information concerning the long-term legislative plans of the corresponding

ministries, a departure from past practice which bore fruit in the form of several substantive pieces of legislation, including: a revised labor code, a charter of teachers' rights and obligations, and other acts dealing with private housing, banks, customs duties, and inland waterways. See ibid., pp. 18-19 and 23.

28. Personal interview with a nonparty member of the Sejm, Warsaw, November 1976. Examples offered of government proposals withrawn as a result of criticism in committee included: one to further tax and restrict the private sector (a policy which has to be reversed starting in the fall of 1976); a second to set up local vigilante groups to monitor changes in the material possessions of citizens (presumably as a deterrent to illegal economic activities); and a third which would have permitted Soviet-style use of psychiatric hospitals to control dissent (see also note 63 below).

29. Jarosz, "Niektore nowe elementy," pp. 6-9. During the 6th term, Premier Jaroszewicz appeared at all 30 "working" plenary sessions, compared with only 11 such appearances during the 5th term--of which 7 took place in 1971. Apart from this change, however, Professor Jarosz is highly critical of the perfunctory and formalized character of plenary "debates."

30. Ibid., pp. 11-12; Bafia, "Dorobek i doswiadczenia," pp. 18-20; Wanda Falkowska, "Rodzina i prawo: zmiany w kodeksie," Polityka, December 13, 1975. This was the only one of the Sejm-initiated policy reviews to produce immediate legislative results.

31. From Chapter II of the Report of the Central Committee; VII Zjazd Polskiej Zjednoczonej Partii Robotniczej, 8-12 grudnia 1975: podstawowe materialy i dokumenty. Warsaw: Ksiazka i Wiedza, 1975, p. 33.

32. For an account of the constitutional debate, which focused on questions of religious freedom, the definition of the party's role and of Poland's relationship with the Soviet Union, see: Radio Free Europe Research (hereafter RFER), "Polish Intellectuals Oppose Change in Constitution," RAD Background Report/183 (December 31, 1975); also

Polish Situation Reports Nos. 1 (January 9 , 1976), 2 (January 16, 1976), 4 (January 30, 1976), and 6 (February 20, 1976).

33. Jarosz, "Dzialalnosc ustawodawcza Sejmu," pp. 21-22 (emphasis added).

34. Ibid., p. 25; the author offers several other examples of the Sejm's failure to enact more comprehensive laws.

35. Ibid., pp. 24-30; also Bafia, "Dorobek i doswiadczenia," pp. 22-23.

36. Curiously enough, this is one point which does not seem to have been raised by the proponents of reform--although Roy Medvedev argues forcefully for full-time representatives in his critique of the Supreme Soviet (in his On Socialist Democracy. New York: Knopf, 1975, pp. 131-47). I was told by a member of the Sejm that approximately 50 deputies are now full-time and salaried, but I have not been able to identify them or what special functions they perform.

37. Sejm PRL, p. 305; in the 6th term, 434 deputies held committee assignments--in some cases two or even three--while 26 did not.

38. Committee chairmen for the 7th term are listed in Trybuna Ludu, March 28, 1976; for the 1st through 6th terms, in Sejm PRL, pp. 516-21. The other positions held by the chairmen can be found in the pre-election lists of candidates to the Sejm (see note 14 above) and in the periodic listings of top party and state officials put out by RFER (see especially the listing of April 5, 1976).

39. See, e.g., Jerzy Wiatr, "Demokracja i samorzadnosc," Zycie Warszawy, December 9, 1976.

40. The term "developed socialism" seems to have emerged in the Soviet Union in late 1966 as an antidote to, and retreat from, Krushchev's reckless vision of a rapid transition to full-blown communism with its unfortunate implications about the withering away of the state. (See Wolfgang Leonhard, "Politics and Ideology in the Post-Krushchev Era," in Alexander Dallin and Thomas B. Larson, eds., Soviet Politics Since Krushchev. Englewood Cliffs,

New Jersey: Prentice-Hall, 1968, pp. 54-58). What little attention "developed socialism" has attracted in the West has been focused almost exclusively so far on the official Soviet interpretation as, among other things, a means of reasserting Moscow's ideological primacy. (See, e.g., Alfred B. Evans, Jr., "Developed Socialism in Soviet Ideology," Soviet Studies, XXIX, No. 3 (July 1977), pp. 409-28). What has gone largely unrecognized is that "developed socialism" has become a code word for the current stage of socialist development throughout the bloc and, as such, provides a forum of framework within which old debates are being carried on with slightly altered terminology. (By "old debates", I mean those going back to the 1903 split between the bolsheviks and mensheviks concerning the nature of the party, the relationship of party and regime to society, the degree of tolerance for spontaneity and initiative from below, etc.). The debate is evident within the Soviet Union itself--e.g., historian Roy Medvedev's view the USSR is not a "developed socialist society" because of its lack of genuine freedom and democracy (Medvedev, On Socialist Democracy, p. 40); it is also echoed in the international communist movement, as in the controversy over Spanish party chief Carrillo's critique of Soviet-type systems in Eurocommunism and the State.

41. Mieczyslaw Rakowski, "Wstep do jesieni," Polityka, September 10, 1977; see also: Stanislaw Widerszpil, "The Advanced Socialist Society: An Analysis," Polish Perspectives, XX, No. 7-8 (July-August 1977), pp. 15-27.

42. There is a tendency for the debate to be carried on in terms of surrogate targets. For example, criticism of domestic proponents of a strengthening of bureaucratic control may be masked as an attack on Western theories of "technocracy" (see, e.g., Sylwester Zawadzki, "Z zagadnien demokracji socjalistycznej," Nowe Drogi, No. 9/328 (September 1976), pp. 44-46). Similarly, attacks on Eurocommunism (as by Moscow) are as often as not also thinly veiled warnings of advocates of socialist pluralism within the bloc.

43. VII Zjazd PZPR, pp. 33, 86, 117-118, 234 and 259.

44. *Konstytucja PRL.* Warsaw: Ksiazka i Wiedza, 1976, p. 52; Article 86 of the new constitution promises the right of citizens to "participate in the exercise of social control, in consultations and discussions on the key problems of the country" and to submit recommendations or lodge complaints with all organs of state.

45. *Ibid.*, pp. 23 and 26 (Articles 30 and 35).

46. Based on numerous interviews in Warsaw, Fall 1976.

47. According to several sources, this "higher option" was under consideration within the leadership all along and was pushed through at the last minute after "consultations" on smaller increases failed to reveal significant opposition.

48. It was widely rumored at the time that, at a briefing for the 49 provincial party chiefs on the eve of the price increases, only one expressed concern that there would be serious trouble; on the other hand, others outside official circles suggested later that the leadership could have gotten a very different reading of the public mood had it consulted social researchers.

49. The views of KOR and other dissident groups will not be discussed here.

50. Zawadzki, "Z zagadnien demokracji socjalistycznej," pp. 40-53. Other items of interest which will not be covered here include: Wiatr, "Demokracja i samorzadnosc"; Jerzy Bafia, "Prawo i praworzadnosc w ksztaltowaniu swiadomosci socjalistycznej," *Nowe Drogi*, No. 5/336 (May 1977), pp. 55-62; as well as a series of articles that have appeared since late 1976 in the weekly *Polityka*, particularly those by editor-in-chief Mieczyslaw Rakowski and Jacek Maziarski. Since the research for this chapter was completed, Professor Zawadzki has published a second article in *Nowe Drogi*, this one dealing specifically with the local People's Councils; see, "Wybory do rad narodowych a rozwoj demokracji socjalistycznej," No. 1/344 (January 1978), pp. 115-28.

51. See, e.g., Zdenek Mlynar, "Problems of Political Leadership and the New Economic System," *World Marxist Review*, VIII, No. 12 (December 1965),

pp. 75-82. It is important to point out, however, that Zawadzki and other moderate reformers are careful never to cite Czech precedents nor to use such terms as socialist pluralism.

52. Zawadzki, "Z zagadnien demokracji socjalistycznej," pp. 42-43 (emphasis in the original).

53. Ibid., pp. 44-47 (emphasis in the original).

54. Ibid., pp. 47-48 (emphasis in the original).

55. See note 10 above.

56. Zawadzki, "Z zagadnien demokracji socjalistycznej," p. 48. While Zawadzki gives precedence to representative organs as the most effective means of popular participation at the policy-making level--and states very forcefully that this role cannot be adequately filled through mechanisms of direct participation--he does not ignore the latter, although he is critical of the tendency of officials to be concerned primarily with numbers of participants at the expense of the effectiveness of their "participation." Ibid., pp. 48-49.

57. Jerzy Kowalski, "Spoleczne-ekonomiczne podstawy socjalistycznego systemu politycznego," Panstwo i Prawo, XXXII, No. 7 (July 1977), pp. 6-7 (emphasis added).

58. Ibid., pp. 9-12 (emphasis added).

59. Krzysztof Jasiewicz, "Artykulacja interesow w polskim systemie politycznym: proba ujecia modelowego" (being revised for publication in Studia Nauk Politycznych). Since this was only a draft for discussion, I was asked not to quote extensively from the text. Comments on the discussion are based on my own recollections.

60. Zawadzki, "Z zagadnien demokracji socjalistycznej," p. 43.

61. I was told on very good authority that such articles are cleared at the highest levels of the Central Committee Secretariat, and sometimes

by Gierek himself.

62. Concerning the regime's approach to consultations, see Zygmunt Szeliga, "Decyzje i wnioski: zmiana struktury cen," Polityka, XX, No. 29 (July 17, 1976). Concerning the role of the Sejm, see especially the report of Gierek's meeting with the leadership of the PUWP caucus: "Doskonalenie funkcji Sejmu: posiedzenie Prezydium Klubu Poselskiego PZPR z udzialem tow. Edwarda Gierka," Trybuna Ludu, March 24, 1977. Also: Wieslaw Grochola, "Sejm od tylu," Polityka, XXI, No. 21 (May 21, 1977); Jacek Maziarski, "Miedzy Wiejska a spoleczenstwem," Polityka, XXI, No. 26 (June 25, 1977); and Krzysztof Krauss, "W Sejmie--sprawy najpilniejsze," Zycie Gospodarcze, XXXII, No. 24 (June 12, 1977).

63. These meetings have been credited by some observers with modifying the regime's policy decisions on such volatile issues as the regimentation of youth and the use of psychiatric hospitals in controlling dissent; as related to me by a visiting scholar who sat in on a number of meetings in 1976. Mention here of psychiatric hospitals raises the question whether it was, as reported above (note 28), the Sejm or professional groups such as the Sociological Association which scotched their use for dissidents; in fact, several other groups, including lawyers and journalists, have also claimed a share of the credit. In another instance, the Sociological Association is reported to have queried the government concerning its censorship practices following the 1977 publication in London of lengthy excerpts from a Polish censor's manual (Czarna ksiega cenzury PRL. London: "ANEKS", 1977).

64. Under a plan that went into effect on January 1, 1978, individual peasants will be eligible for retirement pensions for the first time. However, the scale of payments (which are mandatory) is based not on a peasant's income, his sales to the state or even the size of his holdings, but on "the optimal potential production" of the land if farmed at top efficiency--more often than not an unattainable goal. Despite widely publicized "broad consultations," the peasants were reportedly not made aware of the size of their assessments until shortly before the first payments fell due in June 1978. The result has been widespread

protests, at least scattered strikes, and yet another issue and potential source of support for the dissident movement. See the following RFER reports: "Peasants Protest Against High Pension Contributions," Polish Situation Report No. 14 (June 21, 1978), pp. 3-4; "Peasants Fight Back over Pension Scheme," Polish Situation Report No. 19 (August 11, 1978), pp. 7-10; and "The Dissent Movement: An Exercise in Activist Continuity," Polish Situation Report No. 27 (November 27, 1978), p. 9.

65. Jacek Maziarski, "Co sie zmienia w Sejmie," Polityka, XXII, No. 42 (October 21, 1978). This is an interview with Vice Marshall of the Sejm, Piotr Stefanski, who adamantly contended that, despite the slower pace of legislative business, the overall level of the Sejm's activity and influence had not declined. The interviewer's scepticism is evident throughout.

66. See note 57 above.

67. Maziarski, "Co sie zmienia"; elsewhere in the interview, Stefanski used the term "partnership."

68. As one Pole summed up the mood of his compatriots toward the end of 1976 (and reports indicate that it has continued to deteriorate since then): "If the government declared a Western-style liberal democracy tomorrow, half the people would not notice because they do not read the news, and the other half would just laugh!"

69. The letter is reported on at length in RFER, Polish Situation Report No. 1 (January 13, 1978), pp. 15-19. Among the signers were the following ex-luminaries of the PUWP: Edward Ochab, who served briefly as first secretary in 1956 and later as chairman of the State Council; Jerzy Albrecht, Wladyslaw Matwin and Jerzy Morawski, all relative liberals in Gomulka's post-1956 Central Commitee Secretariat. Another name worthy of mention is that of Professor Andrzej Burda, at one time General Prosecutor of Poland and author of several of the articles on constitutional and parliamentary reform cited in this chapter.

3
Subnational Policy in Poland: The Dilemma of Vertical Versus Horizontal Integration

Daniel N. Nelson

LOCAL POLITICS AND DEMOCRATIC CENTRALISM

As the leading political organization in a polity based upon Marxist principles, the Polish United Workers' Party finds itself confronted with an ideological requirement to maintain ties to "the working masses" via a network of local political institutions, the most fundamental of which are rady narodowe (people's councils). As a Leninist party, however, the PUWP is led by the organizational credo of "democratic centralism." These two ideological claims on the policies and procedures by which communist parties rule cannot be reconciled. In this chapter, I intend to describe how this dilemma is apparent in subnational Polish politics and to explain its implications for policy making and implementation.

Bases for such a tension are not difficult to locate within the ideological heritage of the Polish United Workers' Party. Marx and Engels wrote confidently about the revolutionary potential of an urban-industrial working class, because they reasoned that such a political upheaval would be a mass phenomenon engulfing the entire society. As an inevitable outgrowth of capitalist exploitation, the vast majority of the employed population (i.e., manual workers from the Marxist extrapolation based upon mid-19th century England) would rise up against their natural class opponents. In this version, socialism would be introduced by a mass movement, a popular uprising among the proletarians against the old order. But most of the nation-states where communist parties rule today had no socialist "mass movement", had very small native communist organizations, and lacked a clear-cut majority of urban-industrial workers in their populations. (All of these conditions prevailed in post-World War II Poland). Many of these states continue to have peasant majorities (for whom Marx had disdain), while service-oriented or white-collar occupations are expanding more rapidly than the manual labor segment of the work force. In any case, the "mass movement" from which communist parties were to gain legitimacy and for which they were to rule have rarely constituted a majority or much of a "movement" either.

This background has led communist parties, particularly the PUWP, to cultivate their links with the citizenry to foster ideological legitimacy. While Western observers have often been tempted to disregard ideological image making as a concern of communist governments, the energies expended on doing just that are enormous. Regime-mass intimacy is an objective promoted by party efforts to create viable institutions within local territorial divisions which involve citizens. At the same time, the communist parties resist disseminating power.[1] Notwithstanding strenuous organizational efforts, the ties of communist parties to populations which they rule remain weak because they did not gain power through working class movements or, for that matter, come to power in nations with many industrial workers. Moreover, in the few cases where communist parties came to power with significant popular support (e.g., China, Yugoslavia, Cuba), peasants played the major role in achieving victory, not the supposed working-class "natural allies" of communist parties. Simply put, communists have not been able to rule as a party of the proletarian masses.

Local governmental institutions can play a key role in the maintenance of Marxist credentials for a communist regime such as that in Poland. Such structures allow the claim that Party-controlled systems arise from a broadly democratic base of citizen participation. However, this ideological rationale derived from orthodox Marxism runs headlong into the organizational law of Leninist parties, namely the concept of "democratic centralism." Although Lenin argued in favor of continuing representative assemblies, the role of such local institutions was to be subservient at all times.[2] People's councils, along with their executive organs and standing commissions, are to help the central leadership communicate national policies to the citizenry, recruit and train new cadres, and implement centrally decreed plans. Democratic centralism does not, however, connote a pluralistic input into decision-making channels. This is evident in the statutes of all communist parties wherein "the absolute supremacy of all decisions by higher authorities on subordinate bodies" is an oft-repeated guideline for such regimes.[3] In other words, local political actors are to be concerned that people below them implement decisions of elites above them.

Such an orientation--not toward one's community and its needs, but rather toward the central regime and its goals--has been called vertical integration, and its inverse referred to as horizontal integration.[4] Evidence of such "integration" can be seen in communication links, authority patterns, or psychological ties. If one's primary political identity is within the local system, the individual is "horizontally integrated". The phenomenon of horizontal integration is, of course, ongoing; anytime people work together daily, channels of communication will be established among leaders. If political figures and institutions in the community also possess an aura of legitimacy, such that their statutory power becomes authority, affective or emotional links to the local area may be reinforced. In other words, the ingredients for horizontal integration are always present, but the process remains latent in most subnational units. It can, however, be recognized as a means by which local units can form a united front to influence policy making and implementation at the national level, thereby disrupting the vertically integrated systems Leninist parties must seek to maintain.

The paradox inherent in democratic centralism is implicit when its proponents suggest that both vertical and horizontal integration can be subsumed under the Party's aegis. However, there is no evidence that such a combination can, in the long run, operate successfully. Indeed, the prevailing ethos of communist government is subordination of subnational units to hierarchically superior authorities, with severe constraints on local autonomy. Only on rare occasions have efforts to decentralize or to encourage local initiative been undertaken in communist systems, e.g., Mao's China. In this case, however, the reassertion of centralism quickly followed the discovery of localistic "excesses".[5]

For the Polish communist regime, the need for a legitimizing tie to the masses was apparent from the time the tiny Polish Workers' Party was brought into power on the heels of Soviet armies, through the incidents of social upheaval in October 1956, March 1968, December 1970, and June 1976. The regime's lack of identity with, or sympathy for, the citizenry (particularly the class in whose interests commuists allegedly rule, i.e., workers) has been made painfully evident on too many occasions. Marxist principles have led the PUWP to seek closer links with the masses, for, if it did not, the claims and demands of Poland's volatile public would be exacerbated. Thus, we find in the aftermath of the most recent conflagrations in June 1976, (in the city of Radom, for example) a renewal of rhetorical commitments to "self-government" (samorzadnosc).[6] Meanwhile, Leninist principles account for the PUWP's concern for central control, made explicit in the local government "reforms" of 1972-75 which served to disrupt the accretion of power taking place in wojewodztwa such as Upper Silesia (Katowice).[7]

Since the confrontation between vertical and horizontal integration is endemic to Marxist-Leninist systems, we can expect that the Polish communist regime will exhibit symptoms of such conflict in the arena of local politics, at the level where contact between citizens and government is most constant and salient. In the pages that follow, I shall examine such a dilemma in Poland and its effect on the making and implementation of policy. This consideration will be organized into three parts: 1) local issues, with particular attention to the politicizing role of developmental policies; 2) the accretion of local power; and 3) horizontal linkages and the role of people's councils in effecting those ties.

LOCAL ISSUES AND POLITICIZATION

First impressions of authoritarian one-party states (which Poland is, regardless of the United Peasant Party and Democratic Party), suggest that policy emanates from a small set of people at the apex of the party. In such an interpretation, political participants in counties, cities, towns and communes have no reason for involvement in politics except to climb the party hierarchy, perhaps filling roles in state organs or economic enterprises while they advance their party career. Carrying these assumptions further, there would be little reason for issues to be raised or debated in subnational political environments because of the impotence of those units; decisions, made "above", are to be obeyed and implemented.

Empirical studies have led us to reject such a monolithic view of communist polities. Just as policies are not formulated, decided upon or implemented by the central Party leadership in isolation from the societies they rule, neither do political participants forego debate about and competition over public policies. Autonomous interest groups do operate within the system. At the national level, groups coalesce for economic gains in open defiance of the regime, as have factory workers in Poland and miners in Romania. Ethical convictions and political beliefs cause intellectuals to protest constraints on their liberties via such organizations as the Movement for the Defense of Human and Civil Rights (ROPCO) and KOR, Committee for the Defense of Workers in Poland. Within the limits of acceptable behavior and, therefore, less overt, are broad categories of "interests" whose influence is greater but more difficult to witness. The military-heavy industry complex, students, journalists, educators, the Church and others are important groupings which act in policy processes in communist Poland (and are considered elsewhere in this volume).

These interests, which transcend local units, are nevertheless related to subnational policy inputs. Were a complete portrait of policy making in Poland (or in other communist systems) attempted, occupational and social cleavages that we think of as interest groups would have to be examined in light of subnational distinctions. By way of example, we should not expect educators in Katowice and Bialystok Wojewodztwa to share an entire range of goals, just as different parish councils of the Church ought not be assumed to be of one mind. The more salient an issue is in a particular local unit, the more likely it (the issue) will cause splits within occupational/social groups. Indeed, the norm for most political systems, communist ones included, is for citizens' identities to be tied most strongly with their communities, not occupational/social groups (contrary to Marx). Although the socio-economic changes labeled as "modernization" and "development" mitigate parochialism and localism, the orientations of political actors and the bases for their participation are often unrelated to the nation-state or to the welfare of broad social groups to which they nominally belong.

A variety of theoretical works emphasize that

issues in one's local community that affect daily life, particularly primary group solidarity, will be the main concern for politically active citizens.[8] The accuracy of such a hypothesis will, of course, be greater in developing states than in the most advanced post-industrial societies where media penetration and mobility have lessened parochialism. Allowing for the relative nature of this hypothesis, we can nevertheless expect Polish policy processes to be influenced by such an orientation. We should, therefore, expect that one of the strongest cleavages affecting public policy making and implementation in Poland will be among local units, and that it would be a rare issue that would carry such overriding relevance that people in an occupational/social category would unite across community lines.

The problem of identity and its relevance for political life has been addressed at length elsewhere.[9] From this immense topic, however, a relatively simple argument can be distilled. The actions of a central government which are most often important to citizens are those affecting the community with which the citizen most closely identifies. In Poland, as elsewhere, people have their primary and strongest ties not as part of the "community" of manual workers, but as a family member and resident of a village, town, city or commune. For a religious individual, the closest identity might be with one of the 20,000 churches, for in Poland the closeness of church life (in contrast to the remoteness of Party and State bureaucracy) creates the aura of an extended family, particularly in rural areas. Community ties, and the concomitant saliency of local issues, are then necessary components of any analysis of policy processes in Poland.

Support for these expectations has come from a number of sources. The International Studies of Values in Politics (I.S.V.I.P.) project of the 1960s found, for example, that Polish local leaders (at the now-eliminated level of the powiat) thought local governments should have primary responsibility for more specified functions than did political participants at similar levels in the U.S., India, or Yugoslavia.[10] In a wider survey dealing with media habits, urban dwellers of both white-collar and blue-collar occupations consistently rated city affairs as their primary interest. When cross-tabulated with age and education, local concerns (i.e., city events) retained their primacy above national political news, economic affairs, accidents, sports, humor, and satire, and general announcements.[11]

A more recent and comprehensive Polish sociological survey of people's council members also addressed local orientations. Among the majority of council members (who are "citizen politicians" and whose presence in councils is meant to reflect the social composition of the territorial unit), links to the community are much more evident, not only in terms of place of residence, but also insofar as they act much more frequently in the interest of a few people or a small territorial unit. The same survey, however, uncovered significant differences between "citizen politicians" and local elites categorized as (1) experts and (2) professional politicians. Professional politicians (full-time salaried leaders, who fill PUWP leadership roles as well) and experts (managers of state or cooperative enterprises, i.e., holders of cadre posts) are less often original residents of the local unit, and are somewhat less likely to be known as a people's council member.[12] They are perceived less frequently to act in the interest of individuals or small territorial/organizational units (see Table 3.1).

These findings are particularly relevant to the dilemma facing Polish national leaders. While elites are less integrated horizontally, a majority of citizens who fill roles in local institutions and a plurality of specialists and bureaucrats are primarily tied to the local system. If one interprets these data to mean that a gap exists between local political leaders and the populace, as is quite plausible, Warsaw could find little solace. If one views these data as evidence that local PUWP bureaus can be pressured into the pursuit of local interests due to the strong presence of horizontal integration among local system participants, Warsaw also has nothing to be happy about.

Although we must then differentiate between specific actors in local units, it is important to note that, even in the "expert" category, more emphasis is placed on the "small territorial or organizational unit" than larger units. To be sure, the work of Ostrowski and Przeworski for the 1960s I.S.V.I.P. project tends to confirm that, for the set of participants defined as <u>leaders</u>, "the local community is not a source of <u>political</u> socialization..."[13] Such a finding is not surprising given the periodic transfers of subnational leaders in combination with heavy doses of party education employed by national elites to preempt the socializing effects of local responsibilities and

TABLE 3.1
Local Orientations in Council Activity of Experts vs. Citizen Politicians

In whose interest did the councilman act?	Councilmen: Experts %	Councilmen: Citizen Politicians %
one or few persons	13.5	23.6
small territorial or organizational unit	35.0	51.4
large territorial or organizational unit	21.6	7.4
other	29.9	17.6

Source: Jaroslaw Piekalkiewicz, "Three Elite Groups", p. 8.

the links which bind politicians to their community environment. For the general population, central leaders try to break local ties by implanting new industries in underdeveloped regions which, over time, raise people's social and economic expectations beyond the local systems' capacities. Creating such dependency on the central government serves to reduce local autonomy, thus cementing vertical integration. As cited above, however, local orientations account for more of the actions of people's council members, even in the "expert" category, than other foci.

The threat of local ties is, therefore, recognized and combated by the PUWP leaders. But in Poland, as in most communist states, it is far from certain that the Party has achieved its goal of establishing hegemony over both occupational/social groups and local interests. Other than the circulation of leaders technique and party education, the main weapon against localism has been socio-economic "development". In the omnipresent Five Year Plan, extracting these resources from well-to-do regions and redistributing those resources to underdeveloped locales through the implantation of new industry has been used as the leading edge of the PUWP's efforts to penetrate local communities and overcome horizontal ties. Theoretically, such a redistribution of wealth is necessary since (for a Marxist) economic and social progress are inseparable. Indeed, statistics for the late 1960s and early 1970s demonstrate "a general diminishing...of inequality of expenditures and investments" among wojewodstwa.[14]

That such a policy would be pursued by a communist government is entirely consistent with its ideological heritage, a fundamental tenet of which is the elimination of previous intranational inequalities. The extraction of wealth from already advanced localities and its redistribution to poorer units for investment to promote new industry, modern agricultural methods, etc., is obviously the kind of policy that can affect a community's life significantly. Subnational units receiving new resources may benefit, and advanced locales may find their living standards rising less rapidly. In either case, the local political environment is likely to become politicized. Politicization in local units, the process of becoming more subjectively involved in politics, is often the unintended (and ironic) concomitant of developmental goals pursued by a central government.

Attitudinal data from local Polish leaders confirm the politicizing potential of centrally decreed developmental plans. Hopes and wishes of local leaders for Poland are focused overwhelmingly on improvements in welfare and standard of living. Of 888 subnational leaders interviewed in one survey, 72 percent mentioned "improving welfare and standard of living" as among their desires for Poland, while a closely related response ("industrial development and employment") was second, being mentioned by 49 percent of the subjects.[15] The subnational leaders' desires insure that the political environment in local units is highly sensitized to centrally decreed developmental goals as they affect local socio-economic conditions. We can be somewhat more specific about those areas of "welfare" and "development" which might promote central-local conflict most quickly. Of many "issue-areas" cited by local leaders in Poland in which they lacked autonomy, schools and housing were most frequently mentioned.[16] Because plans involving schools and housing in the local unit are viewed as topics most often beyond the jurisdiction of local political leaders and institutions, plans for development decreed from Warsaw that involve these areas of concern can be expected to be foci of central-local tension.

That development is a politicizing issue in Poland does not mean that there will be a consensus about the effects of developmental plans among political participants (or the public) within or among local units. Indeed, disagreement is greatest among political participants at the local level when examining their positions on economic development and equality.[17] Developmental plans can then politicize the local political environment in either a disintegrative or integrative direction. Stated another way, an increase in the subjective involvement of people in politics due to their concerns about development can mean an increase or a decrease in consensus within the local unit.

What determines whether a politicizing issue such as resource extraction and redistribution will contribute to or mitigate consensus among a community's political participants? In Poland, the key intervening variable appears to be the "national orientation" of actors in local politics, i.e., whether they are of one mind about their concern for and identity with central or local affairs. As indicated previously, most participants outside the local elite are community oriented. For local leaders, a more complex picture is evident. If leaders in a subnational unit are uniformly "centralist" in their orientation (vertically integrated), or are uniformly "localist", then they tend to agree on most other things. Were they (the local leadership) to be divided on their "national orientation", then consensus on other issues is doubtful. Simply put, where Polish local leaders stand on the central/local dichotomy is a lynchpin for their degree of consensus on other politicizing issues, most notably developmental planning that calls for a redistribution of resources (see Figure 3.1).[18] On the basis of these data regarding leaders, one might expect that in Polish subnational units where the majority of political participants are local-minded, a politicizing issue would have an integrative effect; sensing their community has been or would be harmed by central developmental plans, particularly in realms where they perceive a lack of autonomy such as education and housing, central plans become a cause against which to rally local opposition. And, of course, clear-cut negative effects of central plans will move opinion toward a localist consensus. Conversely, the same issue could politicize a community but create discord if the local political participants exhibit no consensus about central/local loyalties. While the latter possibility might appear preferable from the standpoint of central authorities, one should not assume that disintegrative results of developmental plans are desirable, since efficiency is certain to be compromised and the spectre of competing interests is raised where none should exist.

LOCALISM AND LOCAL POWER ACCRETION[19]

If policies related to development are those with the greatest potential to "arouse" a local unit in a political sense, we need to examine conditions enabling community ties and loyalties to have a policy impact and the manner in which local influence is projected. This section deals with the first of those points. Community ties and loyalties can, of course, have a chance to affect central policy only when political actors at the local level present a "united front". When one finds a consensual orientation towards the community and its needs, the potential for concerted action exists. The factors promoting such localism and the conditions enabling such a focus to have policy impact are identical. I have identified these factors

FIGURE 3.1
Variable Impact of Politicizing Issue on Local Systems

National Orientations	Impact of Developmental Plans for Resource Redistributions
Centralist Consensus (Majority of elites experts + citizen politicians are primarily concerned with national goals and issues)	Politicized; vertically integrative mobilized to aid in implementation
No Consensus (elites not wholly united, facing experts + citizens with parochial concerns)	Politicized; disintegrative; implementation impeded
Localist Consensus (majority of local participants primarily concerned with community goals and issues)	Politicized; horizontally integrative; organization and mobilization to change national policy

elsewhere, as I attempted to explain the phenomenon of local power accretion (i.e., the gradual accumulation of the subnational unit's ability and inclination to debate and exert countervailing influence vis-a-vis central authorities).[20] Two variables seem to encourage debate with or defiance of central authorities in Poland. First, one must consider the economic resources of a local unit and the relative importance of the community's wealth to Poland's economy. Second, historical cleavages and rivalries between Warsaw and the region or province should be examined.

Prior to the 1972-1975 reforms of local government in Poland, the position of Upper Silesia (Katowice Wojewodztwo) offered a striking example of local power accretion. The primary impetus for Upper Silesia's strength vis-a-vis Warsaw has been, and continues to be, its economic wealth. The history of Silesia has included the suzerainty of Austrian Hapsburgs, Bradenburg-Prussia after Frederick the Great, Germany, and Poland. Since the 1700s, Silesia has been regarded as a source of wealth because of its bituminous coal reserves. As early as the late 18th century, the beginnings of industrial revolution in central Europe were fed by this energy source. During the 20th century, the valleys of Upper Silesia have become clogged with electrical generating stations and massive steel plants, both relying on coal.

Since the advent of a communist regime in Poland, efforts have been made to disperse industry, somewhat reducing the disproportionate share of the country's GNP in industry concentrated in the six or seven thousand square kilometers in and around the major city of Katowice. Much of the dispersion has not, however, strayed too far. The mammoth Lenin Steel Works at Nowa Huta for example, is in the northeast suburbs of Krakow, a sixty kilometer drive from the heart of Silesia. Roughly 40 percent of Poland's capacity in heavy industry, and 20 percent of all industry thus remains clustered in the southern part of the nation in and around Upper Silesia.[21] The degree to which intranational inequalities persisted well into the communist period must be an anathema for the regime (see Tables 3.2 and 3.3).

As recent data indicate (see Table 3.3), the extent of intranational gaps has closed little. Even when measured in terms of such variables as health, education, and housing expenditures, Katowice still maintains a qualitative lead. There are, however,

TABLE 3.2
Per Capita Economic Differences in Poland (1961)

Province*	GNP	GNP Created in Industry	GNP Created in Agriculture	Net Output in Agriculture Per Capita of Agricultural Population	Personal Consumption
Katowice	138.0	209.3	28.5	111	119.5
Opole	111.8	108.5	128.8	135	103.4
Lodz	111.3	139.2	82.4	86	96.9
Wroclaw	108.5	117.8	95.1	141	105.4
Krakow	107.3	125.8	77.7	75	96.3
Gdansk	102.9	99.8	73.5	124	111.8
Poznan	102.1	88.0	136.3	141	107.1
Szczecin	101.2	73.5	109.3	130	110.0
Warszawa	101.0	90.8	81.4	86	106.8
Bydgoszcz	95.0	76.6	138.8	140	99.7
Zielona Gora	94.6	77.1	114.8	122	96.7
Rzeszow	81.8	64.4	123.9	81	83.6
Olsztyn	74.7	30.8	129.9	98	86.9
Lublin	74.5	35.8	157.9	91	86.7
Koszalin	74.5	31.2	130.3	110	98.2
Kielce	74.4	61.9	109.1	73	78.7
Bialystok	65.5	30.7	130.5	80	80.1
Average for Poland	100.0	100.0	100.0	100	100.0

* City Wojewodztwa omitted; all five (e.g., Warszawa, Krakow, etc. are, as one would suspect, higher in GNP, industrial, and personal consumption.

Source: Kosta Mihalovic, Regionalni razvoj socijalistickih zelmalja, Belgrade: 1972, p. 89, as cited in Paul S. Shoup, "Indicators of Socio-Politico-Economic Development" in C. Mesa-Lago and C. Beck, eds., Comparative Socialist Systems (Pittsburgh: University Center for International Studies, 1975), p. 23.

TABLE 3.3
Differences in Per Capita Public Welfare Expenditures and Investments in Poland (1966-1972)

Province*	Mean Expend. + Invest./Health**	Mean Expend. + Invest./Education	Mean Expend. + Invest./Housing
Katowice	94	74	126
Opole	84	84	insuff-data
Lodz	56	68	insuff-data
Wroclaw	93	insuff-data	54
Krakow	70	insuff-data	76
Gdansk	88	93	100
Poznan	insuff-data	65	81
Szczecin	82	104	insuff-data
Warszawa	insuff-data	insuff-data	insuff-data
Bydgoszcz	67	insuff-data	99
Zielona Gora	insuff-data	93	72
Rzeszow	insuff-data	insuff-data	insuff-data
Olsztyn	75	84	71
Lublin	56	insuff-data	89
Koszalin	86	97	84
Kielce	55	69	92
Bialystok	62	80	87

Source: Adapted from Barclay Ward, "Policy Adaptability in Poland," paper presented at the Midwest Slavic Conference, April, 1978, Bloomington, Indiana, pp. 26-28; calculation of means includes author's estimates for missing data in certain years for certain provinces.

* Cities classified as provinces omitted.

** These are approximate means, in most cases incorporating the author's estimates for cases of missing data.

some redistributive efforts underway, insofar as the least industrial provinces (Table 3.2) are not uniformly low in terms of expenditures and investments in health, education and housing.

In socialized economies, a process of equalization is to universalize the advantages of socioeconomic modernization while redistributing the benefits of industry and urbanization. In Poland, the extent to which some regions possessed disporportionate wealth before communist rule (most obviously Katowice) has not been reversed, with Upper Silesia retaining a preeminent economic position in the country.

Such economic capacities do not, of course, yield economic autonomy for wojewodztwa possessing considerable resources. Nevertheless, the budget director of a large Polish city told me his candid opinion that "Poland needs Silesia more than Silesia needs the rest of Poland."[22] But does this economic weight translate into policy influence for the wojewodstwa or lesser subnational units (after 1975, only the gmina)? Before reforms of the early 1970s, such a question would have been answered affirmatively without hesitation. For higher Party officials and central ministries, Silesia constituted a problem so thorny that it was referred to (with a mixture of admiration and pejorative connotation) as "Poland's Katanga" (i.e., the rebellious province in Zaire during the 1960s).

An obvious example of the potential influence related to economic autonomy is the personal story of Edward Gierek in Upper Silesia. Gierek became First Party Secretary in Katowice Wojewodztwo in 1957 when the provinces numbered only twenty-two as opposed to the current forty-nine. While one can attribute Gierek's rise to his own political savvy and other idiosyncratic factors, the base of popular approval and national renown with which he came to power after the 1970 riots had, no doubt, foundations in Katowice. From Poland's most industrial and most densely populated province, with the country's highest proportion of workers, largest Party membership, and historical distinctiveness (i.e., its ties to Austria and Prussia), Gierek could speak with national impact long before 1970. And, while many of Poland's new industrial cities struggled with inadequate provisioning, housing, and general well-being, Katowice's more established industry provided continuous prosperity. That Gierek did not bring power to the province, but vice versa, was clear when Gierek pushed reforms in the early 1970s to strip local units of their potential to cultivate a power base similar to that which he had enjoyed.

Traditional rivalries or cleavages between the capital city qua central governments versus another major city or region constitute another variable promoting local power accretion in Poland. A trenchant example of this difficulty is the Warsaw-Krakow rivalry. While Krakow was not the first or only center of antigovernment rioting in March 1968, December 1970, or June 1976, it has been the home for much of Poland's avant garde theatre, film making, literature, etc. Subsequent to 1976 riots against price increases, Krakow became a focal point for student activism and some protests by clergy as well, which called for the release of prisoners from the previous year's demonstrations. Perhaps because of the long traditions of Jagiellonian University and its scholarly achievements, the academic community of Krakow sometimes exhibits questioning attitudes about the quality and intent of scholarship produced in the capital. I was asked by a social scientist in Krakow, for instance, whether or not certain scholars in Warsaw had "given me the party line" in explaining 1972-1975 local government reforms, advising me that I could depend on the objectivity of social scientists elsewhere in Poland (which I presumed to mean Krakow). In a broader sense, residents of Krakow regard their city as being the center of Polish culture and history--not the "second" city of Poland, but the first in qualitative terms.

Such traditional cleavages are difficult to denote and, lacking public surveys, impossible to measure. It is likely that communist regimes share this phenomenon with many other political systems. Nevertheless, the centralism upon which a Leninist Party depends makes this kind of localism especially vexing. Whereas economic roots of local power, or ethnic divisions in other European communist states, have a certain rationality to them and can be met by governmental actions, pride and esteem which perpetuate intranational schisms cannot be ameliorated by Party decrees. When Krakow or other Polish locales demur from the cultural, and, by implication, political, leadership of the central government, a Leninist party is certain to be troubled by the challenge this represents to vertical integration, particularly so when local self-assertion has no obvious basis in economic economy or ethnic identity.

At the least, then, bases exist in Poland for

assertive localism. Although the ties of community can be promoted by other conditions as well, most notably ethnic differences (e.g., Hungarians in Romania), it seems clear that local power accretion has been present in Poland where economic resources or historical/cultural rivalries play a role. This does not explain, of course, how a community orientation and the accretion of local power are manifest in policy processes. If community ties and their potential for influence increase when such conditions as economic autonomy and traditional cleavages are present, we need to examine the mechanism by which such potential is translated into action.

HORIZONTAL INTEGRATION AND PEOPLE'S COUNCILS

As described above, the norm for subnational politics in Poland and other communist states is denoted by the phrase "vertical integration", whereby local institutions and elites act to administer centrally decreed policies rather than represent constituents or respond to their needs. People's Councils (rade narodowe), indeed, typically spend about 40 percent of their sessions hearing reports and discussing their own organization and that of subordinate councils, and devote only 5 percent to a matter of such critical concern as housing.[23] The perception by local leaders that they lack autonomy in matters of community concern such as housing and education, reported earlier, no doubt mitigates any effort to spend more time on such matters in meetings of people's councils or party committees. Subnational leaders in the Party hierarchy, people's councils' executive organs, managers of local economic enterprises, etc. have, moreover, less consensus within local units than between units suggesting that socialization of such elites is not determined by community ties alone.

Given these impediments to local self-assertion, it would be easy to overlook the policy impact of localism in communist states. We have, however, seen indications of residual community ties such as the judgment by local elites that their level should have primary responsibility for more functions, their perceived lack of autonomy in areas of citizen need such as education and housing, and the strong localism among citizen-politician and expert members of people's councils. More intriguing is the possibility that Warsaw's goals for socio-economic development can politicize local units, integrating them in opposition to the center.

Inherently involving a redistribution of resources, developmental plans must encounter local leadership highly sensitized to such an issue, who want to see continued improvements in living standards along lines popular in their community.

These latter points suggest, albeit indirectly, that an underlying reservoir of local ties and loyalties exists or develops even among those who are subnational elites. At the same time, the dominant sentiment among nonelite participants at the local level and the public as well is strongly community oriented. There are, in other words, nascent forms of what I earlier defined as horizontal integration. But "orientations" and "sentiments" can exist quite apart from policy processes. Under what circumstances is horizontal integration transformed into a strategy of action, a technique by which local interests are projected beyond the community through efforts of subnational institutions?

Before responding to such a question, one should recognize that there is nothing "automatic" about the use of horizontal integration in Poland to influence public policy. Although building a network of support in a local unit seems to be a reasonable course to pursue to pressure central institutions on a specific issue, the conscious employment of such a technique in communist Poland has been infrequent and surely receives no plaudits from central leaders. Nevertheless, horizontal integration does, occasionally, cease to be merely those ties and contacts related to the orientation of localism and become a political tactic. The impetus for such a transformation comes, in part, from structural limitations on central control which create opportunities for local self-assertion in several ways:

1. Constituent units are diverse, and that very diversity forces superior organs to differentiate the ways in which they deal with subordinate units and "compels them to have local communities with some measure of independence..."

2. The degree of vertical integration is limited by the capacity of channels of communication. "Central actors" cannot "regulate every activity undertaken at the local level".

3. Since "higher authorities are interested in mobilizing local energies and resources" they find it necessary to allow "some local autonomy".[24]

In other words, not only intranational diversity and structural limitations preclude a total absence of horizontal integration, but also the PUWP's goals require "some local autonomy." Seen from Warsaw's perspective, subnational leaders must be free to judge the most efficient means of coordinating local political institutions and mobilizing the citizenry in order to achieve the commune, city, or county economic plan.

Therein, of course, is the problem for all communist governments regarding horizontal integration: while the national regimes need a bit of it, they desire to avoid its spread. All wojewodstwa cannot be governed daily, much less "developed", with decrees from Warsaw. Far less can each gmina be ruled in minute detail from the capital. Broad policy outlines must be translated into contact with the citizenry, and the cooperation, communication and coordination among state, party and mass organizations in subnational units equal de facto horizontal integration.[25] The next step (antithetical to national PUWP aims) is the recognition by local political actors that such contacts can be of use when central policies have negative consequences for them as individuals or for their local community. That is the step which is unacceptable to national leaders since it constitutes a blatant assertion of particularistic interests.

The specific mechanisms and step-by-step actions undertaken by local units in Poland to affect policies decreed from above have been examined in several published studies emanating from the Instytut Socjologii at Warsaw University. Although primarily descriptive in their treatment of decision-making processes, a team of researchers including Marek Kesy, Antonina Ostrowska, Eugeniusz Ryzko, and Jacek Tarkowski considered four locales in depth, giving each powiat a ficticious name for publication purposes: Rolnowo, Borow, Henrykow, and Wolowiec.[26] In cases when each locale was faced by decisions of higher authorities relating to the economic plan which were seen as adverse to the community (or contrary to local needs and wishes), the team of researchers followed community-level actions in policy matters through several stages. As the local unit felt the impact of centrally decreed policies and began to formulate its response, a "predominance of informal contacts" within the local system was found corresponding to a "lack of involvement by formal organizations."[27] In other words, the ties of community (acquaintances, daily contacts, etc.) form the basis for local actions in policy processes. From that point on, through stages of articulation, conflict, mobilization, mediation of the conflict, and final decision, people's council executive organs and the local PUWP committee coordinate their efforts for the mobilization of citizen concern on the issue.

In the specific instance of Rolnowo Powiat, for example, political institutions within that unit were seen to employ means of projecting local policy influence, including delegations to higher echelons within ministerial networks, and the use of personal acquaintances (e.g., former powiat residents) now in national party or state positions. When Rolnowo Powiat was confronted by an adverse decision regarding school construction, local leaders acted to reverse the previous decision by "developing means of influencing the decision-making centers..." The powiat's success was significant; a new school was built as the local unit had originally desired.[28] If policy outcomes of this sort are generalized in Poland, the process by which local units project their influence casts a new light on policy making in communist systems. When the coordination and mobilization of community resources pays off, the network of support created by such efforts increasingly will be viewed by Polish citizens as more beneficial to local interests than any amount of statutory autonomy the Sejm says they (local units) have.

The energies expended by local institutions to extract more of what they want from central decision makers, and the degree to which horizontal integration is a means to achieve those ends, was emphasized by recent interviews I conducted with city officials in Krakow and Poznan. After a series of questions about the extent of local autonomy possessed by Krakow, I inquired from a leading official of that city whether an industrial or agricultural wojewodztwo would have greater independence from central authorities. He responded by saying,

> We never look at it that way, of course...we're not trying to be 'independent'. But, when a locale has a stronger infrastructure due

> to its modernization and development, it can have a more <u>active</u> local government, and pursue the interests of its citizens at higher levels. In this, the expertise and sophistication of a more industrial wojewodztwo is beneficial. Our communications between state, party and mass organizations are excellent, and we know each other's needs. With this more advanced infrastructure, we can work more effectively with national ministries to have the best policies for our citizens.[29]

After formulative stages, horizontal integration becomes an institutional phenomenon. At the core of this effort to project local influence is, interestingly, the people's council executive, specifically the presidium. Local PUWP committees and bureaus qua party organs are unable to initiate such challenges to the center, given that they are part of a "hegemonic system" (Jerzy Wiatr's phrase) in which central control emanates from one national party. Local party organs are very unlikely to be the initial locus of horizontal integration, if for no other reason that their raison d'etre in a Leninist party is precisely the inverse. The primary reservoir of localism in subnational political institutions is not within the PUWP bureau but among the nonelite membership of people's councils (experts and citizens politicians). Notwithstanding local leaders' extra-local socialization, the political milieu is one of community concerns rather than attention to details of socio-economic goals ordained by Warsaw. It should surprise no one, then, that whether we look at the general public, nonelite participants, or local leaders, matters of community concern "matter" most in Poland. The rade naradowe participants outside leadership echelons retain strong local ties, while the council leaders themselves, almost all of whom are simultaneously PUWP Bureau members, must daily reconcile local needs with central policies they are duty-bound to implement. Meanwhile, public opinions regarding people's councils "are formed particularly by their (the council's) activity in fields of social life whose functioning is directly connected with the personal situation of a man."[30] The focus of public and nonelite participants' localism is, then, the institution of people's councils. Since the local PUWP committee and bureau cannot turn overtly to become advocates for particularistic interests, the core institution for amalgamating local needs is the people's council and, more specifically, its executive organs, where the vertical ties of party leaders meet community interests.

Council meetings are themselves brief, infrequent, and perfunctory, involving recitations rather than debate and meaningful voting. Executive committees and presidia, however, include local PUWP elites who fill state offices as well. (Since the "reforms" of 1972-1975, the local party first secretary must be council president as well, a fusion of party and state no doubt meant to control the latter more closely). But the overlap of party bureau and the Presidium of the council has, ironically, offered yet greater momentum for the phenomenon so vexing to a Leninist party trying to implement Marxist social and economic goals, i.e., horizontal integration. As I argued at the outset of this chapter, Marxist principles demand ties to the masses for ideological legitimization, through such mechanisms as people's councils. A Leninist party does not reject organs of local government, but sees them in light of democratic centralism; councils provide, as it were, a "differential axis" through which vertical commands are translated into horizontal power--that is, the penetration of society by the party:

> ...the general acceptance of party leadership and the superiority of central organs does not fully explain the means by which local goals are achieved...In practice, party leadership behavior is, in fact, a horizontal arrangement".31

With the institutional link between the people's council presidium and PUWP bureau in local units, the conditions for horizontal integration as a political tactic are complete. The sentiment of localism, implying community ties and loyalties, is a necessary precondition to local challenges of central authority. In Poland, such an orientation has been identified and measured in the public and among participants in local politics outside the top echelon (i.e., outside the council presidium and party bureau). The solidarity roles with greatest attitudinal impact, in Poland as elsewhere, are usually those with daily saliency such as primary groups and community. Also necessary is the growth of local unit's potential power to countervail national policies. Local power accretion is a key process because, when economic autonomy, ethnic identity, or cultural/historical cleavages provide its foundations, localism is promoted at the same time its potential influence expands. Such a potential effect cannot be realized unless a politicizing issue, such as developmental planning that adversely affects the local unit, raises the subjective involvement of citizens and political actors alike. Although politicization can bring more discord to the local unit if localism is not strong, the possibility exists that centrally decreed policies will galvanize local political institutions, uniting participants against Warsaw. It is at this point that horizontal integration can be, and has been, employed to project local influence beyond the community's boundaries in an effort to change central policy.[32]

Gierek, and Gomulka before him, have not been ignorant of the danger represented by localism and its manifestation in policy processes as horizontal integration. The threat of particularism for a nonresponsive government, where representation is reduced to symbolism, is considerable. There is no room in a Leninist party for the competitive interests of diverse communities, and "democratic centralism" offers no accepted procedure for questioning the absolute supremacy of higher authorities. Thus, PUWP leaders strike preemptively at localism, rotating local leaders, requiring extensive Party education for cadre posts, and "reforming" local government so that vertical ties penetrate even deeper into community politics. But vertical controls are incomplete, limited in part by the ideological needs of a Marxist government legitimized by its ties to the masses of working people. This is a dilemma with no easy solution for Polish communism, and one which is certain to plague the central regime's policy making and implementation processes for years to come.

NOTES

1. For Poland, the best description of this network of state institutions at subnational levels is Jaroslaw Piekalkiewicz, Communist Local Government. Athens, Ohio: Ohio University Press, 1975.

2. V.I. Lenin, State and Revolution. New York: International Publishers, 1968, pp. 40-41.

3. CPSU in Resolution, 7th Edition. Moscow: 1953, pp. 778-779, quoted in Abdurakhman Avtorkhanov, The Communist Party Apparatus. Cleveland: Meridian, 1968, p. 102.

4. Jack Goldsmith and Gil Gunderson, eds., Comparative Local Politics. Boston: Holbrook Press, 1973, pp. 191-192.

5. For a complete description of Mao's encouragement for decentralization in China and his subsequent concerns, see Victor C. Falkenhiem "Decentralization and Control in Chinese Local Administration" in D. Nelson, ed., Subnational Communist Politics: Comparing Participation and Policy-Making. Lexington, Kentucky: University of Kentucky Press, forthcoming 1979.

6. See, for example, Jerzy Wiatr's article, "Demokracja i Samorzadnosc" in Zycie Warszawy (December 9, 1976).

7. For a thorough discussion of these reforms in structural-administrative terms, one can refer to Jaroslaw Piekalkiewicz's essay, "Polish Local Politics in Flux: Concentration or

De-concentration?" in D. Nelson, ed., Subnational Communist Politics.

8. Marion Levy, Modernization and the Structure of Societies. Princeton: Princeton University Press, 1966, p. 806; Charles W. Anderson, et. al., Issues of Political Development, 2nd Edition. Englewood Cliffs, New Jersey: Prentice-Hall, 1974, pp. 62-66; Samuel Huntington and Joan M. Nelson, No Easy Choice. Cambridge: Harvard University Press, 1976, p. 15.

9. See, for example, Lucian W. Pye, "Identity and the Political Culture," in Leonard Binder, et. al., Crises and Sequences in Political Development. Princeton: Princeton University Press, 1971, pp. 101-134; also Karl W. Deutsch, Nationalism and Social Communication. Cambridge: MIT Press, 1953.

10. See Philip Jacob, "Autonomy and Political Responsibility," Urban Affairs Quarterly, Vol. 11, Number 1 (September 1975), p. 43.

11. A. Sicinski, Rola Prasy i Radio w Kulturze Mosowej. Warszawa: Osrodek Badania Opinii Publicznej, 1959; and Funkje Informacyjne Prasy i Radio. Warszawa: Osrodek Badania Opinii Publicznej, 1959, pp. 44-45.

12. These and other findings are reported in Jaroslaw Piekalkiewicz's paper, "Three Elite Groups", presented at the annual meeting of the American Association for the Advancement of Slavic Studies, Washington, DC, October, 1977, pp. 5-8.

13. Krzysztof Ostrowski and Adam Prezeworski, "Local Leadership in Poland," The Polish Sociological Bulletin, Vol. 16, No. 2 (1967), p. 70.

14. Barclay Ward "Policy Adaptability in Poland", paper presented at the Midwest Slavic Conference, April 1978, (mimeo), p. 25.

15. International Studies of Values in Politics, Values and the Active Community. New York: Free Press, 1971, p. 71.

16. Ibid., p. 180.

17. Ibid., p. 149, Table 6.

18. Ibid., p. 153.

19. Portions of sections III and IV are revisions from the author's paper "Dilemmas of Local Politics in Communist States," presented at the annual meeting of the American Association for the Advancement of Slavic Studies, Washington, DC, October, 1977.

20. See D. Nelson, "Dilemmas of Local Politics in Communist States."

21. Roy E. H. Mellor, *Eastern Europe: A Geography of the Comecon Countries.* New York: Columbia University Press, 1975, pp. 264-265.

22. Oral Communication, January, 1977.

23. Jaroslaw Piekalkiewicz, *Communist Local Government.* Athens, Ohio: University of Ohio Press, 1975, p. 127.

24. Jacek Tarkowski, "Wplyw Lokalny w Centralyzowanym Systemie: Zascby Lokalne i Lokalny Aktyw Kierowniczy," (mimeo), December, 1976, pp. 3-13.

25. An excellent summary of institutional integration in local Polish politics is provided in Jacek Tarkowski, *System Polityczny Powiatu Jako System Integracji Poziomej.* Warszawa: Centralny Osrodek Metodyczny Studiow Nauk Politycznych, 1976.

26. See the article by these authors, "Procesy Podejmowania Decyzji...", *Problemy Rad Narodowych,* Vol. 22 (1972), pp. 155-192.

27. *Ibid.*, p. 177.

28. Jacek Tarkowski, "A Study of the Decisional Process in Rolnowo Powiat," *The Polish Sociological Bulletin*, No. 2 (1967), p. 94.

29. Oral Communication, January, 1977.

30. Stefania Dzieciolowska, "People's Councils in the Eyes of the Inhabitants," in Sylwester Zawadzki, ed., *People's Councils in Poland in the Light of Empirical Research.* Warszawa: Instytut Nauk Prawnych, PAN, 1973, p. 213; this article was originally published in *Problemy Rad Narodowych*, No. 13, (1969).

31. Zybmunt Rybicki, "Niektore problemy partyjnego kierownictwa radami narodowymi", Gospodarka i Administracja Terenowa, No. 7-8 (1966), p. 3.

32. There have even been cases when horizontal integration within units has led to tacit alliances between units as was evident in the early and mid-1960s as strong wojewodztwa resisted policies of the Central Committee designed to reduce their authority via decentralizing edicts. See Jaroslaw Piekalkiewicz's description of this period in Communist Local Government, pp. 173-186.

4 Recruitment Policy, Elite Integration, and Political Stability in People's Poland

Jack Bielasiak

Political recruitment has long been recognized as an essential component in the maintenance of systemic stability. The importance of recruitment, of course, lies in the fact that elite selection determines to a large extent who will be provided with access to policy-making positions.[1] Since elite groups play a major role in the authoritative allocation of values and resources, an understanding of decision making depends on the identification of the elites involved in the political process.

It is generally believed that elites in a political system reflect the social, economic, and political forces of that society.[2] At any given time, the leadership must perform those functions necessary for the maintenance of the system. In turn, these functions are to a large degree determined by socio-economic requirements and demands, thereby necessitating some form of response within the elite structure to changing societal conditions. This is especially evident in societies undergoing rapid transformation, such as Poland in the postwar period, where the leadership has had to adjust to demands within the social environment by establishing new elite roles, staffed by personnel with specialized technical and managerial skills, to cope with the conditions created by industrialization and modernization. An examination of the recruitment process, therefore, can tell us much about how the top political elite has responded to the pressures of socio-economic and political developments.

While it is true that the circulation of elites is an important element in assuring the well-being of any society, at the same time we must recognize that opportunities for the acquisition of elite status are limited.[3] Choices have to be made among competing claimants for leadership positions. The criteria applied in elite selection reflect not only the needs and interests of society at large, but also the political position of the incumbent elite. The protection of the existing elite is thus an important factor in the formulation of recruitment policies. Putnam, for example has stressed the importance of the "selectorates"--the incumbent political officials--in fulfilling a "gatekeeping" function for the political structure by determining who will be provided or denied access to policy-making positions.[4] This is especially so in one-party dominant states, where the lack of formal competition for political roles renders the recruitment process the only route for entrance into elite positions. Control over the official channels of the elite selection gives the political leadership in a communist state an important tool for the maintenance of stability in the system. While successful maintenance is tied to the responsiveness of the recruitment process to newly mobilized and politicized segments of society, the extent and locus of the response remain largely the province of the current gatekeepers. In fact, the provision of access to policy making to various constituencies in the system remains a problematic issue in socialist states, with several policy options available for the recruitment of new elites.[5]

The purpose of this analysis is to examine the patterns of elite selection and composition in Poland during the post-Stalin period. Foremost, the aim here is to determine what recruitment policies were adopted by the Polish leaderships in the period from 1954 to 1976, and to relate these strategies of elite selection to the social, economic, and political developments of the country. That there is a conscious policy of elite selection is evident from statements by the Polish leaders. For example, First Secretary Gierek, referring to the recruitment of party personnel, stated at the Sixth PUWP Congress:

> In order to retain its ability to give leadership to the masses and remain in the forefront, the Party must constantly strengthen its ranks by admitting workers, peasants, and intellectuals of the highest quality and freeing itself of people incapable of coping with the responsibilities and duties of a Party member.[6]

The concern with the qualifications of party personnel by necessity translates into a careful evaluation of individuals admitted into the ranks of the political elite. Ideally, our analysis of the recruitment patterns would cover a large sample of the Polish elite from a variety of organizations and at different levels in the leadership hierarchy. Unfortunately, the lack of data for such a diversified sample required another approach in the selection of a representative Polish elite, namely full membership in the Central Committee of the Polish United Workers' Party. Much has been written about the advantages and shortcomings of Central Committee membership as a method for the identification of elites in socialist systems, and there is no need to repeat these arguments once more.[7] It is generally agreed, however, that the Central Committee has significant importance as an institution which grants membership to elites from the most vital sectors of society, and thus includes representative "spokesmen" for different groups. More recently, the Central Committee has also been viewed as an important consultative organ, enabling the transmission of information among key officials and constituencies.[8] Thus, even though the Central Committee may not play an independent decision-making role, it serves as a mechanism for channeling demands and supports between the top political leadership and society. The need to maintain this communication flow makes it most likely that the most important elements in the community will be given status in the central party body.

To ascertain which groups in society were provided with elite status recognition through membership in the Central Committee, biographical career data for each full member was retrieved and classified into categories reflecting the institutional affiliation, the functional tasks and the hierarchial position of each official.[9] Analysis of elite composition and recruitment for post-Stalinist Poland was carried out on the basis of this career information.

ELITE INTEGRATION AND POLITICAL STABILITY

One of the primary functions of recruitment is to integrate the diverse societal sectors into a community responsive to the authority of the political center. During the initial transformation and consolidation phases of the post-revolutionary society, integration is based on a command relationship between the central leadership and society.[10] Recruitment into the elite is limited to committed and reliable political cadres, who penetrate and politicize the entire community by means of ideological appeals, organizational loyalty, and coercion. By these methods, during the Stalinist phase of political development, the population is mobilized to respond to the policies of the central government. The need to modernize society and build socialism are viewed as sufficient reasons for the penetration, and thus integration, of the community.

The success associated with the Stalinist strategy of development, the establishment of an industrial state, increasingly creates severe problems in the new modern society.[11] The argument is that a command political structure relying on ideological conformity and the application of coercion becomes evermore dysfunctional to further economic growth and social development. To assure continued progress, the control mechanisms exercised by a monopolistic political elite must be replaced by a process enabling the newly mobilized sectors of society to participate in the establishment of a value consensus in the polity. Integration based on compliance, relying ultimately on the threat or actualization of violence, is to give way to integration based on participation, relying on the voluntary articulation of interests and policy preferences.[12] The problem in this shift from system building to system management is that it requires an erosion in the dominance of the party bureaucracy in policy making and the opening up of access to political decision making to new elites emerging during the modernization process. In essence, the recruitment policy is to be altered to enable the entrance of heretofore nonpolitical elites into the policy-making structure. However, resistance to the opening up of the recruitment gates occurs on the part of some of the incumbent political cadres. Their fear is that the primacy of the Party and of ideologically defined priorities for policy will be endangered by the diffusion of the elite and the introduction of growing differences into the system's leadership.[13]

The dilemma for the party leadership in the mature socialist society is now to establish a community-wide consensus while maintaining the primacy of the communist party. The latter aim requires an effective limitation on the participation of other groups in the political policy-making process. This in turn places a greater burden on the party leadership to sense diverse group interests and popular sentiments, and most importantly, to respond in some way to the requirements of these newly mobilized constituencies.[14] The maintenance of systemic stability, however, may depend on the ability of the top political elite to institute procedures which will integrate society without constant recourse to command/control mechanisms. An innovative recruitment policy may serve to defuse the issue by opening new opportunities to representatives of socio-economic sectors outside the traditional political bureaucracy, and at the same time succeed in maintaining political stability by effectively limiting the participation of the new recruits in policy making.

For a long time, however, the prevalent view in the literature held that the political leaderships in socialist states were unable to resist the pressures of economic and social development, and thus act as effective "gatekeepers" to the elite structures. Instead, the belief of this "economic imperative" was that political development was simply dependent on and determined by the changes in the socio-economic environment.[15] In particular, the process of modernization was said to affect the selection of new elites into the political process. The need to manage an industrial economy and to integrate an increasingly complex social milieu is beyond the capabilities of political cadres using primarily techniques of mobilization and command. Instead, the modern society demands technical expertise, functional specialization, and differentiation of tasks among the leadership. Elite recruitment will favor more and more specialists in the economic, managerial, and scientific fields, with a resultant displacement of the closely knit, professional political elite. The implication is, first, that the old-line party functionaries with political experience are no longer the best candidates for selection into policy-making positions, but are replaced by experts with functional bases of power. Furthermore, the shift in recruitment is accompanied by changes in decision-making norms, with a decline in ideological compliance standards in favor of the gradual emphasis on technical values. The result is a conflict between the "red" and "expert" elite subsets for positions within the leadership and over the criteria to be applied in policy making.

The important point is that the shift from

political to specialized elites and norms is perceived as a predetermined response of the political leadership to the pressures of modernization. Failure to introduce the heterogeneity increasingly evident in society into the political arena may result in arrested development and the decay of the political system.[16] The political and manipulative skills of the traditional communist cadres are thus depicted as inadequate in the face of the sweeping new forces in society, which demand a share in political decision making in return for contributions to the future development of socialist states. Recently, this view has come under severe criticism for being too deterministic and failing to consider alternative options for the integration of socialist societies.[17] The economic imperative advocates have been especially neglectful of the ability of the political center to initiate policy, particularly in the recruitment area where the gatekeeping function has been ignored entirely. Nevertheless, the incumbent political leadership is well aware of the dangers present in providing even semi-autonomous status in decision making to functional elites. While economic managers and other specialists may seek greater operational autonomy, it does not automatically follow that achievement of that goal is being attained. In fact, the evidence seems to suggest failure to implement such a trend.[18] Jowitt has argued persuasively that the contemporary, i.e., post-consolidation, task of socialist regimes is inclusion: the attempt to prevent the spread of social heterogeneity into the political sector "by revising the regime's format and its relationship to society from insulation to integration."[19] This can be accomplished by maintaining a separation of socio-economic and political functions in society and by directing the leadership tasks to both coordination and mobilization. In fact, Polish and other East European leaders have consistently sought to implement a formula which will assure both continued socio-economic progress and political stability by maintaining the primacy of the political cadres in the formulation of policies.

RECRUITMENT POLICY ALTERNATIVES

The recruitment process presents one of the most effective ways to alter the integration mode of society. A change from a primarily command relationship between the regime and the community to a consensual linkage is likely to be aided by recruiting into the elite representatives of newly mobilized societal sectors. In view of the long-term prevalence of the economic imperative arguments, however, it is essential to stress that an alteration in the the composition of the elite in Poland does not necessarily signify a displacement of the professional political cadres and the incorporation of nonpolitical personnel into the leadership structure. Rather, several recruitment options exist and can be selectively applied by the incumbent leaders to assure inclusion rather than insulation between the political center and society.

One policy alternative for recruitment is indeed the process of adaptation discussed almost exclusively by students of socialist states, namely the horizontal diffusion of the elite. This signifies the extension of political roles to previously nonpoliticized personnel, primarily economic and technical specialists. This recruitment strategy may be termed a rationalization policy, for it aims at the introduction into the policy-making process of elites with expert skills who are concerned foremost with criteria of rationality and efficiency. Essentially this involves the lateral recruitment of elites from the economic and other specialized sectors, resulting in a lateral expansion of the political boundaries.

Recruitment through this lateral policy can be implemented in two ways. One involves a redefinition of political roles, so that managerial or technical elites can maintain their functional responsibilities and bases of power while also acquiring access to political decision making. For example, specialists involved in the direct supervision of production will remain outside the mainstream political agencies, the party and state bureaucracies, but will be recruited to take part in policy making because of their skills and knowledge. Factory directors will thus retain essentially managerial and technical duties, and continue to perform these specialized functions as their primary occupational responsibilities. However, in order to improve the ability of the regime to deal with the problems of industrialization and modernization, the political leadership brings into policy-making deliberations the factory managers and other specialists. The experts, then, are given political roles and functions while continuing to perform basically specialized tasks in society. This pattern of expanding the political boundaries beyond the party apparatus and the state ministries to include technical and managerial personnel, academics, and journalists results in a lateral diffusion of the elite taking part in political decision making. An increase over time in the representation of the specialized elites in the PUWP Central Committeesis an indication that a policy of lateral recruitment is being carried out to some extent by the Polish political leadership.

The other method of lateral recruitment is through cooptation.[20] In this case, elites who have acquired a considerable degree of practical expertise in specialized fields are brought into the party and state bureaucracies, and thus assume direct political roles. Fleron first introduced the distinction between elite members who are brought into the political leadership structure directly, that is without much practical experience in other factors of society, and elites who are coopted into political leadership positions after considerable on-the-job training in economic, cultural, or other specialized fields.[21] The first type of officials includes individuals who assume political functions in the party organization or state ministries shortly after the end of their education, and thus have little exposure to nonpolitical professional careers. These elite members can then be considered primarily as "recruited" politicians. In contrast to this elite, there are individuals who are brought into the party or state organizations only after service in other professional occupations, such as factory management or academics. This type of elite has considerable practical on-the-job exposure to the specialized areas, and thus obtains a substantial degree of expertise in nonpolitical fields. Precisely because of this acquired occupational knowledge, these individuals are then "coopted" into the political elite by assuming positions in the party or state bureaucracies. The operational cut-off point between the professional politicians and the coopted officials is the same as in Fleron's study: the mean number of years spent by the elite members in specialized occupations prior to entrance into political positions in the party or state organizations. For the Polish elite sample under analysis here,this turned out to be six years. That is, for example, a factory technician or journalist who spent five years or less in these professions before being recruited, respectively, to work for the Central Committee Economic Department and the Ministry of Culture are viewed as recruited politicians. On the other hand, individuals whose association with the same specialized vocations exceeded six years prior to their assumption of political offices in the Central Committee apparatus or ministries are described as coopted officials.

The important issue in both the direct lateral and cooptative instances of recruitment concerns the ability of the party leadership to restrict the infusion of the new recruits into policy making. Such an incursion is likely to diminish the control over political decisions hereafter maintained by the professional political cadres. As concerns the direct method of lateral recruitment, limitation on the participation of the newly mobilized elites is most likely accomplished by restricting the specialists to narrow and confined areas of decision making. In contrast, the cooptation policy succeeds in cutting off the expert elites from their prior professional and organizational ties and replacing them by the network of the political bureaucracies. Presumably this places the new coopted officials under the direct control of the political center. Clearly, then, the possibility of restricting the political impact of lateral recruitment is available to the incumbent leadership. The problem is that any restriction may be at the cost of some loss in information about the needs and interests of society. The leadership may be willing to tolerate such a loss to some extent, but is more likely to attempt the development of other means of information retrieval.

One such alternative is a recruitment policy aiming at the vertical diffusion of the elite sector.[22] Entrance into central decision-making roles is increasingly provided to subnational political cadres, with the conscious strategy of altering the exclusively command relationship between the regime and its "representatives" in the periphery. Unlike the previous recruitment option, this policy relies not on specialists but on lower level political officials to provide the center with knowledge about the complex social relations in the mature socialist system. Thus, it is a stabilization recruitment strategy which attempts to assure the continuity of elite personnel through the incorporation of trusted political functionaries into the leadership. The selection, into the 1968 and subsequent Central Committees, of workers and farmers politically active at the factory or cooperative level is an example of this recruitment strategy. Others representing vertical recruitment into the Central Committee are local or regional party apparatchiki and government officials. The allegiance of this personnel to political values is certainly greater than that of elites whose career patterns lie primarily in the specialized sectors. Vertical recruitment is therefore less disturbing to the existing elite and policy arrangements than lateral differentiation, which results in the growing infusion of nonpolitical elements into political decision making. For this reason, a vertical recruitment policy is more likely to be favored by the regime than a policy of lateral elite recruitment.

However, precisely because the political center and the periphery share similar values and goals, vertical elite selection may not be the best means of coping with the demands of modernization, since the cadres at the local level are likely to provide the same type of information as is already available in the top political leadership. In addition, subnational political cadres are very dependent on their superiors within the party and state organizations. This symbiotic relationship may cut down the effectiveness of information flows from the periphery to the center. Both these factors seem to have been present in Poland, where the reactions to the attempted price rises in 1970 and 1976 seem to have caught the Gomulka and Gierek leaderships unprepared, apparently because of a lack of adequate information about grass root sentiments. Nonetheless, it should be noted that a vertical elite diffusion opens up channels of communication between local/regional authorities and central policy makers. Information on popular needs and local problems can be provided by recruits from the periphery having a voice in central institutions, such as the Central Committee. Even though the latter party body may not play an overt decision-making role, it can act as a medium for information exchange between the regime and society. While this would not signify a devolution of policy making from the top political leadership, it could provide a communications and consultative link.[23] Such a formula is likely to be most attractive to the political center, for it permits the replacement of command by "relational skills of persuasion and manipulation" without sacrificing the primacy of political elites and norms in the policy process.[24] In the final analysis, the success of the vertical recruitment policy may depend on the ability of periphery officials to have meaningful inputs into the central policy institutions, without becoming too dependent on the tolerance of political superiors.

We should also be aware that the direct lateral, cooptive, and vertical recruitment strategies are not mutually exclusive. More likely the leaderships of any socialist state will adopt both recruitment policies. In this way, the regime can establish important consensual links to both the specialized and local sectors of society, and thus obtain information of a specific nature from the experts and a general familiarity with grass-roots conditions. In turn, better communications of this kind will improve the integrative capacity of the policy and the community, and facilitate the system's ability to deal with the industrial society. At the same time, given the greater political reliability of vertical recruitment, we expect that elite selection through stabilization will be more prevalent in post-Stalinist Poland than the rationalization strategy.

ELITE INTEGRATION AND DIRECT LATERAL RECRUITMENT

The evidence from the composition of the Central Committees in the 1954-1975 period is that direct lateral entrance of specialists into the Polish elite is a steadily growing phenomenon. Tables 4.1 and 4.2 show that members of the technical and creative intelligentsia have increased their share of seats in the Central Committee from 3.9 percent in 1954 to 8.5 percent in 1975. The undirectional aspect of this trend suggests at first that the inclusion of officials from the specialized sectors into political institutions is a response to modernization, and in particular to the need of the political leadership to have expert personnel among the national elite. Comparison of incumbent and new members of the central party organization (Tables 4.3 and 4.4) also reveals that the percentage of specialists was greater among the new than the old Central Committee representatives, with the sole exception of the latest Committee.

The boundaries of elite roles which are politicized have expanded laterally in Poland during the

TABLE 4.1
Affiliations of Full Central Committee Members, 1954-1975 (N)

	1954	1959	1964	1968	1971	1975
Central Party	14	19	25	19	20	20
Regional and Local Party	9	9	18	25	21	27
Mass Organizations	7	10	4	4	6	6
Central Government	37	28	25	19	25	24
Regional and Local Government	0	1	1	1	2	6
Military	7	6	6	2	3	4
Technical Intelligentsia	0	1	0	2	3	2
Creative Intelligentsia	3	3	5	4	5	10
Workers and Farmers	0	0	1	15	29	36
Other/Unknown	-	-	-	-	1	5
TOTAL	77	77	85	91	115	140

Note: Each full member of the Central Committee was classified into <u>one</u> category only, in accordance with his or her primary occupational status at the time of each PUWP Congress. Assignments of the elite members into the different groups were based on the organizational affiliation, the functional responsibilities and the hierarchial position of each official.

TABLE 4.2
Affiliations of Full Central Committee Members, 1954-1975 (%)

	1954	1959	1964	1968	1971	1975
Central Party	18.2	24.7	29.4	20.9	17.4	14.3
Regional and Local Party	11.7	11.7	21.2	27.5	18.3	19.3
Mass Organizations	9.1	13.0	4.7	4.4	5.2	4.3
Central Government	48.1	36.4	29.4	20.9	21.7	17.1
Regional and Local Government	-	1.3	1.2	1.1	1.8	4.3
Military	9.1	7.8	7.1	2.2	2.6	2.7
Technical Intelligentsia	-	1.3	-	2.2	2.6	1.4
Creative Intelligentsia	3.9	3.9	5.9	4.4	4.3	7.1
Workers and Farmers	-	-	1.2	16.5	25.2	25.7
Other/Unknown	-	-	-	-	0.9	3.6

Note: Each full member of the Central Committee was classified into one category only, in accordance with his or her primary occupational status at the time of each PUWP Congress. Assignments of the elite members into the different groups were based on the organizational affiliation, the functional responsibilities and the hierarchial position of each official.

TABLE 4.3
Affiliations of Incumbent Full Central Committee Members, 1959-1975 (%)

	1959	1964	1968	1971	1975
Central Party	28.6	31.6	32.0	34.8	20.8
Regional and Local Party	10.2	14.0	20.0	8.7	16.9
Mass Organizations	8.2	3.5	6.0	6.5	7.8
Central Government	42.8	38.6	30.0	28.2	22.1
Regional and Local Government	0	0	2.0	2.2	3.9
Military	4.1	7.0	4.0	2.2	5.2
Technical Intelligentsia	2.0	0	2.0	2.2	1.3
Creative Intelligentsia	4.1	5.3	4.0	2.2	7.8
Workers and Farmers	0	0	0	13.0	14.3
Other/Unknown	0	0	0	0	0
TOTAL	49	57	50	46	77

Note: Incumbent elite members are officials who have held full membership in the Central Committee prior to the PUWP Congress in question, while new Central Committee officials have been admitted to full membership for the first time at the equivalent PUWP Congress. Assignments of the elite into the different occupational groupings were based on the organizational affiliation, the functional responsibilities and the hierarchial position of each official.

TABLE 4.4
Affiliation of New Full Central Committee Members, 1959-1975 (%)

	1959	1964	1968	1971	1975
Central Party	17.9	25.0	7.3	5.8	6.3
Regional and Local Party	14.3	35.7	36.6	24.6	22.2
Mass Organizations	21.4	7.1	2.4	4.3	0
Central Government	25.0	10.7	9.7	17.4	11.1
Regional and Local Government	3.6	3.6	0	1.4	4.8
Military	14.3	7.1	0	2.9	0
Technical Intelligentsia	0	0	2.4	2.9	1.6
Creative Intelligentsia	3.6	7.1	4.9	5.8	6.3
Workers and Farmers	0	3.6	36.6	33.3	39.7
Other/Unknown	0	0	0	1.4	7.9
TOTAL	28	28	41	69	63

Note: Incumbent elite members are officials who have held full membership in the Central Committee prior to the PUWP Congress in question, while new Central Committee officials have been admitted to full membership for the first time at the equivalent PUWP Congress. Assignments of the elite into the different occupational groupings were based on the organizational affiliation, the functional responsibilities and the hierarchial position of each official.

post-Stalinist period. Despite that, it is unlikely that this development represents an integrative elite recruitment policy in response to the economic imperatives of modernization. First, the actual increase in the proportion of specialists among the elite is very small. More important, lateral recruitment has not been directed toward the incorporation of individuals engaged in managerial and technical occupations, but has resulted in the increased prominence of individuals in the creative arts and the natural and social sciences (Tables 4.2 and 4.4). This is true of all political leaderships in Poland, from Bierut through Gomulka and Gierek. Even the economic crisis of the early 1960s and the economic riots of 1970 do not alter the situation in favor of officials holding supervisory, managerial, or technocratic positions. Elite integration, then, is not conditioned primarily by a rationalization policy seeking to include, among the leadership, officials directly involved in economic production. The argument that modernization is bound to bring into political roles technical and managerial experts is not supported by the data on elite recruitment in Poland. While it may be true that economic specialists have sought to obtain a more direct voice in political deliberations, these data and other accounts suggest that they have remained essentially in a consultative position.[25]

The regime has thus not extended the political boundaries of the system to include technocrats, but has preferred instead to maintain the economic specialists in an advisory role vis-a-vis the political functionaries. If anything, the growing presence and recruitment of the intelligentsia into the Central Committee signifies that the complexity of modernization makes the support of social elites more significant to the regime than the support of the economic experts. Maintenance of political stability thus depends to a larger extent on elite integration between political and social elites than between the technocrats and bureaucrats. While the attempts by the Polish leaders to achieve either of the above types of integration have not been overwhelming, clearly the attempt to reach the creative elite has been more visible than the establishment of political-technical expert linkages. Nonetheless, the more important observation is that direct horizontal elite recruitment is not a significant part of the elite selection process in Poland.

The corollary of the argument that specialists become an increasingly prominent sector of the elite is the claim that the dominant position of the traditional political functionaries in socialist states is gradually eroded in the face of modernization.[26] Once again, the data on the Polish elite reveal that this traditional dichotomy between "reds" and "experts" is too great a simplification. Just as there are several types of specialists, so we can distinguish between the presence of different political elite subsets. To understand the impact of modernization on elite recruitment, it is necessary to take into account this diversity.

Lateral differentiation of the political elite refers primarily to the party and state bureaucracies, although it also includes the military, police, and mass organizations. The role played by representatives of the latter three institutions was especially significant through the late 1950s. The recruitment of personnel from the mass organizations dropped from 21 percent to 7 percent between 1959 and 1964, and did not pick up in any subsequent period (Table 4.4). The same holds true for the military and police cadres, whose portion among new recruits into the Central Committee decreased from 14 percent to 7 percent in the same years, and then declined even further. From these trends it is clear that the utilization of command and coercion measures was most prevalent during the transformation and consolidation phases of socialist building in Poland, and that elites performing such functions were well integrated into the leadership structure of the time. As the threat of the application of violence decreased in Polish society, the perpetrators of this function lost much of their direct political influence in the system. Similarly, as the tasks of the Polish regime were aimed less at consolidation and more at inclusion, the "transmission belt" role of the mass organizations receded into the background in favor of an integration strategy linking the polity and the community, without need for the intermediary role of the mass organizations.[27] In particular, the manifestations of popular discontent in 1968, 1970, and 1976 made clear to the regime that agencies of coercion and command were unable to curb the expression of mass dissatisfaction and maintain stability in the system. The role of these organizations in society was thus further eroded, and the selection into the Central Committee of functionaries associated directly with command-type politics gave way to the inclusion of grassroot activists.[28]

An important difference in elite selection is evident in regard to the two main components of the political elite: the party and state officials. The proportion of the state bureaucrats on the Central Committee decreased steadily from the Second (48 percent) to the Seventh PUWP Congress (17 percent) (Table 4.2). This downturn in the political fortunes of the state functionaries is in part accounted for by the strengthening of the party institution in Eastern Europe vis-a-vis its state counterpart.[29] In the case of Poland, this trend appears to have been further influenced by the factional struggles rampant among the leadership. For example, the need to dislodge the Stalinists entrenched in the state organization in 1959 and the desire to remove supporters of Moczar in 1968 required Gomulka to move with greater speed against the state apparatus. Nonetheless, the growing displacement of the state bureaucrats from the Central Committee is too systematic a trend to be explained exclusively by factional politics. This becomes more evident when we compare the position of the party _apparatchiki_ to that of the state bureaucrats. Political cadres of the PUWP constituted a growing part of the national elite throughout the Gomulka period: in the fifties, the party _apparatchiki_ made up 30 percent of the elite, placing them below or equal to the state organization, while in the sixties, the 50 percent share held by the party apparatus outstripped the state functionaries. During the earlier period, social transformation was executed by political elites committed to similar goals and means of implementation. As the task of consolidation began to be altered in favor of regime-society inclusion, the resulting disruption to the traditional mobilization techniques required careful supervision by the political center. To perform this function, the most reliable political cadres, those with close affiliation to the party bureaucracy, were recruited into the national leadership structure. For example, among the newly recruited elites into the Central Committee (Table 4.4), the party _apparat_ numbered about 30 percent in 1959, by 1964 had increased to 60 percent, and in 1968 accounted for 45 percent of the membership (although it declined thereafter). The year 1968, however, also witnessed the first recruitment ever into the elite of working class, grassroot, political activists, an innovation which has been continued under the leadership of Gierek. Therefore, even though the party bureaucrats' representation has declined in the 1970s, it has been counterbalanced by the increasing presence of local political activists.

The data on elite recruitment suggests that the complexities of the industrial state continue to require the political brokerage functions traditionally performed by the party. The shift from consolidation to inclusion, however, may signify a change in the type of political cadres needed to fill supervisory roles in society. Party officials committed to ideological, command politics are likely to be displaced by personnel willing to perform the coordination functions of a political manager.[30] Skills of this kind are most likely to be found not among the narrowly trained specialists or functional administrators, but among the most generalist element in the elite: the party cadres themselves. For this reason, the usefulness of the state administrator with well-defined economic or social responsibilities has become more limited with time. Of course, this does not mean that the central leadership can get along without the expertise and support of more specialized sectors of society. Rather, these inputs have been taken over in part by those specialists brought into the elite by direct lateral recruitment and by consultation. At the same time the more general administrative duties of the state bureaucrats appear to have been placed increasingly in the hands of the party functionaries. The state administrators, as a result, have been increasingly displaced in the central leadership structure by elites infringing on the two formerly essential functions of the state bureaucrat: overall administrative supervision and area-specific functional responsibility. The tasks of elite integration in a mature socialist society, such as Poland has become in the past ten years, are significantly more complex than the displacement of "reds" by "experts", as the advocates of the economic imperative would have us believe.

INTEGRATION AND RECRUITMENT BY COOPTATION

Elite integration can also be achieved by a more indirect method of lateral recruitment, namely by cooptation. The cooptation strategy changes the type of personnel staffing the political institutions by recruiting officials with considerable exposure to the specialized sectors of society. Several advantages for the regime are evident in such a recruitment policy. First, it enables the close integration of political and socio-economic sectors through the medium of personnel in the political bureaucracies. Second, cooptation leads to the absorption of individuals with long-term experience in the specialized areas into the organizational and communication networks of the political agencies. Unlike the more direct method of lateral recruitment, it prevents the specialists from maintaining autonomous institutional or functional ties to the nonpolitical areas. Third, it introduces into the party or state organizations the expertise needed to deal with the complex social and economic relations of the industrial state.

The advantages of cooptation are likely to make it an attractive policy for the political leadership, and a preferred recruitment response to the needs of modernization. This is clearly evident in the case of Poland, which shows a considerable increase in the practice of cooptation. Table 4.5 presents the data for the political elite as a whole, and to better distinguish the changes among the elite, for three elite subsets: the party apparatus, government officials with responsibilities in the economic sector, and state personnel working in noneconomic fields.[31] The trend for the entire political elite is a linear increase in the number of coopted officials: from 5 percent in 1954 to 34 percent in 1971.[32] As a consequence of this recruitment policy, then, the nature of the political elite in Poland has changed in the post-Stalin period. Officials who enter political work in the initial stages of their careers have become less and less part of the leadership structure, and have been replaced by individuals with more extensive experience in the economic and social sectors of society. The net effect has been to make the Polish political elite more diversified, with a resultant expansion of the skills and expertise available to the regime. This change presents better opportunities to deal more effectively with the issues of modernization and makes the political center willing to alter the recruitment process in the direction of the cooptation mechanism.

At the same time, the professional political elite has remained the dominant segment of the leadership structure, especially within the party bureaucracy. In 1971 the directly recruited officials in the apparat still numbered over 70 percent of the party cadres (Table 4.5). Most probably the preference of the top Polish leadership is to staff the party organization with cadres who have obtained the majority of their experience in political institutions. In this manner the political orientation of the party personnel is maintained. This situation is more difficult to achieve if the political organizations are predominantly staffed by coopted officials who have extensive former ties to specialized sectors of society. On the other hand, placing coopted personnel among a majority of life-long professional politicians is likely to render them more responsive to political priorities than to the demands for rationalization coming from the specialized areas. The problem with a limitation on cooptation may be that the adaptative capacity of the bureaucracies can become insufficient to absorb the demands stemming from the modernizing society. The ability of the political center to assure systemic stability thus can be endangered, and require additional mechanisms for the integration of the regime and society.

The shift to cooptation into the party and government economic administration is most pronounced beginning with the late 1960s. This trend supports the observation made earlier that, in terms of Jowitt's conceptualization, regime tasks have been recently modified from consolidation to inclusion. One of the characteristics of this attempted movement from the primacy of command political norms to more consensual patterns has been a more extensive recruitment of coopted personnel into political roles. The data also show that coopted officials are more a part of the economic administrative elite than of the party bureaucracy (Table 4.5). Again, this reinforces the perception that the economic administrators in the state bureaucracy have become more narrowly trained in functionally specific areas, and then coopted into supervisory roles in government agencies. The party elite, on the other hand, remains primarily the province of the professional politician, although the elite also obtains technical expertise through cooptation. Nonetheless, the party cadres remain the best qualified elites to assume general political functions in society. This may lead them to become, in the inclusionary polity, "brokers" whose services can best cope with

TABLE 4.5
Recruitment and Cooptation Among Political Elite Subsets in the Central Committees, 1954-1971

		Party Officials		Govt. Officials in Noneco. Areas		Govt. Officials in Eco. Areas		Total Political Elite	
		N	%	N	%	N	%	N	%
1954	Recruited Politicians	23	100.0	17	94.4	17	89.5	57	95.0
	Coopted Officials	0	-	1	5.6	2	10.5	3	5.0
1959	Recruited Politicians	26	92.9	14	87.5	10	76.9	50	87.7
	Coopted Officials	2	7.1	2	12.5	3	23.1	7	12.3
1964	Recruited Politicians	39	90.7	11	84.6	10	76.9	60	87.0
	Coopted Politicians	4	9.3	2	15.4	3	23.1	9	13.0

1968	Recruited Politicians	35	79.5	9	81.8	7	77.8	51	79.7
	Coopted Officials	9	20.5	2	18.2	2	22.2	13	20.3
1971	Recruited Politicians	27	71.1	10	83.3	6	40.0	43	66.2
	Coopted Officials	11	28.9	2	16.7	9	60.0	22	33.8

Note: The distinction between recruited politicians and coopted officials is based on the number of years spent by an elite member in a specialized occupation prior to entrance into a political position in the party apparatus or state ministries. An individual whose association with a specialized vocation was less than five years was classified as a recruited politician, while an individual with more than six years of service in a specialized position before assuming office in the political bureaucracies was classified as a coopted official.

the diversified needs and interests of the modern Polish industrial society.

The question is whether the political center can rely on the party cadres to "manage" properly decision making in the economic area, since their specialized training is not as extensive as that of other elite subsets within the system. Differences between political criteria in policy making and norms of efficiency and rationalization can thus develop, continuing the isolation of the party functionaries from the social and economic elites. The events of the 1970s in Poland suggest that this is indeed the case, resulting in impasses which are resolved through crises.[33]

INTEGRATION AND VERTICAL RECRUITMENT

The above discussion shows that there are definite limits to lateral recruitment by either the direct or cooptation methods. To assure systemic stability and provide for the integration of the various social, economic, and political sectors, the political center needs to develop other inclusionary tactics. One obvious option is to extend the vertical dimension of elite selection.

The data for Poland reveal that members of the subnational elite have acquired a significant presence in the more recent Central Committees. The leadership has increasingly turned to the vertical diffusion of the recruitment process, thereby providing new roles in the political center to "representatives" from the periphery. This policy of elite selection has two aspects. The first involves the recruitment of professional bureaucrats from the regional or local party organizations. As Tables 4.1 and 4.2 show, this is most evident during the period of Gomulka's rule in the Central Committees of 1964 and 1968. The proportion of new recruits from the regional/local party apparatus increased from 14 percent in 1959 to 36 percent in both 1964 and 1968 (Table 4.4). Insofar as there was at this time a modification in regime tasks away from consolidation, it was directed primarily toward the hierarchial integration of the party elite. As a consequence, subnational political cadres were provided with a greater voice in central policy making. As the regional functionaries began to play a more important role in Polish politics during the 1960s, they were provided with symbolic recognition through an increased number of seats on enlarged PUWP Central Committees.

In fact, during the latter years of Gomulka's rule, elite recruitment extension was limited to the professional party apparatus and did not involve the inclusion of elites from other sectors of society. On the one hand, this failure on the part of the regime to bring into the leadership structure experts from the nonpolitical areas explains the stagnation which characterized Gomulka's rule during the final years of his tenure, and accounts to some degree for the lack of economic and social innovation which ultimately spelled Gomulká's downfall. At the same time, the promotion into the national leadership of the younger, more pragmatic regional party personnel also paved the way for Gomulka's removal, since these new officials became increasingly dissatisfied with the policy immobility of the Gomulka government.[34]

The Gierek period is characterized by a decrease in the recruitment of subnational apparatchiki, whose proportion on the Central Committee declines from 36 percent in 1968 to 22 percent in 1975 (Table 4.4). This change in elite selection, however, does not lead to a policy of lateral recruitment and thus the inclusion of other sectoral elites in the leadership structure. Rather the recruitment process moves further down the political ladder to include grassroot political activists. The entrance into the Central Committee of workers and farmers from local production units is thus a major phenomenon in the late Gomulka and Gierek periods. For example, since 1968 this category of recruits accounted for over 30 percent of new Central Committee members, and has increased its representation on the central party body from 16 percent under Gomulka to over 25 percent under Gierek's rule. These officials are not full-time political workers, although most are prominent members of primary party organizations. They are politically active members of society and have the advantage of being in close touch with the masses. Their knowledge of conditions at the local level is likely to be more extensive than that of higher placed elites from the economic and social sectors of society.

The inclusion of the worker/farmer activists on the Central Committee of the party is essentially a response to the strong current of mass dissatisfaction evident in Polish society since the late 1960s, or rather, to the willingness of the workers to voice their demands for change more openly. It is, then, an attempt at inclusionary politics by establishing closer communication links between the regime and the broadest segments of the Polish population. This does not mean that the local political activists have been given a meaningful decision-making role in the political center. The representatives of the grassroots periphery, however, have obtained in the past few years much better direct access to the leadership of the country. They are now in a position to provide information to Warsaw about local feelings and desires, and to serve as a visible link between the center and the periphery. The worker activists' presence among the national elite can be taken as a symbol of the Polish government's willingness to at least listen to the masses and communicate with them. The recruitment policy is part of a larger process characterized by consultative meetings between the leadership and the population, by more frequent and enlarged Central Community plena, and by governmental commissions on various national issues.[35] These actions suggest that the Gierek leadership has sought to go beyond the modification of regime-society relations defined by consolidation tasks to a restructuring of policy-community links. Reliance on command and arbitrary politics has tended to give way to the politics of persuasion and manipulation.[36]

The change in the leadership style of the Gierek regime has not disturbed the primacy of the political organizations and the officials associated with them. The movement from system-mobilization to system-inclusion has focused on the hierarchial integration of the central party elite, the regional apparat, and the local political activists. In the main, the elite recruitment policy of the center has continued to rely on proven political cadres rather than on "outsiders" from the functional economic and social areas. This has been especially true with regard to the party bureaucracy which has not been infiltrated significantly even by the process of cooptation. Therefore, the regime's attempts to meet the pressures associated with the socio-economic development of Poland have been directed primarily toward the retrieval of information from regional and local political cadres. To accomplish this, the subnational political elites were provided with increasingly better access to the political center. Other measures in Gierek's policy of inclusion involved the unification of local party and government positions, the establishment of a two-tiered territorial administrative structure resulting in the breakdown of traditional regions, and the creation of a prefectorial naczalnik position as the representative of the center in the periphery.[37] The vertical diffusion of the elite structure was thus coupled with measures aimed at making the local elites more responsive to the policies of the political center.

The results of all these arrangements are only too well known. The upward flow of information about mass feelings and local conditions was not well tuned to the realities of the Polish situation in the 1970s. The price paid for the lack of adequate communications between the regime and society was, once more, in June 1976, open riots by workers. The long-term consequence is a growing dissatisfaction among the Polish population. In the end, the political leadership's attempts at stabilization depended too heavily on like-minded lower level personnel to forge a link between the new Gierek leadership and the masses. These regional/local political cadres tended to provide only politically correct information and advice. This development, together with the administrative reforms of the early 1970s, only served to reinforce the hand of the political center and render the inputs from society most ineffective. In the final analysis, the political stability of Poland may depend on the leadership's willingness to tolerate more meaningful forms of participation. A recruitment policy going beyond symbolic gestures to provide the new recruits with important influence in policy making would be a big step in that direction.

CONCLUSION: RECRUITMENT AND POLICY CHANGE

In any society influence over the content of policies depends ultimately on access to the centers of decision making. In practice, in socialist societies inputs into policy depend largely on admittance to the leadership structure of the system. The ability of the party leaders to control elite recruitment has therefore an important bearing on the range of policy choices available to the political authorities. For a long time, a widespread expectation in Western scholarship was that the successful building of modern societies in Eastern Europe would diminish the authority of the party and its leadership, and create conditions for the institutionalized expression of multiple views and policy preferences.[38] Changes of this type have not occurred during the post-Stalinist political development of Poland. The examination of elite recruitment during that period reveals that, while new elite groupings have been admitted over time to the leadership system, this process did not culminate in an erosion of the political role of the party and its cadres. Changes in personnel policy have not led to institutional rearrangements in the polity, enabling the new recruits to have a consistent voice in a regularized process of decision making. The political leadership has thus retained a monopoly over the articulation of policy initiatives. The failure to translate the diffusion of the elite into meaningful channels of influence by a variety of interests has extracted a toll in systemic stability. As a number of crisis events over the past decade in Poland testify, the national leadership has been unable to win consistent acceptance of its policies by society or some of its sector, and has had difficulties in implementing several policy programs.

The process of political change in Poland appears to have had an impact on the elite structure without routinely affecting policy making itself. To a large extent, this outcome is due to the fact that the political leadership was able to limit the influence of social groupings in decision making precisely by selectively admitting representatives of these groups into the elite without extending to them overt access to policy deliberations. The selection of recruits into the elite remained, for the most part, a controlled process, accomplished by the implementation of diverse recruitment options by the incumbent political leaders. For example, new participants in the leadership structure were brought in from a diversity of areas by means of direct lateral recruitment, cooptation of specialists into the political bureaucracies, and the vertical selection of grassroot political activists from the factories and cooperatives. Admittance of individuals from these constituencies into the Central Committee represented at least partial responsiveness by the regime to the increasing political interests of the specialized and mass sectors of society. This step can also be interpreted as an attempt to use formal representation to obtain better compliance from those constituencies granted the new status of membership among the societal elite. Apparently, then, extension of elite recruitment is in part a device to "coopt" new personnel, and to increasingly include in the policy social groups heretofore underrepresented in the political community. Understandably, at the same time, the incumbent political leaders were reluctant to jeopardize their policy-making prerogatives, and preferred to contain the new recruitment to symbolic representation without spilling over into decision making.

This does not mean that the PUWP leadership failed to make adaptations to the changing social and economic realities of modernization. In fact, innovations in elite recruitment represent a form of political adaptation, which were accompanied by other measures. Taken together, these steps could not help but have a bearing on policies. The overall pattern of political development in Poland since 1956 can be viewed in terms of three broad phases, with different participatory norms and policy impacts. The movement is essentially a change in the political methods employed by the regime, from mobilization of society through command politics to socio-political integration by means of inclusionary politics.

Polish politics during most of Gomulka's tenure as First Secretary of the PUWP were characterized by the task of political consolidation. In practice, this means the insulation of the political center from society, and the extraction of popular obedience by means of mand.[39] The party's role is given the orthodox ideological interpretation as the vanguard and guiding force of society, and the commanding positions of the organization and its leadership are seen as essential to secure development toward socialism.

> When the activities and the controlling position of the Party are weakened, when the Party organizations and committees lose their hold upon the helm of social life, then the hostile anti-socialist elements are given scope for action.[40]

Political decisions, therefore, must be in the hands of reliable political cadres. During Gomulka's "small stabilization," the system's elite was restricted essentially to political personnel from the party, state, and mass organizations with little experience in the nonpolitical areas (Tables 4.1 and 4.5). Elite recruitment at this time favored the selection into the national leadership of party _apparatchiki_. The policy consequence was reliance on mobilization techniques, with the regime acting upon society. Characteristic of this period was a lack of policy initiative, lack of anticipation of socio-economic problems, _ad hoc_ solutions to these difficulties, and a general immobility in the political arena.[41] It seems that Gomulka was in favor of the status quo as a way to assure systemic stability. This meant that no significant organizational or personnel reforms took place during most of Gomulka's rule, and major specialized and popular interests were not taken into account in decision making. The consequence was the growing isolation of the regime from society, and the intensification of the social and economic problems beseiging Poland in the 1960s.[42] It is highly probable that the failure to rationalize social and economic policies at this time was due to the relatively small recruitment of specialists into the upper echelons of the Polish elite.

The resolution of this policy impasse occurred in 1968, when a number of events coalesced to produce a major crisis in society and the party. This period marked a transitional, post-mobilization phase in the political development of Poland. The political tasks of the time were geared to evaluate the changing socio-economic environment of the country, and to develop policy initiatives aimed at the resolution of the prevalent economic difficulties. To implement these tasks, Gomulka had to abandon the political pattern of the "small stabilization," and give greater authority to the more pragmatic, better educated political cadres recruited primarily from the regional _apparats_. The share of the subnational party elite thus increased in the 1968 Central Committee, while that of the officials associated with the central party and government bureaucracies declined significantly (Table 4.2). The older, more ideologically oriented functionaries were replaced by cadres with better specialized skills, who had been exposed to nonpolitical areas in the initial phase of their careers and then coopted into the political apparatus (Table 4.5). The recruitment pattern signaled the end of muddling through politics, and the initiation of new policies in the economic and social sectors.

The absorption into the party organization of

better skilled and more pragmatic officials brought about an increasing influence of rationality and efficiency criteria into policy making. It is the concern of this personnel with socio-economic issues which culminated in attempted reforms in 1969 to rationalize planning and improve efficiency of production.[43] The difficulty with the proposed reform was that it required the streamlining of the entire industrial system, and therefore signaled an end to price and wage subsidies, the primary beneficiary of which was the working class. Instead, the incentives for increasing production were directed toward the technical and managerial elites.

The 1969-1970 reform thus created a conflict between the policy preferences of the newly recruited political cadres and the specialists on the one hand, and the working masses on the other. Whether as an attempt to counterbalance the recently promoted party cadres by working class representatives, or in anticipation of the workers' opposition to the reforms and a resultant attempt to pacify them with representational status, the 1968 Central Committee had, for the first time ever, grassroot worker activists among its membership. Despite this post-1968 expansion of the elite to include a more diversified type of personnel, the innovative cooptation and vertical recruitment policies did not bring about new participatory modes in policy deliberations. The Gomulka regime continued to exercise control over specific policies and their implementation, without much concrete consultation with the new elements among the elite or much attention to the mood of the masses.[44] The economic reformism of the 1969-1970 years can thus be viewed as a generalized influence of the fusion of political and economic concerns among the new political cadres, who were apparently successful in providing a new overall direction to the socio-economic policy of the government but were unable to bear upon more specific decisions. The centralization of the policy-making process maintained by the Gomulka leadership continued to place the regime out of touch with the sentiments of society, as the ill-timed price reforms of December 1970 demonstrate. The reaction on the part of the mass public was instantaneous, taking the form of workers' riots and strikes which served to bring down the unpopular Gomulka clique and the policies associated with it.

The Gierek leadership rapidly adapted a new

political style and reformulated certain economic and social policies.[45] The new regime responded to the population's discontent by recognizing the legitimacy of the workers' grievances and by reappraising the pattern of economic development. The overall commitment to industrial growth and efficiency was maintained, but without extracting a cost for the reforms from the working class. The prior economic innovations most offensive to the masses, such as price increases and unfavorable wage bonuses, were rescinded, and wages improved. The new economic strategy sought to accomplish the rationalization of the system by technological improvements relying heavily on foreign imports and credits.

These steps were accompanied by new political and social policies aimed at resolving the social issues stemming from economic difficulties, and improving the legitimacy of the government. The measures undertaken by Gierek in the 1970s thus reflect closely the inclusionary political tasks described by Jowitt.[46] The primary goal was the better integration of the polity and the community, and this required the expansion of the political and decision-making boundaries in the system to allow for a fruitful interaction between the leadership and a variety of social elements. Already, in 1971, the party was described less as a commanding force and more "as occupying a special place in the system of organization of the Polish society," striving for "the optimal harmonization of the interests of the various classes and strate."[47]

The best means for achieving this form of integration was through an opening up of political participation and the admission of diverse elite types into the leadership structure. The recruitment pattern under Gierek, analyzed above, stressed the increasing incorporation into the elite of new personnel from the specialized sectors of society, as well as representatives of the working masses (Tables 4.1 and 4.2). The apparent strategy was to establish a consensual legitimacy for the regime by applying concepts of representation to obtain supports from the population.[48] In particular, by bringing into the elite those segments of society traditionally excluded from the political process, the social elites and working class activists, the Gierek government sought to create a common bond between the leadership and the citizens. At the same time, the improved access of a variety of social groupings to the elite structure was to create better communications and information flow between the political center and society. The new Polish Constitution, for example, gave the Polish citizens the right to "take part in exercising social control, in consultations and discussions on key problems of the country's development."[49] The 1970s, in fact, witnessed the proliferation of consultative meetings, regularized meetings of state and party organs, and national debates on major social and economic issues. The leadership style of the Gierek government, therefore, had a definite inclusionary dimension and sought to restructure polity-society relations by the introduction of new modes of representation and consultation, regulation and information diversification, as well as the abandonment of command politics in favor of the politics of persuasion and manipulation.

Despite this innovative style of political rule, Gierek fell prey to the same mistake as his predecessor and misjudged the feelings of the population and its readiness for price increases in June 1976. The open defiance of the workers at this time once again testified to the existing gap between the regime's policies and popular expectations. The continued misunderstanding between society and its leadership can best be explained by the fact that, once again, the expansion of the elite structure's boundaries was not accompanied by a simultaneous expansion of policymaking boundaries. Participation by the nonpolitical elites was therefore limited to formal meetings with few decisional capabilities and to consultation procedures which have slowly lost their earlier effectiveness. The immediate effect was a failure of inclusionary politics, despite the likely belief by the Gierek leadership that it had established successful communication with the population and obtained sufficient supports to introduce new price increases. Instead, reports indicate that the Polish administration has begun to talk primarily with political aktifs, who provided the leadership with information meant to please rather than to appraise them of the conditions and feelings in society.[50]

This development, in turn, is a symptom of a larger problem in the Polish system. The failure to offer the new recruits among the elite more genuine access to policy making and introduce a routine, frank exchange of views between the regime and a diversity of social groupings is due to the leadership's concern about the impact of such openness on the political system. The party elite is faced with a dilemma. On the one hand, the diversity of socio-economic elements present in contemporary Poland necessitates a political integration which may ultimately depend on granting a bigger voice in policy making to the lateral, specialized sectors and the grassroot working class. On the other hand, the continued prevalence of the party organization's views and goals may depend on insulating these policies from the scrutiny of an increasingly heterogeneous society. Under the circumstances, caution is likely to emerge as the most advisable response to the dilemma

The unsuccessful attempt at inclusionary politics during the early part of the 1970s, however, may not be due exclusively to the doubts of the Polish leadership. Political development from mobilization to integration of society requires a change in the style of rule and political behavior on the part of both the party elite and the societal constituencies. These new modes of behavior need to be learned and developed with time by the regime and the population at large. The political elite must develop a better tolerance of different viewpoints, while the diverse societal sectors must learn that their opinions are sought and valued by the leadership. For example, commenting on Poland's consensus socialism, Radio Warsaw stated that consultation "is a relatively new instrument which not everybody can yet use well. One needs some degree of political sophistication."[51] The learning process, for both sides, may take some time.

NOTES

1. For a general discussion of elite recruitment policies see Robert D. Putnam, The Comparative Study of Political Elites. Englewood Cliffs, New Jersey: Prentice-Hall, 1976, chapter 3, and Joseph LaPalombara, Politics Within Nations. Englewood Cliffs, New Jersey: Prentice-Hall, 1974, chapter 12.

2. See, for example, William B. Quandt, The Comparative Study of Political Elites. Beverly Hills: Sage Publications, 1970, pp. 187-191.

3. LaPalombara, Politics Within Nations, p. 476.

4. Putnam, The Comparative Study of Political Elites, pp. 52-59.

5. William A. Welsh, "Elites and Leadership in Communist Systems: Some New Perspectives," Studies in Comparative Communism, IX (1976), p. 169.

6. Edward Gierek, "Party's Tasks in the Further Socialist Development of the Polish People's Republic," Programme Report delivered to the 6th PUWP Congress, December 6, 1971, p. 29.

7. For a more detailed discussion by the author see Jack Bielasiak, "Lateral and Vertical Elite Differentiation in European Communist States," Studies in Comparative Communism (Spring 1979). Also see Mary McAuley, "The Hunting of the Hierarchy: RSFSR Obkom First Secretaries and the

Central Committee," Soviet Studies, XXVI (1974), pp. 477-479.

8. McAuley, "The Hunting of the Hierarchy;" and Peter C. Ludz, The Changing Party Elite in East Germany. Cambridge, Massachusetts: MIT Press, 1972, pp. 120-130. In Poland, the more frequent and lengthier Central Committee meetings and the breakdown of the plena into working groups suggest a similar growth in the consultative, information exchange role of the PUWP Central Committee.

9. The data were obtained from a number of sources. A primary one was the Archive on East European Political Elites assembled at the University of Pittsburgh under the directions of Carl Beck and William Jarzabek. Other important sources were the Reports of Radio Free Europe and the Directories of Officials published by the State Department and the Central Intelligence Agency.

10. For an excellent discussion of the phases of political development in the East European socialist states, see Kenneth Jowitt, "Inclusion and Mobilization in European Leninist Regimes," World Politics, XVII (1975). For a more general discussion of system integration, see the essays in Leonard Binder, et al., Crises and Sequences in Political Development. Princeton, New Jersey: Princeton University Press, 1971.

11. R.V. Burks, "Technology and Political Change in Eastern Europe," and Zvi Gitelman, "Power and Authority in Eastern Europe," both in Chalmers Johnson, ed., Change in Communist Systems. Stanford: Stanford University Press, 1970; Richard Lowenthal, "On 'Established' Communist Party Regimes," Studies in Comparative Communism, VII (1974).

12. Alfred Meyer, "Authority in Communist Political Systems," in Lewis J. Edinger, ed., Leadership in Industrialized Societies. New York: John Wiley, 1967.

13. For this view, see Alfred Meyer, "Authority," p. 103; Jerry F. Hough, "The Soviet System: Petrification or Pluralism?," Problems of Communism, XXI (1972), pp. 32-35; Milton Lodge, "Soviet Elite Participatory Attitudes in the Post-Stalin Period," American Political Science Review, LXII (1968), p. 839; Ludz, The Changing Elite, pp. 4-6;

Gitelman, "Power and Authority," p. 261.

14. Lowenthal, "On 'Established' Regimes;" and Thomas A. Baylis, "Participation Without Conflict: Socialist Democracy in the German Democratic Republic," East Central Europe, III (1976).

15. For a discussion of this point, see Samuel P. Huntington, "Social and Institutional Dynamics of One-Party Systems," in Samuel P. Huntington and Clement H. Moore, eds., Authoritarian Politics in Modern Society. New York: Basic Books, 1970; Lowenthal, "On 'Established' Regimes;" Ludz, The Changing Elite, pp. 1-24, and Welsh, "Elites and Leadership," pp. 165-166.

16. Zbigniew Brzezinski, "The Soviet Political System: Transformation or Degeneration?," Problems of Communism, XV (1966); and Zvi Gitelman, "Beyond Leninism: Political Development in Eastern Europe," Newsletter on Comparative Study of Communism, V (1972).

17. Jowitt, "Inclusion and Mobilization;" and William E. Odom, "A Dissenting View on the Group Approach to Soviet Politics," World Politics, XXVIII (1976), pp. 452-467.

18. Odom, "A Dissenting View," pp. 546-547.

19. Jowitt, "Inclusion and Mobilization," p. 71.

20. Frederic J. Fleron, Cooptation as a Mechanism of Adaptation to Changes" Polity, II (1969), pp. 176-201.

21. Fredric J. Fleron, "Representation of Career Types in the Soviet Political Leadership," in R. Barry Farrell, ed., Political Leadership in Eastern Europe and the Soviet Union. Chicago: Aldine, 1970.

22. Bielasiak, "Elite Differentiation."

23. Alex Pravda, "Gierek's Poland: Five Years On," The World Today, XXXII (1976) p. 275; and Robert W. Dean, "Gierek's Three Years: Retrenchment and Reform," Survey, XX (1974), p. 61.

24. Jowitt, "Inclusion and Mobilization," pp. 72-73.

25. For a discussion in regard to the Soviet Union, see Odom, "A Dissenting View."

26. See the essays in Carl Beck, et al., Comparative Communist Political Leadership. New York: David McKay, 1973.

27. Jowitt, "Inclusion and Mobilization," p. 69.

28. This point is discussed more thoroughly in the next section of the paper.

29. Myron Rush, How Communist States Change Their Rulers. Ithaca: Cornell University Press, 1974, pp. 285-293.

30. Jowitt, "Inclusion and Mobilization."

31. The division of the state bureaucracy into economic and noneconomic functional components follows the practice established by Fleron, and is here intended to facilitate the analysis of how the problems of industrialization, and economic development in general, affect elite recruitment into the economic and noneconomic sectors of society.

32. Unfortunately, since the Archive on Political Elites at the University of Pittsburgh is no longer updating its file, information on the career patterns of more recent recruits into the Polish Central Committee is not available. Therefore the ratio of recruited to coopted officials among the political elite in Poland for the 1975 Central Committee cannot be calculated.

33. For a discussion of these events, see Adam Bromke, "Poland Under Gierek: A New Political Style," Problems of Communism, XXII (1972); Dean, "Gierek's Three Years;" and A. Ross Johnson, "Polish Perspectives, Past and Present," Problems of Communism, XX (1971).

34. For a discussion of the developments surrounding Gomulka's fall, see A. Ross Johnson, "Poland: End of an Era?," Problems of Communism, XIX (1970).

35. See Adam Bromke, "A New Juncture in Poland," Problems of Communism, XXV, no. 5 (1976), pp. 1-17; Peter Osnos, "The Polish Road to Communism," Foreign Affairs, LCI (1977); and Pravda, "Gierek's Poland."

36. For a detailed discussion of the distinctions between consolidation and inclusion politics, see Jowitt, "Inclusion and Mobilization," pp. 77-81.

37. Ibid.

38. See the essays in Gordon H. Skilling and Franklyn Griffiths, eds., Interest Groups in Soviet Politics. Princeton: Princeton University Press, 1971, and Gitelman, "Power and Authority."

39. Jowitt, "Inclusion and Mobilization," p. 70.

40. Wladyslaw Gomulka, "Report on the Activities of the Central Committee," III Zjazd Polskiej Zjednoczonej Partii Robotniczej. Warsaw: Ksiazka i Wiedza, 1959, p. 60.

41. For a description of the Gomulka period, see M.K. Dziewanowski, The Communist Party of Poland. Cambridge: Harvard University Press, 1976, chapter 16, and the articles by Johnson, "Poland: End of an Era?"

42. For a similar analysis of political developments in Poland, see Jan de Weydenthal, "Party Development in Contemporary Poland," East European Quarterly, XI (1977), pp. 354-359.

43. Michael Gamarnikow, "Poland: On Again-Off Again," in L.A.D. Dellin and Hermann Gross, eds., Reforms in the Soviet and East European Economies. Lexington, Massachusetts: Lexington Books, 1972, pp. 102-109.

44. See the report issued by the new Gierek leadership and circulated in a limited edition of Nowe Drogi (undated), translated in Radio Free Europe Polish Press Survey 2313 (July 14, 1971).

45. See Adam Bromke, "Poland Under Gierek: A New Political Style," and Michael Gamarnikow, "A New Economic Approach," in Problems in Communism, XXI (1972).

46. Jowitt, "Inclusion and Mobilization," pp. 75-89.

47. *Rocznik Politiczny i Gospodarczy* 1971, p. 115, cited in David S. Mason, *Elite Change and Policy in Communist Poland* (Ph.D. Dissertation, Indiana University, 1977).

48. For a discussion of consensual legitimacy, see Daniel N. Nelson, "Political Convergence: An Empirical Assessment," *World Politics*, XXX (1978), pp. 415-416.

49. Radio Free Europe, *Polish Situation Report/23*, July 13, 1976, p. 9.

50. See the reports by Flora Lewis in the *New York Times*, September 22, 1976, and Radio Free Europe, *Polish Situation Report/23*, July 13, 1976, and *Polish Situation Report/35*, October 15, 1976.

51. Radio Warsaw, July 11, 1976, cited in Radio Free Europe, *Polish Situation Report/23*.

Part 3

Group Activity and Attitudes: Their Impact on Policy

5
Polish Student Attitudes and Ideological Policy

Maurice D. Simon

According to the prominent Polish political sociologist Jerzy Wiatr, ideology in socialist societies seeks to fulfill three major objectives termed the motivational, legitimation, and programmatic functions.[1] The motivational objective refers to the attempt to create psychic dispositions among the members of society, especially the politically active, which will contribute to the building of a socialist society. The essence of the legitimation objective is the development and strengthening of citizens' convictions that the existing system is rooted in law and merits support. The programmatic objective is manifested in efforts to describe the planned and desired future transformations of the society. Viewed in this manner, we can state that ideology, when given official interpretation and expression by the leadership of the Polish United Workers' Party (hereafter PUWP), is a set of broad policy orientations aiming at the stabilization and strengthening of the existing socialist system, while also seeking to be an important force in guiding societal development and change.

*Research for this chapter was supported by grants from the International Research and Exchanges Board, the Joint Committee on Eastern Europe of the American Council of Learned Societies and Social Science Research Council, the National Academy of Sciences, and the Summer Excellence Fund of the University of North Carolina at Greensboro, whose support is hereby gratefully acknowledged. The guidance of a number of Polish sociologists, who are not responsible for my interpretations and speculation, is also gratefully acknowledged.

In accordance with the above rationale, we find that ideological policy makers in contemporary Poland demonstrate an acute sensitivity toward the values, beliefs, and attitudes of students and recent graduates of post-secondary educational institutions.[2] Youths in this category have been typically viewed as the incipient or emerging socialist intelligentsia, which will eventually play a crucial role in promoting economic, scientific, technical, and administrative advances essential for the construction of developed socialism. As the human products of the extensive ideological and educational efforts of People's Poland, unmarred by direct experience with preceding political regimes, their civic consciousness has been examined in studies as a salient indicator of the degree of success attained in molding the socialist personality type deemed as appropriate for the establishment of a viable and coherent socialist political culture. As one Polish sociologist has asserted, one key criterion by which socialist development can be judged is "the degree of entrenchment of socialist ideology in the consciousness of members of the society and the methods of linking up the system of values and culture with politics and human personality."[3] Ideological policy makers, then, may measure and evaluate the activist, supportive, and transformationist dispositions and potential of socialist man by analyzing the orientations of the new student generation.

In a more specific historical and political sense, ideological policy makers have been sensitive to the capacity for political disruptions displayed by students.[4] Ghita Ionescu and Isabel de Madariaga have pointed out that, because it is difficult to aggregate or channel the dissent or opposition of various groups in authoritarian political systems, "students' movements acquire a supplementary and much more important dimension" than in pluralistic polities:

> They emerge as the group which, because it is young and bears less responsibility, can take the risk of leading public opinion against existing policies...The political debate which the government has tried to suppress in public reopens in the sanctuaries of learning.[5]

In People's Poland, academic and student dissent played an integral role in the liberalization process of 1956. The outcome of the widespread

Polish student demonstrations and protests of 1968 was a repressive political backlash by authorities, but echoes of the student's programs were detectable in the demands of striking workers in 1970 and 1976.[6] Student unrest was openly manifested in 1977 as an element of the Polish human rights movement (which itself was led by some of the academic dissenters of 1968).[7] Given these events, it must be assumed that ideological policy makers seek to keep aware of student opinions in order to detect and block potential sources of instability within the political system.

Although it must be emphasized that students have had no direct role in policy making in People's Poland, the evidence cited above does indicate that they have had an intermittent and sometimes important role in affecting the political environment within which policy has been made. The quiescence of students has usually given the PUWP leadership a sense of assurance and has lent credibility to their ideological claims that People's Poland is constantly gaining in legitimacy. On the other hand, student ferment has been viewed as symptomatic of deeper problems within the policy and has thus coincided with a defensiveness on the part of the leadership marked by a reliance on threatening ideological postures.[8] For some leaders, even quiescence and a compliant "legal consciousness" may be seen as evidence of student passivity and indifference, which can be viewed as an ideological challenge to the desired model of an involved, politically conscious, and activist youthful intelligentsia.[9] Thus, the ideological policy stance adopted by the PUWP toward students has served as a barometer of the leadership's sense of confidence or vulnerability. Ideological policy itself could be viewed as a reflection of empirical and intuitive assessments of student consciousness and behavior.

With these themes in mind, in the pages that follow we will briefly examine and interpret a selection of recent and relevant available survey research data concerning students' values, aspirations, and attitudes.[10] In the first section, we will consider general value orientations, life aspirations, and attitudes toward labor related to the emergence of the ideal socialist personality type. In the second section, we will deal with political attitudes and opinions which are connected to youthful citizen involvement with the socialist polity. In a concluding section, we shall briefly explore the extent to which students' views represent the success or failure of ideological policy, while also noting policy developments affecting students as a group.

VALUE ORIENTATIONS, ASPIRATIONS, AND ATTITUDES TOWARD LABOR

Communist political systems aspire to create "the new socialist man"--a term which denotes a citizen who is superior in his character to "bourgeois capitalist man." Alex Inkeles has described the personal qualities which constitute the syndrome "socialist man" in Soviet treatments of the subject, attributes which are also given primary attention by Polish ideological and pedagogical authorities.[11] For our purposes, what is essential in Inkeles' discussion is the emphasis placed on the formation of both modern and collectivistic values, aspirations, and attitudes. In terms of modernity, Inkeles states that "the modern industrial order requires a man who takes initiative--is autonomous, self-starting, and self-directing." The socialist modern order places emphasis on these qualities, but also demands a collectivistic outlook: "Yet it also requires him to relate to, and to adjust his activities to, the complex patterns of interdependence which modern large-scale organization fosters and rests upon."[12]

In a provocative discussion of the character traits of the ideal capitalist and socialist man, Robert Lane makes a similar point. Socialist man, like capitalist man, ideally has ambitious work motivations, internalized preferences for innovation, and respect for proper authority and control;[13] but in addition he should hold pro-social or altruistic attitudes which demand in some cases "effort without commensurate rewards" and which require that "collective advantage serve as a motivating consideration for the individual in the same way that self-interest narrowly defined motivates him in the market society."[14] Logically there can be tension between these modern and socialist attributes. As Inkeles puts it, "the balance between these elements can at best be a delicate one, and at many points one must expect an outright clash of principles and requirements." This clash might occur when "collective goals...cannot easily be rendered compatible with high degrees of individual initiative."[15]

Polish social scientists have also stressed that the socialist personality and educational ideals include modern and collectivistic character traits. As Jan Szczepanski points out, ideally the supreme values are "self-sacrifice for a common cause, altruism, self-restraint, and discipline" in order to "impose a culture of discipline, organization, and work." The objective to be pursued is "the 'socialized' personality, the hard-working man dedicated to altruistic goals, seeking the fulfillment of his personal goals in the common welfare and in the happiness of others."[16] In the same vein, Jan Jerschina has analyzed the social personality of students, drawing a sharp distinction between two basic personality types. The "desired" personality type from the Marxist perspective is "socio-centric" or oriented toward the collective. A socio-centric individual willingly strives to create and promote new values, specifically seeking to: 1) further scientific knowledge; 2) contribute to social and cultural advancement; and 3) hold an activist perspective, drawing upon positive motives to advance the public good.[17] Thus, the individual with a developed or well-adjusted personality in ideal terms is able to shape his personal aspirations with a sophisticated consciousness of the links between his own goals and activities and the promotion of collective progress.

The undesirable contrasting personality type is described in terms suggesting that such an individual is highly selfish, privatistic, and security oriented. Szczepanski emphasizes that the socialist system rejects "egoism and profit-seeking."[18] Jerschina contrasts the socio-centric student with the "ego-centric" youth, the latter placing a higher value on his own immediate and long-term interests than those of society as a whole. The ego-centric pattern is marked by an aversion to active engagement in work or civic participation unless such activities serve as a means for self-promotion. Ego-centrics are rather materialistic and may tend toward conspicuous consumption, and tend to seek personal power, status, and recognition from society-at-large as a means of personal gratification.[19]

To what extent do students conform to the socio-centric or collectivistic ideal personality type promoted by ideological policy makers? While space limitations prevent a full consideration of this question, examination of responses to several recent survey items permits some tentative conclusions. In 1974 a sample of 827 students from five Krakow higher educational institutions was asked:

"What is it worthwhile striving for in life?" The students were offered alternatives among the following paired combinations of aspirations: 1) directing groups of people, implying holding a responsible managerial position in a hierarchy of authority; 2) productivity, understood as professional activeness bringing measurable results, as well as bringing personal satisfaction derived from these efforts; 3) participation in the cultural sphere of society, which implies gaining intellectual and physical stimulation from leisure-time opportunities; 4) a stable personal life stemming from rewarding interaction with one's family and close friends; and 5) material consumption or a focus on a high standard of living.[20] From the perspective of the ideal socio-centric or collectivistic personality model, we would rate aspirations 1) and 2) as most desired, for they ostensibly contribute to the general welfare as well as provide psychic gratifications for individuals. Aspirations 3) and 4) would constitute lower priority goals of a positive nature (the family unit and cultural life are important elements in the social order). Aspiration 5) would be the least preferred, for overemphasis on this goal is indicative of an egocentric disposition.

As we will see in Table 5.1,[21] students' aspirations are centered on their personal lives, demonstrating what might be considered a rather parochial preoccupation with their families and friends. When all choices are summed, the students chose an emphasis on their personal lives over all of the other aspirations by a margin of 70 percent to 30 percent. This desire for emotional affiliation strongly outweighs the aspirations for material consumption (74.9 percent to 27.3 percent), for a directing position (74.5 percent to 25.5 percent), and cultural participation (72.7 percent to 27.3 percent). There is a more even distribution of selection when productivity is considered (57.9 percent to 42.1 percent), perhaps indicating that finding an interesting job is of prime importance for many students.[22]

The marked rejection of obtaining a directing or managerial position (with concomitant organizational responsibilities) is clearly at variance with the model of the socio-centric personality. When this aspiration is matched with all the other goals, holding a director's post is selected in only 27.6 percent of the choices. Less than 26 percent of the students selected this aspiration as opposed to

TABLE 5.1
Choices of Life Aspirations*
(In Percentages)

	Personal Life	Cultural Participation	Productivity	Material Consumption	Directing Position
Personal Life		27.3	42.1	25.1	25.5
Cultural Participation	72.7		59.4	36.9	15.3
Productivity	57.9	40.6		44.2	49.1
Material Consumption	74.9	63.1	55.8		19.9
Directing Position	74.5	84.7	50.9	80.1	
Total Choices:** (all aspirations)	70.0	53.4	52.1	46.5	27.6

* Each percentage indicates the proportion of those who select the aspiration at the top of the column in preference to those listed in the row.

** Percentages reflect the ratio of the sum of all choices for the aspiration in the column to the selection of all the other aspirations in the row.

cultural participation, material consumption, and personal life goals. There is almost an even distribution of choices when this aspiration is paired with productivity (49.1 percent to 50.9 percent). One possible interpretation of the low popularity of this aspiration is that authority and power (as defined by organizational position) are weakly respected in Poland.[23]

There is a mixed pattern of selections with respect to cultural participation. In an overall sense, this aspiration is only slightly preferred to the sum of the choices for all the other alternatives combined (53.4 percent to 46.6 percent). Yet, the future intelligentsia overwhelmingly chooses this goal over a directing position (84.7 percent to 15.3 percent) and, more positively in an ideological sense, over material consumption (63.1 percent to 36.9 percent). A full intellectual life is slightly less preferred than productivity (40.6 percent to 59.4 percent), but is little desired when matched with aspirations for a fulfilling personal life (27.3 percent to 72.7 percent).

The mixed pattern of selection applies to aspirations regarding productivity, perhaps a disappointing finding in terms of the socio-centric ideal which places an emphasis on labor as a means of contributing to the collective. When all selections are considered, productivity outweighs the total choices for all the other aspirations by only a slight 52.1 percent to 47.9 percent margin. It is only slightly preferred to material consumption (55.8 percent to 44.2 percent), another result which might be judged as negative in terms of the socialist personality ideal.[24] Disavowal of material consumption goals as a high priority should be quite strong according to the socialist personality ideal. Yet this aspiration also draws a mixed response from the students. Material consumption aspirations are far preferred to holding a directing position (80.1 percent to 19.9 percent)--a result that contradicts ideal objectives. On the other hand, students are less consumption oriented than culturally oriented (36.9 percent to 63.1 percent) and far less materialistic than they are family-centered (25.1 percent to 74.9 percent), which can be considered positive findings. However, material consumption nearly matches aspirations for productivity (44.2 percent to 55.8 percent)--not a very positive result from an ideological perspective.

Evidence from other surveys suggest similar patterns of life aspirations or, at least, patterns congruent with the Krakow study. For example, Stefan Nowak has developed a list of life aspirations contrasting a stabilized/instrumental set of goals with a more dynamic/ambitious set of objectives in his studies of youth attitudes and intergenerational continuity and change.[25] Those who have stabilized/instrumental aspirations seek an orderly existence based on an emotionally supportive family, friends who offer respect, a fulfilling job, and a moderate sense of social usefulness. These goals could be interpreted as indicative of security and conformist (even traditional) orientations. Those with more dynamic/ambitious life aspirations seek high professional achievements, the exercise of significant responsibilities, a sense of strong ideological rectitude, and civic activism--a more socio-centric, modernizing perspective. In a more negative sense, they may simply be dynamic and ambitious in the sense of pursuing fame, fortune, and adventure.

Table 5.2 compares students' aspirations from a random sample of 732 students attending the ten major Warsaw higher educational institutions in 1958 and 2,222 students constituting a national representative sample of first and second-year students in higher education in 1972.[26] It is striking how similar are the expressed life goals of students separated by fourteen years. In both studies, the stabilized/instrumental goals (SI) are generally more popular. More than half of the students express the desire to achieve a good professional position and a relatively quiet and comfortable life, while more than 40 percent hope to earn others' respect through their character and actions. Over one-third of the students give evidence of seeking socially useful work, indicating a moderate socio-centric orientation. The desire for fulfilling emotional and affiliative needs is strong in both years (slightly over 40 percent in 1958 and almost 30 percent in 1972). Self-development, in a moral or ethical sense, held little attractiveness in 1958, but was designated as a key life goal by more than 20 percent of the students in 1972.

Turning to the dynamic/achievement (DA) set of goals, we find that among these aims only the objective of contributing new values to humanity receives close to 30 percent of the choices in both years. Less than 13 percent of the students in 1958

TABLE 5.2
Life Aspirations of Polish Students*
(In Percentages)

	Warsaw Students 1958	National Students 1972
1. The achievement of a good professional position, together with a relatively quiet and comfortable life. (SI)	61.2	53.3
2. The winning of other people's respect through your character and actions. (SI)	48.8	42.0
3. Living your life among friends whom you like and who like you. (SI)	41.9	29.7
4. Being able to feel that your activities, even though on a modest scale, are socially useful. (SI)	36.7	33.3
5. The contribution of new values to the heritage of human culture by intellectual, scientific, or artistic achievements. (DA)	29.4	31.4
6. Leading a colorful, eventful life, providing a fullnes of impressions, even at the expense of some risks. (DA)	20.8	19.9
7. The fulfillment of certain valuable ideological and social aims, in accordance with your conviction of their correctness. (DA)	13.1	19.6
8. The attainment of high professional standing and the opportunity to make large-scale decisions. (DA)	12.0	14.3
9. The attainment of notable success, fame, and universal recognition, due to your professional, scientific, or intellectual achievements. (DA)	10.2	9.3

TABLE 5.2 (cont.)
Life Aspirations of Polish Students*
(In Percentages)

	Warsaw Students 1958	National Students 1972
10. Molding your personality to fit some moral ideal that seems important to you personally. (SI)	6.6	21.6
11. Rising to a high position in the field of politics and influencing the course of social and political events. (DA)	3.1	6.5
12. Achieving high earnings. (DA)	3.0	not included

* Percentages represent the proportion of all students selecting each goal with multiple choices permitted.

SI = Stabilized/Instrumental item

DA = Dynamic/Achievement item

and less than 20 percent in 1972 indicated an attachment to or strong conviction for valued ideological and social aims.[27] Moreover, in both years less than 15 percent seemed motivated to advance to highly responsible professional positions. In an ideological sense, the most disappointing finding is the fact that the least attractive life goal in both years was the achievement of a high-ranking political position where one could influence public policies (about 3 percent in 1958 and less than 7 percent in 1972). In both years, about 20 percent of the students were drawn to a risk-filled, adventurous life-style, but only about 10 percent seemed desirous of achieving fame and recognition through their career accomplishments.[28]

In evaluating these life aspirations, it is worthwhile to consider their possible relationship to students' occupational goals. Labor is considered a key Marxist social value and the efforts of the emerging intelligentsia will be vital to Poland's development. As one Polish sociologist states:

> Work is one of the highest values connected with the socialist system. The socialist ideology stresses its great importance both for the society as a whole and for every individual....it is postulated in the socialist society that every man should regard work as something valuable, not only as life necessity or way of earning his living but also as a way of developing one's gifts and skills, as a means of creative expression and of attaining social goals.[29]

Do students seek occupational positions compatible with the stabilized/instrumental (less sociocentric) aspiration patterns or with the dynamic/achievement (more collectivist) perspective? The 1974 Krakow student study provides some suggestive findings. Students were given a list of twenty-two atttibutes of jobs and were asked to designate four which they would find particularly desirable and four that they would particularly like to avoid.[30] The most popular selections conformed to the stabilized/instrumental pattern: interesting work (62.3 percent); permits the realization of personal interests (45.8 percent); earnings providing a high standard of living (43.1 percent); and brings respect in one's surroundings (36.9 percent). From an ideological perspective, the most frequently rejected values suggest some positive internalization of regime norms, for there is an aversion to strictly egocentric or selfish motivations: fame (56.3 percent); allows you to choose your own post (35.4 percent); allows you to transfer to other locales where there are better opportunities to meet your cultural needs (33.0 percent), and does not require physical exertion (29.0 percent). In a similar vein, when the Krakow students were asked to evaluate fourteen attributes of a man's social effectiveness,[31] the lowest evaluations were given to: aspiring to realize one's ideals through membership and activity in political organizations (49.2 percent); spending free time in socially useful activities (43.3 percent); striving for the good name and honor of your workplace (25.0 percent); and offering constructive criticism in order to improve the effectiveness of the workplace (22.1 percent), all of which can be considered the more dynamic, change-oriented traits. The most valued attributes cited are in accord with the stabilized/instrumental orientation, with the positive characteristics designated as: being reliable and having integrity (46.5 percent); effective application of your own intellectual skills in the workplace (30.5 percent); possessing organizational skills useful in the workplace (23.6 percent); and possessing general knowledge (23.2 percent).

Although it could be misleading to overgeneralize on the basis of these particular survey responses, this examination of students' aspirations does indicate that the ideologically-preferred personality patterns have not yet emerged. The socio-centric personality type--described as dynamic, capable of transforming his surroundings, possessing a feeling of personal responsibility for the general social welfare, disciplined and conscientious in his work, and ideologically and politically conscious--is not represented by the majority of student responses in these studies. Instead, on the basis of this evidence, it might be more accurate to express tentative agreement with the author of one of the above studies who characterized the typical student as "...an individual with a lack of dynamism and distaste for changing the structures into which he enters. Such an individual fulfills his duties in a reliable way but within the framework of a concrete assignment of tasks, having insufficient personal activeness and an insufficient amount of social mindedness.[32] Perhaps, as Joseph Fiszman has suggested, the moderate aspirations of Polish youth mean that expectations have been adjusted downward in order to fit existing opportunities.[33] Or perhaps moderate expectancy is consciously promoted by the regime.[34] In any case, students would appear to reject both ideological and idealistic fervor and materialism (including the pursuit of status and power). One Polish journalist's composite portrait of Polish youth seems accurate:

> Positions of authority in the community lie completely outside their aspirations, nor are they attracted by a life full of adventures, travel, and risk, preferring a stabilized existence, "filled with emotional satisfaction" in small informal groups of friends and taking little or no interest at all in the broader concerns of society.[35]

According to this same author, Polish youths value "...Honesty, not diligence, consideration, not go-getting, stability, not risk, friendship in small groups, fulfillment of simple needs, not pleasure, a steady job corresponding to interests and predilections, not power and ambition..."[36] In other words, students apparently possess limited idealism, lack an innovative approach to life, are largely conformist, and seek relative comfort and security--attributes which pose few threats to regime stability, but which do not indicate realization of ideological and pedagogical aims.

POLITICAL ATTITUDES AND OPINIONS

Along with ideological policies promoting the socio-centric or dynamic/achievement patterns of aspirations and goals, there has been a concerted effort to stimulate political involvement and consciousness among the emerging socialist intelligentsia. In the past, Poland's ideological authorities have decried any perceived tendencies toward the formation of a politically unaware or uninvolved student subculture.[37] Since the mid-1960s, the political content of higher education has been expanded, although the curriculum has lost some of its agitation-propaganda characteristics and involves the formal study of political science, political economy, and Marxism-Leninism.[38] Yet the attitudes expressed by Marian Zychowski, one of the key figures in the development of Polish political science in the mid-1960s, remain representative of official ideological policy. Lamenting the fact that students at that time did not appear to have "any particular interest in politics" and were unable to think in broad political categories, Zychowski stated:

> The formation of the new intelligentsia is hard to imagine without equipping them with a possible broad knowledge of the contemporary world, for there is no question but that the young Polish intelligentsia will continue to exert considerable influence upon all spheres of life, including the spiritual development of our society...It is taking over managerial posts and becomes responsible not only for the implementation of professional duties but also for social and moral-political values of our community. It is a well-known fact that these values are not indifferent to people's power. We can say from the very outset that the shaping of socialist consciousness, the ideological attitude of the young generation, must remain the responsibility not only of the political and youth organizations, but also of the whole scientific, didactic staff implementing the university curricula.[39]

At present, Polish ideological authorities still contend that students should be concerned with the key (party-defined) contemporary issues and should be able to analyze them in terms of the approved socialist conceptual categories.[40]

One of the indicators of political involvement and consciousness may be measured by the frequency of student contact with the mass media. As Inkeles has stated, according to socialist ideological doctrine, "The modern man strives energetically to keep up with the news, and within this framework prefers news of national and international import to items dealing with sport, religion, or purely local affairs."[41] Evidence from surveys indicates that Polish students do seem to be anxious to acquire information about current events. In one survey, 941 students at Krakow higher educational institutions were asked about their frequency of contact with the mass media.[42] "Systematic" contact with the media was a response selected by 29.0 percent of the students with respect to the press, 10.0 percent with respect to radio, and 5.5 percent with respect to television. "Very frequent" contact was cited by 44.5 percent of the students for the press, 40.5 percent for television, and 39.6 percent for radio. "Occasional" contact for television was 49.4 percent, for radio 45.0 percent and 23.5 percent for the press. The mass media, especially the press, are highly developed in Poland and it appears that there is a student audience of note, with less than 3.5 percent of the students "never" having interaction.[43] Students as a group seem to overwhelmingly support the notion of wide-scale dissemination of domestic information. A national sample of students was asked whether the full and straight-forward reporting of domestic events would be in accord with national interests and answered 72.2 percent in the affirmative, with 12.4 percent responding negatively and 15.4 percent offering no opinion.[44]

What, specifically, captures the interest of the students? One study of the press indicates that students have a wide range of interests. Asked to cite the "most interesting" problems discussed in the press, cultural affairs proved to be more important than political life (28.2 percent cites the former category, 54.1 percent the latter). The ranking of other items was as follows: popular-scientific news (50.5 percent), travel and life-style items (40.2 percent), sports (33.9 percent), local information (30.8 percent) and socio-economic affairs (18.9 percent). The rather broad interest in a range of problems could reflect the students' current status as not yet employed intellectuals who are able to participate in political life at the national and local level only vicariously. When asked to ennumerate the domestic problems which interested them the most, the national sample of students demonstrated a keen sensitivity to the range of issues directly affecting them in the seventies: housing (50.2 percent), the methods of administering the economy (47.6 percent), the organization of the system of public information (36.9 percent), the development of foreign trade (35.4 percent), problems in the development of private automobile transportation (29.2 percent), the functioning and model of student organizations (25.5 percent), the role of the PUWP in the political life of the country (24.3 percent), agricultural policy and the development of agriculture (19.5 percent), and the tasks of labor unions and their functioning (13.4 percent).[45] Given the stabilized/instrumental goals expressed by students in other surveys, this ranking of interests seems logical and indicative of considerable political awareness. Although ideological authorities could conceivably be disappointed in the relative disinterest in the role of the PUWP, that response could also be interpreted as a sign of acceptance of the existing institutional realities in Poland.

From an ideological standpoint, however, there may be cause for concern in how the students evaluate the mass media. In the Krakow study, the students indicated that they are discerning and critical when they evaluate the mass media. Those who "frequently agree" with the press (46.1 percent) were nearly matched (44.6 percent) by those who only "occasionally agree" with its reports. A considerable portion of the students only occasionally agreed with television and radio (33.2 percent in the former case and 34.3 percent in the latter), thus suggesting discontent with what may be perceived as controlled flows of information. However, those "never" agreeing with the media constituted a tiny minority of the sample.[46] The authors of the Krakow study suggest that the high frequency of negative evaluations shows a lack of confidence in the information transmitted by the mass media, but attribute this to the mistakes of the Gomulka leadership[47]--a Polish credibility gap to be closed under Gierek. We have no later data regarding student opinion on this matter, but Jane Curry's study of the press in this volume would indicate that the press remains severely restricted under the Gierek leadership team.

Communist political systems have an ideological commitment to fostering civic participation and activism. As George Kolankiewicz and Ray Taras point out, socialist man ideally deviates from self-interested bourgeois man in possessing a moral code which subordinates private to public interests: "In this respect participation in collective work can make the new man develop a proper moral relationship to other people. He is to be active, determining his own fate in life rather than having it determined for him as under capitalism."[48] Inkeles stresses the same point, observing that ideally socialist man "shows a strong interest in and takes an active part in civic and community affairs and in local politics."[49] The Polish sociologists Aleksandra Jasinska and Renata Siemienska emphasize that socialist development depends in part on "activeness, commitment to voluntary social activity, participation in the control of collective activity which is to bring about conscious and planned shaping of social relationships."[50] Valuing social activeness, Jasinska and Siemienskaclaim that socialist states "develop various institutional forms to stimulate and involve masses of people in the process of co-creation and participation in the life of society as a whole."[51] The ideal model therefore closely corresponds to the concept of the active-participant citizen developed by Almond and Verba.[52]

Do students behave in ways that are consistent with these policy objectives? Socio-political activism has been examined in a wave of studies carried out between 1968 and 1972 in Warsaw and other academic centers. In the student context, activism has been measured by expressed desires for participation in the work of politically oriented youth organizations and in terms of participation in less overtly political organizations (termed "social organizations"), such as student unions, scouting associations, discussion clubs, and research circles.

Wieslaw Wisniewski of Warsaw University categorizes student participation in terms of those active in primarily political organizations, those participating in social organizations, passive or nominal members of political organizations, passive or nominal members of social organizations, and nonmembers of all organizations.[53] In his studies, he has determined that the declared need for social (or civic) work is approximated by the following percentages: 40 percent of students feel the need for such work, 25 percent state that on the whole they do not feel such a need, 6 to 10 percent definitely do not feel such a need, and 25 percent state that they do not know whether they have such a need (perhaps indicating either ambivalence, indifference, or reluctance to express their feelings). While the 40 percent figure may seem reasonably high, Wisniewski points out that active participation by those who express a positive need has been rather limited. For example, in the academic year 1971-1972 among the 488 first-year students at Warsaw University who declared a need for social (hereafter civic) work, 92 percent were not active participants in any organization two weeks after the start of the terms; this decreased to only 74 percent at the end of the initial year of study.[54] Moreover, during the 1971-1972 academic year only 4 percent of the first-year students were active members of political organizations at the beginning of the year, and this figure increased to only 6 percent by the end of the year.[55]

Only fragmentary published evidence indicates the possible reasons why there is what Wisniewski terms "unharnessed potential" for participation among students.[56] The available data suggest institutional or structural weaknesses. For example, in 1972 among the first-year political activists, 55 percent admitted to encountering disturbing features in their civic work, such as bad interpersonal relations between members, organizational weaknesses, and group tension in the academic setting.[57] Such problems led 13 percent of the second and fourth-year political activists and 27 percent of the social activists to evaluate the work of the Union of Socialist Youth as "insufficient" in 1972, while inactive members of political organizations were even more critical of this organization (41 percent; 23 percent of both the inactive social members and the nonmembers saw the official socialist youth organization in this negative light.[58]

One study which examines student motivations with respect to civic or social participation offers some hints as to why there is a gap between the declared need for participation and the extent of active participation. In a study of 931 second through sixth-year students at the Warsaw Polytechnic,[59] it was found that while 92.4 percent of the respondents were formally members of political and social organizations, only 39.5 percent in fact took part in the different activities of their organizations. The nonactivists (60.3 percent of the respondents) attributed their inactivity mainly to their own lack of desire for civic work, based on an assessment that such action proves to be ineffective (37.5 percent), or that they prefer giving priority to their personal lives (27.8 percent), or that they are unable to see ideals for which it is worth struggling (21.4 percent). Such responses indicate little absorption of the socio-centric personality ideal--a finding congruent with evidence presented earlier in this chapter.

Total responses to a question asking why people spend their time and work in civic activities provide additional indications that activism and activists are evaluated rather negatively.[60] Egoistic motivations for participation (such as deriving satisfaction from leading others, attaining career opportunities, deriving material benefits) were cited by 40.1 percent of the sample. Motivations based upon the desire for prestige and fulfillment of personal ambitions (enjoying overcoming difficulties, obtaining a sense of personal worth, gaining the respect of others) ranked second (28.9 percent). Only 15.8 percent of the students claimed to participate out of idealistic concerns (such as the desire to help others, demonstrating their convictions, valuing this type of activity in itself); 9.9 percent of the students cited as their motivation the need for affiliation (enjoyment of activity in groups of colleagues), while 5.3 percent cited a variety of other reasons.[61]

The activists apparently see themselves in a more positive light, citing the bases for their participation in the following terms: 35.3 percent in terms of the need for affiliation, 28.7 percent idealistic reasons, 10.6 percent past positive experiences in organizations, 5.7 percent ambitiousness and the desire for prestige, and 19.0 percent other assorted reasons.[62] Yet, when their evaluations of other activists' reasons for participation are presented, they do not differ dramatically from the response patterns of the entire sample (35.8 percent egoistic motivations, 32.5 percent ambitiousness and prestige, 16.5 percent idealism, and 9.9 percent affiliation).[63] On the whole, the Warsaw Politechnic study implies that participation is not viewed by students in the idealistic terms promoted by the authorities. Participation, it seems, is valued only in general political terms, but there are apparent psychological and institutional barriers which effectively reduce activism. The attractiveness of participation is evidently limited to only a minority of students, who seem to be viewed rather suspiciously by their peers. Moreover, the activists also tend to identify their coparticipants as driven by the pursuit of material and status benefits. In sum, participation as a means of contributing to the collective and as a way of developing one's character does not seem to be internalized by students.

The ultimate goal of ideological and educational policy is to create support for and commitment to the political system and its institutions. With Poland's history of political turmoil and public resistance to authority in mind, the Polish socialist regime has been striving to attain legitimacy. The Gierek leadership was established as the result of a general crisis of confidence in the political system, which has led to a preoccupation with gaining citizen support. As the respected Polish journalist Mieczyslaw Rakowski states:

> In talking of people's attitudes to work, to their surroundings, to the programmes put forward by the party and the government, we constantly return to one supremely important subject--the state. Does today's Pole respect it, does he identify with it, does he act with the state's interests in mind?[64]

In view of such observations, we shall briefly examine available data bearing on the general evaluation of the political system by students.

Surveys of student attitudes conducted in 1958 and 1961 indicated that there was considerable attachment to socialism in its broadest programmatic form. Moreover, there was considerable support for existing socio-economic institutions but a desire for more flexibility in institutional practice.[65] A 1974 survey of first and fourth-year students at five Krakow institutions of higher education provides some data and insights into more recent attitudes.[66] As in the earlier studies, the vision of the development of a truly socialist Poland is supported by students. Asked whether the future development of Poland is dependent upon the deepening of the socialist transformations of the country, 61.7 percent of the students answered affirmatively; 24.4 percent of the students stated that Poland's future is not necessarily dependent upon transformations of a socialist character, but that history has determined that Poland must develop under a socialist order. Only 7.0 percent of the students indicated that Poland would have a better chance to develop under some other order, while 7.0 percent failed to respond to the question.[67]

Evidently the students view the future with some optimism, for when they were asked to what extent they could be proud of the future the nation can attain, 39.0 percent answered "very proud" and 44.2 percent "sufficiently proud", while only 9.3 percent replied "there is little cause for pride" and 7.5 percent that there is "absolutely no cause for pride."[68] Moreover, feelings of pride with respect to the Polish past were overwhelmingly positive, indicating a strong sense of national consciousness reported elsewhere.[69] The responses "very proud" and "sufficiently proud" were reported for past accomplishments as follows: for the

TABLE 5.3
Krakow Students' Feelings of Pride with the Present*
(In Percentages)

Of what can we be proud?	Very Proud	Sufficiently Proud	Little Pride	No Cause For Pride	Unable to Judge	Totals
Of contemporary achievements in the area of science and technology.	8.1	60.5	25.6	3.1	1.5	98.8
Of Poland's contemporary role in the world and with the influence out nation has on contemporary international politics.	8.4	47.4	32.2	8.3	3.2	99.8
The rapid economic development of our country, the buildup of industry, the modernization of life in the countryside and in cities.	9.6	43.0	36.9	8.3	2.2	100.0
Of the achievements of our contemporary artists and cultural figures.	6.8	44.4	35.6	7.4	5.0	99.0

Of our contemporary capabilities for advancing and building up our country.	6.8	44.2	36.8	9.3	1.8	98.9
Of our social system and that element in it which we specifically term socialism.	8.8	35.3	35.9	12.2	7.2	99.4

* Totals are less than 100% due to some failures to respond.

traditional struggle for national and social liberation (96.5 percent), for the courage and dedication that Poles showed in difficult times in the past (95.7 percent), for the activities of Poles on behalf of the freedom of other nations (92.6 percent), for the attainments of past Polish artists (92.1 percent), and for the accomplisments of past scholars and their impact on world scholarship (92.1 percent). Only the past administration of Polish society was viewed in a strongly negative way, with 70.6 percent stating there was little or no cause for pride.[70] This latter response may indicate dissatisfaction with either presocialist or pre-Gierek governance, or both.

While the past and the future are evaluated in primarily favorable terms, the contemporary period elicits more variation in responses, as is indicated in Table 5.3.[71] Here, we see that there is considerable pride in Poland's accomplisments in the realm of science and technology (68.6 percent), in Poland's role in the world and its influence on contemporary international politics (55.7 percent), in its rapid economic development, the build-up of industry, and the modernization of rural and urban life (52.9 percent), in the attainments of contemporary artists (51.1 percent), and in the country's capacity for development and advancement (50.9 percent). However, the percentage of students who have little or no pride in the latter four categories ranges from 47.9 percent to 40.5 percent, indicating a sizeable amount of dissatisfaction. In fact, 48.0 percent of the students see little or no cause for pride in the Polish social system and that element in it which is specifically termed socialism--a response apparently inconsistent with the 61.7 percent support for the deepening of socialist transformations in Poland cited earlier. One interpretation of this inconsistency would be to suggest that a majority of students desire the achievement of what they consider to be authentic socialism, but are critical of specific current practices and institutions which are officially termed socialist. Supporting evidence in line with this interpretation is available from a response to the national survey of student attitudes in 1971.[72] Students were asked to indicate how social control could be effectively promoted by decision-making authorities. Of those who answered, 50.3 percent stated that this aim could be served by developing press criticism, 31.1 percent by increasing the role of the Sejm (parliament) and the people's councils,

30.7 percent by strengthening internal democracy in the PUWP, 30.6 percent by permitting a legal parliamentary opposition, and 28.9 percent by increasing the role of trade unions. While few survey data have been reported on such explicitly political themes, it would appear that students are anxious for the better functioning of existing political institutions.[73]

EVALUATING IDEOLOGICAL POLICY

Do the aspirations and attitudes examined in this profile of Polish students signify that the ideological goals of the PUWP have been met? We must admit that this question cannot be adequately answered on the basis of the evidence that is available. As is frequently the case in studies of communist systems, the data are of a sensitive nature and are not fully accessible to Western scholars. It is even difficult to ascertain whether the most important questions tapping political beliefs and assessments of current policies have been asked by researchers. Thus, we can only offer some tentative judgements which may shed some light on this crucial question.

If we use existing student aspirations and attitudes as a measure of the success or failure of ideological policy--that is, the extent to which students approximate the ideal socialist personality type--then it would appear that the outcomes fall short of stated regime objectives. The aspirations of the students indicate that "socio-centrism" or the "collectivist" ethic have not been internalized by a large proportion of the students. Instead, students have a very instrumental, moderate set of life and career goals, a security and stability-oriented set of dispositions which are unlikely to promote the dynamism and innovation associated with the ideological objective of building "advanced socialism." The primary concern with economic and emotional stability seems to preclude the desire for wider social involvement and the assumption of major responsibilities. In a society where there is a great emphasis on rapid socio-economic development, the future intelligentsia has a rather moderate change orientation. Writing about Polish youth, one Polish journalist has stated:

> The composite image of the generation shows a respectable, sedate young man, without any yearnings for storms in his private or outside

> life, sticking to a very small stage, properly reliable, staid and level-headed, eschewing any thought of rebellion, moderately straight-laced--the spit and image, in fact, of mum and dad minus the jeans, the long hair, beard, and electric guitar.[74]

This image is that of the conformist or organization man.

A logically complementary pattern of political attitudes seems to exist. Students are not parochial, unaware of politics. They do show an interest in politics, are conscious of current policy issues, especially in the economic spheres most directly related to their personal welfare (such as housing), and give evidence of critically evaluating the existing institutions. At the same time, while they support long-range socialist policies, have a deep-rooted affection for the Polish nation and its heritage, and assert that they would like to participate in social or civic work, only a minority of students can be considered activists. The students themselves seem suspicious of the motives of those who do participate, which could signify a distrust of political authority. Perhaps this distrust is the outcome of ideological overemphasis, as implied by the discussion of character building offered by Mikolaj Kozakiewicz in 1972:

> Teaching citizenship through participation at work and in public life was conceived...as a matter of complying with the patterns laid down by those "who knew better", and not as a kind of feed-back between leaders and led, whereby the latter learn civic responsibility not only by obedience to the wishes of "them" but also by showing up where "they" have gone wrong and making their behavior conform to what they regard as just and proper. The teaching of public-mindedness should not--to paraphrase Makarenko--be confined to drilling people to stand in line, but also encourage them, when necessary, to step out of it.[75]

In other words, the objectives of ideological policies can be undermined by ineffective implementation by agencies of political socialization.

Discussing what we have judged to be the rather

security-oriented, conformist dispositions of Polish youths, Nowak has noted "their fear of the people and the institutions around them." Nowak suggests that such attitudes represent the limited fulfillment of ideological goals and calls for the stimulation of youth's "ideological imagination." This stimulation must be provided in a sophisticated manner:

> But this kind of intellectual stimulation can only produce the desired effects if there is a "remodelling" of the institutional set-ups in which the young function, beginning above all with the school, which does not encourage independence of mind or initiative.
>
> Such remodelling should aim at creating a system of incentives to creative independence of thought, rewarding initiative and spontaneous activeness. Among the younger generations there are potentially great reserves of social activeness. A proper overhaul of the conditions altering the thinking of the young will lead on a mass scale to the creation of creative and active personalities more in keeping with the requirements of the dynamic transformations of our country.[76]

The reforming of institutions and programs of education and political socialization in Poland would appear to be necessary in order to fulfill ideological policy goals.

If we can take ideological discussion and institutional changes as an indicator of PUWP dissatisfaction with the climate of student (and youth) opinion, then there are many indications that the political authorities wish to promote major change. We can only offer a brief outline of Gierek's record in this area, which has been termed an "ideological offensive."[77] The process of educational reform was set in motion in early 1971 with the creation of the expert commission headed by Szczepanski. Among the key objectives of this group was the attempt to increase the political and social consciousness of youth. While the actual policies adopted may fall short of original intentions, the discussion of the nature and projected implementation of the reform reflected the controversy that exists in Poland over ideological and educational policy.[78] During the 1972-1973 academic year, the PUWP Politburo gave special consideration to youth and ideological affairs at its Seventh Plenum, which outlined a program to involve youth in the "building of a second Poland." The discussions and resolutions reflect disappointment by the authorities with the political consciousness of students and youth, whose potential for civic activism has apparently not been realized.[79] In a related step, the Gierek leadership began a consolidation of the fragmented youth organizations, with major organizational changes occurring in 1973 and 1976 which had the effect of placing these agencies of political socialization more directly under the guidance of the PUWP.[80] In this same period, public discussion of political education at all levels of the educational system has been frequent and lively.[81]

While the preponderant aspirations and attitudes of students would indicate a tendency toward passivity, the emergence of movements of dissent and opposition has apparently politicized a portion of the student community.[82] Following the constitutional reform controversy, the workers' strikes of 1976, and the subsequent formation of various human rights' groups in Poland, the PUWP has been especially active in attempting to discredit dissenters and isolate them within the academic community. The "Pyjas affair" and its aftermath are indicative of the sensitivity of the leadership to ideological challenges that could gain support from student groups. There seems to be some fear that a Polish version of Western confrontation politics (drawing on economic discontent and ideological disillusionment) could politicize students and bring about another 1968 outburst. During 1977 and 1978, the PUWP continued to devote attention to these serious problems in ideological sessions and pronouncements.[83]

Despite these indications of a negative evaluation of ideological outcomes, perhaps there is a second alternative interpretation of ideological policy. It has been argued by several Western analysts that perhaps the verbal commitment of the socialist authorities to a politicized, activist pattern for youth and students merely represents the ideal advocated by that segment of the party bureaucracy responsible for ideological affairs--a group which has a vested interest in finding deficiencies in this area as a way of justifying their own activities. Walter Conner has stated that one should consider "whether the 'socializers,' who often point to the work yet to be done, are interested in seeing it completed, if such were possible, or whether they simply seek to insure themselves from redundancy, as the attentions of the Giereks, Kadars, and Husaks are drawn to other concerns."[84] In a similar vein, Joseph Fiszman has suggested that the Polish authorities really only seek the attainment of "legal consciousness" or conformity, rather than a politicized youth.[85]

If these hidden or unstated policy aims do exist, then the student aspirations and attitudes described in this chapter may be an indication of success in ideological and educational policy. The constellation of student attitudes we have examined strongly suggests that students are oriented primarily toward the economic outputs of contemporary Polish society and judge that system in terms of the opportunity structure that serves to promote or block their personal security and comfort. Support for the leadership, then, would depend on its ability to promote development. Socialism is taken as a given fact. Political turmoil would not be rooted in ideological opposition to the system as a whole, but in dissatisfaction with economic outcomes and practices. According to this interpretation, the economic difficulties Poland has been experiencing in recent years would have to be resolved in order to assure active student support. Kolankiewicz and Taras describe this emerging set of values and attitudes as "popular socialism."[86] We might venture that under popular socialism, ideological activism would be a sign of defensiveness about failures in practical policy--a way of diverting attention from the main issues.

A third alternative approach to the evaluation of ideological policy exists. This would be to take a long-range view and posit that the key political values and attitudes held by students and associated with ideological policy are in the process of formation and evolution. Therefore, one cannot at this time adequately measure the success or failure of past policies. For example, Szczepanski states that citizens' attitudes under socialism can only reflect the existing economic and institutional arrangements, which are in themselves constantly undergoing change. This developmental process guarantees that there will be an intermingling of traditional, modern, and socialist values and attitudes that will only become more coherent with time and institutionalization. If this is the case, ideological and educational efforts can be expected to have only limited impact. Szczepanski states:

> In the same way as the social base is formed in the course of a spontaneous process of transformations, the pattern of man requires conscious shaping of personality, overcoming the dependence of consciousness upon the objective living conditions. One should, however, be aware that education conceived this way cannot drastically alter the situation. The practicability of the process of education is nevertheless set in the actual functioning of economic, political, and public institutions.[87]

He suggests that a successful ideological and educational policy will depend upon successful implementation of socio-economic policies rather than ideological statements: "If the social and economic situation does not fully correspond to the recommendations of the educational ideal; it is likely that they could impair the influence of education and that the behavior of individuals will be determined not by the educational ideal but by the socio-economic conditions."[88] According to such a view, ideology can be internalized only when institutions perform effectively.

While this study of student attitudes and ideological policy cannot definitively evaluate success or failure in this area, the description of attitudes and alternative approaches to evaluation does indicate that the role and impact of ideology remains a central policy issue in Poland. It will be worth watching and researching the discussions and policies concerned with ideology as Poland proceeds with its efforts to achieve "advanced socialism."

NOTES

1. For a full elaboration of the "functions" and objectives of ideology, see Jerzy J. Wiatr, "Rola ideologii w spoleczenstwie socjalistycznym," Studia Socjologiczne, 3 (58) (1975), pp. 33-61.

2. Survey research on student attitudes is frequently discussed in mass circulation newspapers and journals in Poland. The reported findings are interpreted from various perspectives and stimulate ideological commentary.

3. Stanislaw Widerszpil, "The Advanced Socialist Society: An Analysis," Polish Perspectives, No. 7-8 (1977), p. 17.

4. See the Ph.D. dissertation by Maurice David Simon, Students, Politics, and Higher Education in Socialist Poland. Stanford University: 1972, especially chapter five, pp. 208-266. See also, Jan B. de Weydenthal, "Academic Dissent as a Catalyst for Political Crisis in a Communist System," Vol. XIX, No. 1 (1974), pp. 17-40.

5. Ghita Ionescu and Isabel de Madariaga, Opposition. London: C.A. Watts and Company, 1968, pp. 176-177.

6. Although students were generally inactive in the strikes of 1970, student demands for a more consumer-oriented economy and a liberalized party-societal relationship were repeated by workers.

7. See the discussion of student unrest and

dissent in 1977 and 1978 in chapter one of this volume by Adam Bromke.

8. Again, Bromke's discussion in chapter one of this volume is relevant. During 1977 and 1978, the Polish press often alluded to the aftermath of 1968 and reminded the public of the involvement of former prominent 1968 leaders (such as Michnik and Kuron) in the new dissent movement.

9. On "legal consciousness," see Joseph R. Fiszman, "Poland: The Pursuit of Legitimacy," in Ivan Volgyes, ed., Political Socialization in Eastern Europe: A Comparative Framework. New York: Praeger Publishers, 1975, p. 27. Two party ideologists who have often attacked mere compliance to political norms (in contrast to active loyalty and participation) are Andrzej Werblan--see his essays in Szkice i polemiki. Warszawa: Ksiazka i Wiedza, 1970--and Mieczyslaw Michalik--see his Moralnosc socjalistyczna. Warszawa: Ksiazka i Wiedza, 1971.

10. In this study I have selected findings from studies conducted primarily in the two main research centers of Warsaw and Krakow. When possible, I have selected findings from studies carried out by prominent social scientists. However, there is a growing number of studies being carried out in other centers that are worthy of future attention. The interpretations offered in this chapter are my own. It is likely that Polish social scientists have drawn other conclusions.

11. Alex Inkeles, "The Modernization of Man in Socialist and Nonsocialist Countries," in Mark G. Field, ed., Social Consequences of Modernization in Communist Societies. Baltimore: The Johns Hopkins University Press, 1976, pp. 50-59.

12. Ibid., p. 57.

13. Robert Lane, "Waiting for Lefty: The Capitalist Genesis of Socialist Man," a paper presented at the annual Meeting of the American Political Science Association, Washington, DC (September 1-4, 1977), pp. 16-17.

14. Ibid., p. 17.

15. Inkeles, "Modernization of Man," p. 57.

16. Jan Szczepanski, Polish Society. New York: Random House, Inc., p. 168.

17. Jan Jerschina, Osobowosc spoleczna studentow uniwersytetu Jagiellonskiego chlopskiego pochodzenia. Wroclaw: Ossolineum, 1972, pp. 21-27.

18. Szczepanski, Polish Society, p. 168.

19. Jerschina, Osobowosc, pp. 21-27.

20. Maria Sozanska, Studenci uczelni Krakowskich: Stosunek do przyszlej pracy zawodowej i cele zyciowe. (Unpublished study). Krakow: 1974, pp. 21-30. The survey was conducted in March of 1974 at the Jagiellonian University, the Higher School of Pedagogy, The Academy of Mining and Metallurgy, the Krakow Politechnic, and the Academy of Agriculture. The sample is representative for the whole Krakow student population.

21. Based on ibid., Table 10, p. 24.

22. The desire to find "interesting work" has been found to be particularly strong in Polish studies of student values. See Halina Najduchowska, "Preferencje wartosci dotyczacych przyszlej pracy," Studia Socjologiczne, 3 (57) (1975), pp. 181-194.

23. In studies of citizens' values, the desire to obtain directing positions in organizations has rated lower as a priority than the other values we considered. See Jadwiga Koralewicz-Zebik, System wartosci a struktura spoleczna. Wroclaw: Ossolineum, 1974, pp. 130-179 and especially p. 135.

24. In comparison with the West, the preference for productivity over material consumption seems quite high. It would be interesting to have comparative data from an earlier period in Poland and from other European countries.

25. Stefan Nowak, Ciaglosc i zmiana tradycji kulturowej. (Unpublished research report). Warsaw: July 1976, chapter 5, pp. 159-192. The dichotomy and terms "stabilized/instrumental" and "dynamic/ ambitious" goals are my own, but draw from the discussion in this report and other literature on Polish students.

26. The 1958 responses are from the well-known

study by Stefan Nowak, Anna Pawelczynska, and Barbara Wilska, Studenci Warszawy. (Unpublished study). University of Warsaw: 1961, Tables 20 and 21, chapter 5. The 1972 responses are from an unpublished study by Barbara Wilska-Duszynska, Postawy Etniczne. Warszawa: 1975, pp. 23-24.

27. Again, it would be interesting to have comparative data for other European socialist states and Western democratic systems on the ideological commitments of students and youth.

28. It cannot be assumed that the slight attraction to a high-ranking political position is very different from attitudes in the West. Only comparative data would be convincing. However, it does appear that politics and political careers are not held in very high esteem by the vast majority of Polish students.

29. Danuta Dobrowolska, "The Value of Work for an Individual in Poland," in N.S. Mansurov, V.A. Yadov, Z. Sufin, and T.M. Jaroszewski, eds., Personal Activity in the Socialist Society. Warsaw: Institute of Philosophy and Sociology, Polish Academy of Sciences, 1974, pp. 227-228.

30. Sozanska, Studenci uczelni Krakowskich, pp. 31-33.

31. Ibid., pp. 41-42. Students assigned a 5 to those attributes highly indicative of social effectiveness, a 3 to those yielding a low indication of social effectiveness. The percentages show what proportion of the students assigned a given characteristic a 5 or a 3.

32. Ibid., p. 44.

33. Joseph Fiszman, "Child Socialization: Comments from a Polish Perspective," Studies in Comparative Communism, Vol. X, No. 3 (1977), p. 270.

34. For a discussion of expectancy, see Walter D. Connor, "Generations and Politics in the USSR," Problems of Communism, Vol. XXIV, No. 5 (1976), pp. 26-28. Connor discusses how a political system may derive support from expectations that it can deliver desired goods and services. This would imply that there is a point where expectations could outpace system capabilities. If expectations

that are developing threaten to strain capabilities, a strategy of promoting moderate demands would seem logical.

35. The journalist is Andrzej Szczypiorski, writing in the weekly Polityka (42) of October 1974, as cited in "Youth and its Values," Polish Perspectives, No. 4 (April, 1975), p. 43.

36. Ibid.

37. This was particularly true in the period of 1968-1970 when the party reasserted its control over higher education.

38. For an overview of the relationship of politics and higher education in the contemporary period, see the essays in Maria Gorska, ed., Ksztaltowanie socjalistycznych postaw ideowo-politycznych studentow. Katowice: Prace Naukowe Uniwersytetu Slaskiego, No. 163, 1976. Also, Stefania Wegrzyn, O socjalistyczne postawy ideowo-polityczne nauczycieli akademickich. Katowice: Prace Naukowe Uniwersytetu Slaskiego, No. 164, 1976.

39. Marian Zychowski, "The Studies of Political Sciences in Poland," in Polish Association of Political Science, Polish Round Table 1967. Warsaw: Ossolineum, 1967.

40. See, for example, Janusz Gorski, "Ideowo-wychowawcze oddzialywanie wyzszej uczelni," Zycie Szkoly Wyzszej, No. 6 (1975), pp. 21-34; and Stanislaw Czajka, "Aktualne problemy pracy ideowo-wychowawczej w wyzszych uczelniach," Zycie Szkoly Wyzszej, No. 6 (1975), pp. 35-50.

41. Inkeles, "Modernization of Man," p. 54.

42. Julian Bugiel, Leslaw H. Haber, and Wieslaw Koson, Uczelnia a Poglady Spoleczno-Polityczne Studentow. Krakow: Akademia Gorniczo-Hutnicza, 1972, pp. 9-19. The sample constitutes 18.5 percent of first and fourth-year students at the Academy of Mining and Metallurgy, the Higher School of Agriculture, and the Higher School of Pedagogy in 1971.

43. Ibid., Table 1, p. 12.

44. Marginal data from a national

representative sample of second and fourth year students (n = 2,115) conducted in 1971 by the Miedzyuczelniany Zaklad Badan nad Szkolnictwem Wyzszym. The responses are to question 26.

45. The responses with respect to interest in domestic problems come from ibid., question 6. The ranking of most interesting problems comes from A. Przeclawska and J.K. Sawa, "Zasob wiedzy spoleczno-politycznej mlodziezy studenckiej a niektore jego determinaty," Miedzyuczelniany Zaklad Badan nad Szkolnictwem Wyzszym Biuletyn Informacyny, No. 7 (1970), Table 1, p. 32. These responses were given in a pilot study of 386 students (an unrepresentative sample) from Warsaw University, the Warsaw Politechnic, the Higher School of Engineering (Bialystock) and the Higher School of Teachers (Bialystock) conducted in 1970.

46. Bugiel, Haber, and Koson, Uczelnia a Poglady, pp. 13-19.

47. Ibid., p. 19.

48. George Kolankiewicz and Ray Taras, "Poland: Socialism for Everyman?" In Archie Brown and Jack Gray, eds., Political Culture and Political Change in Communist States. New York: Holmes and Meier Publishers, Inc., 1977, p. 122.

49. Inkeles, "Modernization of Man," p. 53.

50. Aleksandra Jasinska and Renata Siemienska, "Social Activity and the Socialist Model," in Mansurov, Yadov, Sufin, and Jaroszewski, Personal Activity, p. 293.

51. Ibid., p. 299.

52. Gabriel Almond and Sidney Verba, The Civic Culture. Princeton: Princeton University Press, 1963.

53. In English, see J. Gustaw Borowski and Wieslaw Wisniewski, "Factors Related to Student's Voluntary Social Work," The Polish Sociological Bulletin, No. 1-2 (1973), pp. 88-89. A longer treatment is in Wieslaw Wisniewski, "Aktywnosc spoleczna a ksztaltowanie postaw," in Instytut Socjologii Uniwersytetu Warszawskiego, Oswiata i wychowanie a ksztaltowanie postaw. Warszawa: 1973, pp. 19-40.

54. Wisniewski, "Aktywnosc spoleczna a ksztaltowanie postaw," p. 25.

55. *Ibid.*, p. 22.

56. *Ibid.*, p. 25.

57. *Ibid.*, p. 30.

58. *Ibid.*, p. 33.

59. Data from the unpublished study, *Srodowisko akademickie w opiniach studentow Politechniki Warszawskiej*. Warszawa: 1975, pp. 23-31. The sample consists of 8.2 percent of second through sixth-year students at the Politechnic.

60. *Ibid.*, pp. 24-31.

61. *Ibid.*, p. 25.

62. *Ibid.*, p. 26.

63. *Ibid.*, p. 29.

64. Mieczyslaw Rakowski, "The Pole of 1975," in J. Maziarski, M. Rakowski, Z. Szeliga, and H. Zdanowski, *The Polish Upswing 1971-1975*. Warsaw: Interpress Publishers, 1975, p. 11.

65. See Simon, *Students, Politics and Higher Education*, chapter 4, pp. 160-207, for a fuller analysis.

66. Jan Jerschina and Ewa Stawowy, *Postawy patriotyczne i internacjonalistyczne studentow uczelni Krakowskich*. (Unpublished report). Krakow: 1974. This report is from a survey with a representative sample of first and fourth-year students (n = 739, 482 first-year students, 257 fourth-year students) at the Jagiellonian University, the Higher School of Pedagogy, the Academy of Mining and Metallurgy, the Krakow Politechnic, and the Academy of Agriculture in 1974.

67. *Ibid.*, p. 14.

68. *Ibid.*, Appendix, Table 16.

69. See Kolankiewicz and Taras, "Poland:

Socialism for Everyman?", pp. 100-105 for a discussion of attitudes toward the past and the present.

70. Jerschina and Stawowy, Postawy patriotyczny, Table 6, p. 25.

71. Ibid., Table 7, p. 27.

72. Marginal data from the unpublished survey cited in footnote 41. The responses are to question 32.

73. During 1971, First Secretary Gierek's consultations with various Polish social groupings included students. There were various promises made that youth would be better represented in party and governmental organizations and that their interests would be given just consideration when decisions were made. See, Simon, Students, Politics, and Higher Education, pp. 285-291. Gierek's appeal to youth to engage themselves in the "building of a second Poland," made at the Seventh Plenum of the PUWP in 1972 also implied that youth and students would be given more influence in more responsive political institutions. See, VII Plenum KC PZPR: Podstawowe dokumenty i materialy. Warszawa: Ksziazka i Wiedza, 1972.

74. The journalist was Jerzy Urban in the weekly Polityka, No. 48 (1972), cited in "Youth," Polish Perspectives, Vol. XVI, No. 3 (March 1973), p. 46.

75. Mikolaj Kozakiewicz, "Character-Building," Polish Perspectives, Vol. XV, No. 11 (November 1972), p. 25.

76. Stefan Nowak, "Like Father, Like Son?", Polish Perspectives, Vol. XIX, No. 7-8 (July-August 1976), p. 20.

77. For a discussion of the "ideological offensive," see Adam Bromke, "A New Juncture in Poland," Problems of Communism, Vol. XXV, No. 4 (September-October 1976), pp. 8-10.

78. This observation is based on information gathered by me in 1976-1977. Also, it is the subject of an as-yet unpublished study by Rogene M. Smerage Waite of Vanderbilt University,

"Educational Policy-making in People's Poland: The Role of Experts in the 1978 Reform Project."

79. See VII Plenum KC PZPR.

80. Discussion of the reorganization and of the operations of the youth organizations can be found in Jerzy Mikosz, Panstwo a ideowo-polityczne organizacje mlodziezowe w Polsce Ludowe. Warszawa: Panstwowe Wydawnictwo Naukowe, 1977, especially pp. 79-86.

81. Personal observation.

82. This is briefly discussed in Bromke's introductory chapter in this volume.

83. For example, the Seventh Party Plenum of 1977 focused on the issues of national unity and patriotism. See VII Plenum KC PZPR. Warszawa: Ksziazka i Wiedza, 1977.

84. Walter D. Connor, in his review of Political Socialization in Eastern Europe, The American Political Science Review, Vol. 72, No. 1 (March 1978), p. 349.

85. Joseph Fiszman, "Poland: The Pursuit of Legitimacy," p. 27.

86. Kolankiewicz and Taras, "Poland: Socialism for Everyman?", pp. 123-124.

87. Jan Szczepanski, "System of Education and Pattern of Socialist Personality," in Mansurov, Yadow, Sufin, and Jaroszewski, eds., Personal Activity, pp. 366-367.

88. Ibid., p. 365. Extending the implications of these comments somewhat further, we might hypothesize that dissent in socialist Poland could emanate from those youths and students who have taken the ideological goals very seriously and therefore are prone to demand rapid and fundamental results when doctrine and practice are perceived to be in discord.

6
Polish Journalists in the Policy-Making Process

Jane Leftwich Curry

Journalists in Poland are both highly politicized and highly professionalized. For Polish political leaders, the media are crucial as a conduit to and from the population. Therefore, they are continually involved in evaluating the media and in determining how journalists can participate in forming and pursuing policy alternatives. This close relationship between the profession and the political elite is reflected in journalists' characterization of their professional role as that of a "loyal opposition party." Simultaneously, the profession of journalism has worked to place a distance between their work as professional journalists and their role as political activists. This has involved purging the profession of political appointments,[1] raising the qualifications for membership in the professional association and refusing to modify them under political pressure,[2] and developing the entire professional and academic substructure.[3]

Wladyslaw Gomulka and Edward Gierek have differed on their posture toward the media and on the role which they have felt journalists should play. This chapter will attempt both to show how journalism professionals act in the policy-making process and to look at the impact of regime pressure on the tactics used by Polish journalists to act out their professional roles.

I would like to express my deepest thanks to all of those Polish journalists, academicians, policy makers, and librarians who made this research posible by sharing their time and insights with me. I would like to thank the International Research and Exchanges Board for funding the research.

The press in Communist societies has a number of assigned roles other than reporting the news and providing a minimal level of entertainment for its readers.[4] In fact, providing information for its own sake is not central to the ideological role of the press in these systems. A text on journalism written in 1964 by the leading Polish press scholars listed four functions of the socialist press: organization, propaganda, education, and entertainment.[5] How these four roles are ranked depends on when they are ranked and by whom. The demands of the elite are very different from the desires of the readers. Polish readers press the media establishment to provide them with rapid and thorough information about domestic and foreign events and to engage in searing criticism of various institutions in the Polish system.[6] Gomulka, First Secretary of the Polish United Workers' Party from 1956 to 1970, perceived the press as a problem in the society that had to be dealt with and not as a significant or positive part of party work. Gierek, on the other hand, has considered the media a basic mobilizing force for developing popular support for the policies of the regime.

Journalists have developed their own separate professional goal structure which stresses analysis and criticism of policy and its implementation. Thus, they pride themselves on their ability to be "investigative reporters." The question of what kind and type of criticism should be done is a matter of debate among Polish journalists. They tend to see themselves as checks on the administration of policy and as omsbudsmen for the society. In this role, they tend to act as public organizers and educators.

The multiplicity of professional activities which journalists use to perform their role allows them many potential points of access to the policy-making arena. Aside from the impact of the process of information transmission and selection on public opinion formation, journalists have a number of methods of intentionally influencing policy. These are: 1) intervention and press criticism; 2) press campaigns for legislation or for changes in proposed laws; 3)"clever" presentation of the issues; 4) nonpublished communications; 5) positions in government and party hierarchies; and 6) personal contact or information gathering for the political elite.

BEHIND-THE-SCENES JOURNALISM

The line between the PUWP and the journalism profession is not a firm one. Journalism is the profession with the highest level of PUWP membership. Journalists are prominent in the party leadership,[7] and, party bureaucrats frequently work in the media for short periods in their careers. Leading party officials are frequently assigned to the editorship of a regional or central party organ. This long-term assignment makes party bureaucrats middlemen between their staff and the the party committee. In order to get the cooperation of the existing professional on the journal staff, these editors must earn professional credentials and protect their journalists through the use of their connections in the party and government hierarchy. They serve a broker role in the party not only by giving it an immediate contact with and direct control over the media, but also by providing information concerning the kinds of issues being brought to the paper's attention by the readers and the results of journalists' investigations before they are published. This is further facilitated by the position of the editor on the local or central party committee. From this position he has immediate knowledge of specific policies and of the political tenor among party leaders, which he can carry back to his staff.[8]

The link between local party newspapers and local party committees was very strong during the Gomulka period. The Gierek administrative redivision of 1975 sought to break this strong regional exclusiveness characterized by newspaper-party devotion to protecting the region from criticism. To do this, Gierek made each newspaper responsible to all of the individual party committees of the newly created provincial units (the old wojewodstwo districts). Direction and supervision now comes from a Central Committee official assigned to supervise each newspaper, which puts the paper in the position of servicing competing party hierarchies (of which the editor is only a member of one) with final supervision coming from the Central Committee Press Department. The monthly meeting (involving the top newspaper staff members, the members of the local party committees served by the paper, leading citizens selected by the editor, and the Central Committee official responsible for that paper) became a forum for monthly evaluation and planning of the paper and also for bringing together local elites under the supervision of a central official who can act against regional autonomy.[9]

Since actual deliberations of policy-making bodies are closed, it is difficult to know what role these journalist-politicians play. It appears that, on nonprofessional issues, journalists are divided among the various "opinion groups" which exists in the elite. For instance, in the Gierek era, Kazimierz Kakol, Minister of Religious Affairs, and Mieczyslaw Rakowski, a Central Committee member, have tended to be identified with diametrically opposed groups on such issues as social control, capital punishment, and law enforcement. This split is consistent with the division of their respective journals, Prawo i Zycia and Polityka, during the Gomulka era; but, on professional issues, these journalist-politicians take similar stands about the freedom of information, the need for rapid information on events, and the role of critical discussion in the press. What is unclear is the way these issues are resolved. None of these issues have been resolved in concrete policies. Instead, it has been more effective for individual editors in the political elite to use their position to enhance their own journal and protect their own staff in instances of blocks to information, slow release of information, and censorship. This kind of crisis intervention is very common both in terms of censorship and the release of blocked information. It results from the atmosphere of artificial competition between journals.[10]

Hence, the journalism elite acts on two levels: in nonprofessional issues, it enters into the policy-making process by introducing the issue and setting the parameters of the discussion. On professional issues, which journalists do not feel should be publicly discussed as policy issues, the journalists in the political elite use their position to protect their journal and their staff by influencing the administration of the law.

This same kind of personal intervention and protection is used by journalists, primarily editors, who do not hold political positions themselves but who have contact or personal connections with members of the political elite.[11] Journalists in this position also are able to have an impact on policy and leverage to protect their journal and their staff members.

An excellent example of the power of well-connected editors is provided by the behavior of

Polityka during the Gomulka years. It strayed from the conservative party line to the point that, in 1968, it refused to engage in the press campaign which followed the student riots of March 1968. Although *Polityka* was villified for this in some conservative journals, Gomulka's respect for its editor, Mieczyslaw Rakowski, is credited by those involved with having protected the journal from being shut down as was another major journal.[12]

The most broadranging instance of nonpublic activity by journalists outside the political elite occurred in late 1969 when *Polityka* produced an alternate policy platform in the form of a yearly production plan for that journal. This plan was sent to five members of the Central Committee selected by the top editorial staff as sympathetic potential leaders. One of these was Edward Gierek. The intention of the plan was to suggest an alternate cohesive policy to Gomulka's *status quo* strategy. The basic elements of this plan became the basis for the Gierek "platform" in 1971.[13]

In addition, individual journalists frequently become specialists in one very specific area and utilize this to gain the elite's reliance on them in their specific area of expertise. This occurs particularly in the case of foreign policy, where a number of journalists are considered leading experts on West German policy and on particular areas of the Third World.

At the local level, the journal editor and leading staff members are members of the small circle of local social and political elites. They are frequently able to use these ties to pry information from their colleagues or to assure results from the paper's public or private criticism of an individual or institution.

Much of the journalism profession's function as a "mirror of public opinion" for the elite occurs through private channels. Readers are urged to contact the newspapers either with their comments or for intervention in specific problems. Tabulations of the comments on issues where there is high reader concern or which the journalists deem significant are then made and sent to the regional or central party offices. These "surveys" of public opinion, created by the newspaper itself, are an important base for affecting the administration of a law, introducing an issue, and evaluating alternative proposals. Journalists frequently noted in interviews that "the reader" is often their most effective pressure for policy changes. The intervention role also gives journalists an important function in readers' lives and serves to generate information for the journalist to use in his attempt to rationalize policy.

"Nonpublished communications" also involve the use by journalists of a closed circulation journal, Signals, published by the Central Committee Press Department and distributed to top Central Committee members. Articles which are blocked from publication but which the censors or Central Committee officials feel would be of interest to policy makers are published in this journal. It is particularly significant for journalists on the regional and nonelite papers because their journals are not seen by the central elite. Instead, the elite receives Signals, Trybuna Ludu, Zycia Gospodarcze, Kultura, and Polityka. As a filter, the censorship office also is perceived by many journalists as a "liberating force" since it protects the journalists from publishing controversial articles and, at the same time, can call attention to the problems for policy makers.

Journalists use all of these private communications channels as a matter of course. Since they are concerned with and aware of policy debates, they continually make calculations as to which private or public channel is open to them and is the most efficacious for each issue.

Journalists exert overt and public pressure for policy changes at three levels of specificity and stimulation:

1) intervention in specific issues brought on by complaints from individuals about the treatment they received from specific individuals or institutions.

2) criticism of broader based issues in public life. This criticism of broadly based issues includes, in most instances, suggestions as to the cause and the resolution of the problem. It is expected to be issue specific and to keep its criticism far below the system structures.

3) actions on social needs, as selected by a given journal. This involves journalists as social activists proposing and supervising the implementation of these programs. These grassroots programs generally do not involve policy changes; rather they encourage citizens to resolve low-level issues such as transportation difficulties to local schools, bureaucratic rudeness, misappropriation of vacation facilities, and alcoholism.

Because these three methods of action are the central focus of the work of the journalism profession, the journalist becomes a source for solving conflicts and taking care of the personal problems of his readers. Most daily newspaper and mass circulation magazine journalists feel that success at this task gives them their influence over public opinion. Press criticism is considered significant in calling attention to a general systemic problem in the administrative sphere and in modifying legislative proposals. Press actions stimulate citizen involvement and reduce pressure on the government to invest scarce resources in solving a problem.

"Interventions" are generally handled by the Department of Letters and Contact with Readers. Many "interventions" occur "out-of-print" or are bases for journalists' articles. Mass circulation journals also have a "Letters to the Editor" column which publishes selected letters and the paper's response. These published columns generally include letters about:

1) typical problems which can be cleared up by the presentation of information;
2) information on issues which relate to change in the law;
3) "educational and didactic explanations to readers in the spirit of social norms".[14]

When issues cannot be resolved by the members of the "letters" department (not all of whom are professional journalists) or by contacting the parties involved, or when they require more than advising the reader about personal or family problems or are of general interest, the information is then sent on to journalists who specialize in a given area.[15] The journalists then act as investigative reporters and, finally, as paralegal agents to force change in the situation.

This ombudsmen-like role is based on readers' feelings that journalists are independent agents, opposed to the local power elite.[16] The conflict in which the journalist finds himself because of his sense of responsibility to his readers is clear. Even in routine interventions,

> only the journalist engages <u>publicly</u> in conflicts and disputes. Only the journalist takes a public stand on matters not always and immediately popular. Only the journalist

publicly engages in criticism...in Poland, only the journalist engages in polemics, proclaims his position, etc., not out of a crowd, not in the name of a bigger or lesser collective which, as we know, offers a thousand possibilities for escaping responsibility, but in an article signed with his own name.[17]

This intervention role is encouraged by the political elite. It has been protected since 1964 by the Administrative Code. It sets limits on the amount of time an institution has to respond to either an unpublished letter asking for information or a critical article in the press.[18]

Press criticism is a much more broadly based action than press intervention. It is also, among journalists and the public, the most highly respected form of writing.[19] It involves setting out a problem for public view and discussing the options for handling that problem. Then the journalist is responsible for making a recommendation.

In the mid-1960s, there was a wide-ranging discussion in the press regarding the main aim of press criticism. In this discussion, journalists formed into two camps. Some felt that, after twenty years of socialism, the society should be stabilized enough that public institutions could be expected to act in legal ways and the press should no longer see itself as a professional watchdog of the administration. Rather, "the press should deal with broad issues and set out theses and draw up proposals".[20] Others felt that the ability to intervene in small issues gave journalists direct strength with their readers and the freedom to plant seeds for political consideration of broader issues. Journalists are not yet united on the worth of small-scale interventions, but those who are able to deal with broad issues are considered the most highly influential by their colleagues.

In issues which are not of high salience to the political elite and its ideology, and which journalists consider important, the press attempts to openly manage the search for alternatives. But on issues on which there is a high level of political elite commitment; the press contents itself with nonpublished communication with the elites and with "clever veiling of the issues". For instance, when there were internal discussions of the 1976

Constitutional Reform, the Club of Legal Affairs Journalists, in the Association of Polish Journalists, was the forum for a very bitter questioning of the constitutional reform committee. In further "veiled" discussions of the constitution, Polityka included a number of interviews with legal sociologists and lawyers on the natural tendency for Poles to be law abiding, as a veiled criticism of the strong language in the first draft of the constitution obligating Polish citizens to uphold the law.

Recent open press campaigns have included the proposals for: 1) an anti-parasite law; 2) the psychiatric law; 3) the family law; and 4) the labor code. On all of these journalists claim to have exerted influence.

The close collaboration of journalists is apparent in the cooperation of a group of journals[21] to promote a single reform or policy.[22] It is also apparent in the development of the press campaign against the psychiatric law. The law was formulated in 1969-1970 by a panel of government experts (lawyers and psychiatrists). Legal experts who felt that law was too vague to protect individual liberty initiated professional discussions. These legal experts called a conference at the Polish Academy of Sciences to discuss the law. They invited a "select group of journalists", their personal friends and journalists they respected, to this conference. The journalists then took advantage of the lack of commitment of the Gierek elite to the law and published articles discussing provisions of the psychiatric law (hinting at the need for stringent guarantees against Soviet-like use of mental hospitals). The discussion then moved from the high status small circulation journals to more popular mass journals. This pressure, coupled with specialist pressure against the enactment of the law, resulted in its withdrawal by the government from consideration by the Sejm.

Journalists tend to use both their own articles and interviews with professionals in other fields and, where relevant, workers, to put forward their policy positions. When an issue becomes a national issue discussed in a number of journals, as the psychiatric law did, this does not necessarily involve uniformity of response by the journals. This was particularly the case in the Gomulka era when journalists were more able to carry out their professional adage that conflict draws an issue together and makes it newsworthy.[23]

A final method which journalists use to solve

social problems which come to them is organizing an action under their own sponsorship. These tend generally to be problems which would cause additional strain if the political and economic structures had to respond to them, so the journalist and his newspaper create a structure for individual citizens to work together in solving their own problems. Later these actions may be institutionalized by the government. Some of the press actions which occurred in the 1970s included:

1) serving as a clearing house to assure that all spaces in industrial vacation facilities are filled;
2) organizing volunteer groups in factories to provide transportation for workers' children to regional schools;
3) funding camps for problem children;
4) setting up rewards for bureaucrats to be polite and helpful.[24]

NONELITE FACTORS INFLUENCING JOURNALISTS' BEHAVIOR

While elite pressures are the main factors determining the tactics journalists will use in the policy-making process, three environmental factors affect the press' response to those pressures. First, journalists are caught between pressures from bureaucrats not to portray them in a negative light and from the public to uncover and discuss information about problems in Poland. The pressure from bureaucrats increases as Party interest in performance in an area increases. The extent to which citizens begin vocalizing broad-level criticisms of the society, as they did in 1956, 1968, and 1970, is both a cause and a result of journalists' performance. Once journalists are able to publish more criticism in the press, then readers increase their criticism of the past work of the profession and demand more criticism. Second, there is Soviet pressure on the regime and on the press to limit its treatment of international affairs and of the Soviet Union and other Soviet bloc states. The final environmental limit on journalists' options is the existence of inter-group dynamics within the political elite. The more divided the political leadership, the more press discussion is possible.

How individual journalists behave also depends in part on their personal position in the profession. For instance, if channels of upward mobility are blocked by a shortage of positions and the existence of a stable cadre with long experience, as existed in the 1960s, then young journalists must seek patronage relationships with nonjournalism elites to insure themselves the possibility of upward mobility in their profession.[25] If salaries are based on the amount published by an individual journalist, then his professional risk taking will be lessened. This was the case in the 1960s. Furthermore, journalists found the "unpredictability" of censorship in this period to be a major problem. This became one of their major professional complaints about Gomulka.[26] Most stories, written and researched, had no guarantee of publication. This made heavily researched articles economically risky.[27]

Finally, if the elite of the professional association is made up of highly respected individuals in that field, then individual professionals are more willing to take risks and assume that the Association will work to protect them. This was the case in the period from 1956 to 1968. Journalists interviewed said that they assumed Association officials would appeal to their contacts in the political elite to protect individual Association members. Since 1968 the Association of Polish Journalists has been controlled by relatively unknown journalists. They have been, according to journalists interviewed, unwilling to battle for professional issues and have limited themselves to issues of compensation and working conditions.

GOMULKA VERSUS GIEREK: THE ELITE DETERMINANTS

The methods used by journalists to enter the policy process during a given period depend on the kind of pressure placed on the journalism profession by the political elite. Both in terms of personal predilections and elite dynamics, the periods of Wladyslaw Gomulka and Edward Gierek are in sharp contrast. In addition to their perceptions of the role of the press, the policy on social and economic modernization and the level of inter-elite conflict determine the position of journalists during both periods.

Gomulka dealt with the media by limiting it and reacting to its reporting. What this meant for the press was that it existed with so little financial and material support that its growth was almost stagnant by the middle of the 1960s. In addition, it had virtually no prior guidance as to the direction approved by the elite for its reporting. Stefan Olszowski, Head of the Central Committee Press Department in 1967, outlined this relationship:

> Periodic appraisals of individual newspapers, programs, department and editorial managements play an important role in our system of working with editorial management...These appraisals were aiming, above all, at enabling us to work out the introductory program for a more aggressive activity of the press, radio, and television, on the basis of the careful analysis of the negative tendencies in the journalistic treatment of social subjects... It seems, however, that our serious weakness lies in insufficient control over the fulfillment in this plan and the degree to which the conclusions flowing from these approaches have been taken into account by the editorial management.[28]

This chasm between the press and the political elite is further illustrated by the emphasis placed on the role of the press to rebut the "ideological attacks" on the Polish system by Radio Free Europe and other foreign broadcasting stations.[29]

This divorce between the elite and the press was further emphasized by the lack of contact with the elite. From the first days of his rule in 1956, Gomulka refused to speak to journalists as a group and would only communicate with them through a select group of journalists with whom he worked in other capacities. He maintained this pattern of personal contact with journalist-friends throughout the 1960s. It was a pattern of separation that was characteristic of most of the other Polish leaders of the period, with the notable exception of Edward Gierek, then party chief of Silesia.

In contrast, Gierek always considered the press an important tool of the regime. His system encouraged a dual involvement by journalists: public manipulation of information to support the party's policy and private activism in linking the party elite to the opinions of the population. To carry this out, Gierek has given clear instructions to the journalists regarding what and how they should write, has drawn journalists into the party *activ*, and has met regularly with them.[30] This has served to put the media "in the first rank on the ideological front."[31]

This division in views about the worth and place of the journalism profession and the mass media has a significant impact on the points at which journalists act on policy. Journalists in a Gomulka-style system are external to the elite and, therefore, rely on published discussions and their impact on public opinion, as well as internal party struggles, to affect policy. In a Gierek-style system, journalists are brought into the elite so that their policy-making activity is unpublished, while their published work is intended to present a consistent front to manipulate public behavior.

The impact of elite attitudes toward the press on journalists' behavior is increased by the elites' own policy on social and economic modernization in Poland. During the Gomulka period there was decreasing support by journalists for the regime. Economic and social modernization stagnated while Gomulka was concerned with the maintenance of the status quo. As contact points between the elites and the general population, journalists were forced to answer for the failures of the system when they answered requests for intervention or presented issues to the public. This made them particularly aware of the broad-scale failures of the system. Much of this negative attitude then appeared in the press.

Since policy in the Gomulka period was mainly to maintain the status quo and not to attempt rapid modernization or massive mobilization, there was no need to orchestrate public opinion carefully. This allowed the press to stimulate discussion about an issue by bringing out conflicting points of view. Since devotion to the system was not a primary goal, press criticism could articulate a significant level of disaffection with the system.

This lack of concern about active popular support also resulted in a minimization of the role of the press as a survey instrument to convey to the elite information about public attitudes. It also forced the journalists, at times, into developing unofficial programs to respond to problems that individuals brought to the media for solution. Since increasing investment or changing traditional policies were not legitimate policy options during this period, the journalists took up the slack by presenting voluntary programs.

Edward Gierek's aim, on the other hand, has been to "promote Poland's economic growth and to improve the living conditions of the population" simultaneously.[32] This involves some immediate gains to insure worker productivity and some promises of long-term personal gains. The feasibility of this approach to economic modernization assumes a great deal of popular support and trust in elite policies. Gierek has felt that this requires a monolithic but moderate presentation of policy themes to insure that workers perceive them as the only correct policy. Press criticism, when it occurs, is focused on individual failures as an explanation for problems rather than on errors in policy. Criticism, then, is not to emphasize "temporary" successes or failures, but to stress long-term programs of the PUWP. The need for economic and social modernization is so great that the entertainment function of the press has to be limited to allow for an increase in its pedagogical role in solving social problems.[33] The viable tactics for journalists in a Gierek-style period of pressure for rapid socio-economic modernization with delayed rewards include individual intervention with minimal press criticism of policy or discussion of alternatives; uniform and consistent presentation in the press, making "individualistic" writers an anomaly; much use of unpublished attitude surveys generated by the media or from readers' letters; and increasing use of nonjournalist professional activists to make ideological presentations.

The final factor in elite-press relations, the level of intra-elite conflict, has been much discussed in Western discussions of interest group behavior in Eastern Europe and the Soviet Union. The correlation of intra-elite conflict with open interest group lobbying is a positive one in the case of Polish journalists.

Intra-elite conflict has an impact on the position of journalists. Wladyslaw Gomulka never fully unified his elite. Instead, various factions jockeyed for implementation of their policies. Individual journals were aligned with factions in the elite--Polityka with the liberal technocrats, Kultura with the creative intelligensia, and Prawo i Zycia with the conservative "Moczarists." Individual members of the elite served as patrons for individual journalists, editors, and censors. This meant that censorship was fairly sporadic; articles were sometimes refused by the censors during the day shift and then accepted by the evening shift of censors with only minor revisions. Journalist-editors also reported that during this period they engaged in long battles with censors over the publication of an article. Often they were successful even without turning to someone in the political elite to intervene on their behalf. This unpredictability of censorship, while keeping the options open for journalists, also made the process of writing very risky, since journalists were paid on the basis of how much they published. Censorship itself meant that there were no guarantees of publication. This made the work of journalists very insecure even though actual firing of a journalist was fairly rare.

Members of the elite used press discussions to strengthen their positions, which resulted in open conflict and debate on matters of policy. But it also meant that the elite was so divided that it often could not make a decision on a given policy. Journalists had little positive impact to report to the population. In addition, this elite conflict tied each journalist's future very closely to that of his patron.

Edward Gierek, however, has managed to form a very unified elite.[34] This has meant that, while journals can still appeal to different social groups, they do not have elite patrons. The extent of press discussion is thus reduced. In addition, Gierek has attempted to provide not only positive guidance to the press concerning what it should publish but also predictable censorship. Editors are told regularly what they should write about and what subjects they cannot broach. This means that what appears in the press is more consciously orchestrated. It also means that journalists' entry into the early stages of policy making is only through contacts within the elite. This closing off of options and of the public nature of journalists' policy-making input is a major point of contention between the press and the current elite. Journalists are being denied the opportunity to build their public professional image and, therefore, their prestige. This reduces their contact with their nonelite sources, normally their information base for "monitoring" the system.[35] Their professional options are thus much reduced. As a result, journalists, who are not political activists within the PUWP elite, feel blocked from professional opportunities.

CONCLUSIONS

It is clear that the journalism profession plays a significant role in all stages of policy making. Their policy-related activities are far broader and more colorful than those indicated by what is actually published in the press. What this reflects is the pressure by the journalism profession to carry out its self-defined role as omsbudsman for the society. It also reflects a level of concern by the elite for popular opinion.

While the development of group identity is not encouraged by the political elite, journalists have a group identity and group life. Their identity revolves around the role which they feel they must play in the society and around the common experiences and pressures which they share in their work.

Journalists in Poland act as professional groups do in Western society. They reflect the same autonomy and self-enclosure that professional organizations stimulate within professional communities in the West. Training programs and work experiences, coupled with elite definitions of the expected contributions of journalists, substitute for professional organization in creating the dynamic for the development of a professional community. The formal professional organization merely serves as a forum of interaction.

The existence of an ideologically specific role for the Polish press greatly influences its perception of its professional role. Journalists have integrated political involvement into their professional role. They are the "mirror of society" and the ledger of evil. With this advocacy tradition, journalists in Poland are put in a very conflictual situation in the policy process. Their professional responsibilities to the elite, their self-imposed responsibility to identify system problems, and their identification with the population are roles which are themselves in conflict. In addition, journalists acting as omsbudsmen are put in a position where they are continually in conflict with other professional and white-collar workers. This means that the only secure allies that they have are other journalists (and for some individuals, party elite patrons or popular leadership followings). The profession thus becomes further isolated from direct, "nonprofessional" contacts with the rest of society; as a result, a subculture is spawned.

The professional continually tries to perform his professional functions. How these functions are performed is determined by the parameters set by the political elite both directly and through the manipulation of environmental factors. The sixties were a time of disinterest in the press and the profession of journalism in Poland. Their autonomy and the scope of their opportunities were greater than they were in the seventies when journalists were seen as integral parts of the system. While this allowed them to have more direct access at an early period to the policy process, it reduced their independent professional constituency--popular opinion. This trade-off is a dangerous one for the strength of the journalism profession, for it limits the extent to which they can draw on other groups for support.

Thus, while the journalism profession, because of the very political nature of its role, has played a significant function in policy making no matter what the parameters set by the elite, a disinterested elite provides more fertile ground for journalists to act in the policy process than does an interested elite. No matter what limits the elite puts on journalists, their natural group identity and impetus for acting out a part in the policy process remains. The elite is merely able to strengthen or weaken the impact of the group by cutting them off from their constituency--alternate elites within the system and public opinion.

NOTES

1. In 1956-1957, there was a drop in the number of journalists when journals were forced to drop the unqualified political appointees who had inflated their staffs. This inflation was openly criticized at the 1956 meeting of the National Congress of the Association of Polish Journalists. Stenogram IV Walny Zjazd (October, 1958), p. 88.

2. Following the 1954 and 1956 conventions, there was an increase in the requirements for membership in the professional organization and for using "professional" titles. The current standards specify that journalism must be the prime source of one's livelihood and that one must have served a three-year candidacy period in the professional journalists' organization. This organization has been unwilling to modify the rules or to make exceptions to them. For instance, Kazimierz Kakol was nominated to the Central Committee of the Association of Polish Journalists at the National Congress in 1964. The delegates refused to allow his name to be entered into the slate for the elections because he was still a candidate member of the Association although he was a prominent Party member.

3. All of the elements of Western-style professionalization and professional life are present among Polish journalists in spite of political pressure in each area. Since the end of the war, there has been constant tension between the journalism profession and academics, who want to make the journalism program an independent academic

"school", and the political elite, which wants to integrate the journalism program into a degree program in political science. This integration was carried out in the Stalinist period and again in 1976. Although the course work was highly politicized, the life of students was so isolated and intense that it led to the creation of an autonomous professional peer group. In addition to this, journalists have been involved in the establishment and, to a greater or lesser degree, direction and management of press research programs. This has been particularly the case since 1956. These programs are funded by major press institutions like RSW Prasa and Polish Radio and Television. They do surveys on readership, opinions of the media, content analysis of journals, and correlations between what is reported and what the population appears to believe. Their research focus is suggested by local and central Party groups, journals themselves (sometimes for evidence with which to respond to Party criticism of the work of the journal), or individual intellectual interests of the researchers.

The professional infrastructure, which (along with an academic base) is considered a part of the syndrome of "professional" life in the West, exists at a formal and an informal level. The Association of Polish Journalists is considered by its members to be a service organization and a meeting place for sharing information and making contacts. There is also an internal status infrastructure in the profession. Between ten and fifteen journalists are universally perceived as leaders and examples of proper journalism work. Those individuals are writers on a small number of socio-political weeklies which are "elite" journals in Poland. What and how they write tends to set the tone for how other journalists work in Poland. The work life of professional journalists is so highly pressured, communal, and ridden with conflicts with with other white collar groups that it further professionalizes journalists.

4. Wilbur Schramm, "The Soviet Communist Theory," in Siebert, Peterson, and Schramm, Four Theories of the Press. Urbana, Illinois: University of Illinois Press, pp. 105-146.

5. Mieczyslaw Kafel, "Prasoznawstwo a Nauczanie Dziennikarstwa", in Bartloma Golka, Mieczyslaw Kafel, and Zbigniew Mitzner,

Teoria i Praktyka Dziennikarstwa. Warsaw: Panstwowe Wydawnictwo Naukowe, 1964, p. 31.

6. "Odpowiedzialnosc za Slowo", Kultura, vol. IX, no. 14, (April 4, 1971), pp. 1, 6-7.

7. Encyklopedia Wiedzy o Prasie. Wroclaw: Ossolinium, 1976, p. 73.

8. Interviews with regional press editors, 1976.

9. Interviews with regional press editors, 1976.

10. Interviews, 1976.

11. Interviews, 1976.

12. The journal which was closed was Swiat. Interviews, 1976.

13. Interviews, 1976.

14. Wiktor Gabler, "Dzial Prawny i Jego Rola w Pismie", Biuletyn Naukowy, no. 1/17 (March, 1958), p. 32.

15. Interviews, 1976.

16. In a survey done by Polish Radio and Television in 1974, readers said that they go to the media with a complaint because:

it has influence on other institutions	51.0%
they want publicity	30.3%
individuals sense that Polish Radio and Television is interested in their affairs	26.1%
individuals fear local government	25.5%

Andrzej Duma, "Rola Polskiego Radia i Telewizji Jako Instytucji Skarg i Wnioskow", Osrodek Badania Opinii Publiczna i Studia Programowa (Komitet do Spraw Radia i Telewizja), no. 128 (1974), p. 33.

17. Zbigniew Kwiatkowski, "The Journalist--The Great Unknown", Zycia Literackie, (May 8, 1966), p. 1, translated in Radio Free Europe, Polish Press

Survey, no. 1992, p. 4

18. Andrzej Pociask, "Prasa a Skargi i Zazalenia Ludnosci", Prawo i Zycia, vol XII, no. 6 (March 12, 1967), p. 3.

19. In articles during the "Falkowska debate" of 1964, many journalists held that the only variation in the use of press criticism should be that the most skilled and talented journalists should engage exclusively in criticism, as this was the "elite" function of journalism.

20. Wanda Falkowska, "Interwencje i Mity", Prawo i Zycia, no. 3 (February 2, 1964), p. 2.

21. The Gomulka period was unique in that both the elite and the profession were ideologically divided.

22. The alimony law, for instance was promoted by Przyjaciolka, Trybuna Ludu, Kobieta i Zycia, Prawo i Zycia, and individual journalists on Polityka.

23. Ekran, February, 1972, p. 5.

24. Wladyslaw Maslowski, Akcje Prasowe. Krakow: Osrodek Badan Prasoznawczych RSW "Prasa-Ksiazka-Ruch", 1973, p. 14.

25. This issue was a major topic of discussion in the 1968 National Congress of the Association of Polish Journalists (SDP). It is clear from the explusions from the SDP from 1964 to 1968 that, in some regions, as many journalists were shifting to other professions as were entering the profession. Within the profession this turnover was a result of the stagnant job situation and not directly of political battles.

26. Interviews with members of the Zarzad Glowny, 1964-1968, done in 1976.

27. The change in salary provisions to a set salary scale for journalists was listed, in a survey done in 1976 among Polish journalists, as the single most important achievement of the profession from 1970-1976.

28. "Discussion at the Eighth Plenary Session

of the PUWP", Trybuna Ludu (May 18, 1967), p. 1, translated by Radio Free Europe, Polish Press Survey, no. 2074, pp. 15-16.

29. Ibid., p. 15.

30. "A Press Conference Gierek Style," Radio Free Europe, Background Report, no. 64 (March 15, 1976).

31. Polish Press Survey, no. 1791 (December 4, 1964), p. 8.

32. Adam Bromke, "A New Juncture in Poland", Problems of Communism (September-October, 1976), p. 2.

33. Polish Press Survey, no. 2342.

34. Bromke, "A New Juncture," p. 26.

35. Journalists, in interviews done in late 1976 (after the Radom workers' disturbances over price increases), stated that the number of letters from readers sent to both the newspapers and Polish Radio and Television had decreased and the number of anonymous letters had increased. These anonymous letters are of little use to journalists in gathering specific information for their articles because it is impossible to check on their accuracy. They are also seen as a sign that the public has no respect for the press.

7

Citizen, Voluntary Associations, and the Policy Process

Christine M. Sadowski

INTRODUCTION

To link voluntary associations with public policy in any country is to link voluntary associations with the polity and with the citizen. This is the case for both policy making and policy transmission. The assumption here is that the voluntary associations, while maintaining some degree of autonomy, are not totally independent of either the polity or the citizen. The question of the role of voluntary associations in public policy is particularly interesting in systems such as those of the Soviet Union and East European states, where such associations have been typically described since the early 1950s as "transmission belts," transmitting policy from the top, down. Yet no detailed assessment of this transmission process or of the possibility that voluntary associations represent the interests of the citizen to the state (i.e., transmission from the bottom, up) has been offered in the literature.

This chapter offers some preliminary results of a larger study conducted by the author in 1976-1977 on the function of voluntary associations in Poland. Whether or not voluntary associations in Poland serve the dual roles of policy makers

---

This study was supported by a Fulbright-Hays Research Grant and a National Defense Foreign Language Fellowship administered by the Center for Russian and East European Studies, The University of Michigan. I gratefully acknowledge the helpful suggestions of Walter D. Connor, Zvi Gitelman, Maurice Simon, and David Summers on an earlier draft of this chapter.

and policy transmitters is the question at hand. A brief description of voluntary associations in Poland will be followed by an evaluation of their potential and actual roles as policy makers and policy transmitters.

TYPES OF VOLUNTARY ASSOCIATIONS

Voluntary associations in Poland are divided into three legal categories: common associations, registered associations and associations which are "distinctively useful" to the public. Common associations, composed of at least three members, are usually small, local, and limited in their activity. Discussion clubs, groups which act as voluntary caretakers of monuments and historical buildings, and local folk dancing groups are examples of such associations. They possess no legal status and therefore are not entitled to funding or to a treasury of monies other than membership dues. Barred from soliciting public donations, they are not allowed to engage in broad-ranging activities, to form filiate associations in other parts of the country, or work together with other organizations. Members must live in the city, town, or district in which the organization is based. Common associations cannot have "legal," i.e., group, members. Because of these restrictions, they are unable to play a role in policy making or implementation. If a common association wishes to expand, it may choose to petition for an official change in its status to that of a registered association.

Registered associations (sometimes called "statute associations") are composed of at least fifteen members. Since they enjoy a legal status, they can have their own treasury, be funded by government agencies or other institutions, and collect public donations. These associations must present their statutes to the Council of Ministers for ratification. Registered associations are said to have more social responsibilities and to have a broader social significance. They cover a wide range of interests and include such associations as the Mickiewicz Literary Society, Society of Polish Surgeons, Union of Polish Yacht Clubs, and the Family Planning Society. They are allowed to form branches and to merge or cooperate with other associations.

Those associations which are "distinctively useful" to the public have received this special status from the Council of Ministers. This category enjoys intensive government support. Because of their specific nature, these associations can deviate from the more usual pattern of common and registered association structure. They are allowed and encouraged to coordinate activities throughout the country and have the sole right to activity within their specified field. Because of their "distinctive public usefulness," they may benefit from discounts or be totally relieved of paying taxes or other fees.[1] They may recruit group members and have the special privilege of recruiting youth into their ranks.[2]

This chapter deals with only those associations which have been awarded the "distinctively useful" status, as they would be the associations most capable of playing an active role in public policy. To date, there are fewer than thirty such organizations in Poland. Their limited number is attributed to a conscious effort on the part of the Council of Ministers to maintain variety among existing organizations and to encourage others to be founded. One must remember that an association with a "distinctively useful" status has sole right to activity within its special field, thus precluding the establishment of other organizations with like or overlapping purposes. This also means that the "distinctively useful associations" (DUAs) themselves do not overlap in purpose.[3]

Of the existing DUAs, only the nonhobby, nonyouth, mass social organizations are included in this study, and professional associations which enjoy this status are mentioned only to better illustrate points being made. Ten DUAs remain. They are the Women's League, National Defense League, League for the Preservation of Nature, Voluntary Reserve of the Civil Militia, Polish Red Cross, Polish Social Aid Committee, Social Anti-Alcoholism Committee, Society of Friends of Children, Polish-Soviet Friendship Society, and the Union of Combatants for Freedom and Democracy.

VOLUNTARY ASSOCIATIONS AS POLICY MAKERS

One cannot estimate the potential policy-making power of DUAs without considering their relation to the state. Officially, the role voluntary associations play in socialist society is that of a "partner" to the state, providing services to which the state is unable to devote time and effort.

> Cooperation between state and associations is based on the notion of mutually offering services in the name of general societal good...The state-association relationship, considered at the level of cooperation, is based on the partner principle and not on the superiority of the state over associations. If associations perform a menial or service role in relation to the state, it is only because they recognize the similarity between their own goals and the goals of the state. The state possesses no legal sanctions by which to force associations to cooperate in the realization of its political, economic, or cultural goals.[4]

Yet the means by which the state gives "proper direction" to the DUAs is by determining the purposes and goals of newly created organizations, setting the structure of the organizations, determining the requirements for membership in organizations, determining the range of rights and obligations of associations and their memberships, controlling organizational activity, assisting organizations financially, and assigning to organizations tasks or entire spheres of activity which were previously in the hands of the state.[5] Such direction by the state is said to enhance rather than interfere with organizational goals. Yet the state's detailed delegation of responsibilities and competences to organizations severely limits the types of policy which might otherwise be proposed by the organizations, and makes concepts such as "lobbying" and "pressure groups" irrelevant. While this author certainly agrees that the state and associations in Poland operate as partners, she would like to emphasize that it is not in the form of a business venture, but rather that of an invitation to a waltz. The state assumes the lead, determining direction as well as steps to be taken, allowing improvization (as opposed to experimentation) only to the extent that the dance itself be enhanced.

State support and sponsorship is not, of course, uniform for all organizations. The state has a greater commitment to those organizations which participate in the "building of socialism" and in the development of socialist relations within the society.[6] These organizations include the Women's League, National Defense League, Voluntary Reserve of the Civil Militia, Polish-Soviet

Friendship Society, and the Union of Combatants for Freedom and Democracy.[7] These are the associations most _likely_ to be active in policy making.

Yet despite the fact that DUAs have sole right to activity within their specified fields, all of these associations serve in various ways as voluntary auxiliaries to more powerful institutions which would certainly have the greater input into policy decisions. To the extent that the Women's League attempts to improve the position of women in the national economy, it duplicates the activities of trade unions. Indeed, in the late 1960s the Women's League was forced out of workplaces and sent to residential settings to take part in more domestic matters through the residential self-government organs, with catastrophic consequences for its membership rolls. The auxiliary nature of other DUAs is even more apparent. The National Defense League supplements the activities of the Polish People's military forces; the Voluntary Reserve of the Civil Militia supplements the activities of the regular civil militia; the Polish-Soviet Friendship Society is largely under the auspices of the Polish United Workers' Party (PUWP)[8]; and the Union of Combatants for Freedom and Democracy is the voluntary social counterpart of the Bureau of Veteran Affairs and cooperates very closely with the Ministry of Labor, Wages, and Welfare.[9] While the activities of all of these DUAs go beyond those of their "parent" institutions, most additional activities are educational, cultural, sports-tourist or self-help oriented: a focus underlining their lesser role in policy making than in policy implementation or transmission.

Five organizations--less intensively sponsored by the state--remain: the League for the Preservation of Nature, Polish Red Cross, Polish Social Aid Committee, Social Anti-Alcoholism Committee, and the Society of Friends of Children. The first of these DUAs is under the guidance of the Ministry of Forestry and Timber Industry, while the last four are under the guidance of the Ministry of Health and Social Services. This does not mean that these DUAs cannot in some way influence policy, but it does limit the strength of possible inputs.

These associations can and do provide state institutions with specialized information necessary for the formulation of policy. Their role in this regard whould not be underestimated. Studies are conducted and data gathered on the problems of alcoholism, the unmet needs of orphans and welfare recipients, pollution problems, the double burden of women, etc. The recommendations of the DUAs are taken into consideration, but decisions are made with large-scale political and economic ends in mind, and it would be unreasonable to think, for example, that the League for the Preservation of Nature could ever lobby for legislation requiring state-owned enterprises to install anti-pollution devices within a certain number of years or else be fined or forced to shut down. No legal organization in Poland mobilizes citizens to make demands on the government. This is as much due to the required or predetermined cooperative spirit of organizations as it is to the lack of resources in Poland. State institutions are set up to deal with the most pressing problems. DUAs undoubtedly contribute in some way to the formulation of policy, but they lack real power. Their contributions remain undocumented, officially unacknowledged, and thus difficult to specify as to impact or type.

The exception here are the professional associations, including several with DUA status such as the Chief Technical Organization, the Polish Economic Society and the Polish Society of Architects. Their expertise is recognized by state institutions as a valuable resource. These associations are better equipped to detect problem areas and provide government organs with possible solutions. In this respect, they cannot be described as mere "transmission belts."

Just how instrumental organizations are in policy making is very difficult to measure. Recommendations in specific areas are certainly made by the DUAs to the appropriate ministries or government organs. These recommendations are taken into consideration in policy decisions. Certainly, some decisions indicate change, but less certain is _where_ these policy changes originated. If the ideas originated in the organizations, then we could conclude that voluntary organizations in Poland _are_ influential in policy making. It is possible, however, that the ideas originated within the government organs which, in turn, made requests to the appropriate DUAs to provide necessary details on the matter at hand.

To some extent, the question of the major sources of influence on certain policy decisions--the associations, state institutions, or the PUWP--cannot be untangled because of the overlap at the top of these organizational bodies. The past

Minister of Labor, Wages, and Welfare is now the head of the Polish Social Aid Committee as well as an executive member of the Union of Combatants for Freedom and Democracy. The Chairman of the Council of Ministers, Piotr Jaroszewicz, is likewise the president of the Union of Combatants for Freedom and Democracy. Party First Secretary Edward Gierek himself is an executive member of this organization of veterans. If benefits for war veterans were improved, who was responsible for the change? If the head of the Polish-Soviet Friendship Society, Jan Szydlak, who is also a member of the PUWP Politburo, initiates a change in policy, which organization/institution takes credit for the change? The web of affiliation is too entangled to identify the initiator. The fact remains that the DUAs as such seem neither autonomous nor powerful enough to be credited solely with changes, whatever the power of those who hold leadership positions in them.

Lastly, in order for voluntary associations to participate actively in the policy-making process, they should have close enough contact with the citizen (whether member or nonmember) to know his interests and his needs. The following data were collected in the course of a survey conducted by the author in Warsaw, 1977, on a random sample of Warsaw males between the ages of 30 and 45 (N=113). Respondents were presented with four hypothetical problem situations and asked if and how they would respond to them. The situations were as follow:

Situation A: If you spent your yearly vacation at the same place and noticed that each year the area was more polluted (i.e., the river was more polluted, the forest was more littered, the air was more polluted), would you try to do anything to change this situation? What? To whom would you turn?

Situation B: If a friend of yours at work faced discrimination occupationally only because she is a woman, would you try to do anything to change this situation? What? To whom would you turn?

Situation C: If you had a neighbor who was sick and lived alone, would you try to help her? How? To whom would you turn?

Situation D: If among your close family the following situation occurred: The father is a heavy drinker, the mother is drinking more and more from worry, the children are beginning to drink. Would you try to help them? How? To whom would you turn?

At least one major voluntary association exists which is equipped to deal with each of these problem situations.[10] The interview questions were open-ended and designed to determine the frequency with which voluntary associations came to mind as problem-solving institutions for these situations. The results are presented below in the form of a single table, not so much for purposes of comparison (as the situations themselves cannot to compared) as for purposes of a convenient summary (see Table 7.1).

The percentages presented in Table 7.1 is not particularly surprising. It is understandable that pollution problems would be reported to local People's Councils, that bosses and supervisors would be approached to assist in solving sex discrimination problems at the workplace,[11] and that the sickness and alcoholism situations would be solved by the respondent himself. Note, however, that not only are voluntary associations low in the ranking of problem-solving institutions, but <u>in each case they rank below the percentage of respondents who would solve the problem alone</u>, without turning to others for assistance. This is particularly interesting in situation A: a hypothetical problem which would be very difficult to try to solve individually.

The low percentage (2.4) of respondents who would turn to a voluntary association in the sex discrimination situation is perhaps due to the absence of the Women's League at workplaces. Yet the more relevant interpretation may well be that the Women's League is considered by respondents to be a "do-nothing" organization whose goals are not important and whose activities produce few results.[13]

The situation of the sick and lonely neighbor and the alcoholic family were problems which respondents most commonly felt they could solve themselves. But voluntary associations <u>do</u> exist which were set up to deal with precisely these problems. They are well-known associations with large memberships. In fact, while some 13.3 percent of the entire Polish population are members of the Polish Red Cross, only 2.4 percent of the sample considered turning to this particular voluntary association for help in solving the

TABLE 7.1
Problem-Solving Alternatives in the Opinion of Respondents (given in %)[12]

I would turn to:	Situation			
	A pollution	B discrimination	C sickness	D alcoholism
Myself (solve the problem without turning to others)	14.8	11.3	50.3	46.4
Councils, Ministries, Government Administration	54.7	6.5	7.1	3.2
Voluntary Associations	13.6	2.4	13.0	12.2
Bosses, Supervisors, Directors at workplace		43.5		
Trade Unions		22.0		
Doctors, Hospitals, Clinics			14.8	20.3
Social Services			5.3	7.3
Polish United Workers' Party	1.1	7.1		
Friends		2.4	5.9	.8
Others	9.0	3.6	1.8	6.5
Don't Know	6.8	1.2	1.8	3.3
Total	100.0	100.0	100.0	100.0

problem of the sick and lonely neighbor.[14]

Clearly, voluntary associations are institutions that some would turn to in problem solving. Their importance, however, is diluted by the presence of alternatives which seem more plausible to the respondents. The problem-solving capacity of voluntary associations is considered to be merely "auxiliary" by both polity and citizen. When the state faces a pressing problem, it would sooner turn to the government institutions set up to deal with that problem than to a voluntary association. When an individual faces a pressing problem, he would sooner solve it himself than turn to a voluntary association.

VOLUNTARY ASSOCIATIONS AS POLICY TRANSMITTERS

The most general way in which voluntary associations transmit state policy in Poland is through their efforts to mobilize citizens. That in itself is an avowed socialist policy, i.e., to include citizens and especially workers in the building of socialism and in the managing of the state, and to combine individual interests with societal interests. One of the ways to bring about this combination is through the "involvement" of the individual in society.

> Societal involvement is an act of a socially conscious person and thus it is at the same time a measure of his consciousness, responsible attitude toward society and an indication of his purposefulness...Social involvement is an indication of the degree to which the person has been socialized, and this indication is characteristic of social entities and other social groups rather than individuals.[15]

Thus, not only are social involvement and participation viewed positively and encouraged officially, but they are also seen as a measure of the person's attitudes toward the regime and society.

The 1976 Polish statistical yearbook proudly presents the membership figures[16] shown in Table 7.2.

It would seem, then, that the voluntary associations have been successful in mobilizing citizens. Yet membership figures tell us nothing about levels of participation and involvement. For

TABLE 7.2
Organization Membership (in thousands)

	1960	1965	1970	1975
Women's League	1898.1	5248.8	384.0	453.9
National Defense League	1000.0	1593.1	2310.1	1846.9
League for the Preservation of Nature	126.1	500.3	903.4	1125.2
Voluntary Reserve of the Civil Militia	99.6	246.6	379.4	332.1
Polish Red Cross	2960.0	4535.9	5369.5	4539.8
Polish Social Aid Committee	69.4	582.7	1128.1	1276.2
Social Anti-Alcoholism Committee	—	51.3	83.7	113.4
Society of Friends of Children	90.5	269.1	518.6	870.8
Polish-Soviet Friendship Society[17]				
Union of Combatants for Freedom and Democracy	159.4	187.8	329.5	421.7

such purposes, a more detailed investigation is required.

It is impossible to state here what percent of the members in these DUAs are school-aged children, as none of these organizations compile data on the demographic characteristics of its members. The National Defense League, League for the Preservation of Nature, Polish Red Cross, Society of Friends of Children, and the Polish-Soviet Friendship Society are very prevalent in primary and secondary schools. Entire schools belong to these organizations, and in such cases teachers are expected to join and then act as recruiters, requiring each child to bring in a symbolic membership fee.

A similar recruitment procedure is followed in places of employment. Associations carry out recruitment campaigns with a set goal of a certain number of new members from each place of employment. Organization members, acting as recruiters, approach their coworkers and ask that they help them fill their quota by paying a few zlotys in membership dues. This is by far the most common setting for joining organizations. Of all of the respondents included in the survey, not one joined any of the above-mentioned associations because he was interested enough in a program or a cause to go and knock on the doors of the organization himself and apply for membership. All of the respondents who were organization members were recruited through work places or schools, and it was usually the case that respondents stopped being members of organizations because they finished school, changed jobs, or moved. Membership in organizations is so localized that the Women's League lost 93 percent of its members between 1965 and 1970 when it was asked to move out of workplaces and into the residential self-government setting.

The Union of Combatants for Freedom and Democracy is the exception here. Membership in this organization is sought by war veterans, both to qualify for special pensions and other benefits, as well as for camaraderie found through associating with people who shared similar experiences during the war.

There is little real mobilization indicated by the bare fact of membership. A better means of measuring the success of voluntary associations in mobilizing citizens is the investigation of citizen attitudes toward social activeness and joining organizations. Respondents were asked if they considered themselves to be socially active. To this, 43.4 percent of the sample responded "yes." Of those who were socially active, 40.8 percent expressed the desire to be more active. Of the 56.6 percent who were not socially active, 50.0 percent said they would like to be more active if they had more time, 37.5 percent said they were not and did not want to be active, and 12.5 percent did not know. Respondents were then asked if they felt the need to be socially active with such activity defined as: "the activity of a group of people working together voluntarily to achieve a certain goal." Here, 80.5 percent responded "yes," 15.9 percent "no," and 3.5 percent did not know. Yet when asked the question "Are you a member of a voluntary association?" 24.8 percent responded "yes," and 75.2 percent "no."

Of those who said they did not belong to an organization, 41.2 percent (or 31.0 percent of the entire sample) said they would not join a voluntary association even if they had more leisure time. Those who expressed such reluctance split evenly between those who said that personal situations or characteristics did not allow them to be members (health problems, the feeling that they are too old to join organizations and be active in them,[18] lack of interest in working in groups, etc.) and those who expressed negative feelings toward the system of organizations ("There are no sensible organizations." "Organization members are not equally rewarded--only Party members benefit from organization activities." "Leaders use organizations for their own personal gain," etc.).

Several interesting points can be made here. First, before presenting respondents with a definition of social activeness, 71.7 percent said they either were or wanted to be socially active. Having been given the researcher's definition of social activeness, 80.5 percent expressed the need for such activity. Yet only 24.8 percent said they were members of social organizations. It would seem, then, that organizational membership is not considered a means of fulfilling the need to be socially active. Furthermore, subsequent interview responses determined that 43 percent of the sample were members of organizations (18.2 percent having answered the first question about organizational membership incorrectly). It is difficult to know why so large a percentage of responses to the first question on organizational membership was incorrect, but the most likely reason would be that the respondents simply forgot they were members. These initially unacknowledged memberships covered a wide variety of organizations. What is more surprising is that some 8 percent of the sample said they did not belong to any organization and would not join an organization even if they had more leisure time, when all the while they were members of voluntary associations. Such results are confusing, but strongly suggest that this group of people attach no importance to what are largely pro-forma memberships.

On the whole, the figures suggest that organizations have not been successful in awakening enthusiasm among citizens to become members. Although the Warsaw sample used in the survey was limited in scope, making generalizations to a larger population impossible, informal talks with a wide variety of informants (ranging from school children to retirees and both men and women from various backgrounds) give this author some reason to state that membership in organizations is not viewed enthusiastically among Poles. Although voluntary associations in Poland have been successful in recruiting members, they have not been successful in mobilizing citizens to take an active, spontaneous, and enthusiastic part in their activities.

Although respondents lacked enthusiasm about joining these DUAs, they did evaluate the goals of these organizations and the organizations themselves as important to society. Without being given the name of the organization concerned, respondents were asked whether they felt a particular DUA goal[19] was very important (4.0), rather important (3.0), not so important (2.0), or not at all important (1.0) to Polish society. On the basis of this four-point scale, the organizations were ranked. The mean scores for the goals ranged from 3.73 to 2.70. The ordering from the most to least important was as follows: Polish Red Cross, League for the Preservation of Nature, Society of Friends of Children, Social Anti-Alcoholism Committee, Polish Social Aid Committee, National Defense League, Union of Combatants for Freedom and Democracy, Polish-Soviet Friendship Society, Voluntary Reserve of the Civil Militia, and the Women's League. When asked whether a particular organization (by name) was important or unimportant to the society, the same four-point scale yielded the following ordering from most to least important: League for the Preservation of Nature, Social Anti-

Alcoholism Committee, Polish Red Cross, Polish Social Aid Committee, Society of Friends of Children, National Defense League, Union of Combatants for Freedom and Democracy, Women's League, Voluntary Reserve of the Civil Militia, and the Polish-Soviet Friendship Society, with 3.82 being the highest and 2.74 the lowest mean score. Thus, all of these organizations and their goals were evaluated as "important" to Polish society.[20]

The resulting scales differ somewhat, but the striking similarity remains that, in both cases, the last five DUAs listed (the lesser important half) are the five DUAs most committed to the building of socialism and the development of socialist relations within Polish society. These are the organizations most strongly and enthusiastically supported by the state.

Causality cannot be inferred from the evidence above. It is unclear whether the "socialist orientation" of the more enthusiastic state support of DUAs (or both) make these particular organizations less important in the evaluation of the respondents. Besides, socialist orientation and state support cannot be effectively separated.

CONCLUDING REMARKS

A link is missing in the policy process involving citizens, voluntary associations, and the state in Poland. While the relationship between DUAs and the state in Poland is very close, it is in fact too close to allow DUAs to play an active and significant role in policy making, capable of separate measurement. Their role as research organizations in policy formulation cannot be overlooked, but this role is a powerful one only to the extent that they can provide expertise which is otherwise unavailable. Because most DUAs play an auxiliary role to other, more powerful state institutions, even their potential expertise value is minimized in this respect.

The potential role of DUAs as mechanisms through which citizens can articulate their interests is likewise minimized by the existence of other institutions and people to whom citizens turn in problem situations because of more familiarity, greater confidence, and the simple perception that DUAs are _not_ primarily vehicles for interest articulation.

While DUAs have been successful in increasing membership figures, they have been much less successful in awakening enthusiasm toward joining organizations. While social activeness is valued, joining organizations is not.

The organizations themselves are valued, on the whole. They are certainly valued by the state and seemingly valued by the citizen. It may well be, however, that respondents evaluated the values and causes these organizations represent rather than the organizations themselves. This would mean that the question "Is the League for the Preservation of Nature important to Polish society?" yielded a response "Yes, nature is important," rather than "this organization is important." Such a distinction between causes and the organizations themselves would resolve the discrepancy between the high verbal evaluation of the organizations given by respondents and their actual behavior, which indicates low regard for the organization.

Neither the state nor the citizen turns to voluntary associations in situations which would afford them a greater role in policy making. They are neither powerful nor autonomous enough to be credited with policy making, and their weaknesses are likewise reflected in their lack of success in mobilizing citizens.

The state shows little enthusiasm for increasing the power of voluntary associations. Citizens, when seeking an effective means for the articulation of interests, form their own mechanisms, spontaneously and illegally. There are an estimated twenty-eight dissident newspapers presently being printed in Poland.[21] Some thirty-five university courses are being taught privately in Warsaw and Cracow--courses which would not be tolerated ideologically in the regular university curriculum. Estimates of the number of participants in socio-political action groups range from 2,000 to 10,000 depending on whether or not one includes those whose participation is limited to reading and circulating dissident materials.[22] While the number of participants is small, it is important to remember that these groups do not actively recruit members for the sake of increasing membership figures. They offer no benefits other than personal satisfaction to members whose careers and futures are threatened by the very fact of membership in these groups.

To say that voluntary associations in Poland do not serve as mechanisms for interest articulation is not to say that no such mechanisms exist. When, despite attempts on the part of security guards to prevent the incident, a Warsaw student handed a letter of grievances to UN Secretary General Kurt Waldheim during his 1977 visit to Poland, she had created a mechanism. When workers in Radom and Ursus rioted against increased food prices in 1976, they had created a mechanism. When the parents of in-coming first year university students were summoned by local PUWP cells to be warned against the dangers of their children participating in "ideologically inappropriate" activities at the university, the regime admitted that these citizen-created mechanisms, though not institutionalized, are too powerful to be ignored.

NOTES

1. J. Wiacek, *Stowarzyszenia w panstwie socjalistycznym*. Warsaw: Wydawnictwo Prawnicze, 1962, pp. 30-36; Janusz Romul, *Panstwo a stowarzyszenia w Polsce Ludowej*. Poznan: Uniwersytet Im. AdamaMickiewicza, 1969, pp. 21-22; Leszek Wisniewski, *Model prawny stowarzyszen w PRL.* Warsaw: Panstwowe Wydawnictwo Naukowe, 1974, pp. 20-26.

2. Nonyouth social organizations otherwise have a requirement that members be at least 18 years of age. The privilege of recruiting youth greatly increases membership figures, as well as gives organizations a much larger forum in which to transmit state policy.

3. The various activities of voluntary associations in Poland are coordinated through the United National Front. It is this institution which attempts to prevent the emphasis on certain types of organizational activities from being duplicated.

4. Leszek Wisniewski, *Model prawny*, p. 165.

5. Wladyslaw Ratynski, "Stowarzyszenia w systemie organizacji spoleczenstwa socjalistycznego w Polsce," in Adolf Dobieszewski, ed., *Organizacja polityczna spoleczenstwa socjalistycznego w Polsce*. Warsaw: Ksiazka i Wiedza, 1977, pp. 624-625

6. *Ibid.*, p. 625.

7. Jerzy Rusiecki, Od A do Z o zwiazkach zawodowych i organizacjach spolecznych w Polsce. Warsaw: Ksiazka i Wiedza, 1974, pp. 103-113, 117-126, 133-139, 142-146, 495-498.

8. Polish United Workers' Party members are expected to become members of the Polish-Soviet Friendship Society.

9. The Union of Combatants for Freedom and Democracy, known in Poland by the acronym "ZBoWiD," was a right-wing veterans' organizations led in the 1950s and 1960s by the head of the secret police, Mieczyslaw Moczar. Only recently has it begun to liberalize its policies and been more willing to accept National Army (AK) veterans as members.

10. For situation A: League for the Preservation of Nature, Polish Fisherman's Union; for situation B: Women's League; for situation C: Polish Social Aid Committee, Polish Red Cross; for situation D: Social Anti-Alcoholism Committee, Society of Friends of Children.

11. For more detailed information on problem-solving mechanisms at the workplace, see Aleksander Owieczko, "Samorzad robotniczy w przedsiebiorstwie przemyslowym a zaloga," Studia Socjologiczno-Polityczne, 22 (1967); Zbigniew Maciag, "Funkcjonowanie organizacji spoleczno-politycznych w przedsiebiorstwie (samorzad robotniczy)," 4 Zeszyt Naukowy UJ (Krakow), 1972; and Maciag, part two, "(organizacja partyjna, zwiazkowa, i mlodziezowa)," 5 Zeszyt Naukowy UJ (Krakow), 1973.

12. Percentages were calculated on the basis of multiple responses.

13. The Women's League is held in very low regard by both men and women in Poland. The responses of the all-male sample to questions concerning the Women's League indicated that this organization tries to idealize the "working woman," when in fact women work out of necessity and a "housewife" is a luxury that many men desire but few can afford.

14. Other organizations which would be turned to in the case of the sick and lonely neighbor include the Polish Social Aid Committee and the Polish Boy Scouts.

15. N.S. Mansurov, "Prognosis of the Development and Activity of the Personality--A Basic Theory," in N.S. Mansurov, V.A. Yadov, Z. Sufin, T.M. Jaroszewski, eds., Personal Activity in the Socialist Society. Warsaw: Institute of Philosophy and Sociology, Polish Academy of Sciences, 1974, p. 69.

16. Rocznik Statystyczny 1976. Warsaw: Glowny Urzad Statystyczny, p. 23.

17. Polish-Soviet Friendship Society membership figures are curiously absent from all of the major Polish statistical yearbooks. A separate source indicates that this organization has 38,414 individual members, 17,649 groups members and a cadre of about 25,000 individuals. Jerzy Rusiecki, Od A do Z, p. 498

18. Many Poles believe that voluntary association membership is for school children and not something for adults in society. In fact, most organizations in Poland recruit only adult members. This misperception is perhaps attributable to intensive recruitment in schools by DUAs.

19. Goals were taken directly from organization statutes with only insignificant modifications made to avoid wordiness.

20. Different respondents gave different reasons for organizations being "important" to society. In some situations, a justification for a positive evaluation of an organization was more challenging than in others. Responses to why the Polish-Soviet Friendship Society is important included such statements as: "Individually, people do not want to be friends with the Soviet Union. Perhaps it's easier in a group"; "Because without this organization it would be difficult to prove that friendship exists"; "The organization allows us to keep in contact with our lands of Wilno and Lwow"; "To prevent war"; and "I cannot bluff my way through this one. Why don't you help me think of a good answer?"

21. A Polish scholar (March, 1978) reported that "the dissident newspapers are basically tolerated by the regime. Only occasionally are printing presses confiscated and newspaper contributors and distributors arrested."

22. Well over 1,000 of these activists are known by name to the government because of having signed petitions of protest.

8
The Polish Military and the Policy Process

Dale R. Herspring

In view of the important role played by the armed forces in Eastern Europe in the pre-war period, it is surprising that the West has not paid more attention to their current successors. While contemporary Eastern European armed forces probably do not exert as much influence as they once did, their participation in the policy process may serve as a key, not only to the stability of the political system, but also as an important indicator of the course of Soviet-East European military relations.

POLICY FORMULATION AND IMPLEMENTATION

Conceptually, the role of the armed forces in the policy process may be divided into two general categories: policy formulation and policy implementation.[1] The armed forces of an East European state[2] have the potential to affect the course of policy formulation in a number of ways. First, they may attempt to force their own group interests on an unwilling party leadership through political bargaining; second, they may attempt to overthrow the regime by force of arms; and third, they may be able to guide policy in specifically military areas by the expert advice that they provide when called upon.

The views expressed in this chapter are solely those of the writer and do not reflect official State Department policy. I would like to express my appreciation to the following individuals for their helpful comments on earlier versions of this article: A. Ross Johnson, John D. Scalan and Walter D. Connor.

An Eastern European military may affect the implementation of policies largely dependent on military assistance by its willingness to support the regime's policies and by its technical efficiency in implementing such policies. Vigorous military support for unpopular internal policies can be vital to the Party's ability to enact such policies. On the other hand, failure by the military to support the regime--or even lukewarm support in some cases--ultimately can force the government to back down or to call on the Soviets for assistance. At the same time, the best-intentioned military is of little use to the Party if it does not show a high degree of combat readiness. For example, a military which is technically deficient is not likely to be relied upon by the Soviets. This, in turn, can weaken the regime's ability to get Soviet concessions in other areas as a trade-off for that country's military contribution to the Warsaw Pact.

POLICY FORMULATION AND THE POLISH MILITARY

As an Interest Group

Numerous discussions with a wide variety of East Europeans, including Poles, suggest that the armed forces of Eastern Europe are not involved nearly to the same extent in the discussions of questions of military policy formulation as are their Soviet counterparts in their domestic setting. As a result, the unifying force of a civilian-military confrontation over questions of policy formulation is generally missing. Such confrontations may be vital to the development of the professional officer corps--which is generally split internally over numerous issues--into a cohesive interest group. To a large degree, this situation is a result of Soviet domination of the Warsaw Pact decision-making process of military related matters. The subject of defense expenditures serves as a useful example.

Unlike the situation in the USSR or China, where the subject of defense spending may result in a military-civilian confrontation, armies such as those of Poland are only indirectly involved in fiscal negotiations; these decisions are generally made within the context of the Soviet-dominated Warsaw Pact. In the final analysis, decisions concerning defense expenditures are a subject for political discussion between the Soviet political leadership and the leadership of the country concerned, rather than for military-civilian debate at the national level.

Thus, the Polish army's primary means of influencing the size of the military budget is not lobbying within its own system, although some of this may occur, but rather cultivating contacts with Soviet military colleagues.[3] Polish officers desiring modernization would devote substantial energy to convincing their Soviet contacts of the necessity for more modern weapons systems. Assuming that the Soviets agreed and that new demands were leveled on the Polish armed forces by the Warsaw Pact, the question of whether or not the Polish political system could afford such expenditures ultimately would become a political question for resolution between Brezhnev and Gierek (e.g., would the shift of funds from the consumer to the military sector seriously affect political stability in Poland).

While Polish military writers generally avoid discussing in detail the relationship between the Warsaw Pact and the individual states in the military area, statements by some East European military writers suggest that the comments of the East Europeans cited above are generally accurate, particularly as they relate to the budgetary process. For example, an East German officer has stated:

> The Military Council attached to the Unified Command and the Staff of the Unified Command are <u>obligated to decide problems of military construction and expansion of the unified armed forces, their armament and equipment, the continued improvement of the organization of the troops and increases in the firepower and combat readiness of these troops</u>.[4]

The presence of Polish military officers on both the Military Council and the Military Staff and Joint Command of the Warsaw Pact provide them with an excellent opportunity to make their wishes and needs known to their Soviet counterparts.

Assuming that this model of civil-military relations in Poland is correct, one would expect to find a close relationship between Polish military elites and their Soviet counterparts, thereby maximizing Soviet influence in these armed forces. After all, almost all Polish flag officers attend Soviet service academies and speak Russian. In general, however, this does not appear to be the case. Two factors appear to account for this contradiction: first, the continued existence of national animosities, and second, the growing professionalism of the Polish army. The latter, as Ross Johnson suggests, may be leading to increased dissatisfaction on the part of East European military elites with Moscow's decision to send the latest military equipment to areas outside of Eastern Europe.[5]

One can argue, as one writer has with reference to the GDR, that the presence of the Defense Minister on the Politburo indicates that the military plays an important role in the policy formulation process.[6] While there is no doubt that Jaruzelski occupies an important and influential position in the party leadership, I propose that this is a normal situation in Poland, for his predecessors, Spychalski and Rokossowski, were both members of the Politburo. Jaruzelski's promotion to the four-star rank of General of the Army in 1973 is also not a sign of increased importance for the armed forces. Past Polish Defense Ministers (e.g., Spychalski, Rokossowski, Zymierski) have held the five star rank of Marshal of Poland and, as a result, Jaruzelski, who is the first professional Polish soldier to have attained the position of Defense Minister, is still one rank below his predecessors. Furthermore, his promotion to the four-star rank coincided with the promotion of Heinz Hoffmann, the GDR Minister of Defense, to the East German Politburo. Jaruzelski had been a member of the PUWP Politburo, but only a three-star general. Hoffmann had held the four-star rank, but was not a Politburo member. As a result of these promotions, they became equals, thereby signifying the symbolic equality of the two most important East European armed forces within the Pact.

The lack of frequent direct party-military confrontations in the area of policy formulation may help account for the significantly lower level of military representation on high level decision-making bodies in East European countries as compared with the USSR. Professional military representation on the Central Committee in the USSR, for example, has averaged 7-9 percent since 1952, while in Poland it has averaged about 4 percent.[7] This is particularly true of the period beginning in 1968 as shown in Figure 8.1.

In spite of the higher percentage of profes-

FIGURE 8.1
Central Committee Membership: Professional Military
Poland-USSR

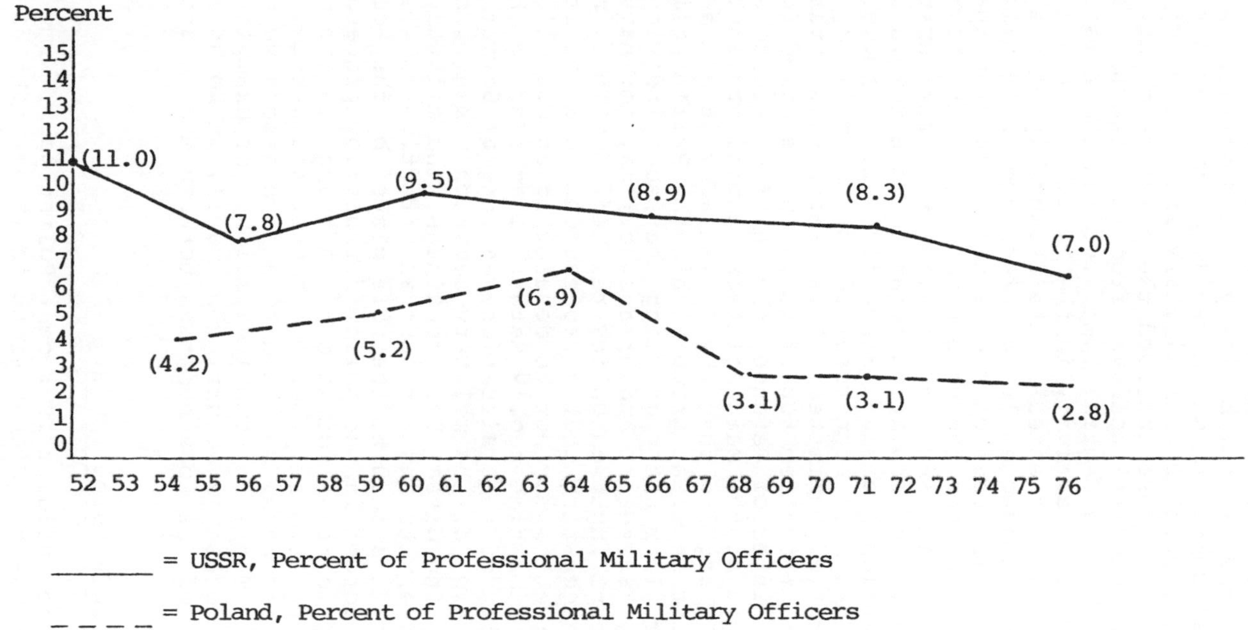

sional military officers on the Central Committee in 1959 and 1964, the military did not function as an effective interest group during those years. Instead, the size of military representation on the Central Committee was a result of two factors that had little to do with military interest group activity. These included the presence of at least one "pro-Soviet" holdover from the Rokossowski period on the Central Committee and the existence of factional activity in the Party, which was inevitably reflected in the leadership of the armed forces. Consequently, a larger number of military men were included on the Central Committee than would have been the case normally. With the defeat of Moczar in 1968, and Borzikowski's retirement, military representation began to move toward an institutional basis. Since 1971, for example, three positions have been reserved for the military on the Central Committee. These seats have invariably gone to the three top officers in the armed forces: the Minister of Defense, the Chief of Staff, and the Head of the Main Political Administration.[9]

In arguing that the Polish army is not a cohesive interest group within the Polish political system, I am not suggesting that some individuals (e.g., Jaruzelski and Urbanowicz) may not have an important input on policy-related questions, nor am I suggesting that a professional and institutional ethos may not be developing as Costello noted some time ago.[10] Rather, I am arguing that, in spite of this situation, as long as Soviet domination of the military decision-making process within the Warsaw Pact continues, the military is not likely to develop into an effective interest group; as a result, the role played by the Polish armed forces in the policy-formulation process is likely to be a limited one. A change in the military relationship between Moscow and Warsaw, on the other hand, may lead to a more assertive military. There is some indication, for example, that this process is occurring primarily in Romania as a result of the loosened ties between Moscow and Bucharest.[11]

The Coup Possibility ...

One incident in recent Polish party-army relations--the Gdansk riots in 1970--might be viewed as a direct civil-military confrontation with the potential of a military coup. According to one account of the events surrounding the riots, the

Polish Army not only ignored commands from Zenon Kliszko, Gomulka's deputy, to use repressive force in putting down the disturbances, but also refused to support Gomulka against Gierek.[12] Neither event, however, appears to have involved an attempt by the armed forces to use coercive force against the political leadership. Rather, they underscore the military's efforts to remain politically neutral.

Two factors appear to have influenced the military leaders in their attitudes toward these two events. First, senior military leaders may have been concerned about the political reliability of the armed forces if employed in a repressive manner against striking workers. Secondly, there has long been a distinction in Poland between the nation and the state. The armed forces have been viewed primarily as serving the interests of the Polish nation, while the police/security apparatus generally is seen as the servant of the state.[13] This is a distinction jealously guarded by the military. As a result, the armed forces may have tried to avoid involvement in civil matters such as the Gdansk riots in order to maintain a "division of labor" which emphasizes their linkage to the Polish "people" (nation). The same is true of the Gomulka-Gierek struggle. The Polish armed forces fought a long battle to get out of politics (Spychalski acted as an inhibiting factor in this regard because of his very close identification with Gomulka). It was only with the appointment of Wociech Jaruzelski as Defense Minister in 1968 that a professional career Polish officer who had not been closely involved in politics was given this important post. The military leadership in 1970 probably wanted to avoid actions which might have reversed this situation.

Providing Expert Advice

The military certainly is called upon to provide expert advice in technical areas, e.g., the effect of agricultural work on the combat readiness of the Polish armed forces. Nevertheless, the military's apparent failure to engage in direct negotiations with the political leadership on such vital issues as the size and composition of the military budget, types of equipment, etc., seriously limits its influence in this area.

While the military's role in policy formulation is limited, this is not true in the area of policy implementation. In fact, the role of the armed forces in this area is of critical importance.

POLICY IMPLEMENTATION AND THE POLISH MILITARY

The Internal Factor

While military involvement in the policy implementation process on the Polish domestic scene is generally limited to projects such as providing assistance at harvest time, or constructing civilian items such as bridges, highways or railroads, the actions of the armed forces may assume a more critical character in times of political turbulence.

Internal disturbances are generally the responsibility of the police/security forces. The military is called in to help deal with such matters only when the police or security forces show themselves unable to resolve them. Consequently, the actions of the military may be vital. Failure to support the regime could force the government either to back down before mass demands, or, perhaps, to call on the Soviets for assistance.

The Polish government has called on the armed forces to put down internal disturbances on three occasions. Unfortunately, from the Party's standpoint, the military's record is not very encouraging. In all three cases, the armed forces failed to support the Party.

Poznan, 1956. Regular army troops refused to disperse the rioters, and in some cases joined them. This made it necessary to bring in special security forces from Warsaw.[14]

Gdansk, 1970. The army strongly resisted involvement in putting down the riots and, according to one observer, disobeyed Kliszko's demand to use "overwhelming force to put down the demonstrations."[15]

Lodz and Warsaw, 1976. Defense Minister Jaruzelski, when asked about the possibility of using any troops to put down the riots, is reported to have stated that, "Polish soldiers will not fire on Polish workers."[16] As a result, the price increases previously announced by Jaroszewicz were rescinded.

A number of factors help to account for this situation. First, the above mentioned hesitancy on the part of the Polish armed forces to become involved in domestic politics probably plays a role. More important, however, is the continued problem that the regime faces in building up what Almond and Verba have called a "normative commitment"[17] to the Polish state. After all, the armed forces are primarily staffed by conscripts. While it is possible to enhance the loyalty of the professional military by offering it rewards not available to the remainder of society (e.g., special stores, special housing), this is not true of conscripts. Conscripts come from society at large and their loyalty to the regime need not reflect that of a special "pampered" semi-isolated societal group such as the professional military. Rather, their orientation to the system mirrors that of society at large. These young men may be asked to fire on their own countrymen--and in some cases on their friends and relatives. Their "definition of the situation" will therefore be important. Based on the three events mentioned above, it would appear that the Polish government must still travel some distance to reach the point of convincing its own people that it is primarily interested in the "national interest" in the internal sphere, and thus worthy of support against internal opponents.

The fact that the armed forces are of rather limited utility in a crisis situation undoubtedly weakens Party control over the larger Polish political process. In the external sphere, however, this fact, when combined with the populace's willingness to defend the Polish "nation" against external threats regardless of the costs, may actually strengthen the PUWP's hand in its dealings with Moscow.

The External Factor

Guaranteeing Polish Independence. While stories about Polish soldiers charging German tanks during World War II may be untrue, as one Polish military historian has argued,[18] the heroic qualities of the Polish soldier in defense of the Polish nation are legend. This is as true of the battles waged by the underground home army as it is of the more conventional battles waged by units of Polish army--both the London-based units and Berling's pro-Soviet forces. As Jerzy Wiatr put it:

> The Polish national hero is typically a military man, distinguished by his sacrifices in the struggle for the future of his country.

> He is not necessarily victorious. In fact, the greatest national heros of modern times have been those whose destiny it was to suffer defeat and death at the hands of enemies.[19]

This attitude toward defense of the Polish nation has continued to the present day. For example, the willingness of important segments of the Polish army in 1956 to support, with military force if necessary, the party leadership's resistance to Soviet pressure over Gomulka's appointment as First Secretary had, in the minds of most observers, an important impact on Moscow's decision to back down.[20] Furthermore, there are rumors that the Polish army took defensive measures to assure the "neutrality" of the Soviet forces in Poland at the time of the Gdansk riots in 1970, and most Western observers agree that a Soviet military intervention in the summer of 1976 would have been opposed by the Polish army.

This situation considerably strengthens the party leadership's room for maneuver vis-a-vis Moscow, particularly in an age of detente. In fact, one could argue, as has Christopher Jones,[21] that this fear of facing military opposition has played an important role in Moscow's hesitancy to "normalize" the situation in Poland. Such an action--particularly if it were bloody and protracted--could cause considerable problems for the Soviets in their relations with Western countries, in addition to the heavy direct costs of such an action. Consequently, the Soviets have tolerated Poland's considerable internal autonomy and have advanced aid during Poland's economic difficulties on more than one occasion, as a means of assuring political stability. Thus, the Polish military serves an important, if unintended, function in assisting the Party in its efforts to maximize its independence from Moscow.

The military also plays other significant roles in the external sphere. For example, Poland remains an important weapons producer, ranking third in the Warsaw Pact behind the Soviet Union and Czechoslovakia as shown in Table 8.1. While the extent of the role played by the military in this area is unknown, if the Soviet case is any indication it is probably an important one. This is particularly true since, unlike the Czechoslovaks who use weapons production as a means of earning hard currency, the vast majority of Polish weapons are intended for internal consumption within the

TABLE 8.1
Arms Transfers: Czechoslovakia, the USSR, Poland; 1965-1976[22]

(Millions of U.S. dollars in current dollars)

Year	Czechoslovakia	The USSR	Poland
1965	161	1310	141
1966	172	1660	142
1967	200	1920	144
1968	77	1550	151
1969	109	1110	154
1970	109	1530	151
1971	122	1610	173
1972	132	2840	86
1973	128	5040	119
1974	223	4880	135
1975	371	3780	106
1976	353	3747	145

Warsaw Pact. Thus the quality of these weapons is important for Poland's relations with other Pact countries. The fact that all of the USSR's Polnocny class landing craft were produced in Poland attests not only to their quality, but probably to the fact that the Polish military was closely involved in their production.

The Polish military also plays an important role in policy implementation as a result of its participation in international peace-keeping forces. Such an action, however, is a two-edged sword. It may be highly advantageous to the Party and state if Poland's military role is not controversial, and if it raises Poland's international prestige. This appears to have been the case, for example, with Poland's military participation in the Middle East Peace Keeping Force. On the other hand, if Polish participation is controversial, as was the case with the International Control Commission in Vietnam, it may complicate Poland's relations with important noncommunist countries. However, even in the Vietnamese case, involvement probably won the Poles points in Moscow, as a result of their willingness to sacrifice their relations with some Western countries for the sake of "proletarian internationalism."

The important role played by the Polish armed forces within the Warsaw Pact also has a significant effect on Polish policy implementation in the external sphere. Geographically, the Polish armed forces play a very important role in Pact strategy. They are located in the Northern Tier region (Poland, the GDR, and Czechoslovakia) and, together with the Czechoslovaks and East Germans, have received the most modern Soviet equipment earlier than other non-Soviet Pact forces. This is also the region where most major military maneuvers have been concentrated.

Poland also has the largest and, by some standards, the most modern of all non-Soviet Pact Forces.[23] In addition, as its performance in past maneuvers and the Middle East indicates, it is a highly professional, well-trained army. While there may be some question about its political reliability in an offensive campaign against the West,[24] it can probably be relied upon to fight well under two circumstances: first, in a defensive war, particularly if Germans are the aggressors, and second, in a preemptive attack on NATO, provided the vast majority of Poles were convinced that the attack was necessary in order to stave off a German invasion. Thus, assuming that Moscow's professed concern about the possibility of German militarism is not meant solely for propaganda purposes. the Polish armed forces can be viewed by the Soviets as a welcome addition to their own forces.

CONCLUSION

The Polish military plays a limited role in the area of policy formulation and, given the combination of the present military relationship between Moscow and Warsaw, this is likely to remain true for the indefinite future. The role of the armed forces in policy implementation, on the other hand, has been significant.

The Party leadership gains several advantages from the military's role in the area of policy implementation. Its apparent willingness to militarily resist a Soviet invasion not only helps increase the Party leadership's freedom of maneuver in the internal sphere, but also limits Moscow's ability to "normalize" the situation in Poland during a crisis. The military's role in the weapons industry helps in relations with other Pact members, while its participation in international peace-keeping forces also has important effects on Poland's foreign relations. Furthermore, while the Soviets may have some doubts about the political reliability of the Polish armed forces in an offensive campaign against the West, the Poles' strong martial tradition and intense love of homeland weigh significantly in Moscow's professed strategy for responding to an attack from the West.

NOTES

1. The author has dealt with this topic in the GDR in Dale R. Herspring, "The Military Factor in the Formulation and Implementation of Foreign Policy in the GDR," forthcoming in Eberhard Schulz, Peter C. Ludz, and S. Scheuner, Hanbuch uber die Aussenpolitik der DDR.

2. When speaking of the Polish army, primary attention is focused on the officer corps. I am not assuming that the officer corps normally acts and thinks as a monolithic entity. Nor do I assume that party-military relations are primarily characterized by institutional conflict. In the normal course of bureaucratic politics, the armed forces are as split by intra-group rivalries as are other bureaucratic organizations. It is only when either vital military interests are challenged by the party leadership or a serious variance in values develops between the officer corps and the party leadership, that the professional military closes ranks in acting against the party leadership and serious institutional conflict may develop. For a discussion of the various conceptual frameworks utilized for analyzing civil-military relations in communist systems (including Poland) see the articles in Dale R. Herspring and Ivan Volgyes, eds., Civil-Military Relations in Communist Systems. Boulder: Westview Press, 1978; and the forthcoming special issue of Studies in Comparative Communism under the author's editorship entitled, "Civil-Military Relations in Communist Systems: First Steps Toward a Theory."

3. Kent Brown has provided an interesting framework for analyzing this type of relationship. See, Kent Brown, "Coalition Politics and Soviet Influence in Eastern Europe," in Jan Triska and Paul Cocks, eds., *Political Development in Eastern Europe*. New York: Praeger Special Studies, 1977, pp. 241-255.

4. Col. Richard Wustner, *Waffenbruder-Vereint Unbesiegbar*. (Comrades in Arms - United, Unconquerable). Berlin: Deutscher Militarverlag, 1975, p. 27. Emphasis added. Additional references on the important role played by the Warsaw Pact in the area include: Col. E. Jedziaka, *Braterstwo Broni*, (Brotherhood in Arms). Warsaw: Ministerstwo Obrony Narodowej, 1975, pp. 499, 505, 506; Col. Gen. P.I. Efimoba, *Boevoy Soyuz Bratskikh Armiy*, (Combat Unity of the Brotherly Armies). Moscow: Ministerstwo OboronySSSR, 1974, pp. 20-22; and Laszlo Serfozo, *Bratok, fegyvertarsak,* (Friends, Conrades-in-Arms), Budapest: Zrinyi, 1976, p. 138. I would like to thank Ivan Volgyes for bringing the Hungarian source to my attention.

5. A. Ross Johnson, "Soviet-East European Military Relations: An Overview," in Herspring and Volgyes, eds., *Civil-Military Relations in Communist Systems*. Boulder: Westview Press, 1978, p. 262.

6. Karl Wilhelm Fricke, "Die Militars in der DDR-Fuhrung," (The Military in the GDR Leadership), *Deutschland Archiv,* Nr. 3, (1974), p. 231.

7. For the USSR, see, Dale R. Herspring, "Why Communist Militaries Don't Revolt - the Polish and East German Cases," paper presented at the 1977 American Political Science Convention. The Polish figures breakdown as follows:

Year	Size of CC	Total Military	Percent of CC
1948	71	2	2.8
1954	94	4	4.2
1959	76	4	5.2
1964	86	6	6.9
1968	95	3	3.1
1971	90	3	3.3
1976	140	4	2.8

Individuals included as professional military include: 1948, Marian Spychalski, Kazimierz Witaszewski; 1954, Jerzy Borzikowski, Konstanty Rokossowski, Stanislaw Poplawski, Kazimierz Witaszewski; 1959, Jerzy Borzikowski, Grzegorz Korczynski, Marian Spychalski, Kazimierz Witaszewski; 1964, Jerzy Borzikowski, Grzegorz Korczynski, Kazimierz Witaszewski, Wojciech Jaruzelski, Marian Spychalski, Czeslaw Waryszak; 1968, Wojciech Jaruzelski, Grzegorz Korcsynski, Marian Spychalski; 1971, Wojciech Jaruzelski, Jan Czapla, Jozef Urbanowicz; 1976, Wojciech Jaruzelski, Sylwester Kaliski, Wodzimierz Sawczuk and Jozef Urbanowicz. These figures differ significantly from those suggested by Carl Beck and Karen Rawling, "The Military as a Channel of Entry into Positions of Leadership in Communist Party States," Armed Forces and Society, III (1977), p. 209. The primary reason for this difference results from Beck and Rawlings' reliance on "military service as a general, admiral, member of a general staff or commander in chief" as the defining criteria for a professional military officer (pp. 208-209), while I have relied on "Ten years service as a military officer primarily in communist militaries, as well as service as an active military officer while a member of the Central Committee" as the defining criteria for professional military representation.

8. Although ethnically Polish, Jerzy Borzikowski was a former Soviet officer who rose to the rank of Lt. General in the Soviet Engineering Corps. His continued presence on the Central Committee well after the events of 1956 was only indirectly a result of his role within the Polish military hierarchy. Rather, it was primarily a concession to the Soviets who were anxious to avoid a complete "Polonization" of the upper ranks of the Polish army, thereby making the break with the pre-1956 period even more explicit.

Mieczysaw Moczar, who spent the majority of his postwar career in the security apparatus, was the leader of a group of veterans of the wartime communist underground movement known as the "partisans," who were militantly nationalistic, anti-intellectual, and anti-revisionistic. During the mid-sixties, Moczar and his followers clashed with Gomulka over liberalizing tendencies within the Party, and may have attempted to challenge Gomulka's primacy within the Party.

9. Although Sylwester Kalicki was a professional military officer, he was a member of the Central Committee from 1976 until his death in August 8, 1978 primarily because he was Minister of Science and Technology, not because he was a professional soldier.

10. Michael Costello, "The Party and the Military in Poland," Radio Free Europe Research, Poland/12, April 26, 1971.

11. See, Walter M. Bacon, "The Military and the Party in Romania," in Herspring and Volgyes, eds., Civil-Military Relations in Communist Systems. Boulder: Westview Press, 1978, pp. 165-180.

12. Costello, "The Party and the Military in Poland," pp. 2-3.

13. In Poland, "the state" generally refers to the governmental structure, while "the nation" refers to the often metaphysical concept of "Polishness." Polish states come and go, but the Polish nation is eternal. For an excellent discussion of the Polish view of the professional soldier, see Jerzy Wiatr, "The Public Image of the Polish Military: Past and Present," in Catherine M. Kelleher, ed., Political-Military Systems: Comparative Perspectives. Beverly Hills: Sage Publications, 1974, pp. 199-208.

14. Flora Lewis, A Case History of Hope. New York: Doubleday 1958, p. 143; Richard Hiscocks, Poland: Bridge for the Abyss? New York: Oxford University Press, 1963, p. 192.

15. Costello, "The Party and Military in Poland," pp. 1-2.

16. The statement has been related to the author by several recent travelers to Poland.

17. Gabriel Almond and Sidney Verba, The Civic Culture. Boston: Little, Brown and Company, 1965, Chapter 1, pp. 1-44.

18. Zbigniew Zaluski, Siedem Polskich Grzechow (Seven Main Polish Sins). Warsaw: Czytelnik, 1962.

19. Wiatr, "The Public Image of the Polish Military," p. 199.

20. Nicholas Bethell, Gomulka, His Poland, His Communism. New York: Holt, Rinehart and Winston, 1969, p. 215; Laszlo Reversz, "Die Polnische Volksarmee," (The Polish People's Army) in Peter Gosztony, ed., Zur Geschichte der europaischen Volksarmeen (Toward a History of the European People's Armies), Bonn-Bad Godesberg: Hohwacht, 1976, p. 33; Adam Ulam, Expansion and Coexistence: The History of Soviet Foreign Policy, 1917-1967. New York: Praeger, 1968, pp. 591-592.

21. Christopher D. Jones, "Soviet Hegemony in East Europe: The Dynamics of Political Autonomy and Military Intervention," World Politics, XXIV (1977), pp. 216-241.

22. Arms Control and Disarmament Agency, World Military Expenditures and Arms Transfers, 1967-1976. Washington: U.S. Government Printing Office, 1978, pp. 128, 145, 149 for 1967-1976. For 1965-1966, see the 1976 edition of this publication, pp. 59, 68, 69.

23. See, Dale R. Herspring, "Technology and the Changing Political Officer in the Polish and East German Armed Forces," Studies in Comparative Communism, X, no. 2 (1977).

24. The question of political reliability in the East European Warsaw Pact forces is treated in some detail in Dale R. Herspring and Ivan Volgyes, "Toward a Conceptualization of Political Reliability in East European Warsaw Pact Armed Forces," forthcoming in Armed Forces and Society.

9
Church and State in Gierek's Poland

Vincent Chrypinski

The incorporation of Poland into the Soviet bloc opened an era of historic encounter between the Catholic Church and the ruling communist party. The circumstance presented both sides with new and difficult problems accentuated not only by doctrinal differences and historically conditioned prejudices, but also by popular attitudes toward both entities.

On the eve of the war's end, Polish communists could not count on a large degree of genuine support among their countrymen. The Communist Party of Poland (CPP) had a narrow base of social support since the industrial working class was relatively small. During the interwar years, the party's peak membership, largely Jewish, amounted to 12,000.[1] The influence of the party was limited by prevailing views that it was a foreign product serving the interests of the Soviet Union. Traditional anti-Russian and anti-communist postures of the majority of Poles were fortified during the war by new bitter experiences of the Soviet occupation of eastern Poland, the Katyn massacre, the Warsaw Uprising, and the behavior of Soviet troops during their westward offensives. The depth of general hostility may be fathomed from a July 1944 report submitted by communists from a county in the Lublin province to their superiors, in which they described their position succinctly as that of a small island in the ocean of ideological enemies.[2]

The situation of the Church was diametrically different. Since Poland accepted Christianity in 966, Catholicism became the national religion and the Roman Catholic Church became a national institution. Imbedded in the national fabric many centuries ago, Polish Catholicism represented not only a system of religious beliefs and sacramental acts, but also an embodiment of Polish cultural values and prescriptions. Quite clearly, it carried implications of a social and political nature, and consequently exerted a considerable impact on popular attitudes toward political ideologies and institutions. As might be expected, the Church--while condemning the evils resulting from capitalism--had a negative attitude toward socialism, class conflicts, and liquidation of private property as contrary to social order and to natural law.

When their country fell under communist rule, very many Poles, perhaps the majority, looked up to the Church not only for spiritual guidance but also for political direction. To many, the communist regime appeared only as a transitional phenomenon, an "interregnum" before a legitimate government would take over. In between, as in the prepartitioned Polish kingdom, the national leadership was to rest in the hands of authorities of the Church, which symbolized the cultural and historical continuity of free Poland.

Beyond doubt, the Polish communists had a strong temptation to strike in the early period and subordinate the Church to their demands. However, this might have been dangerous as it could have provoked an overwhelming reaction and led to a bloody civil war. Thus, it was decided to avoid a violent confrontation and try to realize ideological goals by gradual methods. As is generally known, over the thirty-plus years of uneasy state-church coexistence, there were periods of sharp and dramatic struggles followed by spells of tranquility and compromise. On the whole, the Church has held her ground in the defense of her own spiritual mission and of her place within Polish society. Indeed, the moral authority of the Church grew even larger and was recognized not only by the faithful but by nonbelievers as well.[3]

An historical survey of the postwar era in Poland reveals the existence of several ever-present issues which play a permanent role in influencing the shape of state-church relations in that country. As might be expected, they manifest themselves very strongly in the course of intense controversies. Even then, however, variations and mutations in emphasis placed on some fundamentals by either side occur.

OBJECTIVES OF THE CHURCH

Preservation of the Church's Unity

In postwar Poland, where the new rulers attempted to impose on all organizations the exclusive supremacy of the state, the Catholic Church became a main object of the communist offensive. It was concentrated on two fronts: relations with Rome and the domestic homogeneity of the Catholics.

According to Vatican sources,[4] the ultimate aim of the communist religious policy was to create in Poland a schismatic national church which, separated from Rome, was to submit more easily to political controls. The open hostility was manifested as early as September 1945 when the communist-dominated "Provisional Government of National Unity" abrogated the concordat of 1925. Probably the peak of communist efforts to estrange Polish Catholics from the Vatican came during the 1950-1951 period, and was associated with governmental action to change the canonical status of ecclesiastical administrators in the Recovered Territories where the Holy See refused to appoint regular diocesan bishops before the final signing of a peace treaty.[5]

It must be recalled that external circumstances provided a conducive atmosphere for the communist anti-Vatican offensive. The Cold War strongly accentuated the division of Europe, and the barrier of the iron curtain seriously jeopardized communications with Rome. The Moscow-heralded passage to a higher stage in the process of building socialism brought to Poland intensification of Marxist indoctrination and tightening of political controls. The application of ruthless terror paved the way for communist machinations.

But the events did not catch the Church by surprise. Already in 1945, Pope Pius XII invested the Primate of Poland, Cardinal August Hlond, who was returning to his homeland by way of Rome from war-long exile abroad, with a special personal grant which entitled him to exercise extensive powers in case of an isolation of the Polish Church from Rome. Although the text of the document was never published, it may be assumed that it did not preclude negotiations and pacts with the regime. With the death of Cardinal Hlond in 1948, the authorization was transferred to his successor, Archbishop Stefan Wyszynski. Utilizing his prerogatives, the new Primate concluded, in 1950 and 1956, two unprecedented agreements with the Warsaw government.

More than one appraisal of those compacts is possible, but it cannot be denied that, in the long run, they proved beneficial to the Church. They also ingrained Polish bishops, and especially Cardinal Wyszynski, with the sense of their own independence in coping with domestic problems, including church-state relations. When, in the 1960s, the Vatican started to promote its new Ostpolitik in Poland, it discovered very shortly that the Warsaw-Rome dealings must be accompanied by parallel negotiations between the Polish government and the Polish Episcopate.[6] Of course, the issue had nothing to do with unquestionable obedience of Polish bishops to the pope in matters of religion and morals. The election of Cardinal Wojtyla to Peter's throne will definitely pave the way to deeper understanding and fuller coordination between the Holy See and the Polish Church in other questions as well.

Although communist endeavors had only limited success and were not able to significantly weaken the Church in Poland, Polish bishops became very sensitive to potential dangers associated with the existence of Catholic splinter groups. Their apprehension was fortified by persistent, though not uniform, support extended to "Pax" by governmental officials during the post-October era. Thanks to their benevolence, the movement extended its organizational network throughout the country, and counted toward the end of 1975, i.e., after thirty years of its existence, about 15,000 adherents among whom--according to "Pax" sources--were over 1,800 priests.[7] Not without importance is the fact that "Pax" has permission to publish several newspapers and magazines, some reaching readers far beyond the organizational circle. Among them, the most popular is a well-edited Warsaw daily Slowo Powszechne, which has a circulation of 90,000 copies (200,000 on weekends).

The attempts of "Pax" to infiltrate the ranks of clergymen and to pressure the Episcopate into concessions toward the regime met with vigorous and determined reaction from the bishops. "Pax" periodicals were removed from the list of Catholic publications, and an earlier imprimatur was revoked for issuance of religious books. The leaders of the movement were on several occasions directly admonished, usually in the form of a letter signed by the Secretary of the Episcopate (earlier by Bishop Choromanski, and later by Bishop Dabrowski). In the letter of July 8, 1971, whose full text was published abroad by a Polish journalist,[8] there is a passage which clearly shows the main concern of the Polish bishops. It reads: "the unity of the Church in Poland is one of the greatest values of today, whose preservation the Episcopate considers as its pastoral duty. Therefore, the Polish Episcopate will resist all endeavors which, consciously or subconsciously, attempt to destroy this unity."

For the time being, the danger from "Pax" is not very great. The uncertain political situation in Poland, generational conflict within the organization's leadership, and the prolonged illness and then recent death of Boleslaw Piasecki have imposed definite restraints on the movement. It is doubtful, however, that the communist patrons will abandon it and allow it to slip into oblivion.

As might be expected, the Episcopate is acutely sensitive to any signs of communist infiltration of the Polish clergy. Thus, the bishops categorically objected to attempts at replacing "priests-patriots"--who disappeared in the wake of Polish October--with the "Circles of Priests" formed, since 1955, by the Association of Catholics which administers the remnants of the once vigorous charitable organization "Caritas", taken away from the Church in 1950. While the Association formally abided by the bishops' request, in fact the groups of Caritas priests were retained, and new ones were established under the name of "Communal Circles of Priests".

But this is not all. In order to reach and attract more priests, the association became the prime mover in the creation of a Retirement Fund for Priests. It is obvious that clergymen joining the Fund would expose themselves to extra-clerical influences and would become dependent upon governmental institutions.

Faced with the new threat to the unity of the Church, the Episcopate issued collectively, on August 7, 1978, a strong letter to "Carissimi Confratres"[9] in which the bishops requested all priests connected with either the Association of Catholics, Circles of Priests, or the Retirement Fund to leave these organizations. It is unknown, as yet, how the order has been carried out.

The Struggle Against Secularization

A less dramatic but no less important issue for the Church in Poland is the process of secularization of the Polish masses. Before World War II, the whole system of legal norms and social customs created an environment in which the acceptance and perpetuation of religious elements in the life of a Catholic was an automatic, almost subconscious act. There existed, to be sure, some atheist centers, but they were few in number and small in size, and their influence on the Catholic masses was next to nil. A somewhat greater impact was exercised by anti-clericalism but, since it did not go beyond attacks on priests' profits and morals, it did not lead to crises of faith and to breaks with the Church.

But after World War II, the situation started to undergo many and varied alterations. Most of them occurred under the impact of twin processes of rapid urbanization and intensive industrialization. Both occurrences brought basic transformations in all areas of human life, including religious attitudes and practices of Catholics. Studies among dwellers of Polish urban areas undergoing industrialization demonstrate two phenomena. One shows that, on the whole, religiosity of townspeople remains at a relatively high level[10] and even experiences an increase in comparison to the prewar situation.[11] At the same time, however, it is clearly discernible that industrialization leads to the weakening and gradual atrophy of religious postures and to slackening of bonds with the Church. Characteristically, religious indifferentism is spreading more widely than atheism.[12]

The Church, aware of the dangers of secularization, was obliged to start a not too easy mission of "internal apostolate". Its goal was to protect the diminishing sphere of sacrum against a spontaneous encroachment of profanum. The task was made doubly difficult by communist-sponsored drives toward secularization of public life and legal institutions, as well as an official promotion of atheism.

The secularization impetus, which had already started in 1944 with the elimination of the religious formula of an oath of office, continued after 1956, and--according to a Marxist scholar[13]--resulted in the complete secularization of public life in Poland. The reaction of the Church to various phases of secularization varied with the nature of the problem. In some cases, for instance in those affecting judicial procedures, there was no opposition openly expressed. In others, the resistance was manifested in different forms and degrees.

The reforms of marriage laws and of the school system caused a very pronounced and persistent counteraction. The teaching of religion to school children was an object of permanent confrontation between state and church.

The elimination of religious teaching from Polish schools was high on the list of the communists' priorities. They realized, however, that a frontal legislative attack might provoke an overwhelming reaction of the Church. Thus, they decided to slow the tempo and use not the parliament but rather administrative officials to achieve their purpose. The results were not long in coming. While in 1959-1960 religion was still taught in 21,500 primary and secondary schools (out of 28,000), the following year the number dropped to only 6,500.[14] Clearly, such a dramatic reversal could be produced only by the use of administrative coercion. The statute of July 15, 1961, proclaiming the secularization of schools,[15] put an ex post seal on an accomplished fact which openly violated the modus vivendi of 1956 and marked a serious threat to the Church.

But the bishops were not overwhelmed by a sense of helplessness. In addition to strong protests and pastoral letters reminding parents of their responsibilities, the Episcopate started organizing religious instructions outside of the schools. Already in 1958, a program of catechization was ready for implementation, and early the next year the first "catechetic points" were launched for pupils attending schools without religious instruction. Their number grew with the needs and, by the 1970-1971 school year, reached an impressive amount of over 18,500, of which around 8,500 were accommodated in private homes, the rest in parochial and monastic quarters. It is not publicly known how many pupils attend catechism classes, but Church sources[16] speak of "several million." Instructions are given by about 6,500 priests, 500 members of religious orders, and 600 laymen,[17] of whom many work thirty or even forty hours a week.

The state's attitude toward extramural teaching of religion was mixed. At first, the authorities were tolerant. Later, however, as on many previous occasions, the regime resorted to administrative chicaneries. The harassment of instructors and pupils, pressures on houseowners permitting the use of their premises for religious instruction, and even reprisals towards parents were widely used by local authorities and bitterly protested by the Church hierarchy.[18] There is no evidence of the effectiveness of governmental measures, but the communists claim that a great majority of parish priests followed the orders of lay authorities, registering "catechetic points" and submitting prescribed annual reports.[19]

Be that as it may, the religious instruction of children formed the greatest obstacle for communist efforts of secularization. Under the impact of external adversities, religious instruction underwent significant changes in its scope and methods, and became closer to man and the purpose of his life. The outcome of the reform was definitely positive.

Perhaps the best measures of success of catechization were the pressures and demands within the Communist Party (PUWP) for an intensification of the "ideological offensive". Its foundations were to be provided by schools which were to foster above all the ideological indoctrination of the Polish youth. An integral part of a long-range campaign to win over the souls of the younger generation was constituted by the increased emphasis on the atheistic features of education. In fact, this aspect seemed to be an organic part and one of the key factors in the educational process. Party and governmental efforts were strenuously supported by the Society for the Propagation of Lay Culture (Polish initials: TKKS) which has undergone under Gierek a substantial revamping and revitalization. In the schools, TKKS engaged in a well-planned and coordinated, often highly imaginative and attractive, campaign to eradicate the effects of religious upbringing at home and counteract the "clerical influences" of the Church.

On the secondary school level, TKKS set up for pupils Clubs of Young Rationalists, which were oriented toward discussion of religious questions pertaining to the personal problems of everyday life. Since the selection of topics and the form of meetings were left pretty much up to the students, the clubs became quite popular. By the spring of 1974, some 2,000 of them were already in existence and more were being organized. In addition, pupils were given an opportunity to enroll in Young Rationalists' Universities, at which courses were offered every second Sunday.

The system of ideological indoctrination of youth was complemented by a number of organizations operating within and outside the schools, such as the associations of scouts (ZHP), students (ZSP), Socialist Youth (ZMS), Rural Youth (ZMW), and Circles of Military Youth (KMW), with a total membership of 4,860,000 members. All of them acted under the leadership and control of the party, promoted "socialist ideals", and organized Polish youth for the "realization of the program of the building of socialism" as determined by the party. In order to better integrate and coordinate the activities of these groups, the Federation of Socialist Organizations of Polish Youth (FSZMP) was formed in 1973, and in April, 1976, ZMS, ZMW, and KMW ceased to exist and were merged into one Union of Socialist Polish Youth.[20]

Defense of Human Rights

From the very beginning of Christianity in Poland, the Catholic Church was closely affiliated with the life of the Polish people and with their societal aspirations. The phenomenon was manifested eminently in the time of the partitions (1795-1918) when the Church provided the chief support for efforts to regain independence. During World War II, the Church was again in the forefront of the struggle for physical survival and national liberation. When the postwar communist rule confronted people with problems vital to the preservation of the moral and material substance of national existence, the Church was once more with her flock.

In recent years, the issue of human rights proved anew that the Church is attuned to the concerns of the people and is not hesitant to assume new responsibilities. Long accustomed to fighting for the freedom of the Church, the Episcopate raised its voice in defense of human and civil liberties endangered by despotic actions of the communist rulers.

As might be expected, the posture of bishops caused a number of anxieties and dilemmas among Polish Catholics, clergymen and laymen alike. Not the least important was the theological problem of involvement of the Church in the organization of the world, in the building of a perfect civitas terrena.[21] Those opposed to direct engagement reasoned that the apostolic mission of the Church consisted in promoting the Kingdom of Christ, which is not of this world. Those in favor stressed that there exists an inextricable connection between the spreading of Gospel about the eschatological Kingdom of God and an active pursuit of justice on earth.

Some pointed out that, in taking a stand on the issue of human rights, the Church remained on its own immemorial ground of Christianity, which always maintained that man enjoys certain inviolable and inalienable rights, not due to any grants from a government or a community, but due to the fact that he is a human being.[22]

Another argument of the opponents stressed the predominant importance of prayer and the inner life over an active struggle against evil. The proponents, while not denying the significance of spirituality, argued that avoiding engagement is a manifestation of man's manicheistic dualism which excludes the material world from the domain of God. The Church, they said, must be the conscience of the world, always vigilant and ready to condemn injustice, always aiding in the spread of human solidarity and of social responsibility. In addition, they insisted, keeping religion shut off from terrestrial problems and limited to private efforts of individual salvation means, in fact, a death sentence for the Church.

Theological aspects were not the only ones the bishops had to consider. It can be safely assumed that they were fully aware of the political ramifications of the issue as well. They certainly realized that the question of human rights formed a bridge between the intelligentsia and the workers, the two important social forces that, in 1968 and 1970, fought their battles in separation. In 1976, when the authorities resorted to widespread persecutions of workers involved in the June riots, the intellectuals rallied to their defense and organized, in September, the Committee for Defense of the Workers (KOR).[23] It is clear that this action resulted in a significant popular following for the KOR leaders who, in case of a new outburst of workers' dissatisfaction with the communist regime, might become the acknowledged heads of a massive unrest. The union would immensely inflame the situation, easily lead to a systemic crisis, and almost certainly cause direct Soviet intervention. The consequences would be disastrous for the entire Polish nation and to all national institutions, the Church not exempted.

At the same time, however, the bishops could not overlook the beneficial effects of KOR and the entire opposition movement.[24] Its existence and activities set the Church free from the role, imposed by circumstances, of a para-political opposition. In the new situation, the Church, acting from a purely evangelical position, can better perform its mission of an impartial critic of socio-political relations. What is more, the critical function can be exercised not only toward the rulers, but also toward the opposition and the entire society as well.

A very sensitive appreciation of such a posture of the Church is demonstrated not only by Catholics but also by representatives of the "Secular Left"[25] who, in spite of various temptations and pressures, reject the idea of a political engagement by the Church. Both realize that the Church is the only institution in Poland with authority among the masses and with the ability to reach them. The Church alone can jolt the conscience of the people, inspire them to a greater involvement in public life, and provide moral guidelines for their participation. Only then can one think of a successful struggle for an authentic democracy in Poland.[26]

Nor is this all. Some Catholics are convinced that the Christian mission has by its very nature a political dimension, since the salvation it preaches encompasses the elimination of the socio-political causes of evil. Some still dream of the Episcopate taking an active part in the formation and leadership of a christian-democratic party, of the restoration of the prewar Labor Party. But Polish bishops, and Cardinal Wyszynski in particular, always remained aloof from such pressures, leaving direct political activities to laymen.

Of course, each fundamental issue raised by the Church could be observed from the two perspectives of religion and politics. This is unavoidable. The Episcopate, however, seldom took a stand on clearly political questions, confining itself largely to spiritual, moral, and, at most, cultural topics. But it would be wrong to assume that the bishops fought only for the right to evangelize and for religious freedom for members of the Church. On the contrary, care for human dignity and the freedom of all people were always in their hearts. Episcopal letters, memoranda to the government, and sermons of Cardinal Wyszynski and other clerical leaders bear witness to the Church's concern in th these matters.

The solicitude of the Episcopate for all people, including Marxists who either rejected their former creed or were ostracized by party leaders for nonconformism, manifested itself very strongly in pastoral letters of March 21 and May 3, 1968.[27] In these two missives, the bishops called for respect of basic rights to truth, freedom, justice, and peace, and strongly protested against the use of physical force against those who express dissenting opinions. They asked for freedom of expression and tolerance, and pointed out the harmful consequences of the domination of society by one group.

The same spirit permeated the Episcopate's utterances after the tragic riots of December 1970.[28] Once again the bishops vigorously stressed that the fatherland belongs to all Poles, and that each of them has the right to feel secure and respected. Urging prayers for all those killed and for those who acted in defense of the just claims of the workers, they also enumerated a roster of basic rights. Among them, freedom of cultural life, social justice, and human dignity accompanied the right of religious freedom.

In the aftermath of June 1976, the Church hierarchy openly championed the cause of oppressed workers. Appealing to authorities on their behalf, the bishops reasoned that the only way to restore peace and to win the confidence of the masses necessary to economic success was by an unflinching respect for man, his labor, and his civil rights.[29]

Protection of Institutional Interests

There is no need to argue that, in order to carry out her mission, the Church must enjoy the maximum possible freedom to organize her own internal life without undue interference from secular authorities. But the ethos of the communist state, strongly monistic in spirit and organization, perpetually challenges the independence of the Church. While Polish bishops, under the influence of pastoral reflection and the experience of events, are adapting themselves to the legal regime of the separation of church and state, party officials use a secular juridical order as justification for various forms of intrusion into clerical affairs.

Although flagrant cases of intervention from the Stalinist time seem to be a thing of the past, the state can still interfere in Church affairs. The legal basis for encroachment was provided by the decree of December 31, 1956.[30] Its text, which somewhat softened the harsh regulations of 1953, retained governmental veto power over appointments of bishops and pastors. The burdensome impact of the rule came to full light after the death, in

1974, if the Archbishop of Wroclaw, Cardinal Boleslaw Kominek. Reportedly, over a dozen candidates were vetoed by the Office for Denominational Affairs before, ultimately, a lucky *ternum* met undefined governmental standards and paved the way for the appointment of Archbishop Henryk Gulbinowicz.

It goes without saying that the authorities are not at all concerned with the pastoral qualifications of candidates for clerical appointments. Their consent is based exclusively on their own bureaucratic criteria, which are sharpened or released according to the needs of the moment. Such a situation must adversely affect the choice of clerical leaders whose unique qualities cannot be measured in terms of political reliability.

But this is not all. The decree also empowers governmental authorities to request disciplining and even removing a clergyman from office when he engages in activities "harmful to the state". This is a powerful and dangerous instrument. By means of these provisions, the government could easily blackmail its opponents and perhaps gain unwilling cooperation from weaker clerics.

All this is very painful for the Church and weighs heavily on relations with the state. A *modus vivendi* with any chances of durability must establish not only a clearer division of the domains, but also generate a better reciprocal climate of mutual relationships. Of course, an agreement must take into consideration other claims of the Church as well. One of them relates to the issue of *Caritas*.

The promotion of charity belongs to the essence of the Christian religion, and the bishops of Poland established over the years thousands of beneficent institutions to carry on the work of love and mercy. A great majority of them were operated by members of religious orders. After World War II, they were united into a national association, under a common name of *Caritas.* The Archbishop of Cracow, Cardinal Adam Sapieha, became its national president.

The organization rendered immense assistance to the needy people of Poland who, after the devastating war, suffered a tremendous shortage of food, medicines, clothes, and many other things of vital importance. The range of *Caritas* activities was immense. Among others, the association fed close to 170,000 orphans in 4,500 centers, took care of over 100,000 old people, and maintained 241 field kitchens which daily provided thousands of the hungry with free hot meals. In addition, *Caritas* organized an extensive campaign against alcoholism and venereal disease, maintained several centers of Catholic social studies, supplied liturgical articles to the churches, and supported the Catholic University of Lublin.

The impressive activities were financed by donations from Catholics abroad, especially from the United States, and by voluntary offerings from the Polish people. Since 1945, Caritas has organized a "Mercy Week" each year in October, which has usually brought large sums of money.

The communists were well aware of the achievements of Caritas and of the impact they had on the attitudes of the Polish people, who regarded the bishops not only as their spiritual leaders, but also as some sort of vicarious government which understands and helps to solve everyday problems. Recognizing the situation, they moved in not only to eliminate possible danger, but also to provide themselves with the means of action of their own.

As usual, the communist campaign started with violent attacks by the controlled press, supplemented by various charges and anti-Church declarations and crowned with an investigation into alleged embezzlement, false bookkeeping, and assistance to subversive elements. As might be expected, the accusations were found true, and on January 25, 1950, the government enforced a new management with a "priest-patriot", Rev. Antoni Lamparty, as the national director. A fundamental part of the Church's life passed into the hands of people collaborating with the regime. All of this was done without notifying the Church authorities, who protested, warned the clergy and faithful, but were forced to retreat before physical violence.

But the Episcopate never gave up its struggle to regain lost charitable institutions. During the October 1956 revolt, some hopes existed that Gomulka would recognize the claim of the Church. This was but an illusion. Gierek's friendly gestures during the times of the 1970 and 1976 crises failed to offer any redress either. The matter has not been forgotten, however, and as late as summer 1978 Cardinal Wyszynski once again declared that normalization of relations between the church and the state must start with redressing injuries from the Stalinist period, including the return of Caritas.[31]

The question of ecclesiastical buildings is another burning thorn in relations between the church and the state. The well-known case of the church in Nowa Huta clearly demonstrates the unwillingness of the government to recognize the wants of the population. The authorities argue that the number of ecclesiastical buildings in Poland grew from 7,257 in 1937 to 13,643 in 1973, and consider the figure as fully satisfactory. Yet, even Marxist writers[32] admit this is not the case. The needs exist, and are caused by three main reasons. First, the existing ecclesiastical buildings are often located in places far removed from densely populated areas. Second, very many buildings are temporary barracks or other shelters ill-adapted for permanent use as places of worship. Third, many of the existing churches are too small, and not a few of them show signs of rapidly progressing deterioration.

Every year diocesan bishops submit to authorities annual plans for new constructions and renovations. As a rule, the requests are fully or partly denied although the costs are covered by the Church, usually from local contributions. In the Gierek era the situation improved somewhat, and the government issued, between 1971 and 1974, over 150 permits for construction or renovation of churches and chapels.

However, this is not enough. Since the needs are real and pressing, the people sometimes resort to erecting churches without permits. This, in turn, leads to police reprisals and dramatic encounters between officials and the masses. The situation clearly calls for a negotiated agreement.

FROM CONFRONTATION TO COOPERATION

The Two Crises

Current relations between church and state in Poland are greatly influenced by the religious policy of the government which, in turn, is molded by a variety of international and domestic factors. The global power struggle between the East and West, the evolution of the relationship between Moscow and the Vatican, and the personalities of the leaders of the Catholic Church in Poland as well as the Polish United Workers' Party are but a few elements that shape variations and mutations of an official posture.

During the postwar era, lasting already upwards of thirty years, governmental policy toward the Church has gone through a number of distinct cycles. While there exists a disagreement as to their amount,[33] there is a general accord that a definite evolution is taking place. Despite the underlying, more or less accentuated struggle on the level of moral and metaphysical principles, institutional relations between the state and the Church visibly advanced from the period of initial intensive confrontation to the present stage of normalization. Though still uneasy and vulnerable, it promises a progress toward dialogue and cooperation.

And truly, some impressive steps have been taken since Gierek came to power. Early in March 1971 a meeting took place between Premier Jaroszewicz and Cardinal Wyszynski, followed by other consultations and friendly gestures on both sides. The government made a number of concessions to the Church, including the transfer of title deeds to formerly German sacral building in the Recovered Territories, the repeal of regulations regarding inventories of Church properties, and the issuance of building permits for the construction of new places of worship. A Catholic bishop was invited to become a member of the committee for the reconstruction of the Warsaw royal castle, and, in October 1971, the authorities helped in organizing an airlift of a mass pilgrimage to Rome for the beatification of the Polish martyr of Auschwitz, Father Makymilian Kolbe. Parallel to these developments, the government established contacts with the Vatican aimed at the resumption of diplomatic ties.

And yet, everything was not going quite as well as it seemed from assurances of Edward Gierek, who occasionally claimed that no church-state tension existed in Poland. The Church saw the situation differently. The pastoral letters and other pronouncements of the Polish Episcopate regularly called for the expansion of the Church's rights within the society and denounced government measures aimed at reducing the Church's social initiatives and involvement. A communique issued in late November 1976 contained a list of complaints about the government's "secret conspiracy against God". Clearly, a real "normalization" of state-church relations was far from resolution.

Surely the situation has changed, for, instead of head-on battles of the Gomulka era, the party undertook a long-term transformation of Polish society aimed, among other things at undermining the traditional strength of the Church while expanding the role of the secular state. Socialization of agriculture, followed by the migration of rural youth to the cities, was definitely not working for the benefit of the Church.

Similarly, educational reform with its programs of comprehensive community schools and afternoon classes was perceived by the bishops as a hindrance to children attending catechism classes in their home villages. In the new school curricula there was increased stress on ideological education at the expense of Polish history and culture which, objectively presented, had to emphasize the role of the Church in Polish life.

Included in these efforts were renewed rhetorical attacks against the Church, especially notable because, until then, the communist leadership had taken a quieter approach to the religious question. In March 1974, Politburo member Jan Szydlak lashed out at the "reactionary wing of the episcopate" which, in his words, has at its disposal the institutional structure of the Church, numerous cadres, and whose "political strategy is aimed, above all, at exploiting our difficulties and failures."[34] In the summer of 1976, the Minister for Religious Affairs, Kazimierz Kakol, once again demonstrated official attitudes by telling a group of party journalists that they should be trained in the act of attacking outdated structures of the Church and superficial piety of Polish Catholics. "Normalization" he called, is not capitulation."[35]

A special form of the party's religious policy was aimed at the lay Catholic movement which represents an important segment of nonsocialist public opinion. The purpose of it was to split the movement by fomenting organizational and personal rivalries and isolating more critical centers from their own organizational bases. Through its control of election lists, issuance of commercial licenses, and permits to organize new groups and publish new periodicals, the government was able to make significant progress in undermining the unity of the independent Catholic movement, poisoning the climate in which its leaders operate and undermining its long-term influence within the Polish laity. As might be expected, the Episcopate was aware of the happenings and watched them with anxiety. A bouquet of flowers sent by Premier Jaroszewicz to Cardinal Wyszynski for his 75th birthday certainly did not dispel the Episcopate's skepticism vis-a-vis the regime.

The lack of confidence was clearly manifested during the constitutional debate of 1975. The constitutional amendments, proposed by the party and widely opposed by the intelligentsia, caused the

Episcopate's inquiries as to recommended changes. In addition, the Episcopate submitted to a parliamentary commission on the constitution a list of principles which should be included in the new text. As the issue developed, the bishops made more and more public statements criticizing the amendments. Their voices, joined by many others from the intellectual community, resulted in significant watering down of three controversial amendments which were to institutionalize the leading role of the party, define Polish-Soviet ties as "unbreakable", and make a citizen's rights dependent on his fulfillment of his duties toward the state. The Church's role in Polish politics reached a new high mark.

The strikes and disturbances of June 1976, provoked by the announced price increases, created a highly explosive situation in the country. Any militant pronouncement heralded by the Church at this time could have easily inflamed the populace and lead to greater unrest with unforseeable results. The Episcopate recognized the danger and refrained, in the initial period, from public statements on the events. The bishops, however, dispatched a letter to the authorities in which they criticized the government's economic policy and protested reprisals against workers. Only on August 26, speaking to pilgrims at Jasna Gora, did Cardinal Wyszynski make an overt appeal for leniency toward the protesters and raise the issue of confidence in the government.

But the Church leaders were also aware that the resolution of the crisis, and of economic difficulties as well, required sacrifices from all sides. Thus, the Plenary Conference of the Episcopate, which met early in September, called upon the people to intensify their efforts, show better workmanship, and expand dedication to the common good. In the words of the bishops, "Solid work is a moral obligation and ability to make sacrifices a Christian virtue". At the same time, the communique reminded the government of its obligation to be concerned with and care for the welfare of all citizens. Only then, it said, can the rulers gain confidence of the ruled.

The balanced posture of the Episcopate, combined with a conciliatory speech of Edward Gierek at a Mielec plant on September 3, gave rise to expectations that the communist leadership might be prepared to make a further improvement of relations with the Church and satisfy at least some of the

Episcopate's long-standing grievances. Over a year passed by, however, without anything more than occasional friendly gestures, almost all of which were made toward Cardinal Wyszynski personally.[36] No wonder that in subsequent public statements the Episcopate adopted a more bellicose stand toward the government, returning with persistance to current problems and stressing in particular the crucial importance of freedom in all aspects of everyday life. In the same period, the bishops presented a long list of demands.

Bishops' Demands

Of special significance was a communique issued by the 158th Plenary Conference of the Episcopate on May 5, 1977.[37] It expressed the bishops' views on a number of matters, including normalization of church-state relations. The prelates expressed alarm at the increased attempts to force an atheistic ideology upon the Polish youth, indicated their approval for the government's contacts with the Vatican but added that they must be complemented by concurrent negotiations between the authorities and the Episcopate, and complained about unsatisfactory relations between diocesan bishops and local administrative officials. A pastoral letter read on September 18, the Day of the Mass Media, denounced the state press, radio, and TV for promotion of "godless ideology" and "total dictatorship", and called on the authorities to make radio and television time available for religious broadcasts.

It was only around October 1977 that a new phase in church-state relations was inaugurated. It was opened with the governmental authorization for the building of new churches in the Warsaw area. This step was followed, on October 29, by a lengthy meeting between PUWP First Secretary Edward Gierek and the Primate of Poland, Cardinal Wyszynski. An official communique issued by the government press agency said that the two men "exchanged views on the most important problems of the nation (sic!) and the Church, which are of great significance for the unity of Poles in striving to shape the well-being of the Polish People's Republic."

It was rather obvious that Gierek finally realized the need for the support of the Church and was ready to make some concessions. The expectations were strengthened about a month later when, on December 1, Gierek paid a visit to Pope Paul VI, who assured his Polish guest that the Church was not asking for privileges, "but merely the right to be itself and to carry out its mission unimpeded." The official Polish media presented the unprecedented meeting as a sign that an end to the fundamental conflict between the Church and the state in Poland had arrived.

But governmental statements indicating that an agreement had already been reached between the Church and state did not correspond to the facts. As so many times before, ingratiating hints and small courtesies were not accompanied by any concrete deeds.

The lack of tangible evidence of the government's good will led to the rise of skepticism among some clerics and laymen who started, privately, to question the wisdom of Church leaders for their haste. They argued that Cardinal Wyszynski should meet Gierek only after extracting from him a definite promise of concessions. The criticism must have reached the ears of Cardinal Wyszynski who, in a sermon delivered November 6, justified his action in the following words: "I decided after long reflections over several years that in situations which are especially difficult the bishops and primate of Poland must clearly see the demands of Polish raisons d'etat." His talks with Gierek, he explained, were "directed by the command of my conscience as a bishop and a Pole..."[38]

About a month later, only three days after Gierek's visit with the pope, a pastoral letter was read in all Polish churches. Its contents blamed the government for endeavors to estrange Polish youth from the Church and her moral standards by "brutal sexual instruction" in schools and sexual license in mass media. The anti-religious action was denoted as a segment of a "hidden plan for moral disintegration" conceived and executed by "hostile forces" which aim at the "very biological substance of the nation." There were several intriguing aspects of the document, and especially the reason for its publication at this particular time. It might be safely assumed, however, that the message was directed not only toward the Catholic community in order to obviate possible public dissatisfaction, but also toward the government for the purpose of expressing the bishops' anxiety over the status of church-state relations.

As if to confirm the impression created by the pastoral letter of December 4, the bishops issued another strong statement at the end of the Episcopate's 161st Plenary Conference in the middle of the month. The communication repeated the willingness of the Church to work for the spiritual and material welfare of Poland and reminded the entire Catholic population that it is the duty of every citizen to exert efforts for the common welfare. But it also demanded that the government should respect basic human rights, including "the right to openly state their opinions on society and questions concerning public life."[39]

On the subject of church-state relations, the bishops restated their desire to continue direct contacts "in the hope that they lead to full normalization of relations." They introduced a new element in the situation, however, by stipulating that "a lasting guarantee of those relations must be based on recognition of the public and legal character of the Church (as was the case before the war) and on a corresponding bilateral agreement." While no other conditions of such an accord were specified, the letter referred to a number of grievances that were previously raised by the Church but were disregarded by the authorities. These included restrictions on the free public expression of views, exclusion of practicing Catholics from important public posts, obstructions to religious instruction, the lack of social insurance for clergymen, and the state monopoly of student organizations. On the last point, the bishops explicitly demanded the formation of an independent Catholic student organization.

Current church-state relations in Poland were also discussed in two sermons delivered by Cardinal Wyszynski in Warsaw on December 25, 1977, and January 6, 1978. The primate's assessment of the situation was relatively optimistic. He expressed a guarded hope that at least the "more enlightened section" of the communist leadership might have finally come to recognize the significance of the Church for the preservation of social peace and order. Promising the Episcopate's cooperation in efforts to achieve the moral rehabilitation of the people, he warned that without the Church's involvement no true ethical revival is possible. The Church, however, must be given the necessary means to discharge its mission. Among them, the cardinal listed as most urgent: a broader scope of social liberties, reestablishment of religious associations and sodalities, publication of authentic Catholic newspapers and books, education of the young in the spirit of Christian and national traditions, and most significantly, the formal recognition of the

Catholic Church as a public legal body.[40]

Nothing in the list is, probably, as crucial for improvement of church-state relations in Poland as the recognition of the legal status of the Church. The issue appears to be the cornerstone of endeavors to achieve a speedy normalization. From the bishops' point of view, lack of official legal standing forms a major impediment in the Church's evangelical and social work. It also creates a number of unnecessary difficulties in administrative and financial matters. The position of a "public legal entity" would allow the Episcopate to defend the Church's rights before the courts, give more freedom in organizational matters, and provide better protection of the interests of priests and other religious workers. Naturally, it would also increase the authority of the Church and increase her potential in the struggle for religious and human rights.

But this was exactly opposite to the party's intentions. No wonder, therefore, that the authorities did not show any eagerness to accede to the Episcopate's request. Their hesitation was, at least partly, substantiated by the protesting voices raised by people who worried that granting the Catholic Church a special legal status might have a number of adverse consequences. Some feared for the future of the secularization process of public life; others claimed that concession to the Catholic Church would elevate her over other denominational associations and thus violate the constitutional principle of equality of all religious groups. Still others argued that granting legal personality to the Catholic Church is contrary to the spirit of socialist jurisprudence which, in practice, led to the gradual elimination of the very concept of "public legal person." Not a few pointed out that the Catholic Church in Poland has full legal capacity because its territorial-personal units (parishes, dioceses and diocesan seminaries) possess unrestricted rights, similar to those of physical persons, in matters of acquiring and holding property, in the transaction of business, etc.

After reviewing all these arguments, one comes to the conclusion--shared by Polish legal scholars of distinction[41]--that from the formal point of view, the state can guarantee, in the form of a statute, the status of legal personality either to the organizational units of the Church or to its entire entity. Thus, it is clear that governmental reluctance to assent to the bishops' postulate is caused only by political considerations. Undoubtedly, some of these were generated by the confusion and resentment of party old-timers used to quite a different approach to the Church.

The uneasiness of the officialdom manifested itself in a circuitous way in the Easter (March 25) issue of the party weekly Polityka. A leading article, written by editor-in-chief Mieczyslaw Rakowksi and printed on the front page under the title "Basic Premises of Cooperation and Dialogue", undoubtedly expressed the regime's position on the issues raised by the Episcopate. Characteristically, Rakowski skirted around the specific demands of the bishops, mentioning them only in a general way, dismissing them, in part at least, as absurd in the view of separation between the Church and state, and expressing his "own personal conviction" that "some could be eventually granted conditional on the Church's attitudes toward initiatives instituted by party and state authorities."

The main portion of the editorial consisted of an enumeration of deeds which communist leaders expect the Church to do for Poland. Thus, the Church's efforts should be used for the maintenance of social peace and order, for improvement of public morality, work discipline, and "civic responsibility", and for strengthening of family ties. In other words, Catholics are called upon to avoid any conflicts and tensions and unite with nonbelievers behind Gierek's program to increase the material and spiritual well-being of the nation. Rakowski suggested that any "unnecessary misunderstandings" in these matters could be eliminated in frank discussions between Marxists and Catholics, which could be conducted despite opposition on both sides, especially among conservative "spiritual and lay Catholic leaders."

The tenor of Rakowski's article, as well as later utterances of government officials,[42] indicated quite clearly that there was little likelihood of a more benevolent attitude toward the Church's demands in the near future. There was no significant progress in church-state negotiations, and as 1978 drew to a close the relationship appeared to remain at a standstill. The elevation of Cardinal Wojtyla to the throne of Saint Peter had no immediately discernible effects on the political nature of these interchanges. Nothing could better demonstrate this than the fact that Pope John Paul II's very first message to his former diocese was censured.

CONCLUSION

A review of political events in Poland during the Gierek era indicates a constant interplay of forces whose competition extends beyond a simple conflict as to respective spheres of competence. These powers are the Catholic Church and the communist party. Both are fully aware that the contention results from basic differences in their philosophies of life and as such does not allow for any compromise. Communist materialism and socio-economic messianism project the vision of social order unrelated to God and operating only in accordance with man's reason. The Church opposes the concept with the utmost determination because man's temporal ends can never be fully separated from the final destiny of his existence. Such a stance is not simply tactical ingenuity or an effort to cover interested motives by declarations of lofty principles. In order to exercise her special mission, the Church must act in the area of mundane preoccupations, must defend her present position, and must expand her influence within the society.

For the present and the near future, the Church's position in Poland seems strong. Church attendance remains high, and there are enough vocations[43] to fill the ranks of the clergy. The leadership of the Church, with Cardinal Wyszynski at the helm, is very vigorous, and the whole clergy seems to be united with the Episcopate on the major issues. Despite this positive picture, however, the society in which the Church operates is changing, and this is bound someday to have an effect on the Church's influence. The communist leaders are convinced that the more Polish society is changed by education, urbanization, and economic development, the less important will be the Church's impact on human behavior, while the party's influence will expand. In order to accelerate the process of change, the party is using the state to undermine the Church's opportunities to spread Christian faith and foster Catholic views while, at the same time, promoting secularization. And the secular idea of religious freedom is that the Church shall be free to confine itself harmlessly to the four walls of ecclesiastical buildings. Anything else is condemned as violating the principle of separation of church and state. The Episcopate, of course, is opposed to such a restrictive interpretation and would prefer to see a lay state completely neutral in religious matters with the state administration not taking sides in the controversy.

The party policy of isolating the Church from believers was, however, not very consistent. The reason for this is simple. The communist leadership, faced periodically with dramatic social tensions, was forced to depend on the Church's influence to help calm political storms. The events of 1956, 1970, and 1976 proved it beyond any doubts.

It is evident that the application of this tactic in practice depended on the Church's willingness to cooperate. Failure to fulfill the party's expectations would destabilize the political system, undermine its effectiveness, and consequently jeopardize the communists' ability to enforce their long-term policy of secularization. Why then was the Church not refusing her help?

The answer to this question is contained in the words of Cardinal Wyszynski who once said, "For us, next to God, our first love is Poland, After God one must above all remain faithful to our homeland...."[44] The Church in Poland sees herself as the defender of the faith and of the nation, as the attentive guardian of the country's national interests. When there was a danger that the escalation of domestic conflict might lead to Soviet intervention, or when other overriding interests of the Polish nation were concerned, the Church was willing to use her influence and act in consonant with the party. Thus, the Episcopate supported Warsaw's claim to the Recovered Territories, recognized the necessity of finding a modus vivendi with the Soviet Union, and aided the consumer-oriented economic policy of Gierek after his coming to power.

It is interesting to note that the Episcopate never required concessions as a condition for the Church's cooperation. Instead the bishops stressed that, in order to increase the contribution of the Church to the national welfare, the government should stop interfering with the exercise of the Church's mission and recognize the Episcopate's demands as a necessary premise of the Church's functioning. While as a rule the prelates refrained from complaining when the strains in the society were greatest, they never promised to abstain from criticizing the authorities who undermine the potential of the Church in working for the common good.

One could expect that the party leaders would

respond in kind and redress, if only in a limited way, the Episcopate's grievances. But this was not the case. In these circumstances, a suspicion arises that the communist leaders are abusing the Church's benevolent attitude. They know that the bishops, owing to their own sense of Christian and patriotic duty, will serve national interests without prior compensation. Why, then, show understanding for the Church whose vitality would adversely affect secular goals? Tragic as it is, it seems that only further deterioration of the general situation might force the communist leadership to pay more attention to the voices of the Church.

NOTES

1. M.K. Dziewanowski, Poland in the 20th Century. New York: Columbia University Press, 1977, p. 93. Naturally, one must remember that the CPP was then illegal and operated underground.

2. Krystyna Kersten, PKWN. Lublin: Wyd. Lubelskie, 1965, p. 17.

3. As evidenced by Adam Michnik, Kosciol, Lewica, Dialog. Paris: Instytut Literacki, 1977.

4. Oskar Halecki, Eugeniusz Pacelli, Papiez Pokoju. London: Hosianum, 1951, p. 229.

5. Ryszard Marek, Kosciol rzymsko-katolicki na ziemiach zachodnich i polnocnych. Warsaw: PWN, 1976, pp. 1-77.

6. Hansjakob Stehle, Die Ostopolitik des Vatikans. Munich: R. Piper Verlag, 1975, pp. 379-389.

7. As cited by Andrzej Micewski, Katholische Gruppierungen in Polen. Munich: Kaiser Verlag, 1978, pp. 196-197.

8. Ibid., pp. 188-190.

9. A circular of the Press Bureau of the Episcopate's Secretariat, No. 33/519. (Warsaw: August 7-13, 1978), pp. 1-2.

10. Wladyslaw Piwowarski, Religijnosc miejska

w rejonie uprzemyslowionym. Warsaw: Biblioteka Wiezi, 1971, p. 57.

11. Jan Guranowski, "Istota i metody laicyzacji zycia spolecznego," in Religia i laicyzacja. Warsaw: KiW, 1961, p. 237.

12. Piwowarski, Religijnosc, p. 61.

13. Jerzy F. Godlewski, Kosciol rzymsko-katolicki w Polsce wobec sekularyzacji zycia publicznego. Warsaw: PWN, 1978, p. 196.

14. Ibid., p. 221.

15. Journal of Law, No. 53 (1961), item 295.

16. Pastoral letter to teachers of catechism of September 8, 1974 in Listy Pasterskie Episkopatu Polski, 1945-1974. Paris: Editions du Dialogue, 1975, p. 803.

17. Godlewski, Kosciol, p. 236, footnote 105.

18. For example, pastoral letter of September 4, 1964 in Listy Pasterskie, pp. 365-366.

19. W. Myslek and M.T. Staszewski, Polityka wyznaniowa. Warsaw: PWN, 1975, p. 321.

20. For background see Bodgan Waligorski, "O wychowanie pokolenia epoki socjalizmu," Nowe Drogi, No. 3/286 (March 1973), pp. 86-93.

21. Ludwik M. Wisniewski, "Chrzescijanie wobec walki o sprawiedliwosc," Spotkania: Niezalezne pismo mlodych katolikow (Lublin), No. 1-2 of 1977-1978, pp. 98-107.

22. Tadeusz Mazowiecki, "Chrzescijanstwo a prawa czlowieka," Wiez, No. 2 (February 1978), p. 7.

23. For a full story see Adam Bromke, "The Opposition in Poland," Problems of Communism, Vol. XXVII, No. 5 (September-October 1978), pp. 37-51.

24. Interesting argument presented by Antoni Pospieszalski, "Kosciol i opozycja w Polsce," Trybuna (London), No. 29/85 (1978), pp. 6-10.

25. Michnik, Kosciol, p. 155.

26. Bohdan Cywinski, Wychowanie do podmiotowosci," _Glos_ (Warsaw), No. 7 (May 1978), as quoted by J.S. "Niecenzurowana prasa krajowa," _Kultura_ (Paris), No. 12/375 (December 1978), pp. 23-24.

27. _Listy Pasterskie_, pp. 518-519 and 525-526.

28. Letters of December 29, 1970 and of January 27, 1971 in _ibid._, pp. 614-615 and 619-622.

29. _Dissent in Poland, 1976-1977._ London: Association of Polish Students and Graduates in Exile, 1977, pp. 150-151.

30. _Journal of Law_, No. 1 (1957), item 6.

31. Letter of Cardinal Wyszynski to Minister Kakol from June 10, 1978 as published in _Kultura_ (Paris), Nos. 1/376-2/377 (January-February 1979), pp. 221-224.

32. Myslek and Staszewski, _Polityka wyzaniowa,_ p. 313.

33. For example, Wieslaw Myslek distinguishes four states in _Polityka wyznaniowa Polski Ludowej._ Warsaw: Iskry, 1970, pp. 168-212; Janusz Zablocki--five in "Trzydziestolecie polskiego spotkania," _Chrzescijanin w Swiecie_, No. 30 (1974), pp. 1-9; and Maciej Letowski--only three in "Struktura i dzialalnosc 'Ruchu Znakowego' oraz Kola Poselskiego Znak," Unpublished Ph.D. dissertation, University of Warsaw, 1977, pp. 39-45.

34. Jan Szydlak, "Aktualne problemy pracy ideologiczno-propagandowej," _Nowe Drogi,_ No. 5/300 (May 1974), p. 28.

35. As quoted by Thomas E. Heneghan, "The Loyal Opposition: Party Program and Church Response in Poland," _RAD Background Report/45_, February 28, 1977. p. 6.

36. Probably most significant was permission to condemn publicly the falsification of the Cardinal's book of sermons.

37. A circular of the Press Bureau of the Episcopate's Secretariat, No. 20/453, Warsaw: 9-15 (May 1977), pp. 1-3.

38. Polish Situation Report 27, Radio Free Europe Research, November 9, 1977, item. 1.

39. A circular of the Press Bureau of the Episcopate's Secretariat, No. 51/485, Warsaw: (December 19-25, 1977), pp. 1-4.

40. Authorized text of the January 6, 1978 sermon published in Tygodnik Powszechny, No. 5/1516 (February 12, 1978), pp. 1-2.

41. For example, by the dean of the law department, University of Warsaw, Michal Pietrzak, Prawo wyznaniowe. Warsaw: PWN, 1978, p. 109.

42. For example, Minister of Denominational Affairs Kakol's interview in the Milan daily Il Giornale of June 6, 1978.

43. In 1978, 5,325 young men studied for priesthood in Polish seminaries.

44. Quoted by Adam Bromke, "A New Juncture in Poland," Problems of Communism, Vol. XXV, No. 5 (September-October 1976), p. 11.

Part 4

Issues in Economic and Foreign Policy

10
Victim or Villain: Polish Agriculture Since 1970

Andrezj Korbonski

INTRODUCTION

For more than twenty years, and especially since October 1956 which marked the collapse of the collectivization drive, the official policy toward agriculture has been a perfect example of the schizophrenic nature of the Polish political system. Throughout most of this period, policy consisted of pragmatic and rational thinking interspersed with dogmatic and irrational ideas. On the one hand, it attempted to introduce into the decision-making processes sound economic calculus; on the other, the same policy makers managed to offset the anticipated gains by disregarding not only some basic economic laws but also the elementary rules of human behavior. Major socio-economic reforms decided by the top leadership and intended to improve the overall situation in the farm sector were frequently frustrated, if not sabotaged, by the middle-ranking and local *apparat* entrusted with the implementation of the new policies. The ultimate result was that Polish agriculture, despite substantial increases in the amount of farm inputs and the volume of capital investment, as well as several major concessions granted to the peasants by the government, did not fulfill its goals, and its overall performance fell short of expectations. Consequently, it continued to be blamed in some quarters as the villain responsible for the growing shortages and rising prices of basic foodstuffs,

---

Research for this paper was supported by a grant from the UCLA Academic Senate Committee on Research, whose support is hereby gratefully acknowledged.

while both the peasants and large segments of the remaining population saw agriculture as the major victim of the irrational policies perpetuated by successive Communist regimes.

The purpose of this chapter is to examine certain features of that policy since December 1970, when the Gomulka regime was replaced by a new leadership headed by Edward Gierek. It will be necessary to refer to the pre-1970 policies but, since they have been rather extensively discussed in the literature, there is no need to repeat the various arguments.[1] The main focus will be on the private sector which, as can be seen in Table 10.1, still accounted for the lion's share of total farm output and employment in the first half of the 1970s.

It can be assumed that the major objective of the Gomulka regime, after the mass dissolution of collective farms in the fall of 1956, was to convince the Polish peasants that the government had no immediate intention to resume collectivization. This was no easy task. It required a sophisticated approach as well as a strong commitment to the new course, not only on the part of the top leadership but, more importantly, by the local bureaucracy at the provincial, county and commune levels, which had to execute the policy and which was in direct contact with the peasants. Eight years of outright hostility between the ruling party and the peasants had created a wide chasm that had to be bridged in the name of increased farm output.

Expanded agricultural production was high on the regime's list of priorities for several reasons. Even before Khrushchev bestowed his blessing on it, the Polish party embraced, by and large, the concept of "goulash communism" which, among other things, implied a major increase in food consumption. Moreover, the government was also eager to reduce the import of agricultural commodities, mostly from the West, which represented a serious hard currency drain. Agriculture has also been the traditional source of Polish exports and, hence, increased farm output was bound to improve the country's balance of payments. Therefore, it was not surprising that the regime tried hard to create the atmosphere and conditions favorable to a significant increase in production.

At the same time, there was another side to the official policy which ultimately proved counterproductive, for it minimized the positive effects of the "pragmatic" approach. The official pronouncements, intended to reassure the peasants

TABLE 10.1
Socialized and Private Sectors in Polish Agriculture: 1970 and 1977

Percentage Shares of:	1970	1977
Total agriculture production	100.0	100.0
Socialized	14.9	22.1
Private	85.1	77.9
Total sown area	100.0	100.0
Socialized	15.9	21.9
Private	84.1	78.1
Total employment	100.0	100.0
Socialized	15.4	20.0
Private	84.6	80.0
Production of four grains	100.0	100.0
Socialized	15.3	21.0
Private	84.7	79.0
Production of potatoes	100.0	100.0
Socialized	8.4	9.1
Private	91.6	90.9
Production of meat	100.0	100.0
Socialized	16.3	33.7
Private	83.7	66.3
Production of milk	100.0	100.0
Socialized	12.4	14.4
Private	87.6	85.6
Production of eggs	100.0	100.0
Socialized	5.9	5.9
Private	94.1	94.1
Number of horses	100.0	100.0
Socialized	3.6	2.3
Private	96.4	97.7
Number of tractors	100.0	100.0
Socialized	75.7	51.5
Private	24.3	48.5

Sources: *Rocznik Statystyczny 1977*, pp. 41 and 190-191, and *Rocznik Statystyczny 1978*, pp. 42 and 190.

about the inviolability of their holdings, were frequently interspersed with statements pointing to the socialization of agriculture as the ultimate goal of the government. Although no specific deadline was mentioned, emphasizing the temporary character of the individually-owned farms did go a long way in undermining the confidence of the peasants in the credibility of official promises of support for private agriculture.

Various specific measures tended to increase the dissatisfaction and distrust of the peasants. For example, throughout the 1960s Poland remained the sole East European country which retained the system of compulsory agricultural deliveries, which had been gradually abolished elsewhere in the region. Although a significant share of the revenue derived from these deliveries was, at least in theory, returned to the peasants via the so-called Agricultural Development Fund (Fundusz Rozwoju Rolnictwa), established in 1969 for the purpose of accelerating the mechanization of private farms, compulsory deliveries were strongly resented by the peasants, not only because of their coercive character, but also as reminders of the not-so-distant Stalinist past.

The creation and subsequent expansion of the so-called agricultural circles, supposedly intended to help individual peasants, was also perceived by them as instruments of collectivization "through the back door." This view eventually gained universal currency when the government itself made little effort to deny it. Similarly, neither the pricing nor the investment policies were seen by the peasants as major departures from past practices.

The Gomulka regime was also faced increasingly with a series of developmental and socio-economic problems which required sensitive handling. Among them were continuing exodus from the villages and the resulting aging of the agricultural labor force, progressive fragmentation and subdivision of holdings and the growth of the worker-peasant class, and unresolved questions of land ownership. With the possible exception of the last, these difficulties were not peculiar to Poland alone; yet the predominantly private character of Polish farming made their solution a rather complex task.

All of these politico-economic, legal-institutional, and structural problems would have taxed the capacity of any government, regardless of its political coloration. The fact that the

Gomulka regime was simultaneously faced with a variety of other crises made it difficult, if not impossible, for the government to pursue a rational and consistent policy toward agriculture. Policy eventually acquired a hit-or-miss character, leaving neither the government nor the peasants satisfied with its results.

In view of this, it was not surprising that the objectives set initially by the Gomulka regime were not reached. The peasants responded only partially to the various government initiatives by raising their output only a few percentage points (Table 10.2), and the import of foodstuffs, especially grain, continued to grow, while farm exports lagged behind. Exodus into the cities proceeded apace, and the average age of the peasant population kept increasing, as did the level of fragmentation and the number of peasant-workers. Altogether, in the opinion of one Western scholar, "the end of Gomulka's rule, then, was marked by a situation as desperate as that which had helped his return to power in 1956."[2] While this view appears exaggerated, there is no doubt that, after the early relative successes, the last five years of the Gomulka regime witnessed a serious deterioration in the overall agricultural situation.

AGRICULTURAL POLICY SINCE 1970: FORMULATION AND ADOPTION

Since the changeover in December 1970, the impressive performance of Polish industry, which was largely responsible for the country achieving one of the highest rates of economic growth in the world in the first half of the 1970s, attracted most of the attention and overshadowed to some extent an almost equally impressive performance of the farm sector. After fourteen years of Gomulka's hit-or-miss policy, which had left everybody unhappy, the arrival of Gierek on the scene seemed to inaugurate a new era in the development of Polish agriculture.

The new regime's attention was focused immediately on adopting a new strategy of rapid economic development and growth based on the extensive modernization of industrial capacity with the help of Western credits and technology. However, agriculture was not ignored by the decision makers who, presumably, were well aware of the errors committed by their predecessors, and who appeared determined to avoid repeating the same mistakes.

TABLE 10.2
Indices of Gross Agricultural Production 1965-1970 and 1970-1977

A. 1965-1970 (1965=100)

	1965	1966	1967	1968	1969	1970
1. Gross Agricultural Product	100.0	105.2	107.7	112.5	107.2	109.5
2. Population	100.0	100.6	101.9	102.5	103.5	103.5
3. 1 ÷ 2	100.0	104.6	105.7	109.8	103.6	105.8

B. 1970-1977 (1970=100)

	1970	1971	1972	1973	1974	1975	1976	1977
1. Gross Agricultural Product	100.0	103.6	112.2	120.4	122.3	119.7	118.9	120.1
2. Population	100.0	100.6	101.5	102.4	103.4	104.6	105.5	107.0
3. 1 ÷ 2	100.0	103.0	110.5	117.6	118.3	114.4	112.7	112.2

Sources: *Rocznik Statystyczny 1977*, pp. xxxi and xxxix; *Rocznik Statystyczny 1978*, pp. xxxiii and xli.

How was agriculture viewed in the short and long-term plans of the new leadership? One can assume that, in the short run, the farm sector was expected to perform three basic functions: to provide continuing employment to a large percentage of the population, to serve as the reservoir of labor available to other sectors, and to supply a sizeable share of foodstuffs consumed by households and raw materials utilized by industry. With this in mind, the main objective of the government should have been to maximize productivity of both land and labor. This implied, on the one hand, the provision of adequate incentives for the farm population to increase output and, on the other, the securing of sufficient amounts of inputs and capital to make such an increase possible. Such a policy was postulated on the assumption that agriculture would be considered primarily as an economic sector, in contrast to the past when it was seen mostly as a political and ideological problem. This suggested the short-run official acceptance of the existing status quo, which meant the continuation of the predominantly private character of Polish farming.

In the long run, agriculture was most likely perceived as a marginal sector employing only a fraction of the total labor force. While still serving as an important supplier of certain key foodstuffs and raw materials, it was no longer viewed as the major source of grains and fodder, for substantial amounts of these products would have to be imported. In line with the situation in other European countries with limited availability of arable land, the emphasis was to be on maximizing its productivity. The future farm sector was seen as being fully socialized with privately owned farms playing a minor role. This assumption implied that the government should actively encourage the outflow of people from agriculture and, at the same time, promote the gradual takeover of private holdings by the state.[3]

The official preoccupation with long-run ideological matters at the expense of immediate tasks meant that the regime appeared to pay only scant attention to the various developmental crises--both demographic and structural--which have been plaguing the farm sector for some time. Potentially, the most serious problem was the rapid aging of the farm population.[4] With the continued exodus of the younger age groups into the cities, the average age of the active farm population has been going up, affecting adversely the overall productivity of the sector. The migration to the cities has also accentuated the growing shortage of farm labor which has been only partly offset by increased mechanization. One of the consequences has been a sharp rise in the level of wages paid to farm laborers which, in turn, raised the cost of production on individual farms, reduced farm income, and affected the entire agricultural incentive system.

Could anything have been done to remedy this situation? To begin with, the gradual aging of the farm labor force could not be easily arrested. The only way it could be slowed down would be to reduce the outflow of young people by making farming more attractive as an occupation. A good deal has been done in this respect by bridging the gap between the city and the village through major improvements in the rural infrastructure (roads, transportation, electrification, communications); yet there was still a considerable differential between farm and nonfarm per capita incomes and, until that was reduced and farm work was made less onerous, there was little hope of success in stemming the tide of migration.[5]

The Gierek regime had relatively few options to slow down the exodus and to bring farm incomes closer to those of the nonagricultural population. Apart from the already-mentioned increase in investment and in the supply of farm inputs, which was likely to result in larger output and therefore income, other economic measures, such as raising the level of prices paid to peasants, appeared highly controversial in the context of the 1970s (see Table 10.3 for a summary of prices 1965-1977). As is well known, the June 1976 riots were indirectly caused by the government's decision to close the huge and growing gap between prices paid to the peasants and those paid by the predominantly urban consumers, many of which were frozen since the mid-1960s. A significant reduction in food subsidies was the major objective of the price increase announced in June, and the subsequent withdrawal of the latter meant that the regime was willing to continue paying the subsidies, at least in the immediate future. However, this decision was not tantamount to agreeing to pay still higher subsidies, which would have been the case had the government agreed to grant another price increase to the peasants. Thus, in this particular area, the regime's freedom of maneuver was severely

TABLE 10.3
Indices of Prices Paid to Peasants 1965-1977

(1970=100)

	1965	1970	1971	1972	1973	1974	1975	1976	1977
Wheat	93.5	100.0	105.7	112.5	115.6	112.2	114.5	149.1	146.8
Rye	86.5	100.0	103.4	125.3	128.2	124.9	127.0	185.2	182.7
Barley	96.5	100.0	115.3	119.8	121.4	118.2	119.5	156.5	154.3
Oats	94.0	100.0	113.0	131.5	134.7	133.8	134.7	191.7	188.4
Potatoes	98.7	100.0	124.1	164.6	175.9	178.5	191.1	273.4	287.3
Beef cattle	90.7	100.0	108.8	143.0	154.3	178.3	182.8	202.4	232.2
Hogs	88.7	100.0	126.1	133.5	133.8	134.5	140.9	164.6	197.0
Milk	98.5	100.0	115.9	129.9	131.1	133.0	140.0	175.0	194.3

Sources: Rocznik Statystyczny 1977, p. 332; Rocznik Statystyczny 1978, p. 333.

circumscribed.[6]

With prices paid to the peasants presumably kept roughly constant in the foreseeable future, the only other way to increase farm incomes would be either to reduce the cost of production or to expand the marketable output. Neither was likely to happen soon. The prices of certain key industrial inputs were, in fact, raised shortly after the June riots, while the cost of hired farm labor continued to rise, reflecting increased demand and shrinking supply. Demographic and structural factors made an increase in marketings highly problematical. Thus, in the short run, the probability of a substantial improvement in real farm incomes appeared quite low.

The process of aging and migration has resulted in a relatively recent phenomenon of a growing number of older peasants, especially those without heirs, surrendering their land to the state in return for an old age pension and the right to keep their houses and small garden plots. So far, the major effect of this transfer of land ownership has been a decline in output, for the state farms which were supposed to take over the abandoned land were not properly equipped and prepared and have been unable to cope with the additional farm land which often remained idle or underutilized for a number of years. Until now, the tendency to surrender land to the state has not represented a mass movement, partly because the long waiting period to have the transfer legalized and to receive the pension has discouraged many peasants from making what, for them, was clearly a momentous decision. However, once these problems are ironed out, the transfer of land may acquire a mass character and, unless the state sector is ready for it, the decline in farm output may be considerable, at least for a number of years. Also, until the abandoned land is fully integrated into the state farms, the cost of transfer is likely to be staggering.[7]

Until relatively recently, there has been no evidence that the party apparat has been particularly concerned with this problem or that it has tried to accelerate the process.[8] The alternative, usually preferred by the peasants, has been the sale of land to other private owners willing to add to their holdings; however, as mentioned below, this option has been effectively sabotaged in the past by local officials.

The main structural problem continued to be

the fragmentation of individual holdings, which in 1976 still accounted for 71.1 percent of all agricultural land and 73.1 percent of arable land.[9] While in 1970 individual farms of less than two hectares represented 37.5 percent of agricultural holdings, by 1974 their share rose to 39.2 percent.[10] The respective shares for holdings below five hectares were 64.8 percent of all farms in 1970 and 65.5 percent in 1974, accounting for roughly 28 percent of agricultural land in both years.[11] While exact output data are hard to come by, one may assume that, with some exceptions, the smaller size farms have not been as productive as the farms above five hectares.

Various attempts to reduce the impact of adverse structural features have met so far with little success. In addition to the takeover of abandoned farms by the state, another measure was the creation of a special fund intended to prevent further subdivision of individual farms. The fund was set up to provide loans to pay off deceased farm owners' multiple heirs, who would customarily divide the farm among themselves. Under the fund, loans were to be made available to one heir to enable him to buy out other family members' shares, so that the farm would remain in one piece. Restrictions were also put on those who could purchase and own farm land, in order to prevent agricultural land from falling into the hands of nonfarmers. It is still too early to pronounce a judgement on the success or failure of this measure, which, along with that of allowing individual peasants to enlarge the size of their farms, was clearly one of the most rational policies put forward by the regime.

The major problem facing the Polish rulers has, of course, been the continued presence of the so-called "worker-peasants", individuals who derive the major portion of their income from nonfarm sources--mostly industry and construction--but who also own and live on farms. Without going into the reasons for the persistence of this particular social class, the fact remains that, while owning almost 40 percent of all individual holdings (farms under two hectares), accounting for about 7 percent of agricultural land, their contribution to total agricultural output has been relatively insignificant.[12] Whatever output has been actually produced on these holdings has been largely marginal and intended mainly to supplement the nonfarm income of the owners. The capacity has been clearly underutilized and, for quite some time, the government has been eyeing the worker-peasants' holdings with a view to raising their output. As mentioned below, in early 1976 the government proposed to expropriate the owners who did not farm their land efficiently. Thus far, no action has been taken on this particular measure since any forced expropriation was bound to meet with considerable resistance, especially in the aftermath of the June 1976 events. Moreover, while the small holdings have not been productive, they have been producing enough to satisfy the basic needs of the owners who otherwise would put additional pressure on the food supplies distributed through the retail network at a time when the regime could ill afford it.

POLICY IMPLEMENTATION

The chief problem with all of these approaches was their mutual incompatibility. In the final analysis, this proved to be their undoing. Moreover, neither the short nor the long-run policies were implemented with any degree of consistency; on the contrary, they tended to be contradictory and ultimately ineffective.

Initially, however, the short-run tactics appeared to be working. One of the first measures taken by the Gierek regime after coming to power in December 1970 was the abolition of compulsory deliveries, long a major complaint of the peasants. This was followed by a substantial increase in the level of prices paid by the government for the peasants' products. Furthermore, various restrictions on purchases of farm inputs and producer goods by individual peasants, were gradually lifted. The government itself increased its investment in the agricultural infrastructure and also expanded the output of industrial branches serving agriculture.[14]

The abolition of compulsory deliveries and the increase in prices paid to peasants resulted in a major improvement in the terms of trade between agriculture and the nonfarm sectors, which benefited the peasants and provided additional stimulus to expand production. For example, whereas between 1965 and 1970 the prices received by peasants for grain, potatoes, cattle, and milk remained either stationary or showed only a slight increase, the change between 1970 and 1977 was quite striking, as illustrated in Table 10.3.

The free market prices of farm products also showed a considerable increase in the same period. Between 1970 and 1975, retail prices of such items as building materials (bricks and cement) remained unchanged, the prices of farm implements either remained constant or increased only slightly, and the prices of some fertilizers actually declined.[15] As a result, the real farm income in the same period rose by 24 percent.[16] Since the farm labor force declined by roughly 3 percent during the period 1970-1975, farm income per head increased even more significantly.[17] Although prices of farm inputs rose sharply in 1976, real farm income between 1976 and 1977 increased by 10 percent.[18]

The impressive rise in farm incomes also resulted from an expansion of farm output. As shown in Table 10.2, gross agricultural production increased faster during the first five years of Gierek's rule than during the last five years of the Gomulka regime. It can also be seen that, while gross production stayed ahead of population growth in both periods, the margin in 1970-1977 was considerably larger than in 1965-1970.

Gross animal production actually grew more rapidly than total agricultural output. This was reflected, among other things, in a substantial increase in the production and consumption of meat, by far the most sought after agricultural commodity in the country (see Table 10.4).

However, while various other indicators also pointed to a significant upsurge in agricultural production in 1970-1977, the annual rate of growth, after a rapid increase in 1971-1973, began to drop just as sharply, and the output in 1976 was, in fact, below output levels in 1973, 1974, and 1975.[19] It was this decline that undoubtedly contributed to the worsening in the domestic food supply which led to the unpheaval of June 1976. To put it differently, although the Polish peasants had nothing to be ashamed of, the significant increase in gross output was not sufficient to satisfy the growing popular demand for certain foodstuffs. In addition, this imbalance has left little if any room for the maintenance and/or expansion of the export of agricultural commodities, long a major earner of hard currency for Poland.

EVALUATION

In fact, impressive as it was, the increase in Polish farm output was actually not as striking

TABLE 10.4
Production and Per Capita Consumption of Meat 1965-1977

	1965	1970	1971	1972	1973	1974	1975	1976	1977
Output of meat and animal fats ('000 tons)	2,015	2,187	2,215	2,485	2,735	3,067	3,067	2,902	2,891
Index (1965 = 100)	100.0	188.5	109.9	123.3	135.7	152.2	152.2	144.1	143.5
Index (1970 = 100)	92.1	100.0	101.3	113.6	125.1	140.2	140.2	132.7	132.2
Consumption of meat per head (kilograms)	49.2	53.0	56.1	59.3	62.1	65.6	70.3	70.0	69.1
Index (1965 = 100)	100.0	107.7	114.0	120.5	126.2	133.3	142.9	142.3	140.4
Index (1970 = 100)	92.8	100.0	105.8	111.9	117.2	123.8	132.6	132.1	130.4

Sources: Rocznik Statystyczny 1977, pp. xxxii and xxxix; Rocznik Statystyczny 1978, pp. xxxv and xli.

as one might have suspected, especially when compared with other European countries, both East and West (see Table 10.5).

Moreover, while the period 1970-1976 witnessed a major increase in the availability of farm inputs, such standard indicators as the average yield per hectare, amount of fertilizers per hectare, or the number of hectares per tractor showed Poland still significantly behind not only several West European countries, but also some of its Communist allies, such as Czechoslovakia, East Germany, and Hungary.[20]

All of this suggests that there is still need for more fertilizers, additional machinery and equipment, construction materials, and other inputs. In the final analysis, the decision to allocate additional resources to agriculture and other branches producing inputs for the farm sector lies with the top planners. There is no doubt that, although agriculture has received relatively more resources in the last five or six years than previously, there is also evidence suggesting that the traditional anti-agricultural and anti-peasant bias among the Polish Communist leaders has not diminished markedly since its heyday in the early 1950s.

Moreover, while the heavy industry and other industrial and nonagricultural sectors have traditionally had considerable influence on economic decision making at the top and middle levels, this was never the case with agriculture, which was at no time allowed to establish its own institutionalized pressure group that would articulate its interests. Although the satellite political party, the United Peasant Party (Zjednoczone Stronnictwo Ludowe), especially since 1956, has often been consulted with great fanfare by the ruling Communist party on various agricultural policies, there is little evidence that it has amounted to much more than a traditional transmission belt used as a window dressing to make governmental fiats more palatable to the peasants. Moreover, the relative representation of the peasants in the membership of the Communist party continued to be low and, in fact, it was lower in 1976 than in 1970 and 1960.[21]

The preferential treatment accorded nonagricultural sectors was illustrated by the fact that in 1976 capital investment in agriculture, both socialized and private, accounted for only 13.4 percent of total investment (see Table 10.6). This

TABLE 10.5
Indices of Agricultural Production in Selected European Countries 1961-1965 to 1976

	1961-1965	1970	1971	1972	1973	1974	1975	1976
Bulgaria	100	130	133	140	142	140	151	156
Czechoslovakia	100	125	129	132	140	143	143	139
East Germany	100	121	121	133	134	145	139	131
Hungary	100	115	126	129	138	143	145	140
Romania	100	119	142	155	156	158	163	191
Yugoslavia	100	118	127	127	134	146	150	151
USSR	100	131	132	127	147	142	135	140
Poland	100	117	121	131	141	143	140	138
France	100	116	121	121	128	132	124	122
Greece	100	135	138	142	146	153	154	158
Italy	100	120	119	113	122	122	124	124
Spain	100	123	127	130	139	148	154	147
West Germany	100	116	121	115	119	122	121	117
United Kingdom	100	116	120	121	124	130	121	117
Poland	100	109	117	124	128	125	118	123

Sources: Maly Rocznik Statystyczny 1976, p. 333. Rocznik Statystyczny 1977, p. 491; and Rocznik Statystyczny 1978, p. 497. Gross agricultural production was used as the base for comparison of Poland with the East European countries. Net value added in agriculture was the base for comparison of Poland with the West European countries.

TABLE 10.6
Selected Indices in Polish Agriculture 1970-1977

	1970	1971	1972	1973	1974	1975	1976	1977
Investment in agriculture								
(1) Total (million 1971 zlotys)	36,250	37,841	43,490	50,990	60,173	70,073	72,665	n.a.
Index (1970 = 100)	100.0	104.4	120.0	140.7	166.0	193.3	200.5	225.4
% of total investment	15.9	15.5	14.4	13.5	13.0	13.2	13.4	16.2
(2) Socialized sector	23,570	23,648	27,974	32,348	40,064	49,783	55,408	n.a.
Index (1970 = 100)	100.0	100.3	118.7	137.2	170.0	211.2	235.1	269.7
% of total investment	10.4	9.7	9.2	8.6	8.6	9.4	10.2	12.0
(3) Private sector	12,680	14,193	15,516	18,642	20,109	20,290	17,186	n.a.
Index (1970 = 100)	100.0	111.9	122.4	147.0	158.6	160.0	135.5	149.1
% of total investment	5.6	5.8	5.1	4.9	4.3	3.8	3.2	4.3
Foreign trade (million zlotys)								
(1) Import of farm commodit. and processed foods	1,814	2,429	2,392	3,387	4,324	4,678	5,818	6,118
(2) Export of farm commodit. and processed foods	2,055	1,965	2,676	3,211	3,491	3,348	3,728	3,917
(3) Surplus (+) or deficit (-)	+241	-464	+284	-176	-833	-1,330	-2,090	-2,201
Migration from agriculture ('000)	162	171	165	168	183	251	242	207

Sources: Rocznik Statystyczny 1976, pp. 51, 123, and 337-339; Rocznik Statystyczny 1977, pp. 38; 103; and 286-288; Rocznik Statystyczny 1978, pp. 39; 97-98; and 285-287.

was only slightly higher than the comparable ratio in 1960 but lower than in 1965 and 1970. In contrast, investment in industry has shown a major increase in the same period.[22] Thus the frequent official promises to make agriculture modern and productive remained largely unfulfilled.

It is clear, however, that the lack of available inputs was only one of the causes of deteriorating agricultural performance, and that there were at least two other factors or processes that played a major role. One was the continued presence of a high degree of mistrust between the regime and the peasants. As suggested by one of the most perceptive observers of the contemporary Polish scene, in no other socio-economic sector in Poland could one find so many deeply rooted prejudicies and conflicts, as well as ideas which, although discredited in practice a long time ago, were still considered as dogmas by the ruling party, and especially by its _apparat_.[23]

As suggested earlier, both the ruling oligarchy and the cadres, despite official denials, viewed individual peasants as class enemies who must be tolerated for tactical reasons in the short run. This view was held particularly by the middle and low-level bureaucrats whose intellectual prowess left much to be desired, and who equated the notion of socialized agriculture in the traditional fashion with the total disappearance of private farms. Despite the country's disastrous experience with forced collectivization and the lengthy debates of the 1960s, in the course of which the future model of socialized agriculture was discussed _ad nauseam_, the local officials have frequently acted as though none of these events has occurred.[24]

To put it simply, highly productive individual farms were seen as major obstacles on the road to socialization. Although the notorious epithet of _kulak_ was no longer used in public, the official attitude toward efficient market-oriented peasants remained essentially unchanged for more than a quarter of a century; after all, did not Lenin himself say that small-commodity production begot capitalism "every day and every hour?"

A good example of that attitude was the habitual refusal by the rural _apparat_ to permit individual peasants to purchase additional land in order to increase the size of their holdings.[25] It was only after the June 1976 food riots, when agriculture once again was put in the spotlight, that Gierek himself was compelled to reprimand the party officials and urge them to approve the transfer of land from the less to the more productive peasants.[26]

Similarly, despite the continuing process of fragmentation and subdivision of individual farms which over the years has resulted in a significant increase in the number of small unproductive holdings, there was no evidence that the government has been making a serious effort to stop or at least slow down the process until the spring of 1976. At that time a bill calling for an outright confiscation of inefficient dwarf farms was introduced in the parliament. It can be presumed that, in the eyes of many local officials, the increase in the number of unproductive farms was "good for socialism" and should not be interfered with, just as the presence of productive farms made the construction of socialism in the countryside much more difficult.

In light of this, it is not surprising that many of the individual peasants, aware of the official attitude, preferred neither to increase their output nor to acquire additional land, for fear of being branded class enemies and accused of harboring capitalist tendencies. In a sense, the history of the 1950s was repeating itself in the 1970s.

CONCLUSION

Three major conclusions emerge from the preceding discussion. First, despite good intentions and ideas which, if brought to fruition, were likely to improve the overall agricultural performances, the Gierek regime did not succeed in achieving a major breakthrough after 1970 in the official attitude and policy toward agriculture. Second, despite a significant increase in the availability of inputs and a series of other measures favoring the farm sector, the latter has not been able to expand its output at a satisfactory rate. Third, as a corollary to the second, there has been a growing conviction on the part of the government and the peasants that Polish agriculture, as presently constituted and structured, has either reached or is about to reach the upper limit of its productive capacity, and that further increases in output must be accompanied by major structural changes in the sector, especially with regard to the ownership of land and the scale of operations.

As suggested above, the failure of the regime to gain the confidence of the peasants was a perfect case of history repeating itself. Although the government reached a kind of *modus vivendi* with individual peasants, it was in the nature of a truce or armistice with considerable mistrust remaining on both sides. This failure was particularly attributable to the ruling Communist party which, over the years has failed to eradicate its traditional suspicion of, and contempt for, the peasants, and has continued to treat agriculture as a stepchild of the socio-economic system.

Although the Gierek regime made a sincere effort in its early years to supply the farm sector with capital and inputs and to give the peasants an additional incentive to expand output, many of these measures were either contradictory, frequently offsetting each other and having little or no impact, or were not fully implemented by the bureaucracy. The existing communications gap between the peasants and the *apparatchiki* was also reponsible for the government's habitual ignorance of the actual state of affairs in the countryside.

The growing belief that the time was ripe for major restructuring of the farm sector represents a watershed in the general perception of the future of Polish agriculture. Until now, even the most innocuous official musings about the socialization of the farm sector were treated as anathema by the peasants. Their reaction was so negative that, after the heated debates of the 1960s concerning different methods of and approaches to socialization, the government finally appeared reconciled to the long-run survival of the private farms which, by and large, ceased to be the object of official discussion.

Therefore, the recent change in attitude of the peasants themselves with regard to the future of agriculture is of utmost importance and signifies a radical, almost revolutionary departure from the past.[27] This is not the place to analyze in depth the reasons for this fundamental transformation in the peasant value system. Suffice it to say that, for the first time since the Communist takeover after World War II, the Polish regime finds itself in the position to socialize agriculture without antagonizing the majority of villagers who even in 1976 still represented about 44 percent of the Polish population.[28]

If this is true, then the regime is faced not

only with an opportunity to revolutionize the farm sector but also with a highly complex task of achieving that goal in a most efficient fashion, without causing a major socio-economic crisis manifested in a large-scale disruption of output, reduction in the living standard, and escalating popular dissatisfaction. However, the fundamental restructuring of agriculture can be achieved only if certain conditions are met.

First of all, the regime must make it clear that in the future restructured farm sector there will be room for a certain number of highly efficient and productive private farms, modelled after the type of farms found in Western Europe. In light of this, all current restrictions on acquisition of land, up to the maximum specified by the Land Reform Act of 1944, must be lifted; and the government must also guarantee an uninterrupted supply of necessary inputs to individual owners.

Next, the ruling party must make every effort to educate the local bureaucracy about the importance of the incremental voluntary transformation of the farm sector, including the above-mentioned retention of some privately owned farms. This is a crucial task which is not going to be easily or quickly accomplished in light of the deep-rooted hostility of the cadres toward the peasants.

Third, the regime must mobilize all available resources in order to minimize the economic burden and cost of the transition. As mentioned earlier, the main reason for the failure of the initial attempts by the state to take over private holdings was the lack of adequate resources in the state sector--both capital and labor--which would permit a rapid integration of the newly acquired farms into the productive process without a major decline in output.

Finally, the government must ensure that proper incentives are provided to individual owners to transfer their titles to the state, and that no coercive measures will be applied to achieve that purpose. This is why the question of educating the apparat becomes so important.

To sum up, the present Polish government is faced with a difficult task, but also with a great opportunity to peacefully revolutionize the farm sector--something that has eluded its predecessors for nearly thirty years. Whether the Gierek regime will be able to take full advantage of this unique chance remains to be seen, although the process itself is likely to be a lengthy one, and the final results may be long in coming.

Unfortunately, recent indications suggest that little if any progress is being made under all of the above rubrics. Judging from various pronouncements, the official policy toward the private farm sector is not likely to depart greatly from the past, which does not argue too well for the future and for the hoped-for improvement in agricultural performance.[29] On the contrary, the policy of granting old age pensions to all private peasants, announced with great fanfare in 1977 and hailed as a major departure from the traditional anti-peasant attitudes, was encountering growing resistance among the peasants who found their compulsory contributions to the pensions much too onerous.[30] Clearly, what is needed is a firm commitment to rational thinking on the part of the Polish regime which, until now, has not been strong and confident enough to solve the perennial problem of agriculture.

NOTES

1. Andrzej Korbonski, Politics of Socialist Agriculture in Poland 1945-1960. New York: Columbia University Press, 1965, chaper 11; and "Peasant Agriculture in Socialist Poland Since 1956: An Alternative to Collectivization," in Jerzy F. Karcz, ed., Soviet and East European Agriculture. Berkeley and Los Angeles: University of California Press, 1967, pp. 411-431.

2. Paul Lewis, "The Peasantry," in David Lane and George Kolankiewicz, eds., Social Groups in Polish Society. London: Macmillan, 1973, p. 86.

3. For an excellent analytical survey of official plans concerning the future of Polish agriculture, see Harold Laeuen, "Polens Dorf in der Auflosungsperspective der Partei," Osteuropa, XXVII (1977), pp. 105-124.

4. Over 1.3 million peasants in the mid-1970s were 60 years old or over, and the farms they owned accounted for 40 percent of privately owned agricultural land. Radio Free Europe Research, Situation Report Poland, no. 11, April 29, 1977. This had two additional corollaries: progressive feminization of agriculture and a growing number of farm without heirs. In the early 1970s, women represented the majority of individual farm owners, while already in the late 1960s in 285 thousand farms representing nearly 10 percent of privately owned land, there were no known successors ready to take over the farms upon the death of the present owners. In 1970 women represented about 58 percent

of all persons deriving their income from agriculture. Adam Wyderko, "Spoleczno-demograficzne problemy gospodarki chlopskiej," in Zdislaw Grochowski, ed., Przemiany strukturalne w rolnictwie polskim. Warsaw: Panstwowe Wydawnictwo Rolnicze i Lesne, 1975, p. 150. The estimate of the number of farms without heirs comes from Tadeusz Hunek, Wyzywienie, rolnictwo i wies w Polsce. Warsaw: Ludowa Spolszielnia Wydawnicza, 1975, p. 137.

5. The per capita farm incomes accounted for the following percentages of nonfarm incomes: 1970 - 79.8; 1965 - 84.3; 1970 - 80.6; 1971 - 80,4; 1972 - 85.2; 1973 - 83.4; 1974 - 77.3; and 1975 - 72.4. Zdzislaw Grochowski, "Dochody wsi a rozwoj produkcji rolnej," Nowe Drogi, no. 9 (1976), p. 84. The decline in the relative farm income between 1965 and 1975 is quite striking, despite some increase in the early 1970s. The respective estimated ratios for 1976-1977 were 74.3 in 1976 and 78.0 in 1977. Roman Stefanowski, "The Income of Individual Peasants," Radio Free Europe Research, RAD Background Report/100 (Poland), May 26, 1978.

6. Nevertheless, roughly one month after the June 1976 riots, the peasants did receive another round of price increases. Budgetary subsidies for the food sector in 1977 were estimated at about 12 percent of the Polish domestic net material product or about 70 percent of an average price paid by the population for foodstuffs. Zbigniew M. Fallenbuchl, "The Polish Economy in the 1970s," in East European Economies Post-Helsinki (A Compendium of Papers Submitted to the Joint Economic Committee, 95th Congress, 1st Session) Washington, DC: U.S. Government Printing Office, 1977, p. 860.

7. For an interesting discussion of the cost of private land transfer to the state sector, see Wiktor Herer, "Metoda szacunku ogolnospolecznych kosztow inwestycyjnych przejmowania ziemi przez Panstwowe Gospodarstwa Rolne," Zagadnienia Ekonomiki Rolnej, no. 1 (1976), pp. 18-29; and Urszula Grabowska, "Rachunek Kosztow inwestycyjnych przejmowania ziemi przez Panstwowe Gospodarstwa Rolne," ibid., no. 2 (1976), pp. 84-86.

8. Under a new plan submitted to the Polish Parliament in October 1977, old or invalid peasants will be able to surrender their holdings either to individual successors or to the state, in exchange

for a pension, the amount of which will be dependent on the amount of farm products delivered by the farm owner to the state under contractual arrangements. For details, see "Old Age and Disability Pensions for Private Farmers," Radio Free Europe Research, Situation Report Poland No. 27, November 9, 1977.

9. Rocznik Statystyczny 1977, p. 190.

10. Maly Rocznik Statystyczny 1976, p. 156.

11. Ibid.

12. Ibid.

13. For details on deliveries of building materials, fertilizers, pesticides and other inputs, see Rocznik Statystyczny 1978, pp. 235-238.

14. While the production of agricultural machinery and equipment between 1965 and 1970 increased by nearly 53 percent, a comparable increase in 1970-1977 was 208 percent. Ibid., p. 119.

15. Ibid., p. 328.

16. Rocznik Statystyczny 1976, p. 233.

17. Ibid., p. 55.

18. Rocznik Statystyczny 1978, p. 196.

19. Real farm income in both 1974 and 1975 declined 6 percent in comparison with the preceding year which meant that the 1975 income was roughly 10 percent below that in 1973. However, the real income in 1977 was 19 percent above 1975. Ibid.

20. Ibid., pp. 500-501; 503; 511-512.

21. Individual peasants accounted for 11.8 percent of total party membership in 1960; 11.5 percent in 1970 and 9.3 percent in 1976. Ibid., p. 22.

22. Between 1970 and 1976 the share of investment in industry rose from 39 percent to 44 percent of total investment in the economy. Rocznik Statystyczny 1977, p. 104.

23. Wladyslaw Bienkowski, "Rolnictwo po raz trzeci," Kultura (Paris), no. 3 (1977), p. 75.

24. For a summary of the debates of the 1960s, see Korbonski, "Peasant Agriculture in Socialist Poland," pp. 427-429.

25. While in 1975 about 359 thousand hectares of privately owned land were surrendered to the state, only 17 thousand hectares were either sold back or leased to the peasants, which represented roughly one-third of the 1970 figure. Undoubtedly, the refusal of state banks to grant peasants credit for the purchase of land, which went into effect in 1974, was largely responsible for the decline. In 1977, out of 210 thousand hectares surrendered, some 78 thousand hectares were sold back or leased to private peasants. Rocznik Statystyczny 1978, p. 200.

26. For details, see Gierek's addresses at the Fourth Plenum of the Central Committee of the Polish Communist Party, September 9, 1976, Nowe Drogi, no. 9 (1976), pp. 14-15; at the Fifth Plenum, December 1, 1976, ibid., no. 12 (1976), p. 21; and at the Sixth Plenum, January 21, 1977, ibid., no. 1 (1977), pp. 9 and 12-13.

27. For a discussion of peasant attitudes toward land ownership in other East European countries, see Ivan Volgyes, "Attitudinal and Behavioral Changes among the Peasantry of Eastern Europe," (Paper presented at the Annual Meeting of the American Association for the Advancement of Slavic Studies, Washington, DC, October 1977), pp. 6-10.

28. Rocznik Statystyczny 1977, p. 26.

29. For example, Gierek's address at the Second National Party Conference in January 1978 essentially repeated the old slogans (II Krajowa Konferencja PZPR. Warsaw: Ksiazka i Wiedza, 1978, passim). Gierek's speech at the Eleventh Plenum of the Central Committee of the Polish Communist Party in March 1978 that was devoted entirely to agriculture, contained no new ideas and offered no new suggestions for the solution of the multiple problems facing the farm sector. XI Plenum KC PZPR 17 marca 1978. Warsaw: Ksiazka i Wiedza, 1978, pp. 10-22.

30. Radio Free Europe Research, Situation Report Poland/14, June 21, 1978, Situation Report Poland/19, August 11, 1978, and Situation Report Poland/22, September 25, 1978.

11
Growth, Reform, and Inflation: Problems and Policies

John P. Farrell

In recent years Poland has begun to emerge as a species of "mature socialism," a state whose economy is distinguished from its past by a higher level of economic and financial development and foreign trade dependency. This emergence of the Polish economy, in particular the dramatic change achieved in Poland under the new policies of Gierek, has forced a reappraisal of conventional understanding of the nature and mechanisms of socialist economic growth and the economic policy choices of maturing socialism. This chapter examines these issues.

The first section reviews recent Polish economic growth and outlines the new economic strategy pursued under Gierek. The second section analyzes two principal aspects of conventional wisdom as challenged by recent Polish experience.

RECENT POLISH ECONOMIC GROWTH

By both its own and international standards, economic progress in Poland since 1970 has been impressive. Output, consumption, investment, and foreign trade all accelerated sharply after 1970 (see Table 11.1). In 1972, 1973, and 1974 the increase in investment averaged an extraordinary 24 percent.[1] By the end of 1975 the capital stock in state industry stood at one and two-thirds its 1970 level.[2] The average wage in 1975 was one-third greater than 1970. Consumers experienced an increase in material living standards unprecendented in People's Poland. In short, the economy was booming. By 1974, however, the boom had begun to falter. The investment front had become badly overextended and the balance of

TABLE 11.1
Output, Income, Savings, and Prices, 1961-1970, Poland
(annual percentage change, constant zlotys, unless indicated otherwise)

	1961	1962	1963	1964	1965	1966	1967	1968	1969	1970
(1) Net Material Product	8.2	2.1	6.9	6.7	7.0	7.1	5.7	9.0	2.9	5.2
(2) State Industry[a]	11.0	8.9	5.6	10.4	9.9	7.1	6.9	9.1	8.5	7.3
(3) Agriculture[a]	12.9	-16.4	10.7	1.0	5.3	4.3	-1.6	8.8	-20.5	3.9
(4) National Income Distributed[b]	7.3	2.7	6.3	4.9	8.3	7.4	4.5	8.5	3.5	5.0
(5) Consumption	6.1	3.6	4.6	4.6	6.2	6.2	5.4	6.6	5.1	4.1
(6) Meat, kilograms per capita	6.4	1.3	1.1	1.7	4.4	3.7	2.5	0	.1	.8
(7) Investment	7.3	9.7	2.7	4.7	9.5	8.4	11.3	8.7	8.7	4.1
(8) Household Income, nominal[c]	7.6	7.3	6.4	7.6	9.2	11.6	7.7	8.2	6.2	4.3
(9) Average Net Wage	2.6	.4	2.4	2.1	0	3.3	2.5	1.3	1.7	1.7
(10) Agricultural Income	11.2	-14.8	10.7	2.0	8.6	3.7	.3	8.3	-15.8	2.2
(11) Currency and Savings Deposits nominal	16.4	17.2	16.8	16.7	15.1	19.2	16.0	13.7	12.2	7.5
(12) Average Savings: (Increment in (11)/(8)) x 100	2.6	2.9	3.1	2.4	3.3	4.3	4.0	3.6	3.5	2.3
(13) Consumer Price Index	.1	1.7	1.4	1.2	.3	.6	.8	1.1	.8	1.2

(14) Relative Food Prices: (Private Market Index)/ (State Market Index) x 100	126	141	126	123	127	121	127	126	135	130
(15) Imports, nominal	13.6	12.4	5.6	3.1	15.1	8.0	7.5	8.4	10.6	10.4
(16) Exports, nominal	14.3	11.1	4.6	18.0	8.1	3.9	11.9	15.5	7.7	8.7
(17) Terms of Trade	100	99	102	101	101	101	102	100	100	102

TABLE 11.1 (cont.)
Output, Income, Savings, and Prices, 1961-1976, Poland
(annual percentage change, constant zlotys, unless indicated otherwise)

	1971	1972	1973	1974	1975	1976	1961–1970	1965–1970	1971–1975
(1) Net Material Product	8.1	10.6	10.8	10.4	9.0	7.1	6.1	6.0	9.8
(2) State Industry[a]	9.1	10.5	11.6	12.2	11.6	9.1	7.4	7.8	11.0
(3) Agriculture[a]	8.7	4.7	2.0	-5.2	-11.8	-.2	.8	-1.0	-.4
(4) National income Distributed[b]	9.8	12.7	14.3	12.1	10.9	7.2	5.8	5.8	12.0
(5) Consumption	7.7	9.1	8.1	7.4	11.1	8.8	5.3	5.5	8.7
(6) Meat, Kilograms per capita	5.7	5.7	4.7	5.6	7.2	-.4	2.2	1.4	5.8
(7) Investment	7.5	23.6	25.0	22.5	14.2	2.5	7.5	8.1	18.6
(8) Household Income, nominal[c]	11.1	13.9	13.8	14.5	14.0	6.3	7.6	7.6	13.5
(9) Average Net Wage	5.7	6.4	8.7	6.6	8.5	3.9	2.7	2.1	7.2
(10) Agricultural Income	15.4	15.0	4.0	-5.5	-5.1	9.1	1.9	2.6	4.8
(11) Currency and Savings Deposits, nominal	15.7	21.2	24.5	23.4	17.6	11.2	15.8	13.7	20.5
(12) Average Savings: (Increment in (11)/(8) x 100	4.7	6.4	7.9	8.1	6.6	5.0	3.2	3.5	6.7
(13) Consumer Price Index	-.1	-.3	3.0	4.8	3.2	4.0	.9	.9	2.1

(14) Relative Food Prices: (Private Market Index)/ (State Market Index) x 100	138	145	147	170	173	202	128	128	155
(15) Imports, nominal	13.9	22.1	22.6	14.2	5.0	10.3	9.6	9.0	15.6
(16) Exports, nominal	6.6	15.0	11.0	12.8	8.3	5.4	10.4	9.5	10.7
(17) Terms of Trade	107	109	107	105	105	104	101	101	107

[a] "Czysta produkcja" ("pure production"), a variant of value added.

[b] Differs from NMP (1) in that National Income Distributed ("Dochod narodowy podzielony") includes the trade balance on current account. An export surplus reduces and an import surplus increases this figure relative to NMP.

[c] All money flows from the socialized sector to households (this including private enterprise) less all taxes, fees, and obligatory payments from households.

Sources: S. Rudcenko, "Household Money Income, Expenditures, and Monetary Assets in Czechoslovakia, the GDR, Hungary, and Poland, 1956-1975" (Birbeck College, unpublished paper, 1977), p. 21; Rocznik statystyczny, 1976 (RS76) (Warsaw, 1977), pp. xxivff; 75; RS75, pp. 391; Rocznik dochodu narodowego, 1971 (Warsaw, 1972), p. 19; Rocznik statystyczny handlu zagranicznego, 1974 (Warsaw, 1974), p. 5; RSHZ76, p. 5; RS77, pp. xxxff, 58, 123, 282, 297, 312, 319-20, 413, 420-21, 423.

payments extremely tight. Unmistakable signs of inflation had surfaced: a divergence between free market and state store food prices, an unusually large increase in the official consumer price index, and an improbably high growth rate of private savings (Table 11.1). The state of disequilibrium was evidenced by the government's willingness to instigate very large increases in the prices of basic foods in June 1976.[3] The current Five Year Plan (1976-1980) calls for "regrouping" in the form of a sharp deceleration in investment and a restructuring of priorities in favor of consumer goods, particularly food and apartments (see Table 11.2). By the end of the decade, the ratio of investment to national income is supposed to decline from 32 percent in 1975 to 25 or 26 percent.[4]

Central to understanding this pattern of boom and bust is Gierek's new economic strategy, which can be summarized as follows:[5]

1. Emphasis on international trade. The economy was opened up to an inflow of foreign technology, particularly via licensing. Imports of raw materials and consumer goods, as well as capital equipment, were stepped up. Typical of Eastern Europe during the 1950s and 1960s, Poland had traded relatively little.[6] In addition, in the late 1960s there had been a drive to reduce Poland's dependency on imported fodder. Exports were viewed at worst as a necessary evil and at best as a "vent for surplus." Trade was a source of spontaneity inimical to a planned economy. The new view is that international trade must be an integral part of mature socialism. The instability inherent in world interdependency is an unavoidable cost of progress, part of growing up.

2. Consumption as the "engine of growth" and the ultimate objective of economic activity. In the new doctrine, consumption was not to be treated as an unavoidable residual tossed to the public after investment requirements had been satisfied. This doctrine manifested itself in the so-called "inflationary" incomes policies launched in 1971. To marshall support for the new government, steps were quickly taken to boost real incomes. Prices paid farmers were raised and forced deliveries were abandoned. The momentous price hikes on basic food stuffs decreed in December of 1970 under Gomulka were rescinded, prices of these goods were frozen at their old levels (a freeze still in effect), and the price reductions decreed in December on indus-

TABLE 11.2
Output and Plan, 1971-1975 and 1976-1980, Poland
(annual percentage change, constant zlotys, unless indicated otherwise)

	1971-1975	1976-1980
National Income Distributed	12.0	4.8
Output:		
State Industry	10.5	8.2-8.5
Agriculture	3.7	3.0-3.5
Consumption	8.7	5.6
Investment	18.6	2.3
Apartment Completions, millions	1.14	1.58
Average Net Wage	7.2	3.0-3.4

Sources: T. Checinski, "Priorytety Pieciolatki," *Polityka*, No. 51 (1976), p. 6; "Ciaglosc polityki-nowe elementy realizacji," *Gospodarka planowa*, No. 2 (1977). pp. 61-68.

trial goods were retained.[7] A series of wage increases was decreed during the early 1970s. In general, incomes were allowed to increase more rapidly than historical or anticipated rates of productivity growth. This policy was based on two key assumptions: first, that increasing incomes contribute by work incentives to greater effort and hence production; and, second, at least initially, rapidly increasing demand creates conditions favorable for expanded production. A "shallow" market, on the other hand, only discourages production. The first linkage (the supply effect of increased incomes) has long been recognized. The second, however, (the demand effect) is new, since this effect had been identified by virtually all students of planned economies with capitalism. This point is developed below.

Incomes policy under Gomulka during the late 1960s was niggardly. Plans for wages and secondary money flows from the socialized to the household sectors were rigorously enforced.[8] Agricultural prices were kept low, periodic wage hikes were postponed, and the aborted incentive scheme scheduled for implementation in 1971 would have limited nominal wage increments over the succeeding five years to 15 percent.[9] This financial stringency might have been palatable had there been a healthy increase in real living standards, but there was not; according to official sources, real increases in industrial wages averaged only 2.4 percent for 1961-1970 and 1.4 percent for 1966-1970 (Table 11.1).

3. Social policy. Pensions and minimum wages were increased sharply, medical benefits were extended to the countryside (1973), and efforts were made to bring a broader spectrum of the population into the decision-making process.

4. Economic reform. Major economic reform was to take place on a trial and error basis over several years. The strategic goals of the reform were to strengthen central planning and simultaneously increase the independence and responsibility of enterprises and groups of enterprises. This would move the economy once and for all from the track of "extensive" growth (growth generated mainly by simple augmentation of resources) to "intensive" growth (growth generated mainly by increases in efficiency). The reform actually implemented, which fell far short of the most ambitious hopes, centered on two changes: (1) the formation of very large economic units; and (2) the automatic tying of wage adjustments to increments in value added. The

latter change was a manifestation of the new incomes policies, _inter alia,_ while the former was motivated by the belief that greater industrial concentration facilitates the development and absorption of new technologies.

Economic growth in Poland was fueled by an investment boom, itself sustained in significant degree by foreign credit. By the end of 1976 Poland's foreign debt stood at about 11.5 billion dollars.[10] There were other factors at work. Incomes policies undoubtedly provided significant incentives for better work. No doubt as a new leader Gierek enjoyed at least initial support on the basis of "good faith". External conditions were also favorable, and it is changes in these which contributed heavily to the deterioration of the economic situation by the mid-1970s. Specifically, the recession of 1973-1975 in the West, the continuing energy crisis since 1973, and the persistent stagflation in Western markets made selling products for hard currency more difficult. In the meantime, wages continued their relentless upswing while, on the supply side, Poland has suffered a run of poor or mediocre harvests since 1974. Hence demand outstripped supply.

ECONOMIC REFORM AND ECONOMIC GROWTH

Recent Polish experience has important implications for some common beliefs about the determinants of growth in Eastern Europe. The first of these is the following: acceleration of East European growth rates is possible only if these economies carry through full-fledged market decentralization. This view has been widely accepted by Western economists as well as by some socialist laissez faire economists. But this view is contradicted by events of the early 1970s. Poland's economy has not fundamentally changed since the late 1960s. It is not market decentralization that can be credited with accelerating the growth rate. Rather, it is the policy changes initiated within a fundamentally unchanged structure, aided by favorable domestic and international events,[11] that contributed most directly to the economic success of the 1970s.

However, there was economic reform under Gierek. What was the nature of this reform, and what contribution did it make to the economic performance of the period?

Although the need for comprehensive reform and

some broad principles were announced in 1971, it was not until 1973 that the guiding principles of enterprise reform were crystalized. These can be summarized as follows:

1. Existing enterprises were to be consolidated into large units called "great economic organizations" (_wielkie organizacje gospodarcze_--WOGi). Ideally, these units were to constitute industrial complexes, producers and cooperating suppliers, including research and development and marketing components. The underlying rationale was that large size was necessary to reap the advantage of economies of scale and to cope with the problems of technological change, from design and experimentation through production, marketing, and servicing of new products and processes.[12]

WOGi were to be _the_ basic economic unit of the economy. Thus they were to differ substantively from the old trusts (_zjednoczenia_) which, intentions notwithstanding, often in practice constituted simply another tier in an administrative hierarchy of command planning.

2. Upper level supervision of WOGi would be loose. Indirect instruments of control ("parameters" such as interest rates, depreciation and taxation rates, etc.) would gradually supplant commands. These parameters would be relatively permanent (set for at least three years). WOGi would operate within an environment defined by these parameters, a set of "rules of the game" governing the formation of material rewards, tax payments, credit availability and terms, and, at least temporarily, commands.[13]

3. The wage bill would be tied to value added and the managerial bonus fund to profit by relatively stable coefficients. Material rewards, therefore, were to depend on current "results" in relation to a base period, rather than on the plan for the current period. It was hoped that this tactic would eliminate the venerable process of bargaining for an "easy" plan and would encourage enterprises to exert maximum production efforts without fear of reprisal in the form of a more difficult plan for the next year. Profits and value added were to be expressed in current (as opposed to constant) prices. Hence there was a built-in price sensitivity notably lacking in past arrangements.[14]

4. Substantial price-making authority was delegated to WOGi. Imported consumer goods (those not on a list of exemptions) and "new" products

were to be priced at market-clearing levels. Prices in general are maximum prices; i.e., downward price flexibility was provided. In addition, the turnover tax was eventually to be set as a fixed percentage markup over costs, thus eliminating the traditional isolation between prices received by producers and those paid by users.[15]

5. Small-scale investment was to be self-financed out of enterprise or WOGi profits by fixed formulae, although the bulk of investment was to be centrally determined and financed by bank credit. Central planning was to concentrate on basic questions of macroeconomic structure and development strategy, while WOGi and their enterprises were to occupy themselves with current planning and production. Whatever the locus of formal decision making, investment expenditures were to be recouped from revenue generated by completed projects. Both profit and value added, as defined, were affected by interest on borrowed funds. Hence, investment would affect material incentives in the current period. With wages and bonuses sensitive to investment, enterprises would be encouraged to use capital more efficiently. If the interest charges were high enough, and if efficiency criteria were at least a necessary condition for investment, interest rate charges could be used to regulate investment demand.[16]

Did these guiding principles add up to market socialism? Certainly the indirect instruments of control, the price flexibility, and the role of profits in the reform represent market-oriented changes. Value added as a performance criterion is not part of traditional market socialism, where profit is the immediate objective of enterprise activity, although it is compatible with Yugoslav-type market socialism where wages (the main component of value added, aside from profit) are crucial. Enterprises under the reform would presumably be expected to maximize some amalgam of profit and value added. In this event, the relative attention paid to these criteria would depend upon the associated material rewards, the political complexion of the enterprises (specifically, the weight of worker vs. management representation), and the significance of material rewards in general in explaining enterprise behavior.

Nonetheless, there were fundamental shortcomings in the reform which subverted the declared objective of substituting indirect for direct controls in enterprise management; i.e., of introducing a variant of market socialism. The price system, despite some significant flexibility, was still a cost-based system, and there was little or no provision for changing prices (or other parameters).[17] Under these circumstances, it is unlikely that prices would reflect planners' (or anyone else's) preferences. In general, the reform ignored the role of higher echelons (ministries and the central authorities). While one can appreciate the difficulties of comprehensive organizational change, it is questionable whether partial reform, no matter how many enterprises are included, will work.

As regards decentralization of decision making, the principles were ambiguous. While the WOGi were to gain authority at the expense of ministries, the enterprises were to lose authority to the WOGi. Thus the top and the bottom echelons were to lose while the middle gained authority, a restructuring which cannot be unambiguously labelled in terms of the level of decision making.[18]

Whatever its theoretical characterization, it must be emphasized that reform was implemented only partially and, at that, relatively late. It was a year after the Sixth Party Congress in 1971 that the Government-Party Commission announced the general principles of the reform, and it was not until 1973 that significant parts of that reform were actually implemented. Therefore, the reform really had nothing to do with economic performance for the first two or three years under Gierek. Centralized material allocation, after an initial period of significant suspension, resurged in approximately mid-1974 as the economy was buffeted under the strains and stresses of unusually rapid growth. Other aspects of the reform were abandoned, drastically modified, or simply not implemented.[19] Parametric management above the WOGi level was never seriously tried. The deployment of WOGi did take place, although in an environment considerably more centralized than the one envisioned by the reformers.

While the changes actually made, let alone the broad principles, did not amount to market socialism, they were nonetheless significant. In particular, the increase in industrial concentration engendered by the establishment of the WOGi has had, and is likely to have, a great impact on the way the Polish economy functions. Second and more immediately, the wage reform, however, short-lived in its intended form, was significant. The automatic tie between wages and value added was to be "permanent," not subject to frequent tampering by higher authorities. This approach recognized the role played by workers as a key to economic growth and, therefore, contrasts with the weight of past administrative reforms which have stressed the problem of designing appropriate success indicators for management. While the new emphasis on workers is perhaps ideologically convenient, it proved economically destabilizing.

Instability was brought about by the rigidity of the tie. The tie provided workers and managers a strong incentive to increase output. Both knew more or less what to expect under given circumstances. But the tie was too rigid when other aspects of economic reality, which affected supply-demand relations, went awry. Specifically, the worsening of the balance of trade situation, wrought partly by recession in the West and poor agricultural results at home, called for a reduction in the rate of wage increase. But this could not be effected without discretionary wage authority, which would have contradicted the reform. In this event, the reform was sacrificed.

If wages are tied to output, output is expressed in current prices, and prices are controlled by the enterprise, the stage is set for enterprise-generated inflation. The enterprise can raise prices, output, and wages ad infinitum and generate a perpetual wage-price spiral. This is a wage-price spiral with a vengeance. Capitalist wage-price spirals are not generally self-financing. Only if demand is perfectly inelastic (insensitive to price) will the capitalist enterprise be able to push up prices with impunity, but inelastic demand is much more likely to be the case in East European socialism. The enterprises involved are very large, often monopolists. Moreover, the condition of general excess demand means that, in effect, demand is perfectly inelastic over a significant range.[20]

In fact in Poland the WOGi has a significant measure of price-making authority. And even where that authority was lacking, the Price Commission was evidently willing to abide price increases in light of the general situation of excess demand. Value added was expressed in current prices. Thus the price making by WOGi together with the effects of imported inflation led the central authorities to modify the wage-output link significantly. Wage "reserves" were created, wage increments were taxed, and the coefficient linking value added and the wage bill was changed on an *ad hoc* basis. It may be that the wage reform was suitable as a means of eliciting maximum output in a short period of time, but its suitability was at the expense of long-run equity (as reflected in interindustry wage differentials) and macroeconomic stability.

AGGREGATE DEMAND AND CENTRAL PLANNING

The interdependency of nominal aggregate demand and real aggregate supply is a basic feature of capitalist macroeconomics. An increase in spending is likely to evoke inflation, as well as an increase in real output.

In the traditional view, however, the socialist economies of Eastern Europe have escaped this interdependency. Aggregate supply, after all, is planned, the summation of individual enterprise plans, set at the full-capacity level. Full employment is also guaranteed by fiat. The task of financial planning is to assure that aggregate demand equals aggregate supply at planned prices. A gap between aggregate demand and supply does not elicit adjustment in supply. A deflationary gap, while theoretically possible, is a policy absurdity which makes doubtful the mental equilibrium of central planners.[21] These economies are strictly supply oriented. Demand is no problem. Granted, output may deviate from the full-capacity level, and a variety of real constraints impinge on output, but the essential point is that nominal demand and aggregate supply are independent.

In light of this orthodoxy, the position taken by some economists, particularly in Poland, represents an abrupt departure from conventional wisdom.[22] In their view, aggregate nominal demand and aggregate real supply are not independent. It is argued, in fact, that lagging incomes in Poland during the late 1960s produced a very slow rate of increase in consumer demand which, in turn generated unused labor and capital, and that the new expansionary incomes policies of the 1970s reflated the economy and thereby contributed to the accelerated growth rates of the period.

If this view is correct, our understanding of socialist macroeconomics must be fundamentally revised. Shifts in aggregate demand must be viewed as a determinant of growth rates. In addition, the behavior of financial institutions must be reinterpreted in light of the real aggregate implications of money flows. A policy of a permanently balanced (or surplus) budget, for example, would have much the same destabilizing implications as it has in capitalist economies. Similarly, if one believes that socialist central banks follow "real bills" policies which tie credit rigidly to inventories, the resultant (upward or downward) wages-prices-credit spiral would have real as well as monetary implications.[23]

Unfortunately, the Polish economists concerned with demand management have not developed complete macroeconomic models.[24] However, the following is probably not an unreasonable distortion of their joint views:

1. A deflationary gap can occur under central planning if one assumes (a) stable prices; (b) some degree of decentralization; and (c) that firms respond to market signals. If this is the case, then aggregate demand and supply are, at least within some unspecified limits, interdependent. An expansion in demand creates incentive for expanded output. Expanded demand resolves itself into real and monetary components, depending, in general, on the response of firms and the Price Commission. The multiplier is not in general merely monetary.

2. In fact, there was a deflationary gap in Poland during the close of the 1960s. There were unemployed resources, resources idled by an unduly restrictive incomes policy. This gap was closed in the early 1970s with the rapid expansion of incomes.

3. While a deflationary gap is theoretically possible and, in the case of Poland, empirically important, it nonetheless represents bad policy and should be an exception in the centrally planned economies.

4. Policy errors consisted of (a) a failure to recognize the interdependency between nominal income and real output; (b) the use of a policy tool (incomes policy), too general in its effects; and (c) reliance on partial indicators of disequilibrium. There is, curiously, no suggestion as to why prices were not simply lowered in the face of inadequate demand).

5. The deflationary gap did not apply evenly across all industries, but rather was restricted to consumer durables. (There is no discussion of the "markets" for producer or intermediate goods).

Are these assumptions plausible for a centrally planned economy? What were the central planners doing when firms reduced output in response to inadequate demand shuffling paper?

As an empirical matter and from the macroeconomic perspective, the assumption of stable prices seems to be reasonable. Prices are seldom changed.[25] There is no fetish with equilibrium here.

The adjustment mechanism is the crux of the issue. What are the microeconomic foundations of a Keynesian economics under central planning? For the capitalist firm, with fixed prices, an increase in demand leads to falling inventories and, assuming unemployed resources, to increased real output. Or, conversely, a decrease in demand leads to accumulating inventories and consequently reduced output and reduced use of capital and labor.

But how can this mechanism hold under centralized socialism? A key issue is whether the firm can control, in part at least, its output levels. Let us consider first this issue.

It can be noted that, even in models which assume extreme centralization, some room for managerial manuever is assumed as well. In fact early writers, as well as later ones, have stressed the importance of bargaining between firms and upper administrative levels. Thus, if these studies are to be believed, actual output may differ from "full-employment" output. This possibility is enforced by continuous campaigns launched by central authorities to uncover "hidden productive reserves."

Regarding Poland, another aspect suggests that the power of firms or lower levels to control their output has increased over time. Namely, the central allocation of goods has diminished greatly. Whereas in the early 1950s perhaps 2,000 goods were centrally rationed, today this figure is about 200.[26]

The pattern of plan fulfillment also suggests decentralization. Plans during the 1960s were fulfilled with monotonous regularity and were changed very frequently, often at the last part of the plan period.[27] This is not the pattern of plan fulfillment one expects to see in a traditional Soviet-type economy: large scale and systematic plan underfulfillment in low priority sectors with fulfillment or overfulfillment of plans in high-priority sectors.

A final factor suggesting decentralization is the pluralization of the planning apparatus itself. It is common opinion that there is inadequate centralization of planning in Poland, particularly with respect to investment expenditures. This opinion is heard most often recently and in connection with the introduction of WOGi.[28] It should be remembered, however, that the concentration of industry in Poland, as in other socialist countries, has proceeded by jerks and bounds for the past twenty or so years.[29]

The above tends to establish a necessary condition: firms have some control over output. We must now talk about incentives.

How might the socialist firm respond to lagging demands, assuming output is variable and prices are fixed? If profit were important, excess inventories would mean higher interest charges which, in turn, would impinge negatively on profits. Thus, to the extent that profit is significant--and it has been of some significance as a success indicator in Poland since the late 1950s--the capitalist micro response to flagging demand would be expected. It should be added that the bank, via administrative and economic sanctions, has pressured firms to rid themselves of "excess inventories." Thus there has been an element of khozraschot embedded in the internal incentives of the firm as well as in the configuration of outside control, which encourages firms to respond to demand in a capitalist-like fashion.

Another response--presumably the desired response--is to change the output mix in favor of goods more in demand. This option may be constrained by technology and/or supply problems, or the firm may choose to bargain for a reduced plan. Is this likely to succeed?

If the firm has a significant amount of autonomy, and if full-capacity output is unknown, it is plausible that a socialist firm might respond to flagging demand by slowing output. It would be difficult, however, to reduce output, since the best indicator of capacity is last period's output. Thus, over a period of time, a firm could respond to sluggish demand by planning and executing only small increases in output, increases considerably below "actual" capacity.

It would thus seem reasonable to assume that socialist output is determined, inter alia, by demand, but that there are definite constraints on the amount that output can fluctuate vis-a-vis given fluctuations in demand. Specifically, aggregate output cannot fall below previous levels.

The above assumes a very weak sort of central planning. An alternative hypothesis is to recognize two benchmarks in the bargaining process: the previous year's output, and the planned and actual

TABLE 11.3
Selected Statistics, 1961-1968, 1969-1970, 1971-1972, Poland
(percentage change, unless indicated otherwise)

		1961-1968	1969-1970	1971-1972
	Output			
(1)	NMP	5.5	4.1	9.4
(2)	State Industry	8.6	7.9	9.8
	Nominal Income			
(3)	Total	8.2	5.3	12.5
(4)	Net Wage Bill, State Sector	7.6	6.0	10.0
	Employment			
(5)	Total Nonagricultural	3.5	2.7	3.5
(6)	State Industry	3.7	2.9	3.4
(7)	Unemployment[a]	.60	.78	.65
	Industry			
(8)	Output/Capital Ratio[b]	1.2	.40	1.7
(9)	Shift Ratio[c]	1.54[e]	1.57	1.62[f]
	Monetary Indicators			
(10)	Relative Food Prices (index)	127	133	142
(11)	Average Savings	3.3	2.9	5.6

	Inventory/Sales Ratio[d] (days)			
(12)	Nonfood	94[g]	99	98[h]
(13)	Food	20[g]	19	19[h]
(14)	Consumer Price Index	.9	1.0	-.2

Sources: (1)-(3), (10), (11), (14): Table 1; (4): RS76, pp. xxxvi-vii; (5), (6): *Rocznik statystyczny przemyslu, 1976*, pp. xvi-xvii; (7) RS74, pp. 109, 118; (8): RSP76, pp. xviii-xiv; (9): RSP71 and RSP73, pp. 212-13 and p. 231; (12), (13): RS66, p. 338; RS71, p. 337; RS70, p. 324; RS68, p. 325; RS72, p. 358.

[a]Registered looking for work divided by the number of "actively employed."

[b]Valued added per 1,000 zlotys of gross physical capital, in constant zlotys.

[c]Ratio of "productive" workers employed on the first shift to all such workers.

[d]Average quarterly inventories of consumer goods divided by average daily sales, in current zlotys.

[e]1966-1968

[f]1972 only

[g]1964-1968

[h]1971 only

output of "comparable" firms. Just as it would be difficult for the firm to produce less than the previous year's output, because such a plan would be difficult to justify, so there is pressure to at least match comparable firms. Even in this sort of environment, however, the comparable planned increase is collectively determined in pristine ignorance of real technical conditions; and, in a polycentric economy, there is no guarantee that planned rates will match (or exceed or fall short of for that matter) full capacity.

Having established the plausibility of a demand mechanism which explains the appearance of idle resources in a socialist economy, specifically Poland, let us turn to some numbers. To respectably test the demand hypothesis, one would have to establish that (a) there was a gap before 1970; (b) the gap disappeared after 1970; and, most important, (c) differential incomes policies accounted for both the opening and the closing. The most we can do here is to suggest whether (a) and (b) seem to apply and whether (c) is possible.

Is there any evidence to suggest the existence of unemployed resources in Poland before 1971? Direct measures were taken to limit unemployment. In early 1970 industry was ordered to lay off 200,000 workers.[30] Further, taking the ratio of people registered and looking for work to the total labor force, as a proxy for the intensity of use of labor resources, we observe (Table 11.3) an increase in 1969-1970 compared with the following and preceeding periods.[31] Thus, the official "unemployment" rate supports the gap hypothesis, as do employment growth rates, which reveal a similar slowing at the end of the 1960s.

Unemployment of capital can be gauged by two statistics: the shift ratio and the output-capital ratio (Table 11.3). One would expect that during slack (tight) periods, the shift ration (the ratio of production workers employed on the first shift to all such workers) would increase (decrease). But the ratio was more or less constant. On the other hand, the output-capital ratio dipped sharply in 1969-1970.

Thus, although the picture is mixed, there is some evidence that unemployed labor and capital appeared at the close of the 1960s and disappeared in the early 1970s.

There is little doubt that Poland experienced a very rapid acceleration of real growth after 1970 and that incomes policies differed radically between the late 1960s and the early (and middle) 1970s. If reflation had been the only factor involved, one would have expected a deceleration of growth rates after the 1970s. In fact, however, rates accelerated, although not greatly (Table 11.1). Of course, no one argues that demand management was the only relevant determinant of growth. Undoubtedly the huge imports of foreign goods and technology (which, however, did not begin in earnest until late 1972), auspicious agricultural results, and political commitment all played a role. What can be said is that the hypothesis that demand management is relevant for maturing socialism is consistent with recent Polish experience.

Whatever the role of demand management in explaining Polish economic performance in the late 1960s and early 1970s, it is excess demand, not inadequate demand, which is the problem today.

CONCLUDING COMMENT

The most general problem Poland faces is that of achieving a rate of growth in real consumption adequate to match the rising expectations of the population. These expectations focus most dramatically on food (particularly meat) and housing, an emphasis reflected in the current Five Year Plan. Gains from international trade must be realized and agriculture must be revitalized, issues discussed elsewhere in this volume.

It is clear that decentralization in one form or another is here to stay. This is an inevitable feature of mature socialism, if only because of the complexity of a modern economy and the centrifugal pull of foreign trade. Perhaps the major problem of political economy in Poland is to design an economic structure where the "legitimate" demand for resources does not exceed the ability of the economy to produce. It is a common view that the Polish economy is characterized by inadequate centralization of macroeconomic control. Central authority is fragmented between several power centers: the Planning Commission, the ministries, the Council of Ministers, and the financial authorities. This sort of structure, if the common view is in fact correct, is not likely to generate stable macroeconomic outcomes. Fluctuations have characterized past economic performance. Now conditions are aggravated by the increased concentration in industry brought about with the birth of the WOGi.

An obvious solution is to let money provide the appropriate constraint on demand, but this would require full-fledged market socialism, where prices, profits, interest--value categories in general--are determinant. It would also require that the financial authorities achieve a status and power hitherto vouchsafed to others. This solution is probably ideologically unacceptable. Whether Poland or the other East European countries can, in their command-market economies, even in the best of circumstances, design stable economies is a key question. The experience of the West in this regard, to the extent that it is relevant, is far from encouraging.

NOTES

1. These figures would seem to imply that the ratio of investment to NMP was low in Poland relative to other East European countries, but this was not the case. In 1967 the ratio of net investment to NMP was 27 percent in Poland and 34 percent, 22 percent, 21 percent, and 30 percent in Bulgaria, Czechoslovakia, East Germany, and Hungary, respectively. T.P. Alton, "Economic Structure and Growth in Eastern Europe," in Economic Developments in the Countries of Eastern Europe. Washington, DC: U.S. Government Printing Office, 1970, p. 60.

2. Rocznik statystyczny, 1976. Warsaw: Glowny Urzad Statystyczny, 1977, pp. xxxvii-iv.

3. These price increases, which were announced June 24, 1976, but rescinded before they took effect, were part of a package involving increased prices for agricultural products and differential, partially compensating payments to pensioners, students, and other segments of the population. Sugar was to increase by 100 percent, meat by 69 percent, butter and cheese by 30 percent, and fish by 30 percent to 60 percent. Cf. New York Times, June 25 and June 26, 1976.

4. "Ciaglosc polityki--nowe elementy realizacji," Gospodarka planowa, No. 2 (1977), p. p. 62.

5. For a more detailed discussion of Gierek's policies, see Z.M. Fallenbuchl, "The Strategy of Development and Gierek's Economic Manuever" and "The

Polish Economy in the 1970s," East European Economies Post-Helsinki, J.P. Hardt, ed., Washington, DC: U.S. Government Printing Office, 1977, pp. 826-46; Canadian Slavonic Papers, XV, Nos. 1 & 2 (1973), pp. 52-70; J. Miller, Placa a planowanie gospodarcze w Polsce, 1950-1975. Warsaw: Panstwowe Wydawnictwo Ekonomiczne, 1977, pp. 180ff.

6. Poland traded little even by East European standards. Cf. Trzeciakowski's discussion of Poland's "inward looking" foreign trade posture before 1970 in "Polish Foreign Trade: A Retrospective View," Canadian Slavonic Papers, XV, Nos. 1 & 2 (1963), pp. 71-77.

7. Fallenbuchl, "Strategy," p. 60.

8. Annual wage plans for the state sector were overfulfilled by an average of 2.1 percent for 1965-1970 and 1.1 percent for 1969-1970. Cf. John P. Farrell, "Bank Control of the Wage Fund in Poland: 1950-1970," Soviet Studies, XXVII, No. 2 (1975), p. 267.

9. A. Wiernik, Bank i kredyt, No. 2 (1972), pp. 45-50. On the deflationary aspects of the proposed incentive scheme, see H. Flakierski, "The Polish Economic Reform of 1970," Canadian Journal of Economics, VI, No. 1 (1973), pp. 1-15.

10. Polish foreign debt is relatively high (see table). At the end of 1976, the Polish debt service ratio (interest plus principal over exports to the West) was 30 percent, whereas the rule-of-thumb standard of prudence is 25 percent. Of course if, say, one-third of Polish exports to socialist countries were included in the denominator, the ratio would fall to a solid 15 percent. But since actual hard-currency earnings rather than total export earnings are the more accepted measure of creditworthiness, it seems that Poland is approaching a debt ceiling, in the sense that additional funds would be forthcoming only at premium interest rates. That a "ceiling" is imminent is suggested by recent policy. When the export plan for 1976 went awry, imports were curtailed rather than resort to additional foreign borrowing (cf. Fallenbuchl in this volume). The plan for 1978 calls for an acceleration of exports and a decline in imports from the West (9.2 percent and -1.6 percent respectively). Perhaps the

greatest "reserve" inherited from Gomulka--unused foreign credit--appears exhausted. P. Bozyk, "Wymogi rownowagi," Polityka, No. 2 (1978), p. 18; E. Pietrzak, "Zycie i kredyt," Polityka, No. 33 (1977), pp. 1-4.

ESTIMATED FOREIGN DEBT, POLAND AND SELECTED COUNTRIES, 1975, 1976

		East European Countries		Western Countries	
	Poland	U.S.S.R.	Other	Developed[1]	Developing
End-1975 ($ billions)	7.5	12.5			
% of Exports	172	83	110	66	146
% of GNP	9	2	5	16	27
End-1976 ($ billions)	11.5	8.1			
% of Avg. Exports, 1974-1976	193	80	175	65	133
Debt Service[2]	30	8		10	16
% Real, Growth, 1973-1976[3]	229	105	92	61	44

[1]The sample of developed countries ranged from sixteen to eighteen; of developing countries, from nine to eleven.

[2]Ratio of principal and interest payments to exports of goods and services. For socialist countries, only exports to the West are counted. Poland ranked sixth of thirty countries reported.

[3]External debt outstanding deflated by export prices. Poland ranked first of thirty-three countries reported.

Sources: World Financial Markets (December 1976), p. 6 and June (1977), pp. 8, 10.

11. See Table 11.1 for the behavior of the terms of trade.

12. The best discussion of the WOGi are contained in K. Cholewicka-Gozdzik, ed., Wielkie organizacje gospodarcze: doswiaczenia z lat 1973-1975. Warsaw: Panstwowe Wydawnictwo Ekonomicze and

Polskie Towarzystwo Ekonomiczne; and B. Glinski, ed., Zarys systemu funkcjonowania przemyslowych jednostek inicjujacych. Warsaw: Panstwowe Wydawnictwo Ekonomiczne, 1975.

13. W. Trzeciakowski, Modele posredniego kierowania gospodarka planowa w sterowaniu handlem zagranicznym. Warsaw: Panstwowe Wydawnictwo Ekonomiczne, 1975, pp. 243ff.

14. Specifically, the wage bill was tied to value added by the wage elasticity of value added, meaning that, e.g., if the elasticity was .6, a 10 percent increase in value added would lead to a 6 percent increase in the (legal) wage bill. There are three noteworthy aspects of this reform:

(1) The wage bill was to increase automatically. No attempt was to be made to justify the increase in terms of output mix or employment profile of the firm, as had always been the case in the past. Thus there was a willingness to stimulate output by assuring a payoff to firms which increased value added rapidly, even at the cost of "inequities" at the plant level. In the past the link between wages and output was not automatic at all, and the corresponding coefficient (relating overplan wage bill to overplan output, usually in gross value terms) was regularly manipulated by bodies above the enterprise.

(2) The coefficient was to be set for several years. The object of this relative permancy was to extend the planning horizon of enterprises, reduce uncertainty, and hopefully encourage a longer run point of view conducive to technological change.

(3) Various small funds (for innovation, "quality," "serving unique machines") were consolidated.

In cases of overfulfillment of the value added plan, the extra wages could be spent to increase employment and/or wages, fringe benefits, or social expenditures, at management's discretion. This was significant decentralization as compared to former systems, at least insofar as formal regulations were concerned.

The wage aspect of the reform was not carried out in this pristine form. In practice policy makers found it necessary to restrict increases in wages. K. Gorski, "Zasady tworzenia i gospodarowania srodkami na wynagrodzenia w jednostkach inicjujacych," in Cholewicka-Gozdzik, "Wielkie organizacje,"pp. 166-169.

15. A. Lipowski, "Rozwiazanie w dziedzinie cen," in Glinski, "Zarys Systemu,"pp. 150-166.

16. K. Poznanski, "Finansowanie inwestycji," in Glinski, ibid., pp. 195-215.

17. Lipowski, "Rozwiazanie," pp. 166ff.

18. Decentralization can be defined rigorously only relative to a given partitioning of the economic system. The move to WOGi obviously changed the petitioning of the Polish economy. Cf. L. Hurwicz, "Centralization and Decentralization of Economic Processes," in A. Eckstein, ed., Comparison of Economic Systems. Berkeley: University of California Press, 1971, pp. 79-102.

19. The reform was de facto revoked during 1975 and 1976. In 1977 another attempt was made to implement a "modified" version of the WOGi reform on a "limited scale". J. Mujzel, "Kierunki Ewolucji Polityki Dochodowej," Zycie Gospodarcze, No. 8, (1978), p. 11.

20. The effect, when demand exceeds supply, is that price increases lead to proportional increases in total revenue, so long as the new price is still below equilibrium and supply is given. Thus profits, value added and total revenue (sales) all increase when price increases. If there is no excess demand, the "true" demand curve becomes relevant and price increases are not necessarily in the material interest of the firm.

21. "Deflationary unemployment is thus theoretically possible in a STE, (Soviet-type economy, of the old type--JF), but in such a case the planners heads should be examined." P.J.D. Wiles, Communist International Economics. London: Basil Blackwell, 1968, p. 45. But Wiles also argues that decentralization brings Keynesian problems. My point here is that the view of socialist economies as STEs, at least as regards Keynesian problems, hangs on despite generally acknowledged decentralization.

22. K. Ryc, "Konsumpcja: czynnikiem rozwoju," Nowe drogi, No. 9 (1972), pp. 98-108; Z. Fedorowicz, Podstawy teorii pieniadza w gospodarce socjalistycznej. Warsaw: Panstwowe Wydawnictwo Ekonomiczne, 1975, pp. 191-192; J. Pajestka, Determinanty postepu: czynniki i wspolzaleznosci rozwoju spoleczno-gospodarczego. Warsaw: Panstwowe Wydawnictwo Naukowe, 1975, pp. 75ff.

23. That Gosbank followed a real bills policy is based on R. Powell's pioneering work on Soviet monetary policy, although such a policy has also been ascribed to the Polish central bank by Montias. Cf. R. Powell, "Soviet Monetary Policy," Berkeley: Unpublished Ph.D. dissertation, 1952; J. Montias, "Bank Lending and Fiscal Policy in Eastern Europe," in G. Grossman, ed., Money and Plan: Financial Aspects of East European Economic Reforms. Berkeley: University of California Press, 1968, pp. 38-56.

24. Econometric macroeconomic models of the Polish economy have been built. One of the five major models is Keynesian in that output, or some subset of the output aggregate, is demand-determined and is..."the first of its type for a socialist economy that attempts to handle the problem of the use of productive capacity." Zastosowania ekonometrycznych modeli rozwoju gospodarki narodowej. Warsaw: Panstwowe Wydawnictwo Ekonomiczne, 1976, p. 115.

25. This assumption can be challenged, however. There has always been the problem of "hidden price increases," the substitution of more expensive for less expensive items in the current mix of consumer goods. The problem became particularly intense in Poland in 1973 when "large economic organizations" were allowed considerable freedom in establishing prices of "new" products, and the wage bill was tied rigidly to value added.

26. T. Wojciechowski, Obrot srodkami produkcji. Warsaw: Panstwowe Wydawnictwo Ekonomiczne, 1972, p. 49n. Our interpretation assumes a constant degree of aggregation in "goods" planned. Moreover, goods are allocated from points beneath the "center", and hence this sort of decentralization does not necessarily mean that firms acquire greater choice in their input mixes. However, Polish literature on the subject makes clear that

over the years firms have acquired substantial freedom in input mix determination via more or less free contracting among state firms. There is also in Poland a substantial "secondary market" in allocated goods.

27. Cf. T. Kierczynski and W. Wojciechowksi, Rola zysku w systemie ekonomiczno-finansowym. Warsaw: Panstwowe Wydawnictwo Ekonomiczne, 1972.

28. Cf. Trzeciakowski, Modele, pp. 265-266.

29. By "concentration" we mean size of the average producing unit relative to the total branch or industry. On the evolution of Polish industrial structure, see B. Glinski, System funkcjonowania gospodarki: logika zmian. Warsaw: Panstwowe Wydawnictwo Ekonomiczne, 1977.

30. In addition, the plan for 1971-1975 drawn up under Gomulka envisioned official unemployment of half a million by 1975, about 5 percent of the nonagricultural labor force. M. Gamarnikow, "A New Economic Approach," Problems of Communism (September-October, 1972), p. 21.

31. This is undoubtedly a worse approximation of "true" unemployment than is given by Western unemployment figures, if only because of underemployment. Fortunately, our concern here is more with the trend than the absolute value.

12
Policy Alternatives in Polish Foreign Economic Relations

Zbigniew M. Fallenbuchl

Many of the present difficulties which face Poland's economy in the field of foreign economic relations have their roots in the 1950s. These are the far-reaching consequences of at least three developments: (1) the Stalinist policy of building socialism, with its highly centralized and heavily bureaucratic system of planning and management of the economy; (2) the Soviet-type industrialization drive; and (3) the forced separation of the economy from the West.

There was a strong interrelation between the economic system which was then introduced and the development strategy which was adopted. The centralized command system of planning and management was incompatible with an "outward looking" strategy. On the other hand, the acceptance of the concept of a closed economy, with foreign trade playing a passive role, and of the strategy based on import substitution and the priority development of industries producing investment goods which were required for the development of industry within the country, made rigid controls and administrative commands necessary in order to insulate the economy from the outside forces. Stalin's concept of two separate world markets with only limited contacts between them[1] and the impact of the cold war strengthened both the command system and the policy

The author wishes to acknowledge, with thanks, research grants from the American Council of Learned Societies--the Social Science Council (1974), the Canada Council (1975), and the Ford Foundation (1975) which made it possible for him to visit Poland twice (1974 and 1976) and to collect research materials on which this paper has been based.

of autarky. Under the political circumstances of the decade, no East European country would have been allowed to accept any alternative strategy, the Hungarian limited experiment with Imre Nagy's New Economic Course of 1953-1955 being the best proof.[2] In the field of foreign economic relations no choice was left for the leaders but to follow the policy of a relatively high degree of autarky,[3] which was limited only by special relations with the Soviet Union.

The industrialization drive of the early 1950s was impressive in its scale and speed. The centralized command system facilitated it. Although unable to ensure efficient utilization of resources, the system is a powerful instrument that can ensure the mobilization of the labour force and its full employment, a high rate of capital accumulation, and the allocation of resources for the fulfillment of a few priority targets.[4] It is precisely because it provides the possibility to ignore market forces that it makes possible the creation of new enterprises and industries, in accordance with the planners' preferences, whatever the short-run, or even long-run, profitability of these investment projects. However, it is also because of the lack of signals, which a market provides, that the planners have no guidance concerning the industrial structures to create and the order in which various industries or stages of production should be developed. They are unable to determine whether particular investment projects are profitable in the long-run.

It is now acceptable in Eastern Europe to state that, once the basic industrial structure has been constructed, the centralized command system should be replaced by a more decentralized system utilizing economic parametric signals and material incentives. This new system is often regarded, quite rightly, as necessary to effect a switch from the extensive to the intensive pattern of development,[5] i.e., to make rates of growth of national income, industrial production, and so on depend on increases in the productivity of inputs rather than on increases in their quantities. Systemic modifications and a change in the pattern of development form the economic side of the now fashionable concept of "development under mature socialism," which is the central theme of political programs, speeches and many scholarly works published at present in Poland.

Explicitly or implicitly, it is suggested that

the centralized command system was necessary at the early stages of industrialization and that the pattern of development had to be extensive at that time. This is not, however, obvious. With the intensive pattern, the progress would have been achieved at the early stages at a lower cost. With the utilization of market forces and an "outward-looking" strategy of development, the industrial structure would have been more conducive to the intensive pattern and to the utilization of benefits of specialization and trade.

1950-1955

The Polish Six-Year Plan (1950-1955), like all other East European plans at that time, was based on the assumption that a rapid development of heavy industry should increase the degree of self-sufficiency of the economy. Moreover, this task was expected to be achieved without an increase in the import of raw materials.[6]

The necessary import of investment goods was expected to be financed by almost doubling the export of foodstuffs and other agricultural products, despite the allocation of only limited resources for investment in this sector of the economy, and not taking into consideration that a considerable part of those which would be allocated for this sector would be needed to effect the envisaged collectivization drive, which is always a capital intensive process.[7]

The actual development of trade differed from the planned pattern. The agricultural exports did not increase to the expected level. There was a decline in 1951 and 1952, and the 1955 level was only 38 percent above the 1949 level, despite a drastic limitation of domestic consumption. The growth of raw material imports was controlled until 1953, partly because of a drastically reduced standard of living. Despite all efforts, the import of this group of commodities in 1955 was 23 percent above the 1949 level. Moreover, the import of machines and equipment considerably exceeded the planned quantities. Some targets for domestic production of investment goods were not met, and the planned level of investment could only be secured by additional unplanned imports.[8]

At the same time there was, however, a shortage of exportable commodities. Because of the stress on heavy industry, other sectors of the economy were neglected. Some traditional exports were not produced in sufficient quantities, their output fluctuated widely from year to year, their quality deteriorated, and there were delays in fulfilling orders. The loss of some important markets, in some of which Polish products had been well known before World War II, followed. Disturbances caused by the collectivization drive in agriculture aggravated the situation. At the same time, the high-priority industries were unable to produce for export. Their output was designed to meet domestic needs, above all those connected with the expansion of the domestic productive capacity in heavy industry. An attempt to produce excessively large numbers of investment goods resulted in a limited scale, high cost, and a low level of technological sophistication. The policy of making available for export only some temporary surpluses was not conducive to the long-run expansion of exports. There was a high degree of instability and many transactions were clearly unprofitable,[9] although, with the distorted prices and incomplete calculation of costs, nobody really knew how much of national income Poland was exporting with every item of its exports.

The balance of payments difficulties were met by additional strengthening of the policy of import substitution.[10] This decision, in turn, aggravated the situation even further. The lack of a long-run policy with respect to the expansion of exports restricted the possibility of obtaining additional imports of raw materials and investment goods. International trade developed into one of the main barriers of growth which pushed the rate of growth of national income downward.[11]

The nature of the industrialization drive of the early 1950s is clearly shown by the pattern of investment allocation. In 1950-1955 industry obtained 43.5 percent of total investment funds, agriculture only 10.2 percent, and housing and urban and rural infrastructure 17.9 percent.

Within industry the main stress was on the development of metallurgy (20.9 percent of total industrial investment), fuels (18.0 percent), engineering industry (17.4 percent) and chemical industry, mostly basic so-called "heavy chemical industry" (12.5 percent). Jointly these four industries absorbed, together with power generating industry, 78.5 percent of total industrial investments.

As the result of this policy, an industrial structure was created which ignored developments in the outside world,[12] not only in the West but even in other countries of the bloc, except the Soviet import requirements. This last factor is usually overlooked when the "autarkic period" is discussed in the Polish economic literature.[13] It played, however, a very important role, as exports to the Soviet Union had a powerful impact on shaping the Polish industrial structure.

There was, first of all, the Soviet demand for Polish coal. On the basis of the Soviet-Polish agreement of August 16, 1945, an annual quota to that commodity was exported to the Soviet Union at a special low price. The original quota was halved in March 1947, but it was not abolished until November 1953, and Poland received 2 billion deviza zlotys as compensation after October 1956.[14]

Large exports of mining products to the Soviet Union contributed to the very large share of extractive industries in global industrial production and in total industrial employment.

The Soviet demand also had a considerable impact on the expansion of the Polish engineering industry. Between 1950 and 1955 exports to the Soviet Union represented from 98 percent to 100 percent of the total export of railway passenger cars (total export about 61 percent of output in 1953), from 45 percent to 87 percent of exported railway freight cars (total export 64 percent of output in 1953), from 93 percent to 100 percent of locomotives (total export 77 percent of output in 1955), from 85 percent to 100 percent of ships (total export 93 percent of output in 1953). The heavy transport equipment required large quantities of steel and led to a very rapid increase in the import of iron ore from the Soviet Union. Exports to the Soviet Union increased the import intensity of industrial production and the dependence of the Polish economy on imports from the Soviet Union.

In engineering, the expansion of production was often based on Soviet blueprints and equipment. In effect, instead of building an additional plant within the country in order to increase the output of a particular type of machine, the Soviet Union would let Poland establish that plant exactly according to the Soviet specifications, to utilize Polish steel produced with the iron ore imported from the Soviet Union and domestic coal. There were some adverse consequences of this policy: (1) it was not clear that production of these particular machines in Poland was profitable--at least in some cases the Polish economy was subsidizing that export; (2) the technology was that which had already been in use in the Soviet Union, often for a long time, and the newly established plants were obsolete already at the time of their construction;[15] (3) very often the products could not be sold outside the Soviet bloc; and (4) as the same policy was applied in other East European countries, their economies became "parallel"--they were producing identical products made according to the same blueprints and with the help of the same equipment and technology--this tendency created a serious obstacle for trading among them.[16]

Moreover, mining, iron and steel, and heavy engineering are capital intensive. The priority expansion of these branches of industry required large investment funds and reduced the possibility of allocating sufficient funds for other sectors of the economy.[17] As the result, in some industries producing traditional exports such as high quality foodstuffs and manufactured consumption goods, depleted capital stock was not even replaced. There were many cases of decapitalization in textile and food industries,[18] as well as in residential housing and urban and rural infrastructure.

The industrialization drive had a significant impact on the structure of both exports and imports (see Table 12.1). Between 1950 and 1955 the share of fuels and power in total exports in current prices increased from 41.3 percent to 47.9 percent, the share of metallurgical industry from 6.5 percent to 8.6 percent, and the share of electrical and engineering industry from 9.8 percent to 13.7 percent. The shares of all other groups of exports declined. On the import side, during this period only the shares of fuel and power, and products of the metallurgical industry increased (from 2.8 percent to 4.7 percent and from 9.7 percent to 13.5 respectively).

1955-1960

The industrialization drive ended in economic difficulties which appeared already in 1955. The workers' riots in Poznan in that year and the politically explosive situation, which brought the country almost to the brink of a general uprising, led to a change in leadership, decollectivization, reduction in the pace of industrialization, a greater stress on the production of consumption goods, and a change in attitude toward the expansion of production for export. The share of

TABLE 12.1
(A) The Structure of Export According to the Sectors of Origin
(Current Prices, Percentages of Total Exports)

Sectors	1950	1955	1960	1965	1966	1967	1968	1969	1970	1971	1972	1973	1974	1975	1976	1977
Fuels and power	41.3	47.9	22.7	16.5	15.6	14.3	13.6	12.4	12.5	14.0	13.6	12.7	15.9	20.1	18.0	16.4
Metallurgical industry	6.5	8.6	10.3	7.4	6.8	7.7	7.6	8.3	9.3	8.1	7.2	7.3	7.8	6.8	6.3	6.0
Electrical and Engineering industry	9.8	13.7	30.0	36.9	37.6	38.5	39.9	42.4	41.7	42.3	41.9	41.5	39.4	41.4	43.7	46.2
Chemical industry	3.8	3.4	4.9	6.1	6.6	7.8	8.7	9.3	8.4	9.1	9.2	9.6	11.0	9.3	8.5	8.6
Light industry	10.6	5.9	7.1	7.1	8.2	8.7	9.0	8.4	8.4	9.0	8.9	9.3	8.8	8.9	9.1	9.5
Food industry and Agriculture	21.9	14.7	19.7	19.5	18.6	17.1	15.8	13.8	14.5	12.7	14.7	15.0	12.6	9.8	10.1	9.5
Other products*	6.1	5.8	5.3	6.5	6.6	5.9	5.4	5.4	5.2	4.8	4.5	4.6	4.5	3.7	4.3	3.8

Table 12.1 (cont.)
(B) The Structure of Import According to the Sectors of Origin
(Current Prices, Percentages of Total Import)

Sectors	1950	1955	1960	1956	1970	1971	1972	1973	1974	1975	1976	1977
Fuels and power	2.8	4.7	7.6	7.4	6.7	6.4	6.1	5.7	5.5	9.4	10.1	11.5
Metallurgy	9.7	13.5	16.0	15.1	17.7	16.4	15.2	15.4	17.2	17.5	15.0	13.4
Electromechanical	33.4	32.9	29.3	35.4	38.5	37.9	42.7	44.7	41.9	40.7	42.2	40.3
Chemical	10.1	10.1	9.5	10.1	10.7	11.0	10.4	9.6	12.2	11.8	10.7	11.6
Light industry	16.7	14.3	10.8	8.0	6.8	7.0	6.9	5.6	5.1	4.3	4.1	4.5
Food industry and Agriculture	21.3	20.1	22.6	18.3	12.5	14.4	12.2	13.0	12.4	11.2	12.6	13.3
Other products	6.0	4.4	4.2	5.7	7.1	6.9	6.5	6.0	5.7	5.1	5.3	5.4

*Including: "Mineral industry," "Woodworking and paper industry", "Other industries," "Forestry" and "Others".

Sources: Rocznik Statystyczny 1972. Warsaw: G.U.S., 1972, pp. 393-394; 1976, p. 336; 1977, p. 285; "Polski Handel Zagraniczny w 1977 Roku", Handel Zagraniczny, No. 3, 1978, p. 26.

industry in total investment outlays declined from 43.5 percent to 38.8 percent, the lowest proportion in all five-year periods. The share of agriculture increased from 10.2 percent to 12.5 percent and that of housing and urban and rural infrastructure increased from 17.9 percent to 25.9 percent. Within industry, the share of metallurgy declined from 29.0 percent of total industrial investment to 12.6 percent, and the share of the engineering industry from 17.4 percent to 14.5 percent. However, the share of fuels and power increased even further. There was an increase in the share of the building materials industry and the food industry, as well as small increases in other industries producing consumption goods.

The average rate of growth of Net Material Product (NMP) declined from 8.7 percent in 1951-1955 to 6.5 percent in 1956-1960 (see Table 12.2). However, the newly established industries increased the demand for imported raw materials. Also, because of the potentially explosive political situation, it was necessary to increase import of food and other consumption goods in 1956 and 1957. The average rate of growth of import increased from 7.7 percent in 1951-1955 to 10.7 percent, exceeding both the average rate of growth of export and that of NMP.

As the result of the short-term measures which were adopted by the new leadership, as a matter of necessity foreign trade played an active role, with imports exceeding exports and Western foreign credits being obtained. The adverse balances of visible trade were particularly big in 1957 and 1959 (see Table 12.3). No balance of payments statistics are published in Poland. However, the difference between Domestic Net Material Product (DNMP), or "Produced National Income," represents the balance of commodity trade and of the so-called "productive services" (transport, communications, licenses and technical documentation, services in connection with export, and expenditures on international fairs and exhibitions) plus some "wastes of national income" and "errors", which may be assumed to be relatively unimportant and representing an approximately constant percentage. Discrepancies between the "deviza" prices at which foreign trade is reported and domestic prices at which the rest of the national income is reported make the calculation of an actual inflow or outflow of capital impossible. Nevertheless, it may be assumed that when there is a positive difference between

TABLE 12.2
Rates of Growth of Domestic Net Material Product ("Produced National Income"), National Net Material Product ("Allocated National Income"), Import and Export (Constant Prices)

Year	DNMP	NNMP	Import	Export
1948	29.9	31.6	44.4	64.3
1949	17.7	15.5	32.5	15.7
1950	15.1	15.2	15.0	11.6
1951	7.5	7.5	18.0	-2.4
1952	6.2	6.1	-5.9	5.0
1953	10.4	10.3	1.9	11.8
1954	10.5	10.6	16.9	-2.0
1955	8.4	8.9	3.7	3.0
1956	7.0	7.8	9.6	-3.6
1957	10.7	13.6	19.5	-3.6
1958	5.5	3.2	3.7	26.5
1959	5.2	7.0	15.4	11.7
1960	4.3	3.0	5.3	16.6
1961	8.2	7.3	13.6	14.3
1962	2.1	2.7	12.4	11.1
1963	6.9	6.3	5.6	4.6
1964	6.7	4.9	3.1	18.0
1965	7.0	8.3	15.1	8.1
1966	7.1	7.4	8.0	3.9
1967	5.7	4.5	7.5	11.9
1968	9.0	8.5	8.4	15.5
1969	2.9	3.5	10.6	7.7
1970	5.2	5.0	10.4	8.7
1971	8.1	9.8	13.8	6.5
1972	10.6	12.7	22.1	15.2
1973	10.8	14.3	22.6	11.0
1974	10.4	12.1	14.2	12.8
1975	9.0	10.9	5.0	8.3
1976	6.8	7.0	10.3	5.4
1977	5.0	2.7	0.4	8.8

Average Rates of Growth

Period	DNMP	NNMP	Import	Export	Import/NMP
1948-1950	20.9	23.6	30.6	30.5	1.46
1951-1955	8.7	9.8	7.7	3.1	0.81
1956-1960	6.5	6.9	10.7	9.5	1.65
1961-1965	6.2	5.9	10.2	11.2	1.61
1966-1970	6.0	5.8	9.0	9.5	1.50
1971-1975	9.8	12.0	15.5	10.8	1.58
1976-1977	5.9	4.9	5.4	7.1	0.92

Sources: *Rocznik statystyczny 1978*. Warsaw: G.U.S., 1978, pp. XXXII, XXXIII, XLII, XLIII.

NNMP and DNMP there probably is an inflow of capital, and a negative difference, especially when of a considerable size, suggests an outflow of capital.

From 1947 through 1971 there was only one year when there was a positive difference, and this happened in 1959 (see Table 12.4). The negative difference in 1957 was the third smallest for the whole period, and the average for 1956-1960, the five-year period which followed the "Polish October", was the lowest among all five-year periods until the 1970s. It seems, therefore, that during this period there was the smallest outflow of capital and probably a net inflow in at least one year.

There seems to be some similarity between the policy toward foreign trade in Gomulka's early period and Gierek's new strategy, except that in the late 1950s the policy did not last long, was not connected with the large-scale import of Western technology, and foreign credits were substantially smaller.

Usually 1958 is given as a year after which, throughout Eastern Europe, some serious efforts were made to introduce international specialization within the CMEA. The autarkic tendencies were not, however, eliminated, and the self-sufficiency of the bloc remained one of the top objectives. For example, it was a prevalent view in Eastern Europe that in every country except the Soviet Union serious "disproportions" has been created between the level of development of the processing industry and the domestic raw material base. It was therefore decided that special attention should be given to this problem. The German Democratic Republic, Czechoslovakia, and Poland agreed to make contributions for the expansion of the production of certain raw materials in the Soviet Union. Poland advanced 70 million rubles in the early 1960s for the expansion of potash mines in the region which, until the Second World War, had formed part of the Polish state.[19] A major effort was also made by all CMEA countries, including Poland, to expand their own "domestic raw materials base" with the result that "temporary concentration of investment resources in highly capital intensive branches of production created difficulties for the achievement of high rates of growth of production at that time."[20]

The "Polish October" of 1956 resulted in rather bold proposals for systemic changes; some of them were really pioneering and subsequently had a

TABLE 12.3
Value of Export, Import and Commodity Trade Balance
(Million zld; Current Prices)

Year	Total Trade			Trade With Socialist Countries			Trade With Other Countries		
	Export	Import	Balance	Export	Import	Balance	Export	Import	Balance
1946	506.2	583.1	-76.9	302.9	456.3	-153.4	203.3	126.8	76.5
1947	985.0	1,280.6	-295.6	436.2	442.3	-6.1	548.8	838.3	-289.5
1948	2,125.1	2,065.6	59.5	939.7	981.7	-42.0	1,185.4	1,083.9	101.5
1949	2,475.3	2,529.8	-54.5	1,123.0	1,077.6	+45.4	1,352.3	1,452.2	-99.9
1950	2,537.0	2,672.6	-135.6	1,443.3	1,633.2	-189.9	1,093.7	1,039.4	54.3
1951	3,046.6	3,696.6	-650.0	1,737.3	2,140.7	-403.4	1,309.3	1,555.9	-246.6
1952	3,101.7	3,451.9	-350.2	2,021.1	2,330.5	-309.4	1,080.6	1,121.4	-40.8
1953	3,323.9	3,097.0	226.9	2,275.4	2,223.6	51.8	1,048.5	873.4	175.1
1954	3,475.2	3,613.8	-138.6	2,406.9	2,565.1	-158.2	1,068.3	1,048.7	19.6
1955	3,678.7	3,727.2	-48.5	2,313.4	2,419.8	-106.4	1,365.3	1,307.4	57.9
1956	3,939.0	4,087.4	-148.4	2,320.7	2,709.6	-388.9	1,618.3	1,377.8	240.5
1957	3,899.9	5,006.1	-1,106.2	2,311.8	3,112.2	-800.4	1,588.1	1,893.9	-305.8
1958	4,237.5	4,907.3	-669.8	2,481.6	2,857.4	-375.8	1,755.9	2,049.9	-294.0
1959	4,580.5	5,678.4	-1,097.9	2,727.8	3,692.0	-964.2	1,852.7	1,986.4	-133.7
1960	5,302.1	5,979.9	-677.8	3,320.8	3,797.9	-477.1	1,981.3	2,182.0	-200.7
1961	6,014.3	6,746.8	-732.5	3,756.5	4,216.7	-460.2	2,257.8	2,530.1	-272.3
1962	6,584.5	7,541.6	-957.1	4,137.2	4,984.7	-847.5	2,447.3	2,556.9	-109.6
1963	7,080.1	7,916.1	-836.0	4,492.3	5,304.0	-811.7	2,587.8	2,612.1	-24.3
1964	8,385.7	8,289.0	96.7	5,402.5	5,224.6	177.9	2,983.2	3,064.4	-81.2
1965	8,911.4	9,361.2	-449.8	5,634.7	6,190.0	-555.3	3,276.7	3,171.2	105.5
1966	9,088.4	9,976.2	-887.8	5,600.6	6,415.4	-814.8	3,487.8	3,560.8	-73.0
1967	10,106.2	10,579.1	-472.9	6,444.9	6,947.6	-502.7	3,661.3	3,631.5	29.8

1968	11,431.2	11,412.4	18.8	7,513.9	7,351.9	162.0	3,917.3	4,060.5	-143.2
1969	12,566.1	12,838.6	-272.5	8,255.8	8,454.0	-198.2	4,310.3	4,384.6	-74.3
1970	14,190.5	14,430.1	-239.6	9,064.0	9,892.3	-828.3	5,126.5	4,537.8	588.7
1971	15,489.3	16,150.7	-661.4	9,770.2	10,882.8	-1,112.6	5,719.1	5,267.9	451.2
1972	18,132.7	19,612.4	-1,479.7	11,524.7	12,003.7	-479.0	6,608.0	7,608.7	-1,000.7
1973	21,355.7	26,102.8	-4,747.1	12,959.6	13,485.9	-526.3	8,395.5	12,616.9	-4,221.4
1974	27,624.8	34,822.9	-7,198.1	15,396.4	15,468.3	-71.9	12,228.4	19,354.6	-7,126.2
1975	34,160.7	41,650.7	-7,490.0	20,472.2	19,086.9	1,385.3	13,688.5	22,563.8	-8,875.3
1976	36,600.3	46,070.9	-9,470.6	21,853.0	21,588.0	265.0	14,747.0	24,483.0	-9,736.0
1977	40,747.8	48,558.4	-7,810.6	24,552.0	25,206.0	-654.0	16,196.0	23,352.0	-7,156.0

Sources: Rocznik statystyczny 1967. Warsaw: G.U.S., 1967, pp. 371-372; 1977, p. 289; 1978, p. 288; Rocznik statystyczny handlu zagranicznego 1971. Warsaw: G.U.S., 1971, pp. 2-3; 1976, pp. 2-4.

TABLE 12.4

Domestic Net Material Product (DNMP), National Net Material Product (NNMP), Balance of Foreign Transactions (NNMP - DNMP)* and Accumulation (A)
(Billion zlotys, (Constant 1971 Prices)

Year	DNMP	NNMP	NNMP-DNMP		NNMP-DNMP / DNMP (%)	A	NNMP-DNMP / A (%)
1947	120.2	117.5	-2.7		-2.25	18.4	-14.67
1948	156.2	154.7	-1.5		-0.96	24.4	- 6.15
1949	184.0	178.6	-5.4	-3.9	-2.93	28.2	-19.15
1950	211.7	205.8	-5.9		-2.79	43.2	-13.66
1951	227.6	221.2	-6.4		-2.81	45.3	-14.13
1952	241.7	234.8	-6.9		-2.85	53.8	-12.83
1953	266.9	259.1	-7.8	-7.5	-2.92	72.8	-10.71
1954	295.1	286.6	-8.5		-2.88	66.8	-12.72
1955	319.9	312.1	-7.8		-2.44	70.2	-11.11
1956	342.3	336.6	-5.7		-1.67	69.3	- 8.23
1957	379.1	382.5	-3.4		-0.90	89.2	- 3.81
1958	400.1	394.7	-5.4	-3.4	-1.35	89.6	- 6.03
1959	420.8	422.4	+1.6		+0.38	98.0	+ 0.02
1960	439.2	434.9	-4.3		-0.98	104.3	- 4.12
1961	475.0	466.6	-3.4		-1.77	115.6	- 7.27
1962	485.0	479.3	-5.7		-1.18	115.7	- 4.93
1963	518.7	509.4	-9.3	-10.2	-1.79	129.0	- 7.21
1964	553.6	534.3	-19.3		-3.49	136.1	-14.18
1965	592.4	578.9	-13.5		-2.28	155.8	- 8.66
1966	634.5	621.7	-12.8		-2.02	172.8	- 7.41
1967	670.6	649.7	-20.9		-3.12	176.-	-11.88

1968	731.0	704.9	-26.1	-21.5	-3.57	200.7	-13.00
1969	752.2	729.6	-22.6		-3.00	100.1	-11.35
1970	791.3	766.0	-25.3		-3.20	213.8	-11.83
1971	855.4	841.8	-13.6		-1.59	246.6	- 5.52
1972	945.9	948.4	+ 2.6		+0.27	299.6	+ 0.87
1973	1,048.1	1,083.6	+35.5	+30.6	+3.39	381.9	+ 9.30
1974	1,157.6	1,214.3	+56.7		+4.90	461.0	+12.30
1975	1,237.6	1,309.6	+72.0		+5.82	464.0	+15.50
1976	1,326.0	1,403.3	+77.3	+71.6	+5.83	483.6	+15.98
1977	1,414.1	1,479.9	+65.8		+4.84	500.5	+13.15

Sources: Dochod narodowy 1973. Warsaw: G.U.S., 1973, pp, 1,3, 136, 137, 138, 139; Rocznik dochodu narodowego 1976. Warsaw: G.U.S., 1976, pp. 674; Rocznik statystyczny 1976. Warsaw: G.U.S., 1976, p. XXIV; 1977, pp. 54, 58; 1978, pp. 58, 59.

* Commodity trade and the so-called "productive services" which include transport and communications, licenses and technical documentation, services in connection with export and expenditures on fairs and exhibitions.

Differences between National Net Material Product and Domestic Net Material Product include, in addition to the balance of foreign trade and "productive services", also (1) "wastes of national income" and (2) "amounts unaccounted for". In 1970-1975 the sum of these two items represented about -1 percent of DNMP.

considerable impact on the views held by the economists in other East European countries.[21] The pioneering concepts which were discussed in Polish journals did not, however, lead to any substantial reforms. In the field of foreign trade there was some decrease in the degree of centralization of decisions. At the same time, international trade ceased to be regarded as simply "an instrument with the help of which the national economy could be supplied with necessary commodities which were in short supply," as it had been described until the middle of the 1950s.[22] It was now to serve as a cost-reducing device, but still not as one of the determinants of the rate of growth and the structure of the economy. Both the level of national income and its structure were to be determined by the planners.

1961-1965

In 1961-1965 the share of industry in total investment outlays increased again and reached 40.2 percent, although the share of agriculture also increased (from 12.5 percent to 13.9 percent). Within industry the share of investment allocated to textiles, leather goods, foodstuffs, and building materials declined, while the share of fuels increased to 22.3 percent and the share of power generation to 12.1 percent.

The policy in the field of foreign economic relations during that period had as its objective a reduction in the dependence on foreign borrowing and improvement in the balance of payments by increasing exports. Some efforts were made to reduce imports, for example, by the expansion of the domestic raw material base. Between 1956-1960 and 1961-1965, the average rate of growth of exports increased from 9.5 percent to 11.2 percent, the average rates of growth of imports declined slightly (from 10.7 percent to 10.0 percent), and the average rate of growth of NMP declined from 6.5 to 6.2. The decline in NMP was probably induced by the attempts to reduce imports. There was some decline in the import intensity of the process of growth (see Table 12.2), but the reduction was only marginal. The repayment of foreign loans and contributions to the expansion of the raw materials production in the Soviet Union rapidly increased the outflow of capital, and the average annual difference between DNMP and NNMP reached -10.2 billion zlotys, the highest level so far (see

Table 12.4).

Some serious difficulties appeared by the middle of the 1960s. Although the importance of international economic relations had been recognized, the expansion of trade encountered great obstacles and no significant opening up of the economy took place. Some thinking habits had developed among the members of economic administration which led to the neglect of foreign trade, particularly at the production level. There was the lack of incentives for the expansion of production for export, where the risk of nonfulfillment of the plan is always greater than in the production for the protected sellers' market at home, and greater flexibility in changing the product mix, innovations, and effective quality control is required. There was also a shortage of personnel to staff the foreign trade enterprises.[23]

The strategy of development of the 1961-1965 and 1966-1970 plans was still basically inward looking and the preference was still given to the production of producers' goods for the domestic investment programs which involved a sharp increase in the rate of investment. Neither the basic principles of the development strategy, which had been applied during the first stage of industrialization, nor the planning and administration methods were modified to a significant extent.[24]

The newly created productive capacities, even those which replaced depleted capital, represented a duplication of the technology which had already been in existence within the economy.[25] Even when more recent technology was incorporated in the investment projects, there were serious delays in construction of plants, or their expansion, and in starting new production lines. These delays were caused by the rigidities of the overcentralized planning and management system, excessive rates of investments, and limited productive capacity of the construction industry. The situation was aggravated by the balance of payments difficulties. During the period when efforts were made to repay foreign credits and to prevent imports from expanding too rapidly, decisions were often made to postpone the import of some machines or pieces of equipment which at the time seemed less important. However, these decisions often tended to create a bottleneck effect in the investment process and contributed to the delays. In effect, when the new products were finally available for export, they were in many cases already obsolete. They could, therefore, be exported either to other CMEA countries in exchange for equally obsolete products, or sold in the West only in small quantities at drastically reduced prices, often below the cost of production. In addition, there was the adverse impact of the centralized economic system on innovations, which were in practice discouraged rather than stimulated. As the result of all these factors, the technological level of the rapidly expanding productive capacities in industry was increasingly lagging behind the standards of advanced countries. The acceleration of technological process because a necessary condition for the expansion of export to the West and, more recently, even to other CMEA countries which were increasingly more reluctant to import obsolete machines. The modernization of the capital stock was, therefore, one of the urgent needs.[26]

Equally important was the task of changing the structure of the economy. In Poland, as in other CMEA countries, it became clear during the 1960s that the industrial structure which had been created during the 1950s, was obsolete.[27] Heavy industry dominated the structure, while such "new industries" as the electronic, automotive, precision, computer, and petrochemical industries were underdeveloped. Moreover, the internal structure of even the priority industries was also obsolete, concentrating on relatively material intensive old types of products.

Modernization and restructuring would, however, require large investment outlays, and a large part of investment resources was committed for the expansion of the fuel and raw material basis, including the modernization and technical reconstruction of agriculture which involved, first of all, strengthening of the unprofitable state farms. In the words of a Polish economist, it was "the expansion of the raw material branches of the economy (that) limited, to a great extent, the resources which could have been used for the modernization and reconstruction of the whole national economy" and "as the result, the programme of reconstruction has to be postponed in practice until the 1970s".[28]

A serious conflict appeared between the need to increase investment in order to modernize and restructure the economy and the need to reform the economic system. Reforms of the economic system would require some "slack" in the economy and an expansion in the production of consumption goods to provide material incentives. This was a serious vicious circle.[29]

During 1966-1970, the share of industry in total investment outlays declined and the share of agriculture considerably increased. There was also an increase in the share of transport and communications and construction, but a serious decline in the share allocated for housing and the urban and rural infrastructure. Within industry, the share of coal, other fuels, iron and steel, building materials, and ceramics declined. The biggest increase took place in the share of the chemical industry (to 15.9 percent from 12.5 percent in 1961-1965), machine building industry (to 6.2 percent from 4.5 percent), nonferrous metallurgy (to 5.0 percent from 3.4 percent) and transport equipment industry (to 5.6 percent from 4.5 percent). There were also increases in the share of investment allocated to the metal-working precision, textile, leather, and clothing industries.

During 1966-1970, the average rate of export slightly exceeded that of import, but only because of the determined efforts to keep the growth of import restricted. Both rates were considerably below the 1961-1965 rates. The average rate of NMP declined to 6.0 percent, and the restriction of import was probably one of the reasons. The annual rate of growth of the NMP was only 2.9 percent in 1969, the second lowest increase after the 1962 rate during the whole postwar period (see Table 12.2). The average negative difference between NNMP and DNMP doubled from 10.2 billion zlotys during 1961-1965 to 21.5 billion zlotys during 1966-1970, the highest level during the whole postwar period (see Table 12.4), and this implies a considerable outflow of capital.

Some improvements in the mechanism of foreign trade were already introduced in 1966, when the calculations of the effectiveness of trade were made obligatory and planning in value terms replaced many, but not all, quantitative targets calculated in physical units.[30] In 1968 the Fifth Party Congress adopted the so-called "selective development." The main stress was put on the priority development of certain selected branches of industry and groups of commodities in which Poland was to become one of the major producers. The quality of the selected exports was to reach the highest world standards. The selected branches and enterprises were to receive priority in respect to the allocation of investment funds, skilled labor, research and development facilities, and import of necessary machines and equipment.[31] Unfortunately, not less than 100 enterprises were classified as specializing in production for export. Moreover, the selection was made on the basis of a decision by the central authorities without the benefits of properly operating market signals and calculated opportunity costs.

Some important changes occurred in the structure of exports between 1965 and 1970. The share of electrical and engineering industry increased from 36.9 percent to 41.7 percent (it was even higher in 1969 when it reached 42.4 percent). The share of the chemical industry increased from 6.1 percent to 8.4 percent (again it was higher in 1969: 9.3 percent). The share of the metallurgical industry increased from 7.4 percent to 9.3 percent. There was also an increase in the share of light industry (from 7.1 percent to 8.4 percent). On the import side, the greatest increases took place in the share of the metallurgy and electrotechnical and engineering groups. There were considerable reductions in the share of light and food industries and agriculture (see Table 12.1).

At the end of the 1960s, by far the most important group of exports was composed of goods produced by electrotechnical and engineering industry. It was here that the greatest difficulties appeared in increasing exports to the West and where even exports to CMEA countries were endangered. Fast modernization and restructuring of the economy were needed to stimulate exports. Although many economists were drawing attention to the fact that it was the economic system which created the greatest obstacle to the expansion of international economic relations, not only in Poland but also in other CMEA countries,[32] reforms were brushed aside. The investment drive, which was motivated by the desire to effect modernization and restructuring of the economy in accordance with the requirements of selective development in the shortest possible time, increased the share of accumulation to 27.7 percent of NMP in 1966, 27.1 percent in 1967, 28.5 percent in 1968, 27.3 percent in 1969, and 27.9 percent in 1970.[33] Even during the Stalinist industrialization drive a comparable rate was enforced only in 1952. Together with relatively low rates of growth of the produced national income (DNMP) and a big outflow of capital (the negative difference between NNMP and DNMP ranged from

3 percent to 3.5 percent of DNMP during 1967-1970), there was no possibility to increase consumption. The investment drive ended in the workers' riots in December 1970.

1971-1975

The acceleration of international economic relations was an essential part of Gierek's "new development strategy."[34] The main objective of the strategy was to effect a switch from the extensive to the intensive development pattern and to break away from the vicious circle. This objective was to be achieved by a simultaneous increase in investment and consumption. Large investment outlays were needed to restructure and modernize the economy, while significant increases in consumption were expected to provide incentives to increase labour productivity, in addition to obtaining support for the new leadership and securing political stability.

The strategy had the following implications for foreign economic relations:

(1) Sufficiently big simultaneous increases in investment and consumption were possible only with the help of foreign credits, which were mainly available in the West. Therefore, an excess of import over export in total trade, and especially with the convertible currency area, was expected to appear during the first few years when the import of capital would take place. Subsequently, an excess of export over import, again particularly in trade with the West, would be necessary to repay the loans.

(2) In order to restructure and modernize the economy, the most modern technology should be imported, mainly from the advanced countries in the West. The transfer of technology would take, above all, the form of the import of most modern machines and equipment, but licenses and industrial cooperations agreements would also be utilized. This policy would necessitate rapid increases in the import of machines, particularly from the West. To the extent to which these imports would not be secured by credits, pressures on

the balance of payments would appear.

(3) Higher rates of growth of production would induce greater import of raw materials and this tendency, with a relatively material intensive structure of industry,[35] would create additional balance of payments pressures.

(4) The balance of payments difficulties could also be strengthened if increases in the disposable income of the population were to exceed increases in the domestic supply of goods and services for the population. In such cases some additional imports of consumption goods would be required in order to maintain the domestic balance of the economy.

(5) In order to reduce costs, improve quality, ensure technological progress, and secure high technical specifications of produced goods, it would be necessary to restructure the economy to make it more specialized. This was a condition for increasing the overall efficiency of the economy, for maintaining and improving competitiveness in the CMEA markets in which the buyers were becoming increasingly more selective, to pay for the import of the modern technology from the West, and to repay the Western credits.[36] For these reasons, high priority in the allocation of foreign exchanges for the import of machines and equipment and licenses were to be allocated for the export promoting investments.

It was expected that, as the result of the application of this strategy, the intensive pattern of development would be ensured. Western credits could be repaid easily by expanding exports of modern, highly sophisticated, and efficiently produced goods. They would be produced in new or modernized plants, utilizing the most modern Western technology, according to the Western standards, and in some cases under industrial cooperation agreements with the Western firms. They would, therefore, be sold easily in the Western markets. It would be possible to secure an excess of exports over imports in the future because of the high rates of growth which would be achieved as the result of increased efficiency, with continuous increases in both consumption and the domestically financed investments. This strategy was attractive for the leaders not only because it gave a chance of overcoming the vicious circle, but also because foreign borrowing seemed to provide an alternative to far-reaching economic reforms which had to be de-emphasized for various reasons, including the political risk involved, uncertainty as to their economic results, vested interests at various levels of administration and within the socialist enterprises, as well as, probably, Soviet pressure.[37]

This strategy has been only partly successful. At first, rates of growth of national income, industrial production, disposable incomes, expenditures on consumption, and investment outlays were very impressive. However, the pattern of development continued to depend mainly on extensive factors. Moreover, considerable difficulties had already started to appear in 1974.

Some reasons for this situation were beyond the government's control, such as particularly unfavorable weather conditions which had an adverse effect on agricultural production and the world stagflation which accentuated difficulties in foreign trade.[38] There were also mistakes in the macroeconomic policy: attempts to enforce excessively high rates of investment and the loss of control over increases in disposable incomes, with the existing shares of investment and limited ability to expand the supply of consumption goods and services sufficiently rapidly, especially in view of the difficulties experienced in agriculture and foreign trade. Particularly important, however, was the mistaken assumption that the transfer of foreign technology on a large scale with the help of foreign borrowing was a viable alternative to economic reforms. Moreover, those modest systemic improvements which had been introduced in the early 1970s were withdrawn under the combined impact of domestically generated and foreign induced inflationary pressures.

There were also specific investment, foreign credit, and trade decisions which had a considerable adverse effect on the situation in foreign trade. Indeed, apart from the lack of reforms, foreign trade is now second only to agriculture as the source of current difficulties and the key to the solution of short and long-run problems of the

Polish economy. Moreover, the adverse situation in agriculture creates difficulties in the field of foreign trade, and difficulties in foreign trade make the solution of at least some agricultural problems more difficult.

During 1971-1975 the share of industry in total investment outlays in the national economy increased from 39.4 percent to 43.8 percent, and the share of construction increased from 4.0 percent to 5.1 percent. On the other hand, there was a very serious decline in the share of agriculture (from 16.1 percent to 13.7 percent) and housing and urban and rural infrastructure (from 19.1 percent to 17.2 percent), and a more moderate reduction in the share of trade (from 3.2 percent to 2.6 percent). Within industry, there was an increase in the share of electrotechnical and engineering groups from 19.1 percent to 23.6 percent of total industrial investment and in the share of iron and steel from 6.6 percent to 8.7 percent. Increases in the share of industrial investment allocated to the more consumer-oriented branches were much more limited (the food, textile, woodworking, and clothing industries) or unchanged (the leather and ceramics industries).

In constant prices, the average rate of import increased from 9.0 percent during 1966-1970 to 15.5 percent during 1971-1975, and the rate of growth of export from 9.5 percent to 10.8 percent. They were both above the rate of growth of the NMP, which was the highest since 1951 (see Table 12.2). The role of foreign trade clearly increased and stimulated faster growth of the economy.

The import of foreign capital served as the main agent of growth. Starting with 1972, there were positive differences between the "allocated national income" (NNMP) and the "produced national income" (DNMP), and the average annual positive difference between NNMP and DNMP was 30.6 billion zlotys. This was not only the first five-year period since World War II with a positive average inflow, but the size of the inflow exceeded the average outflow in every previous period (see Table 12.4). The negative balances of commodity trade with nonsocialist countries became very big starting with 1972 (see Table 12.3). This indicates the direction from which foreign capital was obtained. The negative balances with socialist countries, except in 1971, were considerably below their usual levels. This was particularly true in 1974, and in the following year there was a gigantic surplus in Poland's trade with socialist countries. This would suggest that, at the time when Poland had a net inflow of capital from the West, there probably was a net outflow of capital in trade with socialist countries. Equilibruim in balance of payments in Poland is usually achieved with a negative balance of commodity trade because of some transfer payments made by emigrants who support their relatives in the country, revenue from shipping and the use of Polish ports, and from transit through the Polish territories. The balance of invisible trade was negative before 1950, but starting with that year there was a positive balance of that trade.[39] It is probable that, in the absence of such payments, the positive balances between the "produced" and "allocated national income" (NNMP-DNMP) would have been even greater during 1972-1976.

THE 1976-1980 PLAN

The plan for 1976-1980 was built on the assumption that the productive capacity which had been expanded and modernized during 1971-1975 would permit an increase in export and a limitation of the expansion of import, to the extent that investment projects were of the import-substitution type, and that it would be possible to convert a negative balance of trade into a positive one by the end of 1978 or the beginning of 1979.[40] This could only be achieved by slowing down the growth of the economy. For this reason the plan not only envisaged that the total output (DNMP) would be growing more rapidly than the total quantity of goods and "productive" services available for allocation to domestic investment and consumption (NNMP), in order to secure an excess of export over import for repayment of foreign capital, but it also assumed that the rate of growth of DNMP would be considerably lower than the average rate that had been achieved in 1971-1975. The plan accepted, therefore, average increases of 7.0 percent per annum in DNMP and 4.2 percent in NNMP, as compared with the average rates of 9.8 percent and 12.0 percent achieved in the preceding five-year plan period.

The drastic switch from a negative to a positive balance of trade was a completely unrealistic objective and it has not yet been fulfilled. In fact, the very attempt to meet the target had an adverse effect on the economy. In order to reduce the balance of trade deficit, the plan for 1976

TABLE 12.5
Planned and Actual Rates of Growth of Export and Import

Year	Export					Import					
	Plan Total	Actual				Plan Total	Actual				Plan Total
		Total Current Prices	Total at Constant 1971 Prices	Socialist Countries at Constant Prices*	Other Countries at Constant Prices*		Total at Current Prices	Total at Constant 1971 Prices	Socialist Countries at Constant Prices*	Other Countries at Constant Prices*	
1970	7.1	14.9	10.4			4.9	14.5	8.7			+2.2
1971	n.a.	9.2	6.5	6.9	4.9	n.a.	11.9	13.8	11.3	20.7	n.a.
1972	4.9	17.1	15.2	16.0	14.8	16.4	21.4	22.1	10.3	44.8	-11.5
1973	12.9	17.8	11.0	12.0	10.9	20.1	33.1	22.6	13.0	37.8	-7.2
1974	18.9	29.4	12.8	15.7	5.9	22.0	33.4	14.2	11.3	19.5	-3.1
1975	22.3	23.7	8.3	8.6	5.8	14.7	19.6	5.0	-2.2	12.1	+7.6
1976	16.6	7.1	5.4	1.9	13.1	14.4	10.6	10.3	8.6	11.4	+2.2
1977	13.0	11.4	8.2	12.7	-0.2	2.7	5.4	0.4	19.1	-10.6	+10.3
1978	10.0					1.4					
1971–1975	9.2**	19.2	10.8	11.8	8.5	9.8**	23.7	15.5	8.7	27.0	-0.6**
1976–1980	11.8				14.0	4.7				0.0	+7.1

Year	Difference between Rates of Growth of Export (-) and Import (-)			
	Actual			
	Total at Current Prices	Total at Constant 1971 Prices	Socialist Countries at Constant Prices*	Other Countries at Constant Prices*
1970	+0.4	+1.7		
1971	-2.7	-7.3	-4.4	-15.8
1972	-4.3	-6.9	5.7	-30.0
1973	-15.3	-11.6	-1.0	-26.9
1974	-4.0	-1.4	4.4	-13.6
1975	+4.1	+3.3	10.8	-6.3
1976	-3.5	-4.9	-6.7	+1.7
1977	+6.0	-8.2	-6.4	+10.4
1978				
1971-1975	-4.5	-4.7	+3.1	-18.5
1976-1980				

* Calculated from index numbers the 1970 level = 100; not quite comparable with total export and import at constant 1971 prices.

** As of May 1972

Sources: Gospodarka planowa, No. 4, 1971, p. 235; No. 5, 1972, p. 264; No. 4, 1973, p. 240; No. 4. 1974, p. 230; No. 4, 1975, p. 272; No. 5, 1976, p. 216; No. 5, 1977, p. 258; No. 4, 1978, p. 180; Rocznik statystyczny 1978. Warsaw: G.U.S., 1978, pp. XLIII; Ekonomista, No. 4, 1978, p. 890; Handel zagraniczny, No. 3. 1977, p. 18; No. 3. 1978, p. 26.

assumed faster growth of export than import (16.6 percent and 14.4 percent respectively). The actual rate of growth of export was, however, only 17.1 percent, less than half of the planned rate (see Table 12.5). The rate of growth of import was, therefore, reduced. It was considerably below the planned rate (10.6 percent as compared with 14.4 percent), but it was still above the actual rate of growth of export and the balance of trade deficit increased to $9.5 billion from $7.5 billion in 1975. In 1977, again, the planned rate of growth of export was not reached (11.4 percent as compared with 13.0 percent), while the actual rate of growth of import (5.4 percent exceeded the unrealistically low planned rate of 2.7 percent. This time the balance of trade deficit declined, but it was still the second largest ever ($7.8 billion). At the same time, the rate of growth of domestic output (DNMP) declined below the planned average for the new five-year plan period to 6.8 percent in 1976 and 5.0 percent in 1977 (see Table 12.2). The enforced reduction in imports started to choke the economy.

An alternative policy would be to reduce the positive difference between NNMP and DNMP gradually over a much longer period of time, if necessary with some new borrowing but at a slower rate than in the past. It would also involve a drastic reduction in the CMEA commitments which include investing in twelve large joint investment projects in the region, mainly in the Soviet Union, during the five-year period 1976-1980.[41]

In the first half of the 1970s there was a lot of talk, both in Poland and in the West, about the opening of the Polish economy to the West, a rapid expansion in East-West trade, and "reintegration" of Poland into the world economy. Indeed, when calculated at current prices, the share of nonsocialist countries increased with respect to import from 31.4 percent of total Polish imports in 1970 to 55.6 percent in 1974 and with respect to export from 36.1 percent to 44.3 percent (see Table 12.6). The share of trade with socialist countries declined correspondingly: export from 68.6 percent to 44.4 percent and import from 63.9 percent to 55.7 percent. By 1975, however, there was already a reversal of this tendency. On the import side, the share of socialist countries started to increase and reached 51.9 percent in 1977, while the share of other countries declined to 48.1 percent. The share of export to socialist

TABLE 12.6
Geographic Structure of Trade
(Percent of Total Export or Import)

Year	Export				Import			
	Socialist Countries		Other Countries		Socialist Countries		Other Countries	
	Current Prices	Constant Prices	Current Prices	Constant Prices	Current Prices	Constant Prices	Current Prices	Constant Prices
1970	63.9	63.9	36.1	36.1	68.6	68.6	31.4	31.4
1971	63.1	64.3	36.9	35.7	67.4	66.8	32.6	33.2
1972	63.6	64.6	36.4	35.4	61.2	60.5	38.8	39.5
1973	60.7	64.8	39.3	35.2	51.7	55.7	48.3	44.3
1974	55.7	66.8	44.3	33.2	44.4	53.9	55.6	46.1
1975	59.9	67.3	40.1	32.7	45.8	50.5	54.2	49.5
1976	59.7	65.0	40.3	35.0	46.9	49.9	53.1	50.1
1977	60.3	67.7	39.7	32.3	51.9	57.0	48.1	43.0

Sources: Current Prices: *Rocznik statystyczny*. Warsaw: G.U.S., 1976, p. 340; *1978*, p. 288.
Constant Prices: calculated on the basis of *Ekonomista*, No. 4, 1978, p. 890.

countries increased to 60.3 percent in 1977, and that of other countries declined to 39.7 percent.

Although the values of export and import at current prices are relevant for the balance of payments position, the shares of the two groups of countries must be presented at constant prices in order to indicate changes in the directions in the volume of trade. When calculated at constant prices, the share of nonsocialist countries in total import was even greater in 1971 and 1972 than the share at current prices. In subsequent years the constant prices share was, however, considerably lower. Nevertheless, it was continuously increasing from one year to another until it reached 50.1 percent in 1976; then it suddenly dropped to 43.0 percent in 1977. There was a corresponding declining trend in the constant price share of the socialist countries, but it declined below the 50 percent mark only in one single year, 1976, when it was 49.9 percent. In 1977 it increased to 57.0 percent which was the highest share since 1972.

On the export side, the difference between the picture presented at constant and current prices is even more important. At constant prices the share of export to nonsocialist countries was continuously declining from 36.1 percent in 1971 to 32.7 percent in 1975. It increased to 35.0 percent in 1976 and dropped to 32.3 percent in 1977. In every year from 1971 through 1977 the share of export to nonsocialist countries was smaller than in 1970. Correspondingly, the share of export to socialist countries exceeded the 1970 share in all those years. In other words, insofar as the actual volume of trade was concerned, the "opening to the West" took place only on the import side. From 1971 through 1976 Poland was increasing import from nonsocialist countries more rapidly than import from socialist countries, but she was increasing export more rapidly to socialist than to other countries, except in 1976. The differences between the real rates of growth of import and export in trade with nonsocialist countries, were, therefore, very large from 1971 through 1975, and the rates of growth of export to those countries were declining from one year to another between 1972 and 1975 (see Table 12.5). During the same period, in trade with socialist countries there was a positive difference between real rates of growth of export and import in three years (1971, 1974, and 1975). An increase in the rate of growth of export to nonsocialist countries in 1976 was achieved by a drastic decline in the rate of growth to socialist countries from 8.6 percent in 1975 to 1.9 percent in 1976. When the rate of growth to socialist countries was revived to 12.7 percent in 1977, there was a decline in export to other countries by -0.2 percent.

This suggests that, even with the reduced rates of growth of domestic production, the export capacity of the economy is limited, and export cannot expand at high rates of growth at the same time in both directions. In addition, the structure of the economy is still not adjusted to the requirements of the Western markets: the level of technology is still not sufficient; the quality control, servicing, supply of parts, and marketing not adequate; and the system of planning and management tends to reduce flexibility which is necessary in order to meet fluctuations in the world demand. Without sufficiently high rates of growth of export to nonsocialist countries, the repayment of loans to the West will be difficult. It can only take place as the result of a very drastic reduction in import from the West. This is what happened in 1977, when the positive difference between the rates of growth of export to nonsocialist countries and import from those countries was achieved, despite a decline in export in this direction by -0.2 percent, because of a decline in import by -10.6 percent.

This is not, however, a satisfactory policy. A decline in import from the West reduces technology transfer without which it will be impossible to continue the process of modernization and restructuring and to accelerate technological progress in Poland.

An alternative policy would be an attempt to maintain a relatively high rate of import from the West and to give top priority in the development plans to the expansion of export in this direction, so that repayment could be secured with the continuation of technology transfer embodied in imported machines and equipment. The slow recovery from the recession in the world economy makes this task difficult.[42] However, by gearing changes in the structure of Polish industry more closely to the requirements of East-West trade, a considerable improvement in the situation could be achieved. The modernization and restructuring of the economy, including attempts to build a viable export sector, which took place on the basis of the heavy import of

Western technology and capital during the first half of the present decade, were undertaken "from above" by the central planners. They did so in accordance with their understanding of the needs and possibilities, without the benefit of meaningful internal market signals, with distorted price and cost structures, without a significant increase in decentralization and improved flexibility of the production and foreign trade enterprises. In this respect the approach in Poland did not differ from that in other East European countries, with the exception of Hungary, where structural changes were, to a certain extent, allowed to result from micro-economic decisions.[43]

Another argument for more vigorous expansion of export to nonsocialist countries is provided by the terms of trade. During the whole period 1971-1977, changes in the prices of Polish exports were more favorable in trade with nonsocialist countries than in total trade (see Table 12.7). Therefore the Polish export prices were even more favorable in trade with socialist countries. In 1971 and 1972 import prices in trade with nonsocialist countries declined more than prices of import in total trade. Although they increased more than prices in total import during 1973-1977, the differences between the two sets of import prices were considerably smaller than the difference between the two sets of export prices. As the result of these price movements, changes in terms of trade were more favorable in trade with nonsocialist countries than in total trade and, therefore, even more so in comparison with terms of trade in exchanges with socialist countries. It appears, therefore, that a shift of trade from socialist to nonsocialist countries, an opening to the West in real terms, would be beneficial for Poland if the price changes in the remaining years of the current five-year plan period would have the same pattern as that in 1971-1977. The same volume of exported goods could secure a larger volume of import.

In 1971-1975, priority in the allocation of foreign exchange for expansion and modernization of productive capacity was given to the electrical and engineering group of industries. It was expected that the growth of the export of machines and equipment would be more rapid than the growth of total export in 1976-1980. Moreover, the rate of growth of exports to the West was planned to be 14 percent per annum with a considerable increase in the share of machines and equipment in

TABLE 12.7
Export and Import Prices and Terms of Trade
(The 1970 level = 100)

	1970	1971	1972	1973	1974	1975	1976	1977
Export prices								
(1) Total trade	100.0	102.8	104.2	109.9	126.6	144.6	147.7	152.0
(2) Trade with non-socialist countries	100.0	106.3	106.9	122.5	168.5	178.2	169.8	178.3
Difference (2) - (1)		3.5	2.7	12.6	41.9	33.6	22.1	26.3
Import prices								
(1) Total trade	100.0	98.5	94.9	106.6	124.3	142.3	142.9	150.6
(2) Trade with non-socialist countries	100.0	96.2	94.7	113.9	146.6	152.3	148.4	157.7
Difference (2) - (1)		-2.3	-0.2	7.3	22.3	10.0	5.5	7.1
Terms of Trade								
(1) Total trade	100.0	104.4	109.8	103.1	101.9	101.6	103.4	100.9
(2) Trade with non-socialist countries	100.0	110.5	112.9	107.6	114.9	117.0	114.0	113.1
Difference (2) - (1)		6.1	3.1	4.5	13.0	15.4	10.6	12.2

Source: Ekonomista, No. 4, 1978, p. 890.

that export.[44] However, some Polish economists have pointed out that serious difficulties have already appeared, which might restrict the expansion of the export of machines, particularly to the West. They include tariff and nontariff obstacles to trade in the markets of advanced countries; strong domestic demand for machines in Poland which provides an easier alternative; inability to adjust rapidly to changes in foreign demand; the lack of marketing, servicing, parts, and advertising.[45] It is quite possible that the planners' priorities in 1971-1975 have again resulted in the creation of an industrial structure which may hamper rapid expansion of export to the West. The allocation of foreign exchange for the expansion and modernization of less prestigious industries, but with exports less difficult to effect, could have been a better alternative.

Morever, a very large proportion of industries which have been selected for export have more than average material intensity. In 1975, out of sixteen branches of the engineering industry exporting to the socialist countries, ten were highly material intensive, and out of thirteen branches exporting to the capitalist countries, nine were highly material intensive. It is therefore important to: (1) reduce material consumption in those branches of the engineering industry which are material intensive; and (2) expand the production for export of those industries which require relatively small input of raw materials. Therefore, a radical change in the product mix and the branch structure of the machine industry seems necessary.[46]

While the proportion of export to national income has tended to be almost constant, there has been an increase in the import intensity of national income (the share of import increased by 1 to 2 percent annually). Moreover, imports for production purposes have increased particularly rapidly. Their share in total import in constant prices increased from 10 percent in 1968 to 16 percent in 1975, despite considerable increases in import for investment and for consumption by the population which took place during that period.[47] The restructuring of the economy which was effected in 1971-1975 apparently did not take this factor into consideration. On the contrary, some of the main investment projects of that period in the field of steel and iron, nonferrous metals, chemicals, and building materials were heavily import intensive.

It has been calculated, for example, that as the result of the completion of these investment projects alone, the demand for fuels and energy will increase by 30 percent, while the total domestic production of fuels and energy is expected to increase by 18 percent by 1980.[48]

The 1976-1980 plan seems to put a considerable stress on import substitution. It envisages, for example, a reduction in the dependence on imported grain and feeds as soon as possible, a reduction in the import of metallurgical products by 40 percent, and a marked increase in the proportion of domestically produced machines in total investment.[49] Moreover, "on the assumption that the raw material prices will continue to increase in the capitalist markets, and taking into consideration other requirements of the long-run development strategy, it has been accepted as necessary to continue the policy of allocating considerable outlays for capital intensive investments connected with the expansion of the domestic raw material base and for joint investments in the field of raw material production in the CMEA countries."[50] This policy will increase the capital intensity of economic growth. It is likely to prevent the planned reduction in the share of investments in NNMP ("Allocated National Income"), which is assumed to be considerably restricted in the current five-year period, and it can, therefore, make the achievement of the planned average rates of growth of consumption impossible. This would, of course be the end of the "new strategy" and return to another period of relative stagnation at a higher plateau with a high degree of political instability.

These are only some of the problems that exist. The solutions which have been attempted do not seem to be of the type which would ensure dynamic growth based on the continuation of the policy of opening the economy and full utilization of international economic relations in the process of economic development of the country. There are too many analogies with what happened in earlier periods, particularly after the first years of Gomulka's coming to power. It seems that no viable expansion of export can be achieved until a serious reform of the economic system is introduced and the modernization and restructuring of the economy is effected not by an a priori decision from the center, but as an outcome of micro-decisions at the level of production and foreign trade enterprises. In other words, it is necessary to accept in Poland, as it has been accepted in Hungary, that "the starting-point for the actual development priorities should be found in the micro-structure and not in the macro-structure," and that "international economic cooperation should be based, in the first place, on cooperation between enterprises and not between industries."[51]

NOTES

1. J.V. Stalin, Economic Problems of Socialism in the U.S.S.R. Moscow: Foreign Language Publishing House, 1952, p. 35.

2. I. Nagy, On Communism. New York: Praeger, 1957; B.A. Balassa, The Hungarian Experience in Economic Planning. New Haven: Yale University Press, 1959; L. Zsoldos, The Economic Integration of Hungary into the Soviet Bloc: Foreign Trade Experience. Columbus: The Ohio State University Press, 1963.

3. Pavl Bozyk, "Handel zagraniczny a rozwoj gospodarczy Polski w XXX-leciu," Ekonomista, no. 4 (1964), p. 745.

4. Z.M. Fallenbuchl, "How Does the Soviet Economy Function without a Free Market?" Queen's Quarterly, LXX, no. 4 (1966), reprinted in M. Bornstein and D.R. Fusfeld, eds., The Soviet Economy: A Book of Readings. Homewood, Illinois: Irwin, 1974, 4th edition.

5. Pavl Bozyk, Reformy gospodarcze w krajach socjalistycznych. Warsaw: Wydawnictwo CRZZ, 1971. p. 40.

6. A. Karpinski, Zagadnienia socjalistycznej industrializacji Polski. Warsaw: Polskie Wydawnictwa gospodarcze, 1958, pp. 138-141.

7. Z.M. Fallenbuchl, "Collectivization and Economic Development," Canadian Journal of

Economics and Political Science, XXXIII, no. 1 (1967).

8. Karpinski, "Zagadnienia," p. 26.

9. Ibid., pp. 140, 142.

10. S. Albinowski, Handel miedzy krajami o roznych ustrojach. Warsaw: Ksiazka i wiedza, 1968, p. 35.

11. M. Kalecki, Zarys teorii wzrostu gospodarki socjalistycznej. Warsaw: Panstwowe wydawnictwo naukowe, 1963, p. 51.

12. Bozyk, "Handel Zagraniczny."

13. Ibid., pp. 745-750.

14. Prime Minister J. Cyrankiewicz's statement at the Tenth Session of the Sejm, Nowiny z Polski, Warsaw, November 25, 1956.

15. M. Nasilowski, "Systemy zarzadzania gospodarka narodowa a postep techniczny," in L. Gilejko, ed., Rewolucja naukowo-techniczna jako czynnik rozwoju. Warsaw: Panstwowe wydawnictwo naukowe, 1974, p. 225.

16. Z.M. Fallenbuchl, "East European Integration: Comecon," in J.P. Hardt, ed., Reorientation and Commercial Relations of the Economies of Eastern Europe. U.S. Congress, Joint Economic Committee. Washington: U.S. Government Printing Office, 1974.

17. Z.M. Fallenbuchl, "Industrial Structure and the Intensive Pattern of Development in Poland," Jahrbuch der Wirtschaft Osteuropas, IV (1973), pp. 233-254.

18. S. Marciniak, Struktura produkcji a dynamika wzrostu gospodarczego. Warsaw: Panstwowe wydawnictwo naukowe, 1970, pp. 76-77.

19. Oleg Bogomolov, ed., Ekonomicheskaia effektivnost' mezhdunarodnogo sotsialisticheskogo rozdeleniia truda. Moscow: 1965; Polish edition, Warsaw: Panstwowe wydawnictwo naukowe, 1967, pp. 213-214.

20. A. Karpinski, Polityka uprzemyslowienia Polski w latach 1958-1968. Warsaw: Panstwowe wydawnictwo ekonomiczne, 1969, pp. 28-29, 389-392.

21. V.V. Kusin, "Interrelations of Economic and Politic Factors," in Z.M. Fallenbuchl, ed., Economic Development in the Soviet Union and Eastern Europe. New York: Praeger, 1974, I, p. 102.

22. J. Wierzbolowski, "Z problemow socjalistycznej polityki handlowej," Handel zagraniczny, no. 10 (1964), p. 476.

23. A. Bodnar and M. Deniszczuk, Polska 2000: Problemy rozwoju ekonomicznego. Warsaw: Interpress, 1972, p. 21.

24. Ibid., p. 26.

25. M. Nasilowski, Analiza czynnikow rozwoju gospodarczego PRL. Warsaw: Panstwowe wydawnictwo ekonomiczne, 1974, p. 195; Bodnar and Deniszczuk, Polska 2000, p. 58.

26. Ibid., p. 196.

27. Nasilowski, "Systemy," p. 214.

28. Ibid., p. 214-215.

29. Z.M. Fallenbuchl, "The Polish Economy in the 1970's," in J.P. Hardt, ed., East European Economies Post-Helsinki. U.S. Congress, Joint Economic Committee. Washington: U.S. Government Printing Office, 1977.

30. Pavl Bozyk and B. Wojciechowski, Handel Zagraniczny Polski, 1945-1969. Warsaw: Panstwowe wydawnictwo ekonomiczne, 1971, p. 42.

31. U. Plowiec, "Kierunki doskonalenia handlu zagranicznego w swietle tez na V zjazd," Handel zagraniczny, no. 10 (1968), pp. 368-370.

32. J. Soldaczuk and J. Giezgala, "Integracja gospodarcza krajow RWPG," Godpodarka planowa, no. 11 (1968), pp. 3-4; Bozyk, Reformy, pp. 52-53.

33. Rocznik statystyczny 1977. Warsaw: G.U.S., 1977, pp. XXX-XXXI.

34. Z.M. Fallenbuchl, "The Strategy of Development and Gierek's Economic Manoeuvre," in Adam Bromke and J.W. Strong, eds., Gierek's Poland. New York: Praeger, 1973, pp. 52-70.

35. B. Wojciechowski, "Problemy importochlonnosci gospodarki Polski," Gospodarka planowa, no. 12 (1976), p. 642; Fallenbuchl, "Industrial Structure in Poland."

36. H. Kisiel, "Stosunki gospodarcze z zagranica," in K. Secomski, ed., 30 lat gospodarki Polski Ludowej. Warsaw: Panstwowe wydawnictwo ekonomiczne, 1974, p. 156; Bozyk, "Handel zagraniczny."

37. Z.M. Fallenbuchl, "Recent Economic Developments in Eastern Europe," a paper presented at the "MacMaster University Conference on the Communist States in the Era of Detente," October 1975, to be published in A. Bromke and D. Novack, eds., The Communist States in the Era of Detente, forthcoming.

38. Z.M. Fallenbuchl, E. Neuberger and L. D'Andrea Tyson, "East European Reactions to International Commodity Inflation," in Hardt, ed., East European Economies Post-Helsinki, pp. 816-864.

39. Bozyk and Wojciechowski, Handel zagraniczny, pp. 273-274.

40. "Ciaglosc polityki--nowe elementy jej realizacji," Gospodarka planowa, no. 2 (1977), p. 67.

41. Ibid., p. 68.

42. Z.M. Fallenbuchl, "The Impact of External Economic Disturbances on Poland Since 1971," paper presented at the Conference on the Impact of International Economic Disturbances on the Soviet Union and Eastern Europe, Smithsonian Institution, Washington, DC, September 1978; P. Bozyk, "Wspolczesne tendencje w gospodarce swiatowej i ich wplyw na handel zagraniczny Polski," Ekonomista, no. 4 (1978), pp. 889-893.

43. Z.M. Fallenbuchl, "Recent Changes in Industrial Structure and Their Impact on the Export Potential of CMEA Countries in East-West Trade,"

paper presented at a conference on "L'evolution du commerce est-ouest et ses perspectives," Aix-en-Provence, France, November 1978.

44. T. Wrzaszczyk, "Kierunki dalszego rozwoju gospodarki," *Nowe drogi*, no. 1 (1977), p. 14.

45. W. Burzynski and J. Kozinski, "Problemy handlu zagranicznego Polski w zakresie maszyn i srodkow transportu," *Handel zagraniczny*, no. 3 (1977), p. 4; B. Korona, "Aktualne problemy handlu zagranicznego Polski," *Gospodarka planowa*, no. 2 (1978), pp. 101-103; B. Wojciechowski, "Importochlonnosc a jakosc produkcji," *Handel zagraniczny*, no. 7 (1978), pp. 7-9.

46. Borzynski and Kosinski, *Problemy handlu zagraniczny*.

47. A. Jung, "Czy mozna ulepszyc wykorzystanie importu?" *Handel Zagraniczny*, no. 2 (1977), p. 4.

48. "Ciaglosc polityki," p. 66.

49. Wrzaszczyk, "Kierunki dalszegro rozwoju gospodarki," p. 9.

50. "Ciaglosc polityki," p. 62.

51. J. Bognar, "A Contemporary Approach to East-West Economic Relations," *The New Hungarian Quarterly*, no. 34 (1969), p. 34.

13
Poland, the Socialist Community, and East-West Relations

Roger E. Kanet

When Gierek took over the leadership of the Polish United Workers' Party (PUWP) in late 1970, he was faced with a series of major domestic and foreign policy problems inherited from his predecessor. Although the postwar communist political leadership had been quite successful in transforming a rural agricultural Poland into an urban industrial and socialist society, serious economic and political problems remained. The workers' riots of December 1970 which had forced Gomulka's resignation were a clear indication of the dissatisfaction of a substantial portion of the Polish population with the policies of the 1960s. They also acted as a major stimulus for the new economic program introduced by Gierek. In addition, however, unlike other East European communist political elites, the Polish leadership has to deal with a strong and organized domestic political opposition in the Roman Catholic Church. In the foreign policy realm, Poland continued to face a number of serious issues ranging from continuing Soviet domination and the requirement of appeasing

---

This article is part of a larger project on integration within Eastern Europe and its implications for East-West relations. The author wishes to express his sincere appreciation for financial support for the project from the American Council of Learned Societies, the International Research and Exchanges Board (IREX), the North Atlantic Treaty Organization Faculty Fellowship Program, the Office of External Research of the U.S. Department of State, and the Research Board of the Graduate College and the Russian and East European Center of the University of Illinois.

Soviet concerns, to the need for improved relations--especially economic--with the West if the new economic strategy were to succeed.

In the following pages I wish to examine the major developments in Polish foreign relations during the 1970s with special emphasis on the interrelationship of domestic and foreign political and economic developments. The strategy of economic development based on large-scale importation of Western technology introduced in the early 1970s necessitated a substantial expansion of Polish relations with the West. At the same time, however, this has made the Polish economy far more susceptible to the vagaries of the international market than it was in the years prior to 1970.[1] On the other hand, the 1970s have also witnessed an expansion of integration activities within the Council for Mutual Economic Assistance--largely as a result of Soviet initiatives and on the model preferred by the Soviets. This process has included the extension of the system of political consultation between the Poles and the other members of the CMEA community--in particular the Soviets--on economic, political, and social questions.

POLISH FOREIGN POLICY AT THE BEGINNING OF THE 1970s

Throughout modern history the geopolitical position of Poland on the north European plain between two dynamic and much larger countries--Germany and Russia--has been one of the most important factors determining its political history. Lacking effective natural boundaries and a power base comparable to those of their much larger neighbors, the Poles have been unable to maintain a secure political existence independent of German and Russian influence. In fact, for most of the past two hundred years--with the exception of the interwar period from 1919-1939--a truly independent Poland has not existed. Since the defeat of Germany in World War II, Poland has come under the influence and protection of the Soviet Union. Not only did the Soviets provide the major impetus for the creation of a people's republic in postwar Poland--with all that that has meant for the political, social, and economic developments of the past three decades--but also, until the early 1970s, only the USSR among the major powers provided the recognition and support for postwar Polish boundaries required by Polish national security.

This has not meant, however, that Poland's

relations with the Soviets have been based exclusively on a coincidence of interests of the leaders of the two countries. In fact, there is evidence of disagreement--at times serious--between the two communist states. Nor has it meant that Poland's relations with the rest of the world have been determined exclusively by the desires of the Soviets. This has been especially evident in recent years, as the Poles have attempted to expand their political and economic ties with the countries of Western Europe. However, the Polish-Soviet relationship is still the single most important factor in influencing the overall foreign policy orientation of Poland. Even though the limits of acceptable behavior for Poland and the other East European communist states may have broadened in the quarter-century since Stalin's death, ultimate decisions on the acceptability of major policy decisions are still made in Moscow. Given the importance for Soviet security policy of the geographical position of Poland in the "Northern Tier", Soviet interest in and concern for developments in Poland is greater than that for Romania.[2]

During the period of Gomulka's leadership of the PUWP, an evolution in both domestic and foreign policy occurred. Immediately after the events of October 1956, the Polish leadership emphasized both reform in the domestic, political, and economic systems and a substantial degree of autonomy in relations with the Soviet Union. For almost a year and a half they refused to employ the expression "leading role of the Communist Party of the Soviet Union" in official communications concerning relations among the communist states. In fact, during this period the Poles emphasized the autonomy and individuality of national communist parties.[3] After mid-1968, however, they gradually dropped their insistance on equality and autonomy and by the 1960s Poland once again followed a foreign policy line predominantly congruent with that of the USSR.[4]

By the late 1960s, Poland had moved from the position of being among the most liberal of the East European communist systems to virtual political and economic stagnation. Poland, for example, along with the German Democratic Republic, was strongly critical of the new <u>Ostpolitik</u> of West Germany that aimed at improving relations with some of the East European states. In addition, Gomulka strongly criticized developments in Czechoslovakia in 1968 and cooperated fully in Soviet efforts prior to the invasion of August to induce the Dubcek regime to abandon some of its more controversial reforms.

Throughout the postwar period, Polish foreign policy was influenced by two primary, and interrelated, concerns. First of all was the question of the Polish relationship with the USSR and the degree of initiative that would be permitted to Poland in conducting its foreign relations. The second was the security of the Polish state--in particular the potential threat to Poland represented by "West German revanchism." Until the late 1960s the Federal Republic refused to recognize the legitimacy of Poland's postwar borders which included substantial portions of former German territory.[6] As a result of the continuing hostility between the two countries, Poland depended almost entirely upon its soviet ally to guarantee its territorial integrity. In addition, Poland strongly supported the GDR in its effort to gain international stature in the face of the Western refusal to recognize East Germany as more than a "Soviet Occupation Zone."[7] The election of the Social Democrat-Free Democrat coalition government of Chancellor Brandt in 1969, along with Polish initiatives to open up discussions with West Germany,[8] resulted by December 1970, shortly before Gomulka's fall from power, in a bilateral treaty between the two countries.

In the following pages we shall examine the major developments in the foreign policy of Poland since the signing of the Polish-West German treaty. Primary emphasis will be placed on the interrelationship of Poland's policy toward the industrialized West and its relations with the countries of the Warsaw Treaty Organization. In addition, however, we shall treat the mutual impact of Poland's domestic and foreign policies, in particular in the economic realm. During the 1970s Poland's political and economic relations with the industrialized countries of Western Europe and North America have developed substantially. Not only have commercial relations expanded almost exponentially-from total trade turnover of 7,749 million devisa zloty in 1970 to 33,769 million in 1979--but political relations with virtually all of the Western countries have improved significantly. At the same time, however, Poland has continued to commit itself to long-term cooperative economic projects with the other members of the Council for Mutual Economic Assistance (CMEA), and political consultations have been expanded with other socialist countries, especially the USSR, on matters ranging from the coordination of foreign policy to internal ideological vigilance.

The interrelationship of domestic and foreign policy activities is clearly visible in the impact of Gierek's program of rapid industrialization and modernization of the Polish economy, which played the major factor in the improvement of Poland's relations with the West. On the other hand, detente with the West, including the Helsinki agreements, encouraged domestic opponents of the Polish government to organize openly in the attempt to influence governmental policy. Potential domestic instability has also influenced Poland's relations with the Soviet Union.

POLAND AND THE WEST IN A PERIOD OF DETENTE

Probably the two most important developments in Poland's foreign relations with the West during the 1970s have been the phenomenal growth ~~in~~ commercial relations and concomitant improvement of political relations, in particular with the Federal Republic of Germany. Although Poland's contacts with the West had always been substantially greater than those of the other East European communist states in the postwar period--e.g., Polish trade with the West as a percentage of total trade turnover generally remained in the area of 30 percent throughout the 1950s and 1960s, while that of other socialist states ranged between 10 and 20 percent[10]--Gierek's decision to modernize the Polish economy, primarily by means of imports of capital equipment and technology from the West, resulted in an extremely rapid growth in Polish trade with the West (see Table 13.1). The Polish economy was opened to imports of Western goods and credits, as a means of accomplishing both modernization and the rapid increase of the standard of living of the Polish population. The initial result was an unprecedented boom in economic growth in Poland and a substantial increase in the real wages of the Polish worker. During the period 1971-1975 the domestic net material product of Poland grew at an annual rate of 9.8 percent--substantially above the rate originally planned--while real wages grew at 7.2 percent rather than the planned rate 3.4 percent. In addition, investments increased by 18.6 percent per year during these years, compared with the 7.8 percent rate foreseen in the original five-year plan (see Table 13.2). However, Polish political leaders did not foresee the recession in

TABLE 13.1
Poland's Trade With Western Industrial Countries
(In percent of total trade)

	Total	Exports	Imports
1970	27.1	28.4	25.8
1971	28.5	29.8	27.3
1972	32.3	30.4	34.1
1973	39.8	34.2	44.4
1974	44.3	36.2	50.8
1975	41.3	31.5	49.3
1976	41.4	32.0	48.9
1977	37.8	31.3	43.3

Source: G.U.S., Rocznik Statystyczny Handlu Zagranicznego 1978. Warsaw: Glowny Urzad Statystyczny, 1978. p. 4.

TABLE 13.2
Planned and Actual Rates of Growth of Domestic Net Material Product, Investment and Real Wages

		(Percentages)								Average	
		1971	1972	1973	1974	1975	1976	1977	1978	1971-1975	1976-1980
Domestic Net Material Product	Plan	5.8	6.1	7.9	9.5	9.8	8.6	5.7	5.4	7.0	7.0-7.4
	Actual	8.1	10.6	10.8	10.4	9.0	7.1	5.6		9.8	
Investment	Plan	7.2	9.6	12.9	12.4	6.1	5.8	1.4	-5.0	7.8	2.1
	Actual	7.5	23.6	25.0	22.5	14.2	3.5	2.5		18.6	
DNMP/Investment	Plan	0.81	0.64	0.61	0.77	1.61	1.48	4.07		0.90	3.33
	Actual	1.08	0.45	0.43	0.46	0.63	2.84	2.24		0.53	
Real Wages	Plan	4.2	5.6	6.6	5.3	5.0	3.5	2.0	1.8	3.4	3.2-3.4
	Actual	5.3	6.5	8.7	6.6	8.5	3.9	2.3		7.2	
At current price:											
Disposal Income	Actual	10.6	12.7	13.5	13.2	13.6	13.3	n.a.		12.7	
Net Fixed Investment	Actual	10.3	27.5	27.3	22.6	16.5	1.7	n.a.		20.8	
DNMP	Actual	14.1	11.2	12.0	13.6	11.6	18.3	n.a.		12.5	

Sources: Zbigniew M. Fallenbuchl, The Impact of External Economic Disturbances on Poland Since 1971. Occasional Paper no. 44 of the Kennan Institute for Advanced Russian Studies, Washington, DC, September 1978, Table III; based on Gospodarka planowa, no. 4 (1971); no. 5 (1972); no. 4 (1973), no. 4 (1974), no. 4 (1975); no. 5 (1976), no. 5 (1977); no. 4 (1978); G.U.S., Rocznik Statystyczny 1977. Warsaw: Glowny Urzad Statystyczny, 1977.

the West, the phenomenal increase in world energy prices, the long delays in the completion of major industrial projects in Poland, or the substantial increase in domestic consumer demand, all of which have had a negative impact on the Polish economy--in particular on Poland's ability to match imports with exports and to meet consumer requirements.

Two results of the Polish strategy for economic modernization are of special interest at this point. First is the fact that the opening of the economy to Western imports and credits has made the Polish economy more vulnerable to fluctuations in the international market. Second, the significant expansion of economic relations with the West which characterized the early to mid-1970s cut into the percentage of Polish trade with the other CMEA members. This, in turn, raises the question of the compatibility of expanding East-West trade and economic integration within the CMEA.

The most visible indicator of the increased vulnerability of the Polish economy to external economic developments is the inflationary impact of the world market on Polish import prices, as well as on the domestic economy. For example, in 1973 and 1974 prices of goods imported from the industrial West increased by 28 and 32.8 percent respectively. Although this increase was matched by comparable increases in the price of Polish exports, and terms of trade remained virtually stable (a decrease of 8.8 percent in 1973 followed by an increase of 9.4 percent the next year), the fact that Poland's increased imports from the West far outstripped exports resulted in a substantial overall increase in the cost of imports of industrial (and other) goods imported from the West.[11] At the same time the cost of imports of raw materials, including energy, from the CMEA countries also increased substantially after the 1975 price adjustments in intra-CMEA trade, and Poland's terms of trade in intra-CMEA trade worsened by 2.7 percent in 1975. For the domestic economy, one result of the overall increase in import prices has been that Poland has been forced to expand the export of goods for which domestic demand has also been increasing--for example, meat, sugar, and coal, all of which have been in short supply domestically in recent years.[12]

The domestic impact of this increase in import prices, coupled with other domestic economic factors, has been a substantial inflationary trend within the Polish economy, plus a major increase in state subsidies, in order to cushion part of the inflationary pressure. While the visible inflation rate for goods and services was slightly more than 1 percent a year in the late 1960s, the rate increased to about 5 percent by the mid-1970s.[13] Given the recent political history of Poland--most important, the riots of December 1970 which brought Gierek to power, the "price riots" of June 1976, and the commitment of the government to hold basic consumption prices stable--the Polish leaders have been faced with the serious problem of absorbing a very high percentage of the inflation by price equalization taxes and subsidies. By 1975 the net subsidies to hold down inflation equalled almost 17.5 percent of total budgetary revenue. They were somewhat higher than total outlays on investment and repair and substantially higher than expenditures on education, science, culture, and health.[14] Such a large commitment of government resources for price stabilization has obviously had a negative impact on investments and contributed to the major economic difficulties faced in the last few years.

Another of Poland's serious economic problems has been the substantial and growing deficit in its balance of payments with the West. By the end of 1977 the total deficit had reached approximately 12.8 billion dollars--equivalent to three-and-a-half years of Poland's hard currency earnings. The rapid increase of the debt and Poland's continued inability to substantially expand exports to hard currency markets has resulted in the decision to reduce the rate of growth of imports from the West. The increases have been cut from 52, 74 and 53 percent in 1972, 1973, and 1974, to growth rates of 16 and 10 percent in 1975 and 1976. Not until 1977 did the percentage of growth in exports exceed that of imports (8.7 percent compared to a minus 9.7 percent, see Table 13.3).[15] However, in spite of the recent reduction in imports from the West--which clearly has negative implications for the continued development of the domestic economy--Poland's trade deficit with the West continues to increase, for imports still exceeded exports by 65 percent in 1977.[16]

Not only have recent changes in the world economy had a major impact on the domestic economy in Poland, but unplanned developments in Poland's domestic economy have also had significant influence on Polish foreign economic policy. Gierek and his associates have been forced to cut back drastically on investments and on imports from the West--the

TABLE 13.3
Poland's Foreign Trade by Political Region
(in million devisa zloty and in percent)

	1960		1965		1970		1975		1976		1977	
TOTAL TRADE												
Total	11,282	100.00	18,272	100.00	28,621	100.00	75,812	100.00	82,671	100.00	89,306	100.00
Exports	5,302	100.00	8,911	100.00	14,191	100.00	34,161	100.00	36,600	100.00	40,748	100.00
Imports	5,980	100.00	9,361	100.00	14,430	100.00	41,651	100.00	46,071	100.00	48,558	100.00
SOCIALIST COUNTRIES												
Total	7,119	63.1	11,824	64.7	18,956	66.2	39,559	52.2	43,441	52.5	49,758	55.7
Exports	3,321	62.6	5,634	63.2	9,064	63.9	20,472	59.9	21,853	59.7	24,552	60.3
Imports	3,698	63.5	6,190	66.1	9,892	68.6	19,087	45.8	21,588	46.9	24,174	49.8
of which, CMEA w/o USSR												
Total	3,042	27.0	5,053	27.7	7,655	26.7	16,388	21.6	18,710	22.6	20,518	23.0
Exports	1,382	26.1	2,175	24.4	3,597	25.3	8,687	25.4	9,766	26.7	10,450	25.0
Imports	1,660	27.8	2,878	30.7	4,058	28.1	7,701	18.5	8,944	19.4	10,067	20.7
of which, USSR												
Total	3,422	30.3	6,040	33.1	10,448	36.5	21,323	28.1	22,824	27.6	27,007	30.2
Exports	1,561	29.4	3,126	35.1	5,003	35.3	10,766	31.5	11,080	30.3	12,900	31.7
Imports	1,861	31.1	2,914	31.1	5,445	37.7	10,557	25.3	11,744	25.5	14,107	29.1

INDUSTRIALLY DEVELOPED COUNTRIES												
Total	3,357	29.8	4,852	26.6	7,749	27.1	31,307	41.3	34,239	41.4	33,768	37.8
Exports	1,582	29.8	2,557	28.7	4,028	28.4	10,768	31.5	11,711	32.0	12,738	31.3
Imports	1,775	29.7	2,295	24.5	3,721	25.8	20,539	49.3	22,528	48.9	21,030	43.3
DEVELOPING COUNTRIES												
Total	806	7.1	1,596	8.7	1,916	6.7	4,946	6.5	4,991	6.0	5,780	6.5
Exports	399	7.5	720	8.1	1,099	7.7	2,921	8.6	3,036	8.3	3,458	8.5
Imports	407	6.8	876	9.4	817	5.7	2,025	4.9	1,955	4.2	2,322	4.9

Source: G.U.S., Rocznik Statystyczny Handlu Zagranicznego 1978. Warsaw: Glowny Urzad Statystyczny, 1978, pp. 3-4.

so-called "economic maneuver" of 1977.[17]

In addition to the developments in Poland's commercial relations with the West, there has also been a substantial expansion in Polish political relations with the Western industrial countries. Most important has been the evolution of Poland's relations with the Federal Republic of Germany. As has already been noted, virtually the last major political activity of Gomulka's political career was the signing of a bilateral treaty with the Federal Republic that granted full recognition of Poland's postwar boundaries. However, serious problems still existed in relations between the two countries. Most important were the issues of West German payment of compensation to Poles who had worked in Germany prior to 1945, German credits to Poland for the purchase of industrial goods, and German insistance that ethnic Germans be granted the right to emigrate from Poland.[18] Not until a meeting between Chancellor Schmidt and First Secretary Gierek in Helsinki in July 1975--during the European Conference on Security and Cooperation--was a compromise agreement reached. Poland agreed to permit 125,000ethnic Germans to emigrate over a period of four years. In return West Germany granted Poland a long-term economic credit of 1 billion German marks and agreed to pay compensations of an additional 1.3 billion marks to individual Poles who had worked in Germany prior to 1945 and had contributed to the German social insurance fund.[19]

However, Polish criticism of West Germany, especially concerning economic relations, has continued. For example, the well-known journalist Mieczyslaw F. Rakowski complained about blatant West German discrimination against Poland's exports. According to him, about 20 percent of all of Poland exports were subjected to discriminatory measures that West Germany did not apply to other GATT members.[20]

Poland's relations with the other countries of Western Europe have expanded significantly over the course of the present decade. Warsaw has hosted numerous visits by Western heads of state, and Gierek and other Polish leaders have frequently travelled abroad for bilateral and multilateral meetings with their Western counterparts. Among the most important issues discussed in all of these meetings has been the expansion of economic contacts between Poland and the Western countries. In addition Poland has been one of the most active proponents of detente and improved East-West relations.[21] Relations with both the United States and France have developed especially well over the course of the 1970s. Each of the last three American presidents has visited Warsaw, as has President Giscard d'Estaing of France, and First Secretary Gierek has travelled to both Washington and Paris. Under Gierek, Poland has made a concerted effort to develop contacts with ethnic Poles living abroad--so-called "Polonia." This policy represents a substantial change from earlier attitudes toward Polish emigrants.

The expansion of Polish relations with the West has not been limited to political and economic contacts. For example, between 1970 and 1977 the number of Western tourists visiting Poland rose from 279,000 to 924,000, while in 1977 more than 500,000 Poles visited the West.[22] This has meant that Poles have had far greater opportunity to meet with Westerners and to obtain first-hand knowledge of Western standards of living. This has clearly had an impact on the expectations and demands of Poles concerning their own standard of living. More important, perhaps, has been the interrelationship between the evolution of an open domestic opposition in Poland and expanded East-West relations. In Fall 1976, after the arrest and imprisonment of those accused of playing significant roles in the June riots in Ursus and Radom, the Workers' Defense Committee (KOR) was established in Warsaw. The committee, which has found substantial popular support, has continued to speak out on various political issues and has clearly played a role in inducing the government to release the imprisoned workers. In May 1977 the KOR expanded its activities and established an Intervention Bureau to collect and publicize information on officials' violations of human rights and a Social Defense Fund to assist the victims of reprisals. Finally, in late September 1977, the restructuring of the committee under a new name--the Committee for Social Self-Defense "KSS-KOR"--was announced. A communique issued at the time of the reorganization stated:

> We shall continue our action because we are convinced that the most successful weapon against the domination of rules is the active solidarity of citizens, for the major cause of lawlessness by the authorities lies in the helplessness of the public, deprived of institutions independent of the state that

can protect the rights of individuals and groups, in keeping with their interests.

The tasks of the restructured organization include: 1) combating reprisals imposed for political, philosophical, religious, or racial reasons, as well as providing aid to persons persecuted for these reasons; 2) combating lawless practices and providing aid to those suffering from them; 3) fighting for institutional guarantees of civic rights and freedoms; and 4) supporting and defending all social initiatives aimed at implementing human and civic rights.[23]

In addition to the Workers' Defense Committee, other groups have also been active in Poland since 1976. Most important has been the Catholic Church, which has openly and repeatedly supported both the rights of workers fired and jailed in June 1976 and the general principles to which the KOR is dedicated. In fact Church activities in this area began two months before the creation of the Workers' Defense Committee.[24]

In Poland, unlike in the Soviet Union, the opponents of the regime are not made into social outcasts. They came from among the leaders of the Polish academic and cultural community. Their voices carry weight with their fellow citizens to a degree unthinkable at the present time in the USSR, and they represent a serious challenge to the regime. Not only must the Polish political leadership consider the impact that brutal retaliation might have on relations with the West, but they must also take into account the negative impact that such repression might have on the stability of the entire Polish political system.

POLAND, THE SOCIALIST COMMUNITY, AND THE PROCESS OF INTEGRATION

At the same time that Poland's relations with the countries of the industrial West have expanded, Poland and other members of the Council of Mutual Economic Assistance have signed a number of agreements that call for increased economic cooperation and integration of their economies. Throughout the late 1950s and early 1960s, Poland was one of the major advocates of strengthening cooperation within the context of the CMEA. In 1962, for example, First Secretary Gomulka argued that "The forms and intensity of CMEA-cooperation developed until now are inadequate for the competition with capitalism."[25] Gomulka played a leading role in the meetings of CMEA in 1962 and 1963 which approved the principles of the international socialist division of labor, the creation of a multilateral payments system among CMEA members, the establishment of the International Bank for Economic Cooperation, and the coordination of national plans. During this period Poland also advocated the development of a strong CMEA executive and the extension of the transferable ruble from a mere clearing unit to a convertible currency. Poland's proposals were opposed by most of the other CMEA members, including the Soviet Union, and to this day trade within the socialist community continues to be based on bilateral balancing rather than multilateral exchange. As late as 1969-1970, during the development of the Comprehensive Program for Cooperation and Integration, Poland continued to support the development of a convertible currency. However, the document which was finally approved in July 1971 says nothing about convertibility and speaks only in very general terms about the future role of the transferable ruble.[26]

Since the approval of the Complex Program, the official Polish position on CMEA integration has changed substantially. At the 1976 meeting of the CMEA, the Polish prime minister spoke in glowing terms of CMEA involvement in the exploitation of Soviet raw materials and in the expansion of various Soviet industrial projects as indicators of cooperation within the community. He made no mention of the lack of development of economic mechanisms, which Poland had earlier emphasized, and did not support the proposal of the Hungarians to improve the monetary and pricing system within the CMEA.[27] Since the early 1970s the Poles have continued to voice their support for integration within the context of the CMEA, but integration based on planning coordination and product specialization as advocated by the Soviets, rather than on the development of multilateral trade mechanisms.

An important question concerning Poland's foreign economic relations concerns the degree to which expanded trade with the West is compatible with integration within the CMEA. At the theoretical level, the Polish position has been that integration and expanded East-West economic contacts are processes that reinforce one another. For example, in 1973, Z. Kamicki, an advisor on economic affairs to the Polish Ministry of Foreign Affairs, argued that "The Progress in integration foreseen in the (Complex) program should not cause any difficulties in the Comecon countries' trade with the West. What is more, it seems that implementation of the program may even introduce some additional incentives for a further expansion of trade between East and West...." The reasons for this, according to Kamicki, are: 1) integration will stimulate their economic growth and, therefore, increase demands for imports from the West; 2) the integration model being pursued is not oriented toward economic autarky; 3) the implementation of the program will require additional imports of machinery and equipment; and 4) the implementation of the program will give the CMEA economies a more export-oriented character.[28] This argument, which has been repeated on numerous occasions in both Poland and in other CMEA countries, is persuasive--at least at initial glance. One of the major expectations has been that the integration program will result in the development of more efficient and competitive industrial production within the CMEA countries themselves. Not only will the implementation of the program require substantial industrial imports from the West, but, if successful, it will also enable the CMEA countries to improve production, increase labor productivity, and generally upgrade their industrial production to the level where they will be able to expand exports to the West.

An examination of the Polish case during the past six or seven years leads to no clear conclusions. First of all, most of the integration projects in which Poland has been involved relate to the expansion of raw materials production in the Soviet Union--most notably the new oil and gas pipelines from Western Siberia which will provide additional supplies of Soviet energy to Eastern (and Western) Europe.[29] Although these projects have definitely resulted in an increase in imports from the West--most of the pipe and the equipment for the pumping stations has been imported from the West--there is little indication that they have added to Poland's ability to compete in world markets. In fact, one of the developments that influenced the Polish turn to the West for the credits with which to modernize its economy was the unavailability of investment funds within the CMEA community. Between 1971 and 1974, the CMEA's International Investment Bank granted Poland credits for twelve projects totaling only 68.4 million transferable rubles (two-thirds in convertible currency).[30] It has only been in the West that Poland has been able to find the credits which have enabled it to undertake the major investment program of the 1970s.

Although the expansion of Polish commercial relations with the industrial West did cut into the relative overall position of Polish trade with the other CMEA countries, and Poland continues to depend heavily upon Western credits to fuel its domestic investment program, economic ties with the Soviet Union and the other communist states retain fundamental importance for the Polish economy and, since 1975, have expanded once again relative to Polish trade. A very high percentage of Polish raw material requirements still comes from the Soviet Union.[31] In addition the number of bilateral and multilateral agreements on production specialization within CMEA has continued to grow--in particular with the USSR--thereby tying the Polish economy more closely into the CMEA economic network.[32]

To date it seems clear that the expansion of Polish economic ties with the industrial West, although not significantly retarding the integration of Poland into the CMEA network, has also not contributed to that process. In fact, the recent expansion of Poland's trade with its CMEA partners has been largely the result of Poland's balance of payments problems in the West and its inability to significantly expand its export of industrial products to world markets (see Table 13.4). Probably the most important development in Poland's external economic relations has been the fact that the Polish economy has been opened up far more than in the past to external economic influences--from both West and East. As Polish economic planners have discovered in recent years, although this expansion has provided a stimulus to the dynamics of the Polish economy, it has also added a degree of dependence and uncertainty that was not present in the past.

Poland's past political relations with the Soviet Union and the other CMEA members have generally been excellent during the 1970s. Poland has become one of the strongest supporters of Soviet policy in virtually all areas, and Polish leaders never miss an opportunity to emphasize the growing strength and importance of the fraternal ties that bind the two countries together. At a special session of the Polish parliament devoted to

TABLE 13.4
Poland's Trade with the CMEA Community
(Percentage of total trade)

	1970	1971	1972	1973	1974	1975	1976	1977
Exports	60.6	59.4	60.6	58.1	53.0	56.9	57.0	57.5
Imports	65.8	64.4	58.2	49.4	42.3	43.8	44.9	49.6

Source: G.U.S., Rocznik Statystyczny Handlu Zagranicznego 1978. Warsaw: Glowny Urzad Statystyczny, 1978, p. 4.

the thirtieth anniversary of People's Poland, for example, Gierek stated:

> The fundamental factor determining our country's place in the world is the class and national alliance with the USSR. It is a solid and reliable guarantee for all vital interests of Poland, enabling it to play an important part in safeguarding international security and peace and enhancing its prestige.[33]

Gierek has clearly attempted to impress upon the Soviet leadership that, in spite of internal political developments in Poland and the expansion of ties with the West, Poland is a faithful ally of the Soviet Union. However, the repeated efforts of the Polish leadership to emphasize their loyalty to the Soviets have been viewed by many Poles as a form of toadyism that has reached unacceptable levels.[34] The proposed constitutional amendments that were to bring the Polish constitution more in line with those of the other communist states met widespread opposition in early 1976. For example, the reference to Poland's "inseparable and unbreakable ties" with the Soviet Union was dropped from the final document and references to the socialist nature of the Polish state and the leading role of the PUWP were watered down.[35]

Consultation among Polish and Soviet leaders has become a regular element in both state and party relations. In recent years, for example, Gierek--as well as other East European party chiefs--has vacationed in the Crimea near Brezhnev's summer villa. These "vacations" have been interspersed with political consultation. Almost immediately after his appointment as the new Polish foreign minister, Emil Wojtaszek visited Moscow in mid-January 1977.[36] During Prime Minister Jaroszewicz's visit to Moscow in January 1978, the discussion concerned mutual "satisfaction with the results of the work done (in the area of economic cooperation) and emphasized the importance of expanding and deepening national economic ties...." According to the communique issued after the visit, there existed an "identity of views between the heads of government."[37] In August 1978, however, during Gierek's annual meeting with Brezhnev in the Crimea, the need to speed up the program of specialization and production cooperation between Poland and the Soviet Union was emphasized.[38]

In addition to the regular meetings among the top Soviet and Polish leaders, however, there has been an increase of meetings among other officials.[39] In December 1976, for example, CPSU Central Committee member Mikhail Zimianin visited Poland to discuss with his Polish counterparts experiences in ideological, educational, and propaganda work.[40] This was apparently part of the Soviet effort to insure that Gierek's regime does not relax efforts to strengthen ideological vigilance and to continue the construction of socialism--of the Soviet variety--in spite of strong and continuing domestic opposition.

Both Poland and the Soviet Union are faced with potentially serious problems in their mutual relations. The Soviets have been clearly aware of the internal weakness of the Polish regime and the possibility of serious problems--witness the uprising that brought Gierek to power in 1970 and the riots of June 1976. In November 1976 the Soviet leadership came to the assistance of their colleagues in Warsaw with a substantial loan to help mitigate the domestic economic problems in Poland.[41] In addition, they have not intervened directly in domestic Polish politics, even though the rise of internal opposition is clearly inimical to their interests.[42]

For the Polish leadership, a major problem concerns the need to balance the demands of the Polish population with the requirements set by the Soviet Union. So far, Gierek and his associates have responded to domestic opposition quite leniently--at least when compared with the behavior of political leaders elsewhere in Eastern Europe. In recent years the PUWP has been forced to change or adapt a number of policies in the face of widespread domestic opposition--e.g., the proposed constitutional amendments of 1976, the food price increase of June 1976, and the jailing of participants in the June riots.[43] Overall the Polish communist party and government are no longer leading the country, but to a substantial degree must respond to popular pressures.[44] Yet the danger clearly exists that, should the regime go too far in permitting open domestic opposition, the Soviets may intervene more directly in the Polish political process than they have done in the recent past. As Peter Osnos has noted, "the question remains, however, how far the Soviets are prepared to go along in allowing challenges to State supremacy that are far more basic than the complaints of intellectuals."[45]

IN LIEU OF CONCLUSIONS

In the present discussion I have pointed to at least three sets of interrelationships that affect Poland's foreign relations: 1) the interdependence of domestic and foreign developments; 2) the clear interrelationship between economic and political factors in both domestic and foreign relations; and 3) the reciprocal impact of Poland's Western and Eastern policies. The present political leadership is beset with a number of seemingly insurmountable problems. Efforts to resolve a difficulty in one area often run counter to the means necessary to deal effectively with problems in other areas. For example, given the serious problems faced by Poland in its economic relations with the West, the regime has been forced to cut back on imports from the world market. This, however, is likely to retard the growth of the Polish economy and to exacerbate many of the consumer goods shortages that have plagued Poland and have added to popular discontent. In other areas, the emphasis on heavy industry, chemicals, and electronics in the modernization program of the early 1970s resulted in a failure to upgrade production in other areas. According to Jerzy Kleer, this has already resulted in the danger of Poland losing some of its traditional consumer goods market in the Soviet Union.[46] Such a loss would clearly compound Poland's foreign economic problems. Finally, efforts to respond to domestic discontent and to the demands of the Soviet-Polish relationship are often contradictory.

Polish leaders must somehow bring the domestic economy under control by reducing irrational investment policies and introducing a pricing system that brings production costs more into line with prices. At the same time, however, they must also satisfy domestic consumer demands and gain popular support for the measures needed to stabilize the economy. These tasks, and the many others that have not been dealt with in this chapter, will require a willingness on the part of the leadership to innovate--both in the system of economic decision making and management and in the development of a more open approach to the discussion of major problems with the population at large. At the same time, Gierek and his associates will have to continue to retain Soviet support, even for policies that differ substantially from those preferred by the Soviet leaders. Failure to accomplish these tasks effectively will result, at best, in the continuation of the present situation of economic and political instability. At worst, widespread upheavals, political and economic chaos, and direct Soviet intervention loom as distinct possibilities.[47]

NOTES

1. For a discussion of this question see the author's "Polish Foreign Trade: The Interrelationship of Domestic and Foreign Economic Policy," Revue comparative d'Etudes Est-Ouest, forthcoming. For an excellent discussion of the implications of growing Polish economic relations with the West see Sarah Meiklejohn Terry, "The Implications of Interdependence for Soviet-East European Relations: A Preliminary Analysis of the Polish Case," unpublished paper prepared for the U.S. Department of State, Office of External Research, June 1977. Unfortunately the study came to the attention of the author of the present article only after he had completed his research and writing.

2. For an interesting elaboration of the argument that geographical position, among other factors, has enabled Romania to exert a substantial degree of foreign policy independence see Aurel Braun, Romanian Foreign Policy Since 1965: The Political and Military Limits of Autonomy. New York: Praeger, 1978, passim.

3. For an excellent assessment of this period in Polish-Soviet relations see Jacques Levesque, Le Conflit sino-sovietique et l'Europe de l Est: Ses Incidences sur les Conflits sovieto-polonais et sovieto-roumain. Montreal: Les Presses de l' Universite de Montreal, 1970, pp. 9-96.

4. For a survey of the major issues in Polish foreign policy during the 1960s see James F. Morrison, "The Foreign Policy of Poland," in

James A. Kuhlman, ed., The Foreign Policies of Eastern Europe: Domestic and International Determinants. Leyden: A.W. Sijthoff, 1978, pp. 129-165. See, also, M. Kamil Dziewanowski, "Poland's International Position under Gomulka and Gierek," in George W. Simmonds, ed., Nationalism in the USSR and Eastern Europe. Detroit: The University of Detroit Press, 1977, pp. 352-363.

5. Already in late 1957 the explusion of PUWP members considered "revisionist" was begun. Within a year approximately 800 individuals were removed from the membership lists. See the report of Gomulka to the XII plenary session of the Central Committee of the PUWP published by Radio Free Europe, News and Information Service, December 9, 1958, and in Bulletin d'information du Comite central du POPU, Warsaw, December 1958.

6. For an inciteful and balanced discussion of Polish-West German relations see W.W. Kulski, Germany and Poland: From War to Peaceful Relations. Syracuse New York: Syracuse University Press, 1976.

7. Until the mid-1960s popular and official usage in West Germany referred to East Germany by this term and to the Polish Western Territories as "Eastern Germany." For an indication of Polish support of the GDR see Gomulka's speech at the Seventh Party Congress of the Socialist Unity Party on April 19, 1967. According to him: "Our party (the PUWP) and the government of People's Poland have always considered the security and sovereignty of the GDR and the inviolability of your borders as synonymous with the security and inviolability of the borders of Poland, and with the peaceful stabilization of our continent." Protokoll des VII. Parteitages der SED. Berlin: Dietz Verlag, 1967, Vol. I, pp. 461-467.

8. In a speech in May 1969 Gomulka proposed a bilateral treaty between the two countries in which West Germany would recognize the Oder-Neisse border. For a discussion of the implications of the speech see A. Ross Johnson, "A New Phase in Polish-West German Relations (II): Gomulka's May 17 Proposal and Its Aftermath," Radio Free Europe Research (hereafter RFER), Polish Background Report, 14, July 3, 1969.

9. See Glowny Urzad Statystyczny, Maly Rocznik

Statystyczny 1977. Warsaw: Glowny Urzad Statystyczny, 1977, pp. 199-200; G.U.S., Rocznik Statystyczny Handlu Zagranicznego 1978. Warsaw: Glowny Urzad Statyztyczny, 1978, p. 4.

10. Comparable data on the trade of the European communist states with the West as a percentage of total trade is included in the following table:

	1952	1958	1967	1973	1975	1976
Bulgaria	9.4	10.5	16.4	14.6	17.0	14.6
Czechozlovakia	19.9	17.0	19.1	23.6	22.4	21.7
East Germany	23.3	19.1	19.8	27.9	25.9	28.3
Hungary	21.2	22.8	25.0	28.2	24.4	33.5
Poland	30.7	32.1	28.7	39.8	41.3	41.5
Romania	11.7[a]	18.4	31.8[b]	41.7	36.7	54.5[a]

[a]These figures include trade with noncommunist developing countries which in 1952 may have totalled 3 percent of total trade and in 1976 18-19 percent.

[b]This estimate made by Franklyn D. Holzman, differs substantially from the estimate of 38.1 percent that appears in U.S. Congress, Joint Economic Committee, Economic Developments in Countries of Eastern Europe. Washington: U.S. Government Printing Office, 1970, pp. 545-550.

Sources: 1952, 1958, 1967: Franklyn D. Holzman, International Trade Under Communism: Politics and Economics. New York: Basic Books, 1976, p. 129 which is calculated from Paul Marer, Soviet and East European Foreign Trade, 1946-1969. Bloomington: University of Indiana Press, 1973; 1973, 1975, 1975: Sovet Ekonomicheskoi Vzaimopomoshchi, Sekretariat, Statisticheskii Ezhegodnik Stran-Chlenov Soveta Economicheskoi Vzaimopomoshchi. Moscow: Izdatel'stvo "Statistika," editions for 1974, 1976, and 1977.

11. See Zbigniew M. Fallenbuchl, Egon Neuberger, and Laura D'Andrea Tyson, "East European Reactions to International Commodity Inflation," in John P. Hardt, ed., East European Economies Post-Helsinki: A Compendium of Papers submitted to the Joint Economic Committee, Congress of the United States. Washington: U.S. Government Printing Office, 1977, p. 56. Fallenbuchl also provides

information on gains and losses of income resulting from changes in Poland's terms of trade for 1971 through 1975 in his The Impact of External Economic Disturbances on Poland Since 1971. Occasional Paper no. 44 of the Kennan Institute for Advanced Russian Studies, Washington, DC, September 1978, Table XII. In 1973 and 1974 Poland had a net loss in income of more than 2,200 million devisa zloty from changes in terms of trade. After modest gains of 145 and 467 million zloty in the next two years, Poland suffered a loss of almost 1,000 million zlotys in 1977.

12. Exports of meat increased from 38,384 thousand tons in 1970 to 99,834 and 90,977 thousand tons in 1974 and 1975--in the latter year this represented 55 percent of total production. However, the domestic meat crisis, which resulted from stagnating production and increasing demand, led to a drastic cutback of exports in 1976 and 1977 to 48,215 and 43,001 thousand tons respectively. See Rocznik Statystyczny Handlu Zagranicznego 1977, p. 41, 1978, p. 39.

13. In 1978 prices of consumption goods and services increased by 4.9 percent and those of nonconsumption goods and services by 14.7 percent. See Rocznik Statystyczny 1978, p. 319.

14. For an excellent discussion of this question, from which my summary has been taken, see Fallenbuchl, et al., "East European Reactions to International Commodity Inflation," pp. 79-84.

15. In the first half of 1978 exports to the West were up 9.7 percent while imports dropped by an additional 9.6 percent compared to the same period a year earlier. See the report of the Main Statistical Administration reported in Trybuna Ludu, July 24, 1978.

16. The growth of the Polish hard currency debt is indicated in the figures which follow:

Polish Hard Currency Debt:

(Billions of U.S. Dollars)

	1970	1973	1974	1975	1976	1977
Year end debt	0.8	1.9	4.0	6.9	10.2	12.8
Debt-export ratio[a]	.80	.92	1.38	2.29	3.02	3.50
Debt service ratio[b]	.20	.21	.27	.43	.49	.60

[a]Debt-export ratio equals net indebtedness divided by hard currency export earnings.

[b]Debt service ratio equals the repayment of principal on debt and interest divided by hard currency merchandise export earnings.

Sources: The Scope of Poland's Economic Dilemma, a research paper published by the National Foreign Assessment Center of the Central Intelligency Agency; reprinted in Roman Stefanowski, "Poland's Western Debt: A Progress Report," RFER, RAD Background Report/ 251 (Poland), November 22, 1978, p. 9.

17. See "Economic Developments in Eastern Europe," Intereconomics, no. 5/6 (1978), pp. 150-151.

18. See Kulski, Germany and Poland, pp. 284-285. For a statement of the Polish position see Czeslaw Pilichowski, "FGR Indemnities for Poles," Studies on International Relations (Warsaw), no. 5 (1975), pp. 85-98. See, also, Karl Hartmann, "Vier Jahre deutsch-polnischer Vertrag," Osteuropa, XXV (1975), pp. 246-256.

19. The treaty was ratified by the German Bundestag on March 12, 1976 and by the Polish Sejm three days later. See Trybuna Lundu, March 13, 1976 and March 16, 1976.

20. Official Polish statistics for 1977 indicate that Rakowski's criticism may well be exaggerated. In 1977 Poland's exports to West Germany increased by 11.7 percent, while imports dropped by 12 percent. Rocznik Statystyczny Handlu Zagranicznego 1978, pp. 224-227.

21. See, for example, the Polish Institute of International Affairs publication entitled Conference on Security and Co-operation in Europe:

A Polish View. Warsaw: PWN--Polish Scientific Publishers, 1976.

22. Rocznik Statystyczny 1978, p. 412.

23. The communique is cited in RFER, Situation Report, Poland/25, October 13, 1977, p. 7. Although most issues of RFER, Poland published after October 1976 included articles on the activities of KOR, this issue has the most complete summary of its early activities.

24. Ibid., p. 23. A second major civil rights organization--the Movement for the Defense of Human and Civil Rights--was created in March 1977. Its members, unlike most of the KOR activists, are not primarily Marxists, although the goals of the two organizations seem to be quite similar. See RFER, Situation Report, Poland/16, June 15, 1977, p. 1-2.

25. Trybuna Ludu, November 6, 1962.

26. Comprehensive Programme for the Further Extension and Improvement of Cooperation and the Development of Socialist Economic Integration by the CMEA Member-Countries. Moscow: Progress Publishers, 1971. The present discussion has benefitted from Adam Zwass, "Costs and Benefits of CMEA-Integration: Poland's Perspective," unpublished paper presented at the Conference on Integration in Eastern Europe and East-West Trade, Bloomington, Indiana, October 28-31, 1976.

27. Trybuna Ludu, July 9, 1976. Several years earlier the noted Polish economic analyst Jerzy Kleer had criticized exactly this type of "specialization" based on economic credits in investment projects as senseless. "Na porzadku dziennym," Polityka, July 4, 1972.

28. Z. Kamicki, "Economic Integration of the Comecon Countries and Possibilities of Expanding Trade Between East and West," Sprawy Miedzynarodowe (September 1973); translated in RFER, Polish Press Survey, no. 2434, December 13, 1973, pp. 13-14. For additional statements of this argument see Pawel Bozyk, Wspolpraca Gospodarcza Krajow RWPG. Warsaw: Panstwowe Wydawnictwo Ekonomiczne, 1976, pp. 396-399 and Aleskander Czepurko, "Mozliwosci rozwoju handlu Wschod-Zachod," in Pawel Bozyk, ed.,

Integracja Ekonomiczna Krajow Socjalistycznych. Warsaw: Ksiazka i Wiedza, 1974, pp. 289-310.

29. For a recent discussion of economic cooperation between Poland and the Soviet Union see Kazimierz Starzyk, "Polsko-radziecka wspolpraca gospardarcza w systemie integracji sochalistyczne," Sprawy Miedzynarodowe, no. 4 (1978), pp. 7-24.

30. See L. Skibinski, "Poland in CMEA," Nowe Drogi, (April 1976), cited in Zwass, "Costs and Benefits of CMEA-Integration," p. 18.

31. Forty-two percent of all Polish raw material imports come from the USSR. Of that amount energy and fuel imports account for 80 percent of Polish requirements; iron ore imports account for 80 percent, cotton for 60, nonferrous metals for 55, and asbestos for 45 percent. See Zycie Gospodarcze, November 14, 1976.

32. For a survey of recent Soviet-Polish trade and cooperation agreements see RFER, Situation Report, Poland/7, March 17, 1978.

33. Citied in N. Ponomaryov and V. Zhuravlev, "USSR-Poland: Fraternal Alliance of Peoples," International Affairs (Moscow), no. 1 (1977), p. 89. In his speech at the Twenty-Fifth Congress of the CPSU in Moscow, Gierek has also emphasized the importance of the ties of Poland and the PUWP with the Soviet Union. Trybuna Ludu, February 27, 1976.

34. See Adam Bromke, "A New Juncture in Poland," Problems of Communism, XXV, no. 5 (1976), p. 17.

35. See Peter Osnos, "The Polish Road to Communism," Foreign Affairs, LVI (1977), pp. 213-214. 214. The proposed amendments were made public on January 24-25, 1976 in Trybuna Ludu and the revised version was approved by the Sejm on February 10.

36. Trybuna Ludu, January 20, 1977. Wojtaszek has emulated Gierek's behavior in lauding the development of Polish-Soviet relations. See his article on "Poland's Foreign Policy and European Security Problems," which appeared in the Soviet journal International Affairs, no. 8 (1978), pp. 19-30. Wojtaszek maintains that "The all-round development of cooperation between Poland and the

Soviet Union has led to a qualitatively new stage in Polish-Soviet relations. This is reflected in in every sphere of life and is marked by more intensive scientific and cultural exchanges and people-to-people contacts, which help to deepen the friendship of the two nations." (p. 22).

37. Soviet News, February 7, 1978, p. 54.

38. Trybuna Ludu, August 4, 1978.

39. See, for example Wojtaszek, "Poland's Foreign Policy," p. 23.

40. Trybuna Ludu, December 22, 1976.

41. See RFER, Situation Report, Poland/38, November 12, 1976.

42. For an excellent survey of dissent in Poland see Adam Bromke, "Tne Opposition in Poland," Problems of Communism, XXVII, no. 5 (1978), pp. 37-51.

43. Most recently the peasantry has organized in opposition to various aspects of the pension program proposed by the government in 1977.

44. For an excellent discussion of the failure of the Party to socialize the majority of the Polish population to the major tenets of Marxist-Leninist political and social values see George Kolankiewicz and Ray Taras, "Poland: Socialism for Everyman?" in Archie Brown and Jack Gray, eds., Political Culture and Political Change in Communist States. London: The Macmillan Press, 1977, pp. 101-30.

45. Osnos, "The Polish Road," p. 219.

46. Polityka, March 4, 1978. According to Kleer, Poland's share of the Soviet clothing market (minus knitted goods) fell from 26.2 to 24.6 percent during the period 1974-1976--a drop of 6.1 percent.

47. For an argument that the United States should do everything possible--including the granting of large-scale economic assistance--to help to stabilize the Polish economic and political system see Daniel M. Duffield, Jr., United States Security Interests in Eastern Europe: The Case of

Poland. National Security Affairs Monograph 77-76. Washington: National Defense University, Research Directorate, 1977, especially pp. 47-57.

Part 5

Conclusion

14
Poland Enters the Eighties

Maurice D. Simon

As Poland enters the 1980s, its political leadership faces a set of vexing policy dilemmas that defy easy resolution. The expressed optimism of the early seventies--voiced in slogans like "we are building another Poland" or couched in concepts such as "developed socialism"--has evaporated. Instead an atmosphere of uncertainty, perhaps even anxiety, prevails. At present the Polish political system appears to be stalled, locked into what can be termed policy immobilism.

The key economic, social, and political factors that confront Polish policymakers are summarized in the following list:

1) The Polish economy is in dire straits, with a slowing (even negative) rate of growth, mounting consumer discontent, and a worsening balance of payments problem.

2) The Polish social structure has become more complex and differentiated, fostering tensions and competition between various social strata and groups. As a result, social integration has become increasingly difficult to maintain.

3) The government and party institutions of Poland appear ill-adapted to deal effectively with the new economic, social, and political forces. Groups expressing dissent and opposition to the PUWP continue to operate and draw public attention. The Catholic Church remains a potent organization challenging the leadership. Party leaders' promises to enhance citizen participation and influence in decision-making processes go unfulfilled. Compli-

---

This chapter was completed in May before the final manuscript was scheduled for printing.

cating matters even further, the constraints imposed upon Poland by its membership in the "socialist community" limit its ability to adopt responsive and innovative policies.

These factors are clearly interrelated. Thus, tensions and problems in any one of these areas promote difficulties elsewhere. In the discussion that follows, I will briefly explore the policy and political environment of contemporary Poland as it bears upon the 1980s.

ECONOMIC PRESSURES

Recent official Polish discussions of economic progress during the seventies hail the system's accomplishments--the rapid acceleration of growth, technological modernization, the emphasis on social welfare, considerable increases in the population's standard of living, and the rise in stature of the Polish economy in the international arena.[1] In a characteristic statement, Gierek declared:

> During the past decade...we lifted our country onto a qualitatively new level. This was achieved mainly thanks to the undertaking of a broad investment programme, thanks to the creation of new jobs for the exceptionally numerous young generation, thanks to the expansion and modernization of the production potential. Our gross national product grew considerably providing foundations for the marked improvement of the material and cultural living standards of the population.[2]

Gierek's defense of his economic program rests largely on the 130 percent increase in industrial production and 85 percent increase in national income achieved under his leadership, increases which have indeed brought considerable improvements in many areas of Polish life.[3]

Yet current trends and events indicate that the outlook for the immediate future is quite bleak. The maintenance of the high growth rates of the 1970s is proving to be untenable in light of a number of factors. Scarcities in raw materials and fuels, especially oil, are placing constraints on the capacity of the Polish economy to grow at a rapid rate. Here, increases in the price of Soviet oil and the world spot market play an especially adverse role.[4] Moreover, Poland's labor force will increase by only a small increment in the 1980s, necessitating increases in labor productivity.[5] Since labor efficiency has been a long-standing weakness of the Polish economy there is little reason to expect dramatic improvements in productivity to occur. These are just two of the major barriers to rapid growth, with the lengthier list provided in the recent economic diagnosis of Prime Minister Babiuch providing additional grounds for pessimism.[6]

The economic picture becomes even darker when we consider the problems begrudingly endured by the Polish consumer. The chronically-ill agricultural sector has shown few signs of improvement in recent years. Thus, rampant discontent over the availability of meat and other essential food products persists. According to one source, agricultural production has increased by only thirty percent since 1970, with 1979 production of domestic grain falling five million tons short of the planned target.[7] Consumer demand for meat continues to outstrip supply. In 1979 there was a 500,000 ton shortfall and it was recently acknowledged that in 1980 demand will exceed supply by twenty-five percent.[8] Although there has been some progress in housing construction, it is admitted that difficulties persist in fulfilling planned targets both qualitatively and quantitatively, especially in the largest urban areas.[9] Pressures from consumers for goods and services are clearly intensifying, just as the leadership calls upon citizens "to adhere to...rational economizing in their own best interests and those of society."[10] One Western analyst suggests that the PUWP "is fighting for a breathing spell...of economic reprieve in order to either succeed on the economic front or to prepare the population for a more difficult maneuver on the consumption front that would require more sacrifices from the population."[11] It remains to be seen whether Polish consumers will accept delays in satisfaction of their heightening demands.

The international economy provides additional complications. Poland financed much of its development during the seventies by securing Western credit which now amounts to about $18 billion. Indebtedness to the West has brought estimates that Poland will need to borrow up to $6 billion in hard currency this year in order to repay some of its standing obligations. Moreover, it is estimated that 75 to 80 cents of every hard currency dollar Poland earns this year will be utilized for debt repayment.[12] As a result, Poland needs to achieve considerable improvement in its balance of trade by promoting its own exports and reducing its Western imports. Yet the Polish leadership admits that the terms of foreign credit are worsening and that Western assistance is "becoming more costly and hard to obtain."[13] Given international economic trends, Poland obviously faces difficult economic readjustments.

Finally, we must draw attention to some persisting features of the Polish socialist economy which require major changes. Throughout the 1970s, wage and price policies, the system of economic planning, and administrative-management practices have needed fundamental reform. However, policy decisions in these areas have been insufficient. Prime Minister Edward Babiuch recently labeled the price structure as "an obstacle which impeded setting the market situation in order" and admitted the need to "counteract an excessive increase in the cost of living and to maintain the proper plan-sanctioned relationship between the cost of living and wages and other sources of income." Moreover, he emphasized the pressing need for improving methods of planning and managing the economy by warning, "We shall consistently put the criteria of economic analysis into practice and use them to gauge the efforts of everybody, but especially of those who, by virtue of the positions they occupy and functions they fulfill, bear special responsibility for the results of management."[14] Similar promises have been made in the past, but have borne little fruit."[15]

The 1979 performance of the economy illustrates how difficult the situation has become. Industrial production increased by only 2.6 percent, while national income decreased by 2 percent.[16] The leadership has conceded that its investment program must be cut back in light of current economic realities and has limited the 1980 goal for increased industrial production to 3-4.2 percent.[17] Thus, a sense of economic crisis dominates the society and poses immense challenges for the political leadership.

SOCIAL FACTORS

The postwar modernization of Poland has produced significant changes in its social structure. The landed aristocracy which dominated traditional rural Poland has disappeared. Socialist industrialization has brought about the elimination of a powerful bourgeoisie (although the small private enterprise sector remains important in providing certain goods and services). Moreover, urbanization has reduced the size and influence of the peasantry. In today's Poland we find a numerically and economically important working class, the influential intelligentsia, and the politically powerful category of PUWP leaders and governmental officials. Although space permits only a limited discussion of these groups, we will briefly examine some key developments.[18]

The disturbances of 1956, 1970, and 1976 demonstrated that the Polish working class is a potent force for change. During the seventies, there has been a notable surge of working class assertiveness which has required the PUWP to be increasingly sensitive to the demands of this group.[19] Workers have shown that they are especially concerned with policies that bear directly upon them. Of special note are wage and price policies which affect their buying power, management reforms which determine their working conditions and sense of personal security, housing patterns which influence their families' personal comfort, educational opportunities which can control their children's destinies, and, of course, the availability of consumer goods. As Walter D. Connor has observed, collective social mobility in Poland has slowed down and many members of the working class are no longer grateful to the PUWP for their social promotion. The contemporary Polish working class is looking for concrete results and views life under socialism quite critically.[20] In his recent discussion of the economy, Prime Minister Babiuch made special efforts to reassure workers on such sensitive policy issues as income differentials, taxation, housing, and health care, but it is difficult to see how the working class can feel calm in light of the government's call for austerity.[21] Their interests rest in seeing that the various economic and administrative reforms intended to promote efficiency do not lessen their own security and material welfare. During the seventies they have gained a sense of their power to influence governmental actions and thus their behavior will remain a critical factor determining system stability.

While the peasantry has derived some material and social benefits during the seventies, peasants remain relatively disadvantaged. Despite the increasing attention paid to the peasantry during recent years, young male peasants continue to escape the countryside resulting in the aging and feminization of the rural population. Rural conditions continue to lag behind the urban areas. Moreover, Polish private farms remain too small and economically inefficient. Prime Minister Babiuch has promised that the Polish government will make strenuous efforts to foster agricultural moderization and growth during the 1980s, but peasants have evidenced restlessness over governmental purchasing policies for produce, land transfer policies, pension plans for the aged, rural schooling, social services, and living conditions.[22] An awareness of how food shortages can affect the political system gives the peasants heightened influence politically.

There is little doubt that the intelligentsia, which has grown numerically and in complexity under socialism, has enjoyed a favored position in postwar Poland. Members of this stratum have benefitted from the dynamic socioeconomic change by experiencing upward social mobility and by receiving material rewards.[23] However, as Connor has pointed out, a "second-generation" intelligentsia is in the process of formation, which is less beholden to the communist authorities for having provided such opportunities.[24] The current socialist intelligentsia is primarily concerned with rationalization and reform of the economy, income differentiation based upon merit criteria, a socially just distribution of national wealth, and enhanced opportunities for influencing policy decisions. The intelligentsia, while not necessarily unified and anti-system, is change-oriented and demands more effective governance from the party leadership. During the seventies intellectuals and professionals have been candidly critical of existing conditions. Consequently, a minority of the intelligentsia have been in the forefront of the dissident movement. While the majority of members of this stratum are likely to remain either passive or active supporters of the status quo, deteriorating economic conditions and political inflexibility by the PUWP could push more of them into the ranks of the dissenters.

The growing social complexity of Poland in a period of economic hardship means that it will be more difficult to moderate social tensions in the future. Polish researchers who have examined the "social transformation" of the society have begun to explore "structural collisions of interests" and "articulated conflicts." In other words, there is a recognition that competition and conflict between social strata and groups will occur and must be dealt with by policymakers.[25] Among the frequently cited contradictions are the following: those connected with the uneven distribution of key consumer goods (primarily housing and food); those derived from income differences associated with varying educational attainments; those associated with the provision of social services (health care, education, transportation, access to cultural facilities); and those emanating from one's position in the authority structure and the consequent ability to influence social decisions (party versus non-party membership).[26] From the discussion above, it is clear that rising tensions within and between key social groups will critically affect Poland during the eighties.

POLITICAL TRENDS

The inability of the PUWP under Gierek to make significant headway in resolving the host of economic and social problems of the past decade has lowered the political credibility of the party leadership. At the Eighth Congress of the PUWP (February 11-15, 1980) important leadership changes demonstrated that both inside and outside of the party, there is substantial dissatisfaction with existing patterns of political management. The removal of Prime Minister Jaroszewicz provided a convenient scapegoat for recent economic failures. His replacement, Edward Babiuch, is a trusted Gierek associate. Moreover, the ouster of Stefan Olszowski from his Politburo and Secretariat posts and the removal of Politburo members Jozef Tejchma and Jozef Kepa may have consolidated Gierek's hold at the top of the party. Gierek and the PUWP leadership, however, appear only to have bought time. A continuation of the hesitant and often contradictory policies of the seventies certainly will provoke additional criticism and discontent.[27]

The events of the past two years have yielded evidence that crucial segments of the Polish population are deeply frustrated with PUWP rule. The enormous outpouring of sentiment for Pope John Paul II during his summer visit of 1979 has strengthened the capacity of the Catholic Church to pose as the symbol of national unity in contrast to the PUWP. Since the Church can (and has) operated at times to support and shield members of the various dissident groups, the PUWP must continue to seek a proper relationship with this organization.[28] Given the ideological gulf between the two groups, it remains to be seen whether the party can achieve "amicable coexistence" and cooperation with the Church "in pursuance of important national goals," but an escalation of tensions undoubtedly would foster discontent.[29]

The PUWP is also confronted with a bolder, increasingly diversified, and more resolute dissident movement.[30] The persistence and ingenuity of the dissident movement is a source of frustration for the PUWP. Its continued existence demonstrates, as Jan Gross has observed, an "underlying weakness of the government and an underlying strength in the opposition."[31] Although the party has consistently pledged to oppose the "enemies of socialism--both those descending from old right-wing political orientations and newer, revisionistic ones," it seems to have acknowledged that repression will not work. Instead, it proclaims that "of decisive importance is...the strengthening of our socio-economic system and intensification of political activeness and propaganda-educational work."[32] The tacit admission that dissent thrives on the poor performance of the leadership is an illustration of the growing defensiveness of the PUWP.

The main source of the PUWP's difficulties, however, appears to inhere in its unflagging commitment to the single-party pattern of leadership and consequent inability to respond effectively to the more complex and competitive political environment of contemporary Poland. As Tellenback has argued, the PUWP has attempted to strengthen its leadership capacities by upgrading the technological and administrative competence of its own personnel and by rationalizing policy implementation. This "technocratic pragmatism", however, avoids full recognition of the pluralistic nature of Polish society and the burgeoning demands by groups to share in the formulation of national policy.[33] Gross makes a similar argument, but adds that the denial of legitimacy to the diverse, competing social groups of contemporary Poland induces these groups "to manipulate the system by feeding it with slanted information in order to extract from it favorable rulings" or forces them "to circumvent the existing institutions, to articulate outside of the officially sanctioned establishment."[34] The result is the distortion of information fundamental to the making of sound decisions. Poor decisions promote frustration and public disorders which in turn can frighten party authorities and lead them to clamp down on various social groups. The solution to this problem would be the legitimation of pluralism, an increase in effective citizen participation, and a recognition of the value of public discussions of alternative policies.

Indeed, the PUWP under Gierek continually has expressed a commitment to "socialist democracy" which is to be manifested in "consultations" with citizens, a greater role for voluntary associations, a better system of workers' self-management, expansion of the activities of the local people's councils, and the development of the Polish Sejm. Yet most studies of these institutions indicate that there has been minimal progress in fostering authentic socialist democracy.[35] The hesitancy of the PUWP to make these institutions legitimate and effective actors in the policy process tends to validate the arguments of Tellenback and Gross. The political leadership under Gierek has been willing to offer a new political style, but has failed to offer meaningful new political forms and processes.

Poland's membership in the "socialist community" is certainly a factor contributing to its political immobilism. While the Soviet Union did not intervene during the 1970 and 1976 disturbances, the lessons of Czechoslovakia in 1968 and Afghanistan in the current period undoubtedly constrain the Polish leadership in developing economic, social, and political reforms. Participation in the Warsaw Treaty Organization insures cautiousness. Moreover, the international economic situation guarantees that the Polish leadership will continue to feel dependent upon the Soviet Union for key energy resources and essential economic assistance. Thus, Poland will, for the most part, toe the line in foreign policy and act with circumspection in domestic policy. Nonetheless, the PUWP has lacked inventiveness and dynamism in ways that simply cannot be accounted for by the Soviet factor.

The successful future of policy and politics in Gierek's Poland, then, may depend upon a new willingness on the part of the PUWP to develop political mechanisms that will promote an authentic national discussion of economic, social, and political issues. There are few observers of the Polish polity who would not argue that in a crunch, the

PUWP has both the resources and the will to muddle through. The postwar pattern of crisis-relaxation-consolidation could go on. Alternatively, the party could adopt a more authoritarian stance, while striving to achieve greater technocratic efficiency. Since either of these approaches probably would widen the existing gap between citizens and the leadership, movement toward political reform and greater public participation seems the most effective--but perhaps not the most probable--choice for Poland in the 1980s.

NOTES

1. See "For Further Development of Socialist Poland and Prosperity of the Polish Nation," (Guidelines of the Central Committee for the 8th Congress of the PUWP, adopted at the 16th CC Plenary Session on October 19, 1979), Contemporary Poland, XIII, no. 22 (1979), pp. 20-29.

2. "Further Progress in Meeting Social Needs is Supreme Objective of Party Policy," (Speech delivered by Edward Gierek at the 16th Plenary Session of the PUWP Central Committee on October 19, 1979), Contemporary Poland, XIII, no. 21, p. 22.

3. Pedro Ramet, "Poland's Economic Dilemma," The New Leader, LXIII, no. 8 (1980), p. 4.

4. See John Darnton, "Political Chill Gives Shivers to Economy of E. Europe," The New York Times: The Week in Review, (May 18, 1980), p. 2E.

5. See "Main Directions of Government Activity," (The report of Edward Babiuch, Chairman of the Council of Ministers, delivered in the Sejm of the Polish People's Republic on April 3, 1980), Contemporary Poland, XIV, no. 8 (1980), pp. 23-24.

6. Ibid., pp. 20-41.

7. Ramet, "Poland's Economic Dilemma," p. 4.

8. See Eric Bourne, "Some Plain Speaking in Poland," The Christian Science Monitor (April 23, 1980), p. 13.

9. "For Further Development of Socialist Poland..," p. 22.

10. "Main Directions of Government Activity," p. 30.

11. Bogdan Mieczkowski, "The Political Economy of Consumption in Poland," Soviet Studies, XXIV, no. 3 (1979), pp. 83-84.

12. See Bradley Graham, "Leaders Urge Poles to Face Up to Economic Austerity," The Washington Post (March 16, 1980), p. A26.

13. "Main Directions of Government Activity," p. 29.

14. *Ibid.*, p. 32.

15. See, for example, Mieczkowski, "The Political Economy of Consumption in Poland" and P.T. Wanless, "Economic Reform in Poland 1973-1979," Soviet Studies, XXXII, no. 1 (1980), pp. 28-57.

16. Graham, "Leaders Urge Poles to Face Up to Economic Austerity," p. A26.

17. Ramet, "Poland's Economic Dilemma," p. 5.

18. Two excellent treatments of this subject are Walter D. Connor, "Social Change and Stability in Eastern Europe," Problems of Communism, XXVII, no. 6 (1977), pp. 16-32 and Sten Tellenback, "The Logic of Development in Socialist Poland," Social Forces, 57, no. 2 (1978), pp. 436-456.

19. For a good treatment of this subject, see Jan B. de Weydenthal, "The Workers' Dilemma of Polish Politics: A Case Study," East European Quarterly, XIII, no. 1 (1979), pp. 95-119. A recent provocative analysis of working class assertiveness is Walter D. Connor, "Dissent in Eastern Europe: A New Coalition?" Problems of Communism, XXIX, no. 1 (1980), pp. 1-17.

20. See Connor, "Social Change and Stability in Eastern Europe," especially pp. 27-30.

21."Main Directions of Government Activity," pp. 38-40.

22. For discussion, see Andrzej Korbonski, "Social Deviance in Poland: The Case of the Private Sector" in Ivan Volgyes, ed., Social Deviance in Eastern Europe. Boulder: Westview Press, 1978, pp. 94-98. Also, see his chapter in this volume.

23. See, for example, Maria Hirszowicz, "Intelligentsia versus Bureaucracy: The Revival of a Myth in Poland," Soviet Studies, XXX, no. 3 (1978), especially pp. 344-356. Also, see Tellenbach, "The Logic of Development in Socialist Poland," especially pp. 437-439 and 445-447.

24. Connor, "Social Change and Stability in Eastern Europe," pp. 26-27.

25. See the studies in the Polish Sociological Association, Polish Sociology 1977: Social Structure. Wroclaw: Ossolineum, 1978. The terms "structural collisions of interests" and "articulated conflicts" are used by K.M. Slomczynski and W. Wesolowski. For a brief discussion of Polish social science literature on this subject see Maurice D. Simon, "A Window on Poland's Social Transformation," Problems of Communism, XXIX, no. 2 (1980), pp. 76-80. Also relevant is a discussion by Sarah Meiklejohn Terry, "The Case for a 'Group' Approach to Polish Politics," Studies in Comparative Communism, XII, no. 1 (1979), pp. 28-34.

26. See, for example, the discussion by Andrzej Tyszka, "Diagnosis and Vision of the Structure of Socialist Society" in the Polish Sociological Association, Polish Sociology 1977, pp. 33-52.

27. For an analysis of the Congress and the leadership changes, see J.B. de Weydenthal with Roman Stefanowski, "The Eighth Congress of the Polish Communist Party," Radio Free Europe Research, RAD Background Report (Poland), 46, February 29, 1980, especially pp. 14-22.

28. For a recent discussion of the Church and the opposition, see Jacques Rupnik, "Dissent in Poland, 1968-1978: the end of Revisionism and the rebirth of the Civil Society" in Rudolf L. Tokes, ed., Opposition in Eastern Europe. Baltimore: The Johns Hopkins University Press, 1979, especially pp. 86-92. Also see the chapters by Bromke and Chrypinski in this volume.

29. "For further Development of Socialist Poland and Prosperity of the Polish Nation," p. 41.

30. See the sources cited in footnote 28. Also, see Connor, "Dissent in Eastern Europe: A New Coalition?" and Abraham Brumberg, "The Open Political Struggle in Poland," New York Review of Books, XXVI, no. 1 (1979), pp. 29-34.

31. Jan P. Gross, "Thirty Years of Crisis Management in Poland," in Teresa Rakowska-Harmstone, ed., Perspectives for Change in Communist Societies. Boulder: Westview Press, 1979, p. 150. This is an excellent interpretation of some factors behind Poland's turmoil.

32. "For Further Development of Socialist Poland and Prosperity of the Polish Nation," p. 40.

33. Tellenback. "The Logic of Development in Socialist Poland," p. 447.

34. Gross, "Thirty Years of Crisis Management in Poland," p. 60.

35. See the studies in this volume by Sarah Terry, Christine Sadowski, and Daniel Nelson for evidence of this minimal progress. Also, see Zvi Gitelman, "Development, Institutionalization, and Elite-Mass Relations in Poland" in Jan F. Triska and Paul M. Cocks, eds., Political Development in Eastern Europe. New York: Praeger Publishers, 1977, pp. 119-143, and Maurice D. Simon and David M. Olson, "Evolution of a Minimal Parliament: Membership and Committee Changes in the Polish Sejm," Legislative Studies Quarterly, V, no. 2 (1980), pp. 211-232.